Strategic Brand Management and Development

Bringing together theories and concepts from brand management, consumer culture theory, marketing, communications, and design, this book provides an understanding of how organisations can successfully develop, market, and manage their brands. It draws extensively from scholarly research published in social sciences and humanities to provide a detailed discussion of the process of brand management and development.

This book explores how organisations can design brand identities, develop brand marketing programmes, measure brand performance, and sustain brand equity, combining psychological, sociological, cultural, and management perspectives. It provides numerous examples that contextualise theory, enabling the reader to understand how past and present branding campaigns and strategies can be deconstructed, analysed, and evaluated, using these theoretical insights. With end-of-chapter case studies on *Burberry*, *Juventus F.C.*, *Pukka Herbs*, *YO!*, and many other European and global brands, *Strategic Brand Management and Development* is an essential text for students in marketing, brand management, and consumer research, or for anyone interested in understanding the extraordinary power and scope of brands and branding in contemporary post-modern society.

Sotiris T. Lalaounis is a Senior Lecturer in Marketing and Design Management in the Department of Management at the University of Exeter Business School. Following a postgraduate degree in Design and Digital Media from the University of Edinburgh, he worked in design consultancies, and earned his PhD in Design Management from the Centre for Creative Industries at Glasgow Caledonian University. His thesis explored business development issues in the creative industries, and his current research interests include organisational paradoxes, ambidexterity, and creative firms. He is the author of *Design Management: Organisation and Marketing Perspectives* (Routledge, 2017; Japanese translation, 2020).

Strategic Brand Management and Development

Creating and Marketing Successful Brands

Sotiris T. Lalaounis

LONDON AND NEW YORK

First published 2021
by Routledge
2 Park Square, Milton Park, Abingdon, Oxon OX14 4RN

and by Routledge
52 Vanderbilt Avenue, New York, NY 10017

Routledge is an imprint of the Taylor & Francis Group, an informa business

© 2021 Sotiris T. Lalaounis

The right of Sotiris T. Lalaounis to be identified as author of this work has been asserted by him in accordance with sections 77 and 78 of the Copyright, Designs and Patents Act 1988.

All rights reserved. No part of this book may be reprinted or reproduced or utilised in any form or by any electronic, mechanical, or other means, now known or hereafter invented, including photocopying and recording, or in any information storage or retrieval system, without permission in writing from the publishers.

Trademark notice: Product or corporate names may be trademarks or registered trademarks, and are used only for identification and explanation without intent to infringe.

British Library Cataloguing-in-Publication Data
A catalogue record for this book is available from the British Library

Library of Congress Cataloging-in-Publication Data
Names: Lalaounis, Sotiris T., 1980– author.
Title: Strategic brand management and development : creating and marketing successful brands / Sotiris T. Lalaounis.
Description: Abingdon, Oxon ; New York, NY : Routledge, 2021. | Includes bibliographical references and index.
Identifiers: LCCN 2020037224 (print) | LCCN 2020037225 (ebook) | ISBN 9780367338749 (hardcover) | ISBN 9780367338756 (paperback) | ISBN 9780429322556 (ebook)
Subjects: LCSH: Branding (Marketing) | Brand name products–Management. | Product management.
Classification: LCC HF5415.1255 .L35 2021 (print) | LCC HF5415.1255 (ebook) | DDC 658.8/27–dc23
LC record available at https://lccn.loc.gov/2020037224
LC ebook record available at https://lccn.loc.gov/2020037225

ISBN: 9780367338749 (hbk)
ISBN: 9780367338756 (pbk)
ISBN: 9780429322556 (ebk)

Typeset in Sabon
by Newgen Publishing UK

To Graham

Contents

List of figures	*xiii*
List of tables	*xv*
List of images	*xvi*
Foreword	*xviii*
Acknowledgements	*xxiii*

1	Introduction: History and the importance of brands	1
2	Developing brand equity, positioning, personality, and values	23
3	Creating brand identity: Brand aesthetics and symbolism	59
4	Brand communications and the attention economy	100
5	Holistic brand experiences and emotional branding	135
6	Consumer collectives, brand avoidance, and political consumption	171
7	Brand ethics, social responsibility, and sustainable consumption	211
8	Brand performance and metrics	246

9	Brand growth: Brand architecture and brand extensions	275
10	Brand futures: Technology and innovation in branding strategies	308
Index		*342*

Detailed Contents

List of figures   *xiii*
List of tables   *xv*
List of images   *xvi*
Foreword   *xviii*
Acknowledgements   *xxiii*

1 Introduction: History and the importance of brands   1

   Chapter aims and learning outcomes   *1*
   Defining brands   *1*
   History of brands and branding   *5*
   Importance of brands to consumers, organisations, and society   *11*
   Book structure   *17*
   Chapter review questions   *19*
   Recommended reading   *19*
   References   *19*

2 Developing brand equity, positioning, personality, and values   23

   Chapter aims and learning outcomes   *23*
   Developing brand equity   *23*
   Brand positioning   *41*
   Brand personality and brand values   *49*
   Chapter review questions   *51*
   Recommended reading   *51*
   Case study: Union: (Re)positioning a Slovenian icon   *52*
   References   *55*

3 Creating brand identity: brand aesthetics and symbolism   59

   Chapter aims and learning outcomes   *59*
   Brand identity development process   *60*
   Brand aesthetics   *71*

	Chapter review questions	*89*
	Recommended reading	*89*
	Case study: The Lakes Distillery	*89*
	References	*95*

4 Brand communications and the attention economy — **100**

Chapter aims and learning outcomes — *100*
Brand communications options and their contributions — *100*
Traditional and digital media platforms — *110*
Planning and implementing brand IMC programmes — *114*
Social media and the (over)democratisation of marketing — *118*
Social media, hyper-narcissism, and the attention economy — *126*
Chapter review questions — *128*
Recommended reading — *128*
Case study: Burberry *and "brand heat" strategy* — *128*
References — *131*

5 Holistic brand experiences and emotional branding — **135**

Chapter aims and learning outcomes — *135*
Holistic brand experiences — *135*
Emotional branding: Nostalgia and retro branding — *152*
Chapter review questions — *162*
Recommended reading — *163*
Case study: Building the YO! *brand: From kaiten belts to multi-format Experiences* — *163*
References — *167*

6 Consumer collectives, brand avoidance, and political consumption — **171**

Chapter aims and learning outcomes — *171*
Collectivist and constructivist aspects of consumption — *171*
Subcultures of consumption — *174*
Brand communities — *177*
Consumer tribes — *187*
Brand publics — *190*
Brand avoidance and anti-consumption — *193*
Political consumption — *195*
Chapter review questions — *200*
Recommended reading — *200*
Case study: Beyond the football borders: Going ahead to grow the relationship with fans and entertainment enthusiasts — *200*
References — *207*

7 Brand ethics, social responsibility, and sustainable consumption — 211

Chapter aims and learning outcomes — 211
(Post)postmodernism and social responsibility — 211
Moral philosophy and ethical branding — 213
Corporate social responsibility and branding — 217
Incorporating ethics and CSR in brand development and marketing — 221
Social marketing programmes and branding — 225
Green marketing and sustainable consumption — 229
Cause-related marketing and consumer philanthropy — 233
Chapter review questions — 236
Recommended reading — 237
Case study: Pukka Herbs: A budding brand creating change through Commerce — 237
References — 243

8 Brand performance and metrics — 246

Chapter aims and learning outcomes — 246
Assessing brand value — 246
Brand audit — 256
Understanding the brand ecology: Consumer ethnography — 264
Chapter review questions — 269
Recommended reading — 269
Case study: From measuring to impacting performance — 270
References — 272

9 Brand growth: Brand architecture and brand extensions — 275

Chapter aims and learning outcomes — 275
Brand architecture and brand hierarchy — 275
Brand extensions — 280
Chapter review questions — 299
Recommended reading — 300
Case study: A case for divergent brand extensions? — 300
References — 303

10 Brand futures: Technology and innovation in branding strategies — 308

Chapter aims and learning outcomes — 308
Consumer engagement and its dimensions — 308
Big data and consumer analytics — 311
Measuring and facilitating consumer engagement — 317
The Internet of Things (IoT) — 321

Neuromarketing and branding	*326*
Chapter review questions	*332*
Recommended reading	*333*
Case study: Village Hotels *and the Internet of Things (IoT)*	*333*
References	*338*

Index — *342*

Figures

1.1	The history of brands	6
1.2	Strategic brand management process and book plan	17
2.1	Strategic brand management process and book plan	24
2.2	Stages of brand development	26
2.3	Customer-based brand equity pyramid model	27
2.4	An example of a brand concept map for *Mercedes-Benz*	31
2.5	An example of a brand concept map for *Absolut*	31
2.6	Competitive point-of-parity (POP) associations	43
3.1	Strategic brand management process and book plan	60
3.2	Managerial approaches to creating style	66
3.3	Dimensions of semiosis	69
3.4	Types of semantic relationships	70
3.5	Conceptual framework of sensory marketing	73
4.1	Strategic brand management process and book plan	101
4.2	Traditional communications options and their contributions to consumer decision-making	104
4.3	Digital communications options and their contributions to consumer decision-making	109
4.4	The marketing communication tetrahedron	115
4.5	Strategic ladder of engagement	122
4.6	Themes in digital consumption landscape	123
5.1	Strategic brand management process and book plan	136
5.2	Experiential aspects of consumption framework	138
5.3	Progress of economic value	140
5.4	The four realms of experiences	141
5.5	Impact of brand experience on consumer satisfaction and loyalty	151
5.6	Retro brand antinomy: Animating brand allegory, aura, and arcadia	162
6.1	Strategic brand management process and book plan	172
6.2	Types of consumption communities	173
6.3	Characteristics of subcultures of consumption	175
6.4	Characteristics of brand communities	178

6.5	Characteristics of consumer tribes	188
6.6	Characteristics of brand publics	192
6.7	Types of brand avoidance	194
6.8	Types of political consumption	196
7.1	Strategic brand management process and book plan	212
7.2	Strategic CSR brand framework	219
7.3	Integrating ethics in brand marketing	222
7.4	Socially responsible brand development process	224
7.5	Stages of change theory	227
8.1	Strategic brand management process and book plan	247
8.2	The brand value chain model	248
8.3	Components of brand audit	257
8.4	Dimensions of qualitative research goals	258
9.1	Strategic brand management process and book plan	276
9.2	Brand–product matrix	279
9.3	Brand architecture	279
9.4	Brand hierarchy	280
9.5	Types of brand extensions	281
9.6	Advantages of brand extensions	282
9.7	Disadvantages of brand extensions	284
9.8	Consumer processes for evaluating brand extensions	288
9.9	Moderating factors of brand extension evaluations	293
10.1	Strategic brand management process and book plan	309
10.2	Dimensions of consumer engagement	311
10.3	Dimensions of big data	312
10.4	Big data, value creation, and competitive advantage	314
10.5	Framework of consumer connectivity	324
10.6	Cognitive methodologies in neuromarketing	328
10.7	Applications of neuromarketing in branding	331

Tables

2.1	Example of brand associations and core brand associations for *Mercedes-Benz*	46
2.2	Example of brand associations and core brand associations for *Absolut*	46
2.3	Example of brand mantras for *Mercedes-Benz* and *Absolut*	46
3.1	Visual sense and its characteristics	80
3.2	Auditory sense and its characteristics	82
3.3	Haptic sense and its characteristics	84
3.4	Gustatory sense and its characteristics	86
3.5	Olfactory sense and its characteristics	88
5.1	Consumption emotions set	152
5.2	Typology of consumption emotions	152
5.3	Categories of nostalgic objects	155
6.1	Types of consumption communities – similarities and differences	173
6.2	Brand community practices	181
8.1	Ten factors in brand strength analysis	255
8.2	Questions for assessing consumers' brand usage and brand attitudes	264
8.3	Brand exploratory: Qualitative and quantitative techniques	265
10.1	Measuring consumer–brand engagement	318
10.2	Consumer–brand engagement metrics for the main social networking sites	322

Images

0.1	Culture-jamming Starbucks's mermaid logo	xx
1.1	*Heinz Baked Beans* (image courtesy of H.J. Heinz Foods UK Ltd)	10
1.2	*Heinz Baked Beans* advertising (image courtesy of H.J. Heinz Foods UK Ltd)	10
2.1	*Absolut*'s 'Metropolis' advertising campaign (image courtesy of Absolut)	47
2.2	*Absolut*'s 'Metropolis' advertising campaign (image courtesy of Absolut)	48
2.3	*Absolut*'s 'Kiss With Pride' advertising campaign (image courtesy of Absolut)	49
2.4	*Union* and *Laško* products (image courtesy of Pivovarna Laško Union d.o.o.)	53
2.5	*Union*'s packaging (image courtesy of Pivovarna Laško Union d.o.o.)	53
2.6	Similarity of *Union*'s packaging with a private-label brand's packaging (image courtesy of Pivovarna Laško Union d.o.o.)	54
3.1	Procter and Gamble (P&G) logo	62
3.2	*Gillette* razors	63
3.3	*Lenor* fabric conditioner	64
3.4	*Herbal Essences* shampoo	65
3.5	*Absolut* iconic bottle (image courtesy of Absolut)	75
3.6	*Absolut* 'Unique' special edition bottles (image courtesy of Absolut)	76
3.7	*The Lakes Distillery* brand essence (image courtesy of The Lakes Distillery)	91
3.8	*The Lakes Distillery* brand purpose (image courtesy of The Lakes Distillery)	92
3.9	*The Lakes Distillery* re-brand packaging (image courtesy of The Lakes Distillery)	93
3.10	*The Lakes Distillery* – The Quatrefoil Collection (image courtesy of The Lakes Distillery)	93
3.11	*The Lakes Distillery* – The Quatrefoil Collection (image courtesy of The Lakes Distillery)	94

3.12	*The Lakes Distillery* guidelines and toolkit (image courtesy of The Lakes Distillery)	94
5.1	*YO!* logo (image courtesy of YO!)	164
5.2	*YO!* kaiten belt (image courtesy of YO!)	164
5.3	*YO!* food (image courtesy of YO!)	165
5.4	*YO!* restaurant experience (image courtesy of YO!)	166
6.1	Culture-jamming (image courtesy of Adbusters Media Foundation)	197
6.2	Culture-jamming (image courtesy of Adbusters Media Foundation)	198
6.3	New branding and marketing strategy launch event, Milan, 16 January, 2017 (image courtesy of Juventus)	201
6.4	*YourIcon* contest entry (image courtesy of Juventus)	202
6.5	*YourIcon* contest entry (image courtesy of Juventus)	203
6.6	*YourIcon* contest entry (image courtesy of Juventus)	203
6.7	*YourIcon* contest entry (image courtesy of Juventus)	204
6.8	*YourIcon* contest entry (image courtesy of Juventus)	204
6.9	*YourIcon* contest entry (image courtesy of Juventus)	205
6.10	*Live Ahead* marketing story at the Allianz Stadium (image courtesy of Juventus)	205
6.11	*Juventus* capsule collection in collaboration with *Adidas* and *Palace* (image courtesy of Juventus)	206
6.12	*Juventus* fans (image courtesy of Juventus)	207
7.1	*Pukka Herbs'* founders Tim Westwell and Sebastian Pole (image courtesy of Pukka Herbs)	238
7.2	*Pukka Herbs'* logo (image courtesy of Pukka Herbs)	238
7.3	*Pukka Herbs'* packaging (image courtesy of Pukka Herbs)	239
7.4	*Pukka Herbs'* certifications (image courtesy of Pukka Herbs)	240
7.5	*Pukka Herbs'* carbon footprint targets (image courtesy of Pukka Herbs)	241
7.6	*Pukka Herbs'* social activism (image courtesy of Pukka Herbs)	241
9.1	*Samsung* shipyard (image courtesy of Samsung)	277
9.2	Procter and Gamble's (P&G) portfolio of brands	278
10.1	*Village Hotels* arrival and departure experience (image courtesy of Village Hotels)	335
10.2	*Village Hotels* arrival and departure experience (image courtesy of Village Hotels)	335
10.3	*Village Hotels* arrival and departure experience (image courtesy of Village Hotels)	336

Foreword

Russell W. Belk

Professor of Marketing; Kraft Foods Canada Chair in Marketing; York University, Toronto, Canada.

LOVEABLE HELLO KITTY MEETS EVIL RONALD MCDONALD

In the following pages you will find an exciting introduction to strategic management and development of brands in a digital age. Yet as the first chapter discusses, brands themselves are thousands of years old. This suggests that there is something about branding that serves a very useful purpose in commerce. Successfully branded products and services can command a premium price, enhance consumer loyalty, facilitate the introduction of new items sharing a family brand name, instantly register in the consumer's mind with a brand symbol or logo, help extend a brand's accumulated goodwill to a related product or service offering, and carry the essence of this goodwill as the company's offerings change. With a well thought out brand image, a product can be marketed globally even though its local offerings are unique. For example, *McDonald's* and its golden arches are well known in the West for their French fries and beef hamburgers. But in predominantly Hindu and Muslim India the unacceptability of beef makes this combination taboo. Accordingly, there is no beef or pork on the Indian menu. Instead it includes such popular offerings as *McAloo Tikki* and the *Maharaja Mac*. Because nearly a third of Indians are also vegetarians many items on the menu involve veggie patties. Everything is sourced locally and as of early 2020 the firm was serving 320 Million customers a year. Besides high quality locally appropriate products, the *McDonald's* brand also takes scrupulous pride in uniform courteous service, clean facilities, and modern decor.

Nevertheless, when *McDonald's* was about to open in India in the early 2000s, Hindu nationalists seized on the fact that *McDonald's* in the United States uses beef extract for its fries – something they saw as a plot to undermine their religion. Although the extract was never exported to India these claims did scar the brand in India for a time (Watson, 2006).

The leading brand in a product category must be resilient for it is usually the one singled out by protests and by brand-related urban legends like the mouse in the *Coke* bottle, *McDonald's* hamburger meat being made out of worms, or snakes in the pockets of *Wal-Mart* coats made in Asia (Fine, 1992). In India and elsewhere, these American brands are also symbolic of the United States, capitalism, and imperialism (Varman & Belk, 2009).

Besides the taste of its products, its service, and local adaptations, a part of what makes the *McDonald's* brand so successful globally is its consistency and speed. This is achieved by principles that Ritzer (1993) labels efficiency, calculation, predictability, and control. These comprise what he calls *McDonaldization*, a term that he does not intend as a compliment. As McDonaldization suggests, academia too is apt to go after the most popular brands, especially when they are seen as producing products that are harmful to the individual, the environment, or society (e.g., Schlosser, 2004; Spurlock, 2011; Star, 1991). But beyond just the particular brand, once again the target is larger—in this case American fast food.

More often a brand can take advantage of these same national associations. Back in the days of a communist Eastern Europe having a pair of *Levi's* or a *Beatles* record was an instant status symbol (Belk, 1997). Even knowing the names of Western brands, movies, cars, and popstars was a ticket to admiration by peers. In the former Yugoslavia, Drakulić tells of:

> ...going into the bathroom, taking my chewing gum out of my mouth, putting some lipstick on it, and mixing the chewing gum until it became pink; then going out and pretending to the girls it was it was the original "Bazooka Joe", ... so they would envy me.
>
> (Drakulić, 1991, p. 187)

As Gronow (1997) details, the communist countries of Eastern Europe produced faux luxuries including crystal chandeliers, 'Champagne', chocolates, and resort hotels, even if they were pale imitations of their Western counterparts. There was also Eastern European brands of foods, cars, televisions, and other consumer goods. But the difference was highlighted before the fall of the Berlin Wall in special 'hard currency stores' where foreign goods and those with Communist Party connections and international currencies could buy them (Manning, 2009). This separation made foreign brands even more magical (Taussig, 1993). In a popular 2003 film, *Goodbye, Lenin!* an East German young man's mother is in a coma for eight months and misses the fall of the Berlin Wall. When she recovers the doctor tells her son that she should experience no sudden shocks. Therefore, he proceeds to try to re-create East Berlin for her by covering signs for *Coca-Cola*, *Burger King*, *Volvo*, and *Ikea* and trying to find the old Eastern German brands like the *Trabant* automobile, *Neus Deutschland* newspaper, and *Spreewaldgurken* pickles (Berdahl, 2010). It is a good depiction of the quick triumph of popular Western brands, but it also shows lingering nostalgia for the consumption compromises made under communism (Boym, 2001; Todorov & Gille, 2010). Brand attachments are hard to shed, even if the brands are ostensibly inferior. They are like old friends who may not have succeeded in life but are still our friends with whom we once shared a bond (Fournier, 1998).

One way in which brands form bonds with us, in addition to repeatedly mentioning their brand name in advertising, is by using an animal, cartoon, or avatar icon (Brown & Ponsonby-McCabe, 2014). Familiar examples are the *Michelin Man*, *Mr. Clean*, *Tony the Tiger*, and the *Geico* gecko. In Japan, Minowa (2014) notes that brand icons are most often small familiar characters that are perceived as *kawaii* (cute). The characters also have qualities of immaturity, childishness, and femininity. One such character, *Hello Kitty*, has inspired a cult of followers alleged to resemble a "new spirituality movement" (Minowa, 2014, p. 102). Members of the *Hello Kitty* cult have enjoyed their favourite feline from infancy well into adulthood. The brand has been imprinted on an array of merchandise from toasters, wines, and airlines to facemasks, thongs, and sex toys (Minowa, 2014, p. 97).

This is not to say that popular global brands are universally revered. As with urban legends, some very popular brands like *Starbucks*, *McDonald's*, and *Disney* not only have their detractors, they also spawn brand parodies. These inversions of brand image are referred to as *Doppelgänger* brands (Giesler, 2012; Luedicke, Thompson, & Giesler, 2010; Thompson & Arsel, 2004; Thompson, Rindfleisch, & Arsel, 2006). Some of the satiric mock logos made for the *Starbucks* doppelgänger included names like 'Starbucks Sucks'. None of this detracts from *Starbucks* being a tremendously successful brand. Like the brand-related urban legends it is part of what comes with being number one. It is also a bit like counterfeit branding. No one likes having their brand image potentially damaged by cheap counterfeits, but no one likes being left out because their brand isn't popular or desirable enough to be imitated. Lin (2011) notes that counterfeit brands helped to create greater awareness of the brands they imitated in China. Perhaps the ultimate *doppelgängering* of popular brands was the 2010 Academy Award-wining short film *Logorama* (https://vimeo.com/10149605). The film features over 3000 brand mascots and logos in a cops and robbers scenario in which an evil *Ronald McDonald* is the villain chased by two overweight *Michelin Man* policemen (Lawrence, 2010). The film irreverently treats a disastrous chase through a commercially decadent Los Angeles, which ultimately suffers an earthquake and falls into the sea. One thing that

IMAGE 0.1 Culture-jamming Starbucks's mermaid logo.

doppelgänger brands, urban legends, and counterfeits illustrate is that branding is no longer entirely in the hands of the marketer. Brands are instead a co-production by marketers and consumers leading to what Craciun (2014, p. 11) calls the inherent instability of the brand.

Besides being co-created by consumers the unstable brand is also mediated by influencer bloggers, unboxers, and YouTubers who gain a following that can sometimes include millions of consumers. They specialize in particular domains like cosmetics, shoes, or clothing fashions, and have even in some cases displaced 'mainstream' fashion magazine writers at fashion shows in Paris, Milan, and London (Dolbec & Fischer, 2015; McQuarrie, Miller, & Phillips, 2013). In an effort to gain better control of their brands, marketers have turned to supporting these influencers with merchandise and other incentives. The long tail of Internet marketing also facilitates finding micro-bloggers with smaller more specialized audiences who can be pursued as micro-market segments.

What does this brave new world of attempting to cope with consumer co-optation mean for brand management? The book you are about to read holds some answers. But it is well to remember that the *brandscape* (Sherry, 1986) is ever-changing. The same is true of the *consumptionscape* (Ger & Belk, 1996). But there is more to the world than just brands and consumers. We live in a globally connected neoliberal world. Thus, Appadurai (1996) adds ethnoscapes, technoscapes, financescapes, mediascapes, and ideoscapes. With this book you will be armed with many tools and examples to help navigate these flows.

REFERENCES

Appadurai, A. (1996). *Modernity at large: Cultural dimensions of globalization*. Minneapolis: University of Minnesota Press.
Belk, R. W. (1997). Romanian consumer desires and feelings of deservingness. In L. Stan (ed.), *Romania in transition* (pp. 191–208). Aldershot: Dartmouth Press.
Berdahl, D. (2010), Goodbye, Lenin! Aufwiedersehen GDR. In M. Todorova & Z. Gille (eds), *Post-communist nostalgia* (pp. 177–189). New York: Berghahn.
Boym, S. (2001). *The future of nostalgia*. New York: Basic Books.
Brown, S., & Ponsonby-McCabe, S. (eds) (2014). *Brand mascots and other marketing animals*. London: Routledge.
Craciun, M. (2014). *Material culture and authenticity*. London: Bloomsbury.
Dolbec, P., & Fischer, E. (2015). Refashioning at field? Connected consumers and institutional dynamics in markets. *Journal of Consumer Research*, 41(6) 1447–1468.
Drakulić, S. (1991). *How we survived communism and even laughed*. New York: W. W. Norton.
Fine, G. A. (1992), *Manufacturing tales: Sex and money in contemporary legends*. Knoxville: University of Tennessee Press.
Fournier, S. (1998), Consumers and their brands: Developing relationship theory in consumer research. *Journal Consumer Research*, 24(4), 343–373.
Ger, G., & Belk, R. W. (1996). I'd like to buy the world a Coke: Consumptionscapes of the "less affluent world". *Journal of Consumer Policy*, 19(3), 271–304.

Giesler, M. (2012). How doppelgänger brand images influence the market creation process: Longitudinal insights from the rise of botox cosmetic. *Journal of Marketing*, 76(6), 55–68.

Gronow, J. (1997). *The sociology of taste*. London: Routledge.

Lawrence, R. (2010), Logorama: The great trademark heist. *Hein Online*, Summer. Available at: https://heinonline.org/HOL/LandingPage?handle=hein.journals/inprobr2&div=5&id=&page= [accessed 10 April 2020].

Lin, Yi-Chieh, J. (2011), *Fake stuff: China and the rise of counterfeit goods*. New York: Routledge.

Luedicke, M. K., Thompson, C. J., & Giesler, M. (2010). Consumer identity work as moral protagonism: How myth and ideology animate a brand-mediated moral conflict. *Journal of Consumer Research*, 36(6), 1016–1032.

Manning, P. (2009). The epoch of Magna: Capitalist brands and postsocialist revolutions in Georgia. *Slavic Review*, 68(4), 924–945.

McQuarrie, E. F., Miller, J., & Phillips, B. J. (2013). The megaphone effect: Taste and audience in fashion blogging. *Journal of Consumer Research*, 40(1), 136–158.

Minowa, Yuko (2014), Feline fetish and marketplace animism. In S. Brown & S. Ponsonby-McCabe (eds), *Brand mascots and other marketing animals* (pp. 91–109). London: Routledge.

Ritzer, G. (1993). *The McDonaldization of society*. Newbury Park: Pine Forge Press.

Schlosser, E. (2004), *Fast food nation: The dark side of the all-American meal*. New York: HarperCollins.

Sherry, J. (1987). Cereal monogamy: Brand loyalty as secular ritual in consumer culture. Paper presented at the Eighteenth Annual Conference of Association for Consumer Research, Cambridge, MA, 8–11 October, 1987.

Spurlock, M. (2011). *Supersized: Strange tales from a fast food culture*, Milwaukee: Dark Horse.

Star, S. L. (1991). Power, technologies and the phenomenology of conventions: On being allergic to onions. In J. Law (ed.), *A sociology of monsters: Essays on power, technology and domination* (pp. 26–56). London: Routledge.

Taussig, M. (1993). *Mimesis and alterity: A particular history of the senses*. New York: Routledge.

Thompson, C. J., & Arsel, Z. (2004). The Starbucks brandscape and consumers'(anticorporate) experiences of glocalization. *Journal of Consumer Research*, 31(3), 631–642.

Thompson, C. J., Rindfleisch, A., & Arsel, Z. (2006). Emotional branding and the strategic value of the doppelgänger brand image. *Journal of Marketing*, 70(1), 50–64.

Todorova, M., & Gille, Z. (eds). *Post-communist nostalgia*. New York: Berghahn.

Varman, R., & Belk, R. W. (2009). Nationalism and ideology in an anti-consumption movement. *Journal of Consumer Research*, 36(4), 686–700.

Watson, J. (2006). *Golden arches east: McDonald's in East Asia* (2nd edn). Stanford: Stanford University Press.

Acknowledgements

Throughout the process of writing this textbook, there has been a number of people who have provided me with great support and encouragement.

First, I would like to thank my colleagues in the Department of Management at the University of Exeter Business School, and my very bright and passionate students, who over the years, have provided me with great inspiration and feedback while teaching them the content presented in this textbook.

I am extremely grateful to staff at Routledge, and in particular Sophia Levine and Emmie Shard, for their continuous guidance and support throughout the process of writing this textbook.

I would also like to extend my warmest thanks to the following people for their contribution (case studies): David Zappe, David Shanks, Nina Van Volkinburg, Victoria Mathers, Luca Adornato, Lidi Grimaldi, Edward Latham, Mathilde Leblond, Radu Dimitriu, and Martin Jordan. Special thanks to Cassie O'Neill at Interbrand. Furthermore, I would like to thank Professor Russell W. Belk for writing the foreword of this textbook. Your contribution and feedback on the final manuscript is truly appreciated.

Finally, my deepest love and gratitude to Graham, Mum, Dad, Antonia, Spyros, Liz, Graham Sr., Susie, Luca, Ruby, Wiz, and George, as well as my extended family and friends – thank you all for your continuous love and support.

Dr Sotiris T. Lalaounis
Bristol, UK

CHAPTER 1

Introduction: History and the importance of brands

CHAPTER AIMS AND LEARNING OUTCOMES

Understanding the exact meaning of important concepts can be a good starting point for developing thorough knowledge of a subject. A better understanding of the tangible and intangible characteristics of brands can enrich our grasp of the topic of branding (Moore & Reid, 2008). Thus, before we embark on our exploratory journey on how brands can be developed, marketed, and managed successfully, it is important to introduce brands, reflect on their history, and understand their importance to economy and society. In particular, this chapter aims to achieve the following:

1. Define the concept of brands and branding.
2. Discuss the role of brands in the economy and the society by exploring the history of branding from ancient civilisations to post-modern contemporary societies.
3. Explore the importance of brands to consumers, organisations, and society.

DEFINING BRANDS

Agreeing on a definition of a concept which is so dynamic and multifaceted can be extremely difficult. Over the years, scholars and practitioners have come up with a plethora of different definitions of brands. Etymologically, the origins of the word *brand* can be traced in Germanic language, meaning 'to burn' (*Oxford English Dictionary*, 2019). In the past, criminals were stamped with hot irons so that they could be identified (Henning, 2000). Nowadays, as in the past, farmers brand by marking their livestock so that they can identify and distinguish their livestock from those of their competitors. Transferring this notion to branding or marking products and services, the American Marketing Association (AMA) defines brand as:

a name, term, sign, symbol, or design or a combination of them intended to identify the goods and services of one seller or group of sellers and to differentiate them from those of competitors.

(*American Marketing Association*, 1960)

This is one of the most prominent definitions, and one that has been around for years, yet many critics regard it as one dimensional and outdated. De Chernatony and Dall'Olmo Riley (1998) argue that it limits the scope of brands because it focuses on the organisation's *input* in terms of differentiating its product or service through a name or visual identity. Most importantly it ignores the role of the consumers who, as nowadays scholars and practitioners recognise, are not passive recipients of the organisation's marketing activity; "branding is not something done to consumers, but rather something they do things with" (de Chernatony & Dall'Olmo Riley, 1998, p. 419). Conejo and Wooliscroft (2015) echo this view. They find AMA's definition rather simplistic as it does not represent how brands have evolved over the last few decades. Furthermore, they argue that brands should be conceptualised as "broad multi-dimensional constructs with varying degrees of meaning, independence, co-creation, and scope" (Conejo & Wooliscroft, 2015, p. 291). In fact, these four elements point to four limitations with AMA's definition.

First, with regard to *meaning*, brands have evolved to "sophisticated networks of information, associations, and feelings, and complex bundles of multidimensional meaning" (Conejo & Wooliscroft, 2015, p. 289). Brands are not merely organisational legal trademarks but instead have become consumer symbolic devices that enable consumers to construct, communicate, and maintain their identity (Belk, 1988). There is a continuum of meaning on which we can place brands; on the one hand, there are brands that are very basic in their meaning (e.g. *Vodafone* telecom services or *Soxo* salt), and on the other hand, brands that are rich and complex (e.g. *Gymshark* or the *BBC*). Brands are dynamic entities and their meanings are fluid. Brand meanings have to be managed across all brand touchpoints, i.e. the points where different publics come into contact with the brand, in order to create identification, differentiation, and value for consumers and organisations (Hales, 2011).

Second, as far as *independence* is concerned, AMA's definition creates the notion that brands are part of finished products, and that products are more important than brands. Current thinking challenges this notion because brands have become independent of, and more valuable than, their products. Brand names and symbols do not only refer to products. In our contemporary post-industrial world, organisations outsource the manufacturing of their products and focus on the development of their brands. As Klein explains, many organisations are able to "have their products made for them by contractors, many of them overseas. What these companies [produce] primarily [are] not things…but images of their brands" (1999, p. 4). Brands gain a life of their own beyond products and organisations, and even if products are discontinued or firms go bust, brands can live on as important parts of popular culture (Conejo & Wooliscroft, 2015) if they have gained over the years a certain level of iconicity (Holt, 2004). Similar to meaning, there is a continuum of independence on which we can place brands where, on the one end, some brands are closely linked, or even subordinated, to their products (e.g. *Kellogg's* corn flakes), and on the other end, brands are independent of their products (and even of their organisations) (e.g. *Nike*).

Third, in relation to *co-creation*, AMA's definition does not take into account the fact that brand meaning is co-created by consumers with organisations. Consumers are not merely passive recipients of messages but active co-creators of value (Vargo & Lusch, 2004, 2008). Instead, the definition "assumes that since organisations create brands, they therefore largely control brands meanings" (Conejo & Wooliscroft, 2015, p. 290). This assumption does not reflect post-modern reality; meaning is dialogic (Morris, 2003) and brand meaning is generated through a dialogue between consumers and organisations. The Internet and social media provide a variety of platforms on which such discussions can take place. On a continuum of co-creation, some brands might still be solely created by their organisations, while at the other end of the spectrum, other brands are collaboratively co-created by consumers (Vargo and Lusch, 2004, 2008) acting as a community of 'co-designers' (Garud, Jain, & Tuertscher, 2008). As explored in Chapter 6, consumers-enthusiasts often form brand communities that construct brand meanings beyond the organisation (e.g. *Harley-Davidson*) (Fournier & Lee, 2009; Muñiz Jr. & O'Guinn, 2001; Schau, Muñiz Jr., & Arnould, 2009).

Finally, AMA's definition has an important limitation in regard with brands' *scope*. The co-creation of brand meaning activity is not limited to the consumer–organisation dyad; there is a range of external and internal stakeholders involved in the co-creation process: suppliers, distributors, employees, government, competitors, media, pressure groups (e.g. *Greenpeace* or *Friends of the Earth*), investors, the local community, and the wider public. All these different stakeholders bring their own backgrounds and worldviews to process and re-distribute brand meanings (Cova, Kozinets, & Shankar, 2007). On a continuum of scope, some brands may still be closely linked to the company (e.g. *Samsung*), while other brands bring together a variety of internal and external stakeholders (e.g. the *International Olympic Committee*) (Conejo & Wooliscroft, 2015).

The AMA sought to provide an added definition of brands, perhaps as a response to the criticism its initial definition had received. They specify that:

> A brand is a customer experience represented by a collection of images and ideas; often it refers to a symbol such as a name, logo, slogan, and design scheme. Brand recognition and other reactions are created by the accumulation of experiences with the specific product or service, both directly relating to its use, and through the influence of advertising, design, and media commentary.
> (*American Marketing Association*, 2015, cited in Dall'Olmo Riley, 2016, p. 4)

The above reinforces the argument that the initial AMA definition had been too restrictive and preoccupied with the product. Through a content analysis of extant literature at the time, de Chernatony and Dall'Olmo Riley (1998) identified 12 main themes as accurate categorisations of brand definitions, namely the brand defined as a legal instrument, a logo, a company, shorthand, risk reducer, identity system, image in consumers' minds, value system, personality, relationship, added value, and an evolving entity. As we can see these themes demonstrate "a shift in emphasis from a notion of brands as logos to a more integrated view as the matching of a firm's functional and emotional values with the performance and psychosocial values sought by consumers" (de Chernatony and Dall'Olmo Riley, 1998, p. 418). Each categorisation has its advantages and disadvantages and each explore the concept of the brand from a different perspective.

Shifting our thinking from conceptualising the brand as a legal instrument or logo to a value system, a personality, and an evolving entity means that we move from a 'small b' brand notion to a 'big B' brand notion. AMA's initial definition mirrors the US Federal Trademark Act definition of legal trademarks, hence it is more in line with the 'small b' brand notion where the focus is mainly on the organisation's input activity (de Chernatony, 1993; de Chernatony and Dall'Olmo Riley, 1998; Dall'Olmo Riley, 2016; Keller, 2006). Instead, the 'big B' brand notion views the brand as a more dynamic system of values with its own personality (Aaker, 1997). As de Chernatony explains, a brand "is a cluster of functional and emotional values that enables a promise to be made about a unique and welcomed experience" (2010, p. 17). We must have a more holistic view of the brand which brings together the organisation's messages (input), i.e. the *brand identity*, elements, and personality, with the consumers' processing (output), i.e. the *brand image* in their minds which includes a set of mental associations (Dall'Olmo Riley, 2016). Brands are great sources of value for the firm and the consumer; they are "multidimensional concepts capable of capturing content, images, feelings, lifestyles, personalities, culture, and other characteristics that help a consumer deeply and uniquely associate, or disassociate, with a brand" (Baalbaki & Guzmán, 2016, p. 32). The wonderful amalgamation of tangible and intangible characteristics that is a brand is eloquently explained by Bastos and Levy (2012) with the following:

> Branding reflects the reality of the core product, its facts and features, its functions and benefits, as well as the surrounding aura of its aesthetic, its music, its texture, its visualisation, and its fantasy-like existence in the culture as it relates to societal and customer mythology. Ultimately a brand is an opus, a complex design, a mosaic, a symphony, an evolving cultural construction that benefits from a knowledgeable, and perceptive director, and that fires the imagination. The most successful and iconic brands go beyond the ordinary elements (the four essences of earth, air, fire, and water), to become quintessential, and transcendentally so.
>
> (Bastos & Levy, 2012, p. 360)

Bastos and Levy (2012) point to *Apple* as the epitome of a successful brand due to its integration of innovative technology, human-centred design, and widespread appeal. The aforementioned statement represents the ethos of this book in that we consider brands and branding not only as a commercial and managerial phenomenon, but one that has a multifaceted nature. Hence, brands and branding need to be explored from a combination of sociological, psychological, cultural, and managerial, perspectives. As Schroeder (2015) argues,

> brands and branding are not just managerial tools or marketing concepts, they represent a contested cultural, managerial and scholarly arena. Understanding brands and branding implies an awareness of basic cultural processes that affect contemporary brands, including historical context, ethical concerns, consumer response and regulation.
>
> (Schroeder, 2015, p. 3–4)

HISTORY OF BRANDS AND BRANDING

It has been a popular misconception that brands are a Western outcome of capitalism and the Industrial Revolution. Contrary to popular belief, historians, archaeologists, and marketing scholars have indicated that brands and the act of branding have been around for thousands of years in earlier societies around the world. Wengrow (2008, p. 21) claims "brands have been a long-term feature of human cultural development, acting within multiple ideological and institutional contexts". Over millennia, brands have been cultural symbols and agents of marketplace growth. Exploring how branding systems developed in different sociocultural, economic, and historic contexts can help us gain a better understanding of brands and their role within social systems (Eckhardt & Bengtsson, 2010). Besides, exploring the history of a subject is always the best starting point for gaining an understanding of its contemporary theory and practice (Tadajewski, 2009).

Moore and Reid (2008) argue that from ancient to modern times, brands have played two key roles; as *conveyors of information* about origin and quality, and as *conveyors of image or meaning* in terms of status/power, value, and personality. They make a distinction between two types of brands: 1) *proto-brands* (from the Greek πρῶτος = *protos* meaning first or primitive), the early type of brands, which are found in ancient civilizations and the pre-Industrial Revolution era, and 2) *modern brands*, emerged with the Industrial Revolution and developed ever since (see Figure 1.1). Such distinction is made in order to indicate that some dimensions of brand can be found in earlier societies but not in the same modern sense of the word, and to demonstrate the gradual shift to greater complexity of brands as multidimensional constructs (Moore & Reid, 2008). Moore and Reid's main thesis is that proto-brands conveyed information which was "physically or inherently attached to a product or product vessel (packaging)" (2008, p. 430), yet they did not include complex image

6 HISTORY & THE IMPORTANCE OF BRANDS

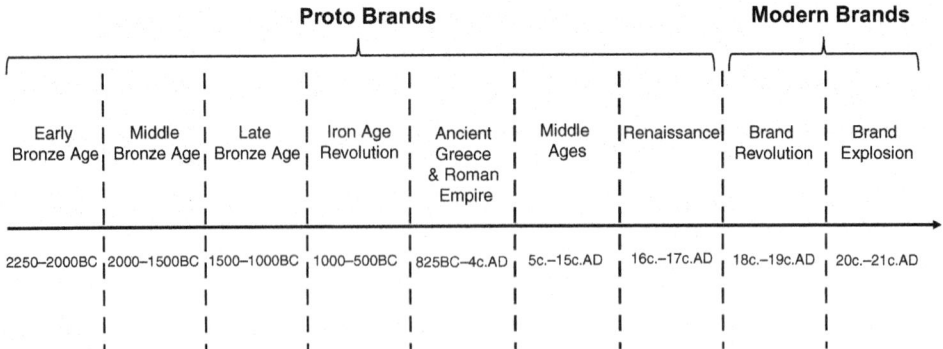

FIGURE 1.1 The history of brands

or meaning characteristics found in modern brands. Generally speaking, there was a gradual transition from the *transactional* to the *transformational*, with brands in the pre-modern era concentrating on *utilitarian* information regarding the maker's identity, origin, and quality of produce, to brands in the modern era conveying, in addition, *image-building* brand characteristics regarding status/power, inherent value, and brand personality (Moore & Reid, 2008), i.e. human personality traits associated with the brand (Aaker, 1997).

Proto-brands: From Brahma bulls and Zu crests to Sophilos

As mentioned above, a proto-brands' role is essentially informational; this role involves at least one of three functions. First, proto-brands carried information about the place of origin by "utilising a known mark, signature or through the known physical properties of a given raw material" (Moore & Reid, 2008, p. 430). Second, proto-brands elaborated this information to enable some basic marketing functions, such as sorting, transportation, and storage, to occur. Such logistical information is provided in modern brands by using barcodes or separate labels, but these are not combined with the brand itself (Moore & Reid, 2008). Third, proto-brands communicated information about the quality of the product through designating the origin of the product which removed consumer uncertainty and reduced purchase risk, hence increasing the perceived quality in consumer's mind (Moore & Reid, 2008). In the pre-modern economy, proto-brands were "an instrument used to solve information asymmetries between producers and consumers" (Belfanti, 2018, p. 1138), evolved through time, and differed from region to region.

The earliest examples of branding can be found in Early Bronze Age (2250–2000 BC) in the Indus Valley. Merchants used seals of tigers, elephants, Brahma bulls, and other Indian animals, along with associated text, to brand their products (Wolpert, 2000). Manufacturers, re-sellers, and government authorities used these seals to communicate information regarding origin of the product and to facilitate sorting, storage, and transportation (i.e. the first and second function mentioned earlier) (Moore & Reid, 2008). Taking into consideration Keller's (2003) notion of brands as having intangible and abstract qualities on top of their more tangible informational elements to achieve a more transformational (image-related) character communicating cultural meaning (McCracken, 1986), the brands found in the Indus Valley during the Early Bronze Age are indeed an early type of brands (proto-brands) (Moore & Reid, 2008).

In Shang China during the Middle Bronze Age (2000–1500 BC), the kingdom was organised on the basis of towns where *Zu*, i.e. kin groups, were settled, all subject to *Wang*, the king who owned the land. These kin groups traded specific produce with other groups and were organised as different occupational units (Moore & Reid, 2008), each having their own family crest and their name based on the product they were responsible for. These crests can be considered a type of proto-brand as they communicated information about the origin of the product based on the location of the Zu, as well as information about quality which was regulated by the king (Moore & Reid (2008). It is also assumed that they conveyed information for sorting, distribution, and storage, however "imagery was limited to the utilitarian images associated with the use of the product" (Moore & Reid, 2008, p. 425). Nevertheless, Eckhardt and Bengtsson (2010) challenge Moore and Reid's (2008) conceptualisation to demonstrate that Chinese pre-modern brands had imagery elements that conveyed meaning besides functional characteristics that merely provide logistical and place of origin information. Their analysis yields some important findings regarding the use of brands in Imperial China because it demonstrates that these brands were associated with the human desire for differentiation and quality assurance and acted as agents of consumer culture in those social systems, which according to Holt (2006a, 2008) is a central characteristic of modern brands. There is evidence that "the advent of the brand as marketplace mediator and as an important cultural and social force occurred before the evolution of modern brands" (Eckhardt & Bengtsson, 2010, p. 218).

The development of the Late Bronze Age (1500–1000 BC) economy was based on the growth of seaborne commerce as a trade model for Canaanites (Phoenicians), Minoans, and Mycenaean Greeks, and was significantly influenced by the mining of copper on the island of Cyprus in the Mediterranean Sea (Moore & Reid, 2008). Merchants started branding in a more sophisticated way because of a trade model that allowed more market freedoms. Nonetheless, these brands were still a type of proto-brands. Interestingly, Cypriot copper was "a special example of a brand characteristic which is often affiliated with raw and other high-end processed materials as a symbol of inherent quality" (Moore & Reid, 2008, p. 426). During the Iron Age revolution (1000–500 BC), merchants from Tyre (in present Lebanon), the greatest city in the Phoenician civilisation, traded with many regions and often established their own settlements around the Mediterranean Sea. The main produce from Tyre was purple-dyed garments and red-slip ceramics, similar to how Cyprus was famous for its copper. These garments and ceramics were often adorned with depictions of *Melqart*, the Supernatural-King of Tyre, which acted as a proto-brand conveying informational characteristics with regards to origin and quality, "while also utilising image in a powerful combination for the purpose of showing power or status and value of partaking in the cult" (Moore & Reid, 2008, p. 427).

A more market-oriented culture that encouraged entrepreneurship flourished in ancient Greece and the Roman Empire (825 BC–fourth century AD) and branding was used to distinguish between merchants through the use of imagery. In the early seventh century BC, potters in Euboea started labelling their produce, a practice which spread to Athens and Corinth a century after, with Sophilos being the first Athenian potter to identify his own work. Competition was encouraged by the layout of the *agora*, the marketplace where merchants were arranged by product category, and competing brands of pottery sat side by side (Dixon, 1995; Moore & Reid, 2008). The agora was a very busy and vibrant place where sellers and buyers negotiated on the price, and the former always tried to undercut their competitors (Shaw, 2016). As with most cultural diffusion of innovation, early market innovations and the use of brands spread to other ancient Greek city-states (Shaw, 2016). With the conquest of the Hellenic world by the Romans, the use of brand continued well into the prime of the Roman Empire. The entrepreneurial culture nurtured in ancient Greece brought significant changes in branding practice. Beyond the traditional proto-brand strategy of communicating information, place of origin, and quality, pottery depicted imagery such as that of *Aphrodite*, the goddess of love, beauty, and sexual rapture, to suggest the maker's personality. Yet, "the large scale growth of the development of brand personality is truly a phenomenon of the twentieth century" (Moore & Reid, 2008, p. 428).

After the fall of Rome (476 AD), the market system developed in ancient Greece and the Roman Empire disintegrated (Blackett, 2003), and during the period known as the Middle Ages (fifth–fifteenth century), "warlords took what they wanted; law and order collapsed…so industry and trade deteriorated to near nothing. Europe returned to self-sufficient agriculture…as it had before Greek and Roman times thousand years earlier" (Shaw, 2016, p. 34). Any use of brands was reduced to local scale with some exceptions such as marks used by royal families, governments, and noble groups (Blackett, 2003). Conditions started to improve after 1000 AD, with Crusades bringing the need to fix old Roman roads that had been damaged. This increased the opportunity for the transport of produce, and as the armies needed supplies, there was an increase in trade. Slowly, law and order returned, and villages started holding market days once a week. This era brought marketing innovations such as trade fairs, new payment methods such as promissory notes and bills of exchange, and guilds (Shaw, 2016): "Medieval guild regulations served [the] purpose of controlling unauthorised imitation by other guild members, but guilds had to seek legal protection to prevent imitation by those outside the guild" (Petty, 2016). However, Schechter (1925) argues that such guilds were more of a liability to users than a method of promoting their products because they were policing quality instead of promoting it, hence they cannot be considered a basis for modern brand marketing.

During the period of the Renaissance (sixteenth–seventeenth century) there was an increase of volume manufacture of products such as fine porcelain, furniture, and tapestries with support from Europe's royal houses. In addition, laws for watermarking paper and hallmarking gold and silver objects were established in the seventeenth and eighteenth centuries, and are still in use today (Blackett, 2003). Brands gradually started to emerge as ways to signify authority, ownership, and status, as factories started manufacturing durable products (Moor, 2007).

Modern brands: From Bass beer and Quaker Oats to iPad and Instagram

The Industrial Revolution of the eighteenth and nineteenth century brought profound changes in trade and to society in general. Economic developments, such as mass production, better product distribution, and increased transportation occurred in tandem alongside significant social changes, with the increase of urbanisation, the formation of working and middle classes, and more interactions among consumer cultures. Products were especially designed and produced to satisfy the needs of the low-income workers, other products targeted the bourgeoning luxury consumer who looked for more hedonic purchases. This brought "the necessity for firms to be identified and represented by a symbol, recognisable by the consumer" (Belfanti, 2018, p. 1138). Gradually, manufacturers started packaging and labelling their products that in the past had been sold in general stores as staples in bulk (Bastos & Levy, 2012). Buyers started recognising the names of the manufacturers, which added value to the products sold.

The brand names adopted by manufacturers "marked the development from marks as descriptions of origin to brands as items of artifice, from conveyors of information to evocative contrivances" (Mercer, 2010, p. 35). Brands such as *Coca-Cola*, *Heinz Baked Beans*, *Quaker Oats*, *Chesterfield Cigarettes*, all still widely available to this day, originate from the period described by Blackett (2003) as the *brand revolution* era, where advances in manufacturing and communications led to the mass-marketing of consumer products. The first registered trademark in the United Kingdom is *Bass* beer's red triangle (registered in 1876), which the company still uses on its bottle. The brand revolution brought the establishment of advertising agencies such as *Lord & Thomas*, *J. Walter Thompson*, and *McCann Erickson*, which are still very successful, creating some of the world's most innovative communications campaigns.

Following the end of the Second World War, the market witnesses a *brand explosion*, a burst in the use of brands with developments such as improved transportation, the collapse of communism, the birth of the Internet, and the advances of social media, accentuating this phenomenon further (Blackett, 2003). In a seminal paper published in the *Harvard Business Review*, Gardner and Levy proclaimed that "people buy things not only for what they can do, but also for what they mean" (1955, p. 39). This inspired the advertising world as it confirmed the importance of brand personality (Bastos & Levy, 2012). Moore and Reid argue that brand personality could not have been a component of brands prior to the Industrial Revolution because the developments of media communications facilitated a "greater richness and complexity of brand messaging, and greater marketing research techniques

IMAGE 1.1 *Heinz Baked Beans* (image courtesy of H.J. Heinz Foods UK Ltd)

IMAGE 1.2 *Heinz Baked Beans* advertising (image courtesy of H.J. Heinz Foods UK Ltd)

allowing for more in-depth knowledge of target markets" (2008, p. 429). It is evident that brands in modern and post-modern societies evolved beyond the primitive nature of proto-brands to convey not only informational characteristics but also image characteristics including elements such as status and power, inherent value, and brand personality. Nowadays, we recognise that a brand has its own identity and personality, it evokes intellectual and emotional associations, which together create a brand image in the mind of the consumer. These are concepts and mechanisms that we will explore in greater depth in Chapter 2.

The evolution of brands over the millennia demonstrates the strong connection between branding and societal development. In our post-modern society, with its high level of consumerism, we all seek to satisfy our functional and emotional needs as successfully and efficiently as possible. Branding has been elevated to a commercial (and personal) process of storytelling whence we gain most of our shared knowledge about ourselves (Twitchell, 2004). Nowadays we recognise that *anything* can be branded. The list is very long, from commodities (e.g. *Saxo* salt, *Chiquita* bananas, *British Gas*), durable and perishable physical products (e.g. *Nike* trainers, *iPhones*, *iPads*, *Innocent* smoothies), different types of services (e.g. retail, travel, professional), and online platforms (*eBay*, *LinkedIn*, *Facebook*, *Instagram*, and *Snapchat*), to arts, sports and entertainment (e.g. *Tate Modern*, *Olympic Games*, *Formula 1*), geographical locations (*Visit Scotland* tourist board), ideas and notions (e.g. *Cool Britannia* in the 1990s, or the UK's *Conservative Party*'s *One Nation* agenda), charities (*Macmillan Cancer Support*, *The Red Campaign*), and even people (e.g. the *British Royal family*, and the *Beckham* and *Kardashian* families). In addition, with the clothes we wear, the stores where we do our shopping, the places we frequent, we can even brand our individual self to people around us. Such an act of *self-branding* where an individual controls his/her brand identity in order to stand out and create a desirable image in other people's minds (Peters, 1997) has become a widespread phenomenon through social networking on social media apps, allowing each of us the potential to become micro-celebrities (Khamis, Ang, & Welling, 2017). The aforementioned social media platforms are brands themselves, but also they offer the platform to every single one of us to take our own self-brand onto the global stage. Our *Instagram* photos, *Facebook* updates, *Snapchat* stories, *Twitter* feeds, and *LinkedIn* resume, can help us continuously feed information about ourselves to those people we choose as our followers, and to those online groups we choose to join as members, creating a certain image about us in other people's minds.

IMPORTANCE OF BRANDS TO CONSUMERS, ORGANISATIONS, AND SOCIETY

If a brand resides in people's minds, "it is simply a collection of perceptions held in the mind of the consumer" (Fournier, 1998, p. 345); if an individual perceives something (physical or intangible) as a brand, then it is. Branding is ubiquitous, and brands are fluid and dynamic as they morph and develop over time. Brands are of great importance to consumers, organisations, and the society in general. In this subsection we will discuss the reasons for their importance in more depth.

Importance of brands to consumers

Recognising the importance of exchange, Kotler and Zaltman stated that "marketing does not occur unless there are two or more parties, each with something to exchange, and both able to carry out communications and distribution" (1971, p. 4). A consumer-centric approach to branding means it is essential to start our exploration of the importance of brands by looking at the case of the consumer as one of the main parties in the marketing exchange (the other being the organisation).

Brands enable consumers to identify the source of the product or service, i.e. to recognise which organisation is the producer or service provider (Keller & Swaminathan, 2020). When you look at a box of cereal on the supermarket shelf, its packaging can help you identify that it is produced by *Kellogg's* or *Nestle*. Over the years consumers develop their own *brand knowledge*, i.e. "the personal meaning about a brand stored in consumer memory [including] all descriptive and evaluative brand-related information" (Keller, 2003, p. 596), which they use to make quick and effective decisions about what to consume. This means that brands can represent this knowledge and the connection consumers have with the product maker/service provider.

As a result, brands allow consumers the power to assign responsibility to these product makers/service providers (Keller & Swaminathan, 2020). The organisational offering needs to deliver what consumers expect; in fact, in most cases, it must exceed consumers' expectations. If it does, consumers will be satisfied and will (probably) consider buying the brand again in the future, if it does not, then they will (probably) avoid this brand next time. For example, if the box of cereal you purchased from the supermarket did not taste as expected or you did not like the taste, you can avoid this particular product or the brand altogether.

Buying a product from a brand that you know and trust can reduce the risks associated with purchasing and consuming a product. By consumption, we mean *using* the product (once when it is perishable, e.g. a soft drink), or many times (when it is durable, e.g. clothing), incorporating it in your lifestyle (e.g. your wardrobe) (Roselius, 1971). These risks include 1) the *functional* risk (will it work/deliver what is expected?), 2) the *physical* risk (will it harm me and/or others around me?), 3) the *financial* risk (will it be worth the price?), 4) the *psychological* risk (will it communicate to my family, friends, colleagues, acquaintances, and the general public around me the messages I want?), 5) the *social* risk (will it reinforce my expectations and contribute to my well-being?) and 6) the *time* risk (will I have to look for another product or service to replace it because it did not deliver what I expected?) (Roselius, 1971). *Brand trust* can reduce all these aforementioned risks. Delgado-Ballester and Munuera-Alemán (2001, p. 1242) argue that "trust is a feeling of security held by the consumer that the brand will meet his/her consumption expectations". This means that the consumers will look for a trustworthy brand as the important criterion for making a decision to purchase a product in order to avoid the associated risks of a product class. Trust can be developed from direct sources such as the consumer's own trial, use and satisfaction from the product or service, as well as from indirect sources such as advertising messages, word of mouth (WOM), and reputation (Delgado-Ballester & Munuera-Alemán, 2001). For example, when a female consumer wants to purchase a make-up product, she will most likely purchase a product from a brand (e.g. *Clinique* skin foundation) she has used before (experience), because she was happy with its quality (satisfaction). Thus, she trusts this branded product (trust) to deliver what is expected (avoiding the functional risk), to not harm her skin (avoiding the physical risk), to communicate to other people the right message in relation to her looking after her appearance with a quality brand (avoiding the psychological and social risks). As a result she will not have to look for another product to replace it (avoiding the time risk) and she will be certain that the product was worth the price paid (avoiding the financial risk). Delgado-Ballester and Munuera-Alemán (2001) suggest that when consumers feel higher commitment to a brand, they are more price tolerant, i.e. they are willing to pay a higher price; this connects with the concept of *brand equity* as we will discuss later.

From the above, we can also see that brands reduce the cost of searching for a new product or service. Because consumers are likely to return to the brands they know from direct and/or indirect experience, they do not need to spend (or waste) time and effort searching for new products or services. Especially in the case of low-involvement habitual purchases, such as buying a bottle of soft drink or a sandwich, this simplifies decision-making and speeds up the consumption process (Jacoby, Szybillo, & Busato-Schach, 1977). Brands signal quality and provide a sort of guarantee to consumers, which means brands can achieve their risk-reducing function.

Brands are important to consumers because they are symbolic devices; they allow consumers to satisfy not only their functional needs but also their emotional needs. Consumption has become meaning-based and symbolic; brands enable consumers to express their personality and values. Of course, we do not see ourselves represented by single products; instead we bring together a constellation of brands, a portfolio of possessions (Chaplin & Lowrey, 2010; Solomon, 1988). The constellation of brands we incorporate into our lives help us to construct and maintain our identity, an identity we wish to retain in response to an ever-changing environment (Elliott & Wattanaasuwan, 1998). Over time, these brands become part of our 'extended self'. As Belk explains

> we learn, define, and remind ourselves of who we are by our possessions ... we seek to express ourselves through possessions, and use material possessions to seek happiness, remind ourselves of experiences, accomplishments, and other people in our lives, and even create a sense of immortality after death. Our

accumulation of possessions provides a sense of past and tells us who we are, where we have come from, and perhaps where we are going.

(Belk, 1988, p. 160)

This means that we usually consume brands whose personality and values correspond to our own personality and values. There is a greater preference for a brand when there is congruity between the characteristics of the consumer's actual self (how an individual perceives him/herself) or ideal self (how an individual would like to be perceived) and the brand's characteristics (Aaker, 1997; Malhotra, 1988; Sirgy, 1982). However, this is not always the case as "there is no reason that an object seen as expressive of self needs to share our characteristics" (Belk, 2016, p. 71). In addition, it is not likely that our identity will be *fully* expressed through brands, because, naturally, we have certain personal characteristics that cannot be expressed through the brands we consume. Still, in our post-modern world, brands play a fundamental role in people's identity construction and management, as consumption has become an inherent aspect of human life and development (Belk, 1988).

Importance of brands to organisations

Powerful brands are treasure troves, horns of plenty, pots of gold. They are exceptionally valuable corporate assets. More often than not they are included on the balance sheet of the company that owns them. Brands and analogous intellectual properties may be intangible, but they are much more valuable, for the most part, than bricks and mortar and the machines that make them.

(Brown, 2016, p. 9)

The above statement illustrates the importance of brands to organisations. From a practical and logistical perspective, a brand provides identification, i.e. the organisation can identify its own products, which simplifies the handling or tracing of products. From a legal perspective, a brand also allows the organisation to legally protect unique features of its products or services and secure the copyright of its brand elements. For instance, an organisation can prohibit its competitors from using the same name or brand colour in the product or service category. If a new airline firm was to be set up to operate in the UK air travel market, this firm would not be able to call itself *British Airways* or use *EasyJet*'s orange insignia as these are legally protected against use by other organisations in the same sector.

As we explored in the previous subsection, brands also signal quality to consumers who, as a result, trust the organisation's offerings. This means that organisations can be more successful in marketing their offerings to the audiences they choose to target because their brands act as a guarantee of quality (de Chernatony & McWilliam, 1989). Most importantly, however, a brand bestows the product and service with unique associations in consumers' minds (Erdem & Swait, 1998). This means that when consumers think of the product or service, certain associations (e.g. thoughts, images, feelings, experiences) come into their minds because of the brand. Consequently, if these associations are positive, a brand is a source of competitive advantage for the organisation leading to differentiation and brand equity.

Brand equity is the added value the brand endows a product or service beyond the product's or service's objective quality (Farquhar, 1989). A brand with high equity can command a higher price from consumers who are willing to pay this price for the branded product or service. In addition, the organisation can demand lower costs from suppliers, which means that the profit margins increase. Hence, a brand is a source of financial return for the organisation. The financial value of the brand is the "financial representation of a business's earnings due to the superior demand it creates for its products or services through the strength of its brand" (Hales, 2011, p. 146). For example, consumers are willing to pay a higher price for a pair of *Levi's* jeans than an unbranded pair of jeans, even when the two products are comparable, i.e. they are exactly (or almost) identical in terms of objective quality (e.g. fabric and cut). The concept of brand equity will be explored in more depth in Chapter 2. In general, branding matters to organisations because it connects the firm with its various external and internal audiences; even in times of crisis or uncertainty, e.g. the 2008 economic downturn, strong brands can be a guarantee to protection and growth for organisations (Farquhar, 1989; Hales, 2011).

Importance of brands to society

Brands do not only satisfy people's functional, emotional, and symbolic needs, and enable organisations to successfully market their offerings, they contribute to society in general. Brands are important to society because they contribute to sustainable wealth creation, security and stability of employment in the countries in which they operate, which bring associated social benefits (Hales, 2011). From an economic point of view, brands own a big part of global wealth, and they are often wealthier than entire nations. According to *Interbrand* (one of the world's leading brand consultancies) and its global brand rankings, the top-10 global brands have a combined financial value of around $880 billion, with *Apple* being the world's top global brand (Interbrand, 2018).

Successful branding requires everyone in the organisation to understand what the brand stands for – its core purpose – and deliver this to society. This means that the brand has to connect with a breadth of people: current and prospective consumers, current and prospective employees, suppliers, distributors, shareholders, and the general public. The societal approach to marketing emphasises three essential foci for any organisation, i.e. to satisfying consumers' needs and desires (consumer), generating corporate profit (organisation), but also contributing positively to social welfare (society) (Kotler, 1972). If a brand delivers what it promises, behaves responsibly, and continues to innovate and add value, people will continue to consume, respect and love it (Hales, 2011).

Schroeder (2009) encourages a cultural perspective to understanding brands as this highlights their importance to society and complements managerial and psychological perspectives of branding. He asserts that "brands are not only mediators of cultural meaning – brands themselves have become ideological referents that shape cultural rituals, economic activities, and social norms" (Schroeder, 2009, p. 124). Brands often display the metaphorical signals of what a society values at a specific point of time (Hales, 2011). Perhaps this is why *Apple* is very successful at present as our post-modern society values technological products that work seamlessly with human intuition. In a *McDonaldised* world which values efficiency, predictability, quantity, and is dominated by technology (Ritzer, 2015), *Amazon* provides to all of us an efficient platform for searching and purchasing products, and getting them quickly delivered at our door with a click of a button.

Indeed, brands can reflect many societal values and ideologies (Holt, 2004, 2006b; McCracken, 1986). Brands can reflect different characteristics of a person's society and its dominant ideology, hence they can reflect what the person likes or dislikes about his/her society and what it represents (Shepherd, Chartrand, & Fitzsimons, 2015). There can be differences in an individual's support of his/her social system; some people are satisfied with their social system while others are not. For instance, in the United States, there are two main components of the country's dominant ideology, *power* (social status, control and dominance over people and resources) and *universalism* (concern for others, equality, and social justice) (Shepherd et al., 2015). Schwartz and Bardi (2001) explain that Americans tend to value power more than people from other countries, and "power and universalism are more equivalent in the minds of many Americans" (Shepherd et al., 2015, p. 77). A person's satisfaction with his/her socio-cultural setting influences the person's values, and has implications for how [he/she responds] to different ads, packaging, brand information, and consumer-related policy" (Shepherd et al., 2015, p. 89). It also has implications in relation to whether or not a person considers a brand as a cultural icon (Shepherd et al., 2015).

Globalisation is a phenomenon (or ideology) often associated with successful brands, since such brands tend to operate on a global scale. *McDonald's*, *Nike*, and *Starbucks* have all evolved into global brands, hence are often targeted by those in support of the anti-globalisation movement. Brands can certainly become political symbols or take a stance in political debate. In the United Kingdom, the *Brexit* debate dominated socio-political discourse from 2016 to 2019, and many organisations came out to support (e.g. *Dyson*) or oppose (e.g. *Virgin*) the UK's departure from the European Union. Similarly in the United States, some brands might be perceived as *anti-Trump* (opposing US President Trump's rhetoric) as a result of their communications campaigns, e.g. *Nike* and its advert featuring former *National Football League (NFL)* athlete *Colin Kaepernick*, whose kneeling during the playing of the US anthem (in support of the *Black Lives Matter* movement) had been condemned by President Trump. However, brands might also "pre-empt cultural spheres of religion, politics, and myth, as they generally promote an ideology linked to political and theological models that equate consumption with happiness" (Schroeder, 2009, p. 124). The role of brands in society and as expression of ideologies will be explored in more depth in Chapter 6.

BOOK STRUCTURE

Recognising the economic, social, and ideological importance of brands in postmodern society, *Strategic Brand Management and Development: Creating and Marketing Successful Brands* seeks to provide a thorough understanding of brand development and management by achieving the nexus of sociological, psychological, cultural, marketing, and management perspectives. Established models and frameworks in branding and brand management provide a solid foundation and structure for this book, yet this book adds more depth to these models and frameworks by incorporating a wider base of literature from multiple disciplines spanning the social sciences and humanities, such as sociology, psychology, consumer culture theory, marketing, management, communications studies, and design studies. We use Keller and Swaminathan's (2020) *strategic brand management process* as the roadmap for our journey (see Figure 1.2) but go beyond merely explaining this process. Each stage is thoroughly discussed bringing numerous theories and concepts to develop a deeper knowledge and insight into the development, marketing, and management of brands and branding.

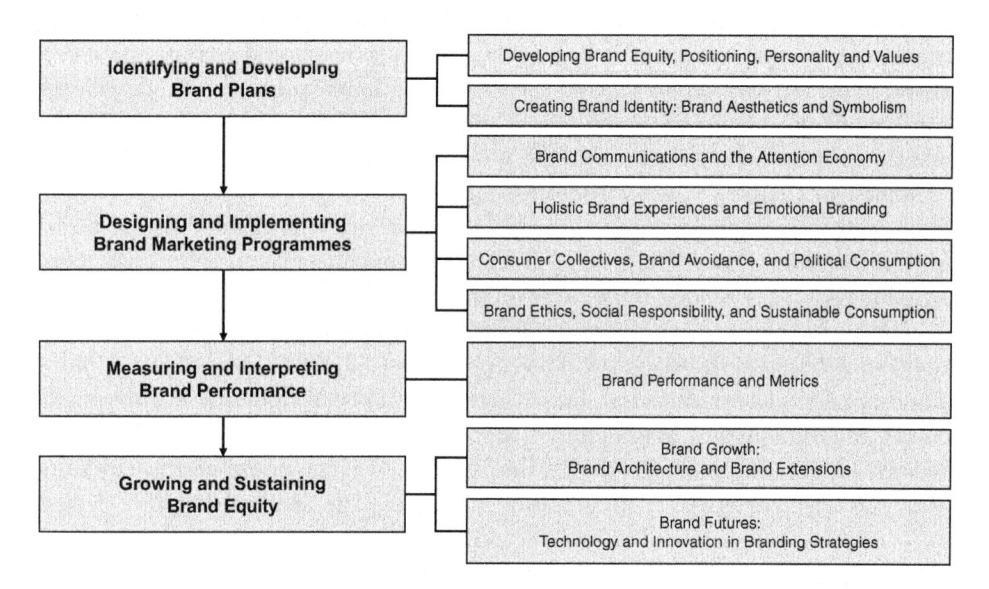

FIGURE 1.2 Strategic brand management process and book plan

Chapters 2 and 3 correspond to the first stage of the process: identifying and developing brand plans. In Chapter 2, we will discuss the concept of brand equity and the components of the *Customer-Based Brand Equity* (CBBE) pyramid model (Keller, 2001), how organisations build successful brand positioning to develop brand equity, and how brand personality and brand values enable organisations to create successful brand positioning. Chapter 3 explores how organisations can develop a successful brand identity through aesthetics and symbolism, and draws from literature in marketing, management, consumer culture theory, communication and design studies, as well as, semiotics.

Moving to the second stage of the process, designing and implementing brand marketing programmes, will be discussed in Chapters 4, 5, 6, and 7. Chapter 4 will explore the characteristics of brand communications options and media platforms, and how these have an impact on consumer decision-making and brand equity development. It will also explore how organisations can plan brand integrated marketing communications (IMC) programmes and will discuss the implications of social media for consumer culture, through the concepts of digital consumption, co-creation, and the (over)democratisation of marketing. Finally, it will discuss the role of social media in the wider society through the concepts of self-branding and the attention economy. In Chapter 5, we will discuss human experiences and experiential perspectives on consumption. We will explore the application of the human experiences construct on branding by discussing the concepts of the experience economy and experiential marketing. The chapter also delves deeper into the realm of emotions and explores how organisations can pursue emotional branding. In particular, the chapter focuses on nostalgia and retro branding, and their contribution to the development and management of brand meaning. Chapter 6 will explore the scope and power of consumer collectives, i.e. subcultures, brand communities, consumer tribes, and brand publics, and their branding implications. It will also discuss brand avoidance and anti-consumption, as well as different types of political consumption, making connections with the notion of brands as expressions of political ideologies. In Chapter 7, we will discuss ethics and corporate social responsibility (CSR), and their implications for brands and branding. This chapter will also provide a discussion of social marketing, green marketing and sustainability, and cause-related marketing activities, drawing from theories in human behaviour.

The third stage of the strategic brand management process, measuring and interpreting brand performance, will be explored in Chapter 8. This chapter explores a conceptual model for understanding the creation of brand value and identifying the sources and outcomes of brand equity (Brand Value Chain Model). It also discusses the way organisations can carry out a brand audit to gauge brand performance and assess the effectiveness of their branding strategies. The chapter will also explore ways organisations can understand the ecology of the brand by pursuing ethnographic studies.

Finally, the fourth stage of the strategic brand management process, growing and sustaining brand equity, will be discussed in Chapters 9 and 10. With Chapter 9, we will explore brand architecture and brand hierarchy, and the power and scope of brand extensions along with their advantages and disadvantages. Chapter 10 will discuss the potential of technology and innovation in branding strategies. Organisations need to continuously find innovative ways to grow and sustain their brand equity. This chapter explores the dimensions of consumer engagement and how it can be measured, as well as the contribution of big data and consumer analytics to value creation and competitive advantage. It also discusses the Internet of Things (IoT) and its implications for brands, in addition to the application of neuromarketing research studies in branding strategies.

CHAPTER REVIEW QUESTIONS

You can use the following questions to reflect on the material covered in Chapter 1:

1. Discuss the various phases in the history of brands and branding.
2. Think of two brands you really like. What do you think your attitude to these brands say about you?
3. Think of two brands which you do not like. What do you think your attitude to these brands say about you? What do these brands say about the people who love and/or consume them?
4. Why are brands important to consumers, organisations, and society? Are brands important to you, and if so, why?

RECOMMENDED READING

1. Dall'Olmo Riley, F. (2016). Brand definitions and conceptualizations. In F. Dall'Olmo Riley, J. Singh, & C. Blankson (eds), *The Routledge companion to contemporary brand management* (pp. 3–12). London: Routledge.
2. Moore, K., & Reid, S. (2008). The birth of brand: 4000 years of branding. *Business History*, 50(4), 419–432.
3. Eckhardt, G. M., & Bengtsson, A. (2010). A brief history of branding in China. *Journal of Macromarketing*, 30(3), 210–221.

REFERENCES

Aaker, J. L. (1997). Dimensions of brand personality. *Journal of Marketing Research*, 34(3), 347–356.

American Marketing Association. (1960). Marketing definitions: A glossary of marketing terms. Chicago: American Marketing Association.

Baalbaki, S., & Guzmán, F. (2016). Consumer-based brand equity. In F. Dall'Olmo Riley, J. Singh, & C. Blankson (eds), *The Routledge companion to contemporary brand management* (pp. 32–47). London: Routledge.

Bastos, W., & Levy, S. J. (2012). A history of the concept of branding: Practice and theory. *Journal of Historical Research in Marketing*, 4(3), 347–368.

Belfanti, C. M. (2018). Branding before the brand: Marks, imitations and counterfeits in pre-modern Europe. *Business History*, 60(8), 1127–1146.

Belk, R. W. (1988). Possessions and the extended self. *Journal of Consumer Research*, 15(2), 139–168.

Belk, R. W. (2016). Brands and the self. In F. Dall'Olmo Riley, J. Singh, & C. Blankson (eds), *The Routledge companion to contemporary brand management* (pp. 3–12). London. Routledge.

Blackett, T. (2003). What is a brand? In P. Barwise (ed), *Brands and branding* (pp. 13–25). London: *The Economist*.

Brown, S. (2016). *Brands and branding*. London: Sage.

Chaplin, L. N., & Lowrey, T. M. (2010). The development of consumer-based consumption constellations in children. *Journal of Consumer Research*, 36(5), 757–777.

Conejo, F., & Wooliscroft, B. (2015). Brands defined as semiotic marketing systems. *Journal of Macromarketing*, 35(3), 287–301.

Cova, B., Kozinets, R. V., & Shankar, A. (2007). Tribes, Inc.: The new world of tribalism. In B. Cova, R. V. Kozinets, & A. Shankar (eds), *Consumer tribes* (pp. 3–26). Oxford: Butterworth Heinemann.

Dall'Olmo Riley, F. (2016). Brand definitions and conceptualizations. In F. Dall'Olmo Riley, J. Singh, & C. Blankson (eds), *The Routledge companion to contemporary brand management* (pp. 3–12). London: Routledge.

de Chernatony, L. (1993). Categorizing brands: Evolutionary processes underpinned by two key dimensions. *Journal of Marketing Management*, 9(2), 173–188.

de Chernatony, L. (2010). *From brand vision to brand evaluation*. Oxford: Elsevier.

de Chernatony, L., & Dall'Olmo Riley, F. (1998). Defining a "brand": Beyond the literature with experts' interpretations. *Journal of Marketing Management*, 14(5), 417–443.

de Chernatony, L., & McWilliam, G. (1989). The varying nature of brands as assets: Theory and practice compared. *International Journal of Advertising*, 8(4), 339–349.

Delgado-Ballester, E., & Munuera-Alemán, J. L. (2001). Brand trust in the context of consumer loyalty. *European Journal of Marketing*, 35(11/12), 1238–1258.

Dixon, D. F. (1995). Retailing in classical Athens: Gleanings from contemporary literature and art. *Journal of Macromarketing*, 15(1), 74–85.

Eckhardt, G. M., & Bengtsson, A. (2010). A brief history of branding in China. *Journal of Macromarketing*, 30(3), 210–221.

Elliott, R., & Wattanasuwan, K. (1998). Brands as symbolic resources for the construction of identity. *International Journal of Advertising*, 17(2), 131–144.

Erdem, T., & Swait, J. (1998). Brand equity as a signalling phenomenon. *Journal of Consumer Psychology*, 7(2), 131–157.

Farquhar, P. H. (1989). Managing brand equity. *Marketing Research*, 1(3), 24–33.

Fournier, S. (1998). Consumers and their brands: Developing relationship theory in consumer research. *Journal of Consumer Research*, 24(4), 343–373.

Fournier, S., & Lee, L. (2009). Getting brand communities right. *Harvard Business Review*, 87(4), 105–111.

Gardner, B. B., & Levy, S. J. (1955). *The product and the brand. Harvard Business Review*, 33(2), 33-39.

Garud, R., Jain, S., & Tuertscher, P. (2008). Incomplete by design and designing for incompleteness. *Organization Studies*, 29(3), 351–371.

Hales, G. (2011). Branding. In J. J. Kourdi (ed.), *The marketing century: How marketing drives business and shapes* society (pp. 139–167). Chichester: John Wiley & Sons.

Henning, S. (2000). Branding harlots on the brow. Shakespeare Quarterly, 51(1), 86-89.
Holt, D. B. (2004). *How brands become icons: The principles of cultural branding*. Cambridge: Harvard Business Press.
Holt, D. B. (2006a). Toward a sociology of branding. *Journal of Consumer Culture*, 6(3), 299–302.
Holt, D. B. (2006b). Jack Daniel's America: Iconic brands as ideological parasites and proselytizers. *Journal of Consumer Culture*, 6(3), 355–377.
Holt, D. B. (2008). Commentary to prehistories of commodity branding. *Current Anthropology*, 49, 23.
Interbrand. (2018). *Activating brave: Best global brands 2018*.
Jacoby, J., Szybillo, G. J., & Busato-Schach, J. (1977). Information acquisition behavior in brand choice situations. *Journal of Consumer Research*, 3(4), 209–216.
Keller, K. L. (2001). *Building customer-based brand equity: A blueprint for creating strong brands* (pp. 3–27). Cambridge: Marketing Science Institute.
Keller, K. L. (2003). Brand synthesis: The multidimensionality of brand knowledge. *Journal of Consumer Research*, 29(4), 595–600.
Keller, K. L. (2006). Branding and brand equity. In B. Weitz and R. Wensley (eds), *Handbook of marketing* (pp. 151–178). London: Sage.
Keller, K. L., & Swaminathan, V. (2020). *Strategic brand management: Building, measuring, and managing brand equity* (5th edition). London: Pearson Education.
Khamis, S., Ang, L., and Welling, R. (2017). Self-branding, "micro-celebrity" and the rise of social media influencers. *Celebrity Studies*, 8(2), 191–208.
Klein, N. (2009). *No logo*. London: HarperCollins Publishers.
Kotler, P. (1972). What consumerism means for marketers. *Harvard Business Review*, 50(3), 48–57.
Kotler, P., & Zaltman, G. (1971). Social marketing: An approach to planned social change. *Journal of Marketing*, 35(3), 3–12.
Malhotra, N. K. (1988). Self concept and product choice: An integrated perspective. *Journal of Economic Psychology*, 9(1), 1–28.
Mercer, J. (2010). A mark of distinction: Branding and trade mark law in the UK from the 1860s. *Business History*, 52(1), 17–42.
McCracken, G. (1986). Culture and consumption: A theoretical account of the structure and movement of the cultural meaning of consumer goods. *Journal of Consumer Research*, 13(1), 71–84.
Moor, L. (2007). *The rise of brands*. Oxford: Berg.
Moore, K., & Reid, S. (2008). The birth of brand: 4000 years of branding. *Business History*, 50(4), 419–432.
Morris, P. (2003). *The Bakhtin reader: Selected writings of Bakhtin, Medvedev, Voloshinov*. London: Arnold.
Muñiz Jr., A. M., & O'Guinn, T. C. (2001). Brand community. *Journal of Consumer Research*, 27(4), 412–432.
Oxford English Dictionary. (2019). Available at: www.lexico.com/en/definition/brand [accessed 10 June 2019].
Peters, T. (1997). The brand called you. *Fast Company*, 10(10), 83–90.
Petty, R. D. (2016). A history of brand identity protection and brand marketing. In D. B. Jones & M. Tadajewski (eds), *The Routledge companion to marketing history* (pp. 121–138). Abingdon: Routledge.
Ritzer, G. (2015). *The McDonaldization of society*. London: Sage.
Roselius, T. (1971). Consumer rankings of risk reduction methods. *Journal of Marketing*, 35(1), 56–61.

Schau, H. J., Muñiz Jr., A. M., & Arnould, E. J. (2009). How brand community practices create value. *Journal of Marketing*, 73(5), 30–51.

Schechter, F. I. (1925). *The historical foundation of the law relating to trade-marks*. New York: Columbia University Press.

Schroeder, J. E. (2009). The cultural codes of branding. *Marketing Theory*, 9(1), 123–126.

Schroeder, J. E. (2015). Introduction. In J. E. Schroeder (ed.), *Brands: Interdisciplinary perspectives*. London: Routledge.

Schwartz, S. H., & Bardi, A. (2001). Value hierarchies across cultures: Taking a similarities perspective. *Journal of Cross-cultural Psychology*, 32(3), 268–290.

Shaw, E. H. (2016). Ancient and medieval marketing. In D. B. Jones & M. Tadajewski (eds), *The Routledge companion to marketing history*. London: Routledge.

Shepherd, S., Chartrand, T. L., & Fitzsimons, G. J. (2015). When brands reflect our ideal world: The values and brand preferences of consumers who support versus reject society's dominant ideology. *Journal of Consumer Research*, 42(1), 76-92.

Sirgy, M. J. (1982). Self-concept in consumer behavior: A critical review. *Journal of Consumer Research*, 9(3), 287–300.

Solomon, M. R. (1988). Mapping product constellations: A social categorization approach to consumption symbolism. *Psychology & Marketing*, 5(3), 233.

Tadajewski, M. (2009). A history of marketing thought. In E. Parsons & P. Maclaran (eds), *Contemporary issues in marketing and consumer behaviour* (pp. 13–36). London: Butterworth-Heinemann.

Twitchell, J. B. (2004). *Branded nation: The marketing of Megachurch, College Inc., and Museumworld*. New York: Simon and Schuster.

Vargo, S. L., & Lusch, R. F. (2004). Evolving to a new dominant logic for marketing. *Journal of Marketing*, 68(January), 1–17.

Vargo, S. L., & Lusch, R. F. (2008). Service-dominant logic: Continuing the evolution. *Journal of the Academy of Marketing Science*, 36(1), 1–10.

Wengrow, D. (2008). Prehistories of commodity branding. *Current Anthropology*, 49(1), 7–34.

Wolpert, S. A. (2000). *A new history of India* (6th edn). Oxford: Oxford University Press.

CHAPTER 2
Developing brand equity, positioning, personality, and values

CHAPTER AIMS AND LEARNING OUTCOMES

This chapter corresponds to the first stage of Keller and Swaminathan's (2020) *strategic brand management process*, i.e. identifying and developing brand plans (see Figure 2.1). More specifically, it aims to achieve the following:

1. Provide an in-depth discussion of the Customer-Based Brand Equity (CBBE) pyramid model and its components.
2. Explore how organisations can build successful brand positioning and how this contributes to brand equity development.
3. Discuss the concepts of brand personality and brand values and highlight their role in creating successful brand positioning.

DEVELOPING BRAND EQUITY

Defining brand equity

"If you ask ten people to define brand equity, you are likely to get ten (maybe 11) different answers as to what it means" (Winters, 1991, p. 70). This statement is still relevant today despite the fact that, over the years, there have been numerous research studies published on the subject of brand equity. Brand equity is a multifaceted concept with a diversity of conceptualisations, and a multiplicity of studies has explored different characteristics of an intangible asset (Christodoulides & de Chernatony, 2010). As mentioned in the previous chapter, one of the most widely accepted definitions indicates that brand equity is "the added value with which a given brand endows a product" (Farquhar, 1989, p. 24). However, scholars have pointed out that this added value has been examined from a

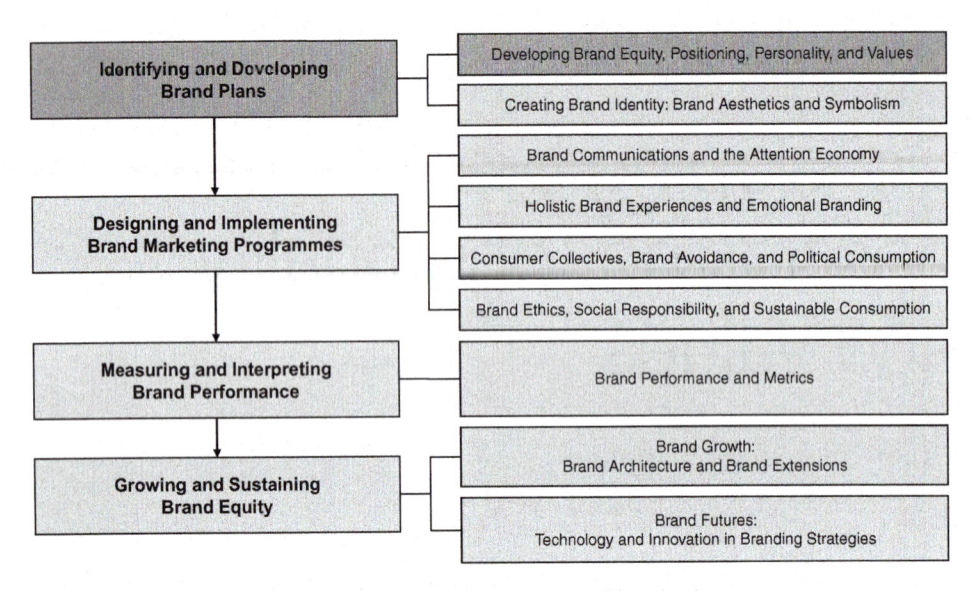

```
┌─────────────────────────┐     ┌─────────────────────────────────────────────────────────┐
│ Identifying and Developing │────▶│ Developing Brand Equity, Positioning, Personality, and Values │
│      Brand Plans        │     ├─────────────────────────────────────────────────────────┤
└────────────┬────────────┘     │ Creating Brand Identity: Brand Aesthetics and Symbolism │
             │                  └─────────────────────────────────────────────────────────┘
             ▼
┌─────────────────────────┐     ┌─────────────────────────────────────────────────────────┐
│                         │────▶│ Brand Communications and the Attention Economy          │
│ Designing and Implementing │     ├─────────────────────────────────────────────────────────┤
│ Brand Marketing Programmes │────▶│ Holistic Brand Experiences and Emotional Branding       │
│                         │     ├─────────────────────────────────────────────────────────┤
│                         │────▶│ Consumer Collectives, Brand Avoidance, and Political Consumption │
│                         │     ├─────────────────────────────────────────────────────────┤
│                         │────▶│ Brand Ethics, Social Responsibility, and Sustainable Consumption │
└────────────┬────────────┘     └─────────────────────────────────────────────────────────┘
             ▼
┌─────────────────────────┐     ┌─────────────────────────────────────────────────────────┐
│ Measuring and Interpreting │────▶│ Brand Performance and Metrics                           │
│   Brand Performance     │     └─────────────────────────────────────────────────────────┘
└────────────┬────────────┘
             ▼
┌─────────────────────────┐     ┌─────────────────────────────────────────────────────────┐
│                         │────▶│ Brand Growth:                                           │
│ Growing and Sustaining  │     │ Brand Architecture and Brand Extensions                 │
│     Brand Equity        │     ├─────────────────────────────────────────────────────────┤
│                         │────▶│ Brand Futures:                                          │
│                         │     │ Technology and Innovation in Branding Strategies        │
└─────────────────────────┘     └─────────────────────────────────────────────────────────┘
```

FIGURE 2.1 Strategic brand management process and book plan

plethora of different perspectives (Baalbaki & Guzmán, 2016; Christodoulides & de Chernatony, 2010). First, the *financial perspective* explores the financial value brand equity generates for an organisation (firm-based brand equity). Second, the *consumer perspective*, drawing from cognitive psychology, focuses on the added value created by the different ways consumers perceive the brand and how their perceptions influence their behaviour (customer-based brand equity). Individuals interpret brands in different and highly idiosyncratic ways, which means that the value each consumer draws from the brand is entirely subjective (Baalbaki & Guzmán, 2016). Third, the *economics perspective* examines the added value created by the extra utility a brand gives to a product or service. Fourth, the *employee perspective* is about the "differential effect that brand knowledge has on employee's response to their work environment" (King & Grace, 2009, p. 130).

Indeed, both accounting and marketing scholars have discussed brand equity, which suggests the significance of a long-term focus in brand development and management (Wood, 2000). In accounting terms, Wood (2000), drawing from Feldwick (1996), defines brand equity as "the total value of a brand as separable asset – when it is sold, or included on a balance sheet" (Wood, 2000, p. 662). Contrastingly, when defining brand equity, marketing scholars have concentrated on the marketing results that are exclusively an outcome of marketing an organisational offering under a specific brand name, i.e. on marketing effects that would not have occurred if the same organisational offering did not have that brand name (Keller, 1993). Developing brand equity can provide the organisation with many competitive advantages, including: 1) an increase in the strength of consumers' positive attitudes for the branded product, 2) higher perceived product or service quality, 3) easier retail acceptance and distribution, 4) increased effectiveness of marketing communications, 5) brand resiliency to survive crises and market uncertainties, as well as to safeguard the organisation from competitive attacks, 6) greater barriers to competitive entry, 7) better profit margins as consumers are willing to pay a higher price for the branded product and suppliers are more inclined to agree on lower costs, and 8) a solid base for launching new products (brand extensions) in the future as well as for licensing agreements (Chaudhuri & Holbrook, 2001; Erdem, 1998; Farquhar, 1989; French & Smith, 2013; Keller, 2001).

In this chapter, the vantage point for our discussion shall be the consumers' cognitive and emotional processing of brands, thus we will concentrate on customer-based brand equity, defined by Keller as "the differential effect of brand knowledge on consumer response to the marketing of the brand" (1993, p. 2). The way a consumer perceives a brand determines his/her behaviour towards it. Brand equity demonstrates the strength of the relationship between the consumer and the brand (Feldwick, 1996; Keller, 2001; Wood, 2000). As mentioned above, higher brand equity means greater consumer willingness to accept a higher price for the branded product or service. For example, consider how much more a consumer might be willing to pay for a *Burberry* trench coat than any other coat with the same quality of fabric and design. This is because the brand has, over the years, developed strong equity in the category of trench coats, associating itself with heritage, status, and luxury, which influences the perceived quality of the *Burberry* brand in consumers' minds. This means that

> customer-based brand equity involves consumers' reactions to an element of the marketing mix [product, price, place, and promotion] for the brand in comparison with their reactions to the same marketing mix element attributed to [an]...unnamed version of the product or service.
>
> (Keller, 1993, p. 2)

Brand equity is generated when there is a greater consumer confidence towards a brand than its competitors (Lassar, Mittal, & Sharma, 1995). Of course, brand equity cannot be developed unless there are two elements: consumers' brand awareness and brand image (Keller, 1993; Aaker, 1991). This means that consumers need to be aware of the brand in the first place; this is the starting point in developing strong brands. Then they have to hold strong, favourable, and unique associations for the brand, which will bring together a positive brand image in their minds. Brand awareness and brand image contribute to consumers' brand knowledge (Keller, 2003).

Customer-based brand equity model

In order to develop strong brand equity, the organisation must follow four important stages: 1) make the consumer aware of the brand and associate the brand with a specific category or consumer need (*brand identity*), 2) create brand meaning in consumers' minds by linking certain properties of the brand with a range of

```
┌─────────┐    ┌─────────┐    ┌─────────┐    ┌─────────┐
│ STAGE 1 │───▶│ STAGE 2 │───▶│ STAGE 3 │───▶│ STAGE 4 │
└─────────┘    └─────────┘    └─────────┘    └─────────┘
```

| Make consumers aware of the brand and associate the brand with a specific category or consumer need. | Create brand meaning in consumers' minds by linking certain brand properties with a range of tangible and intangible brand associations. | Generate rational and emotional consumer responses to brand identity and brand meaning. | Transform consumer responses to long-term loyalty relationships. |

| BRAND IDENTITY | → | BRAND MEANING | → | BRAND RESPONSES | → | BRAND RELATIONSHIPS |

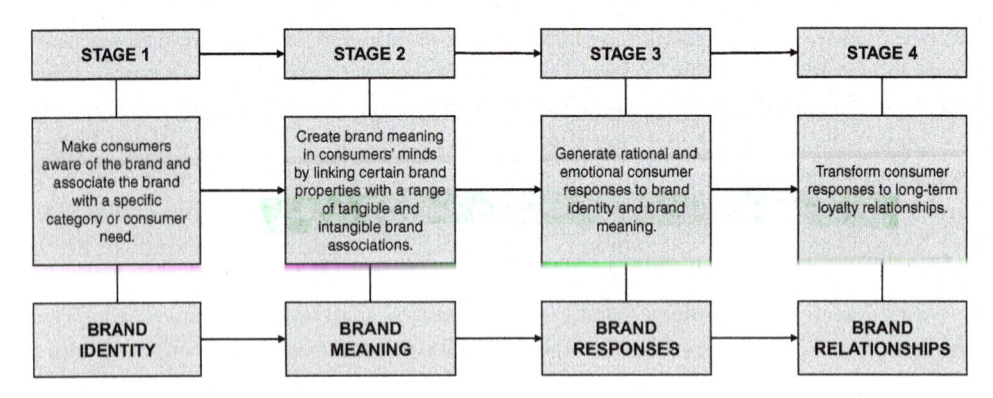

FIGURE 2.2 Stages of brand development

tangible and intangible brand associations (*brand meaning*), 3) generate rational and emotional consumer responses to this brand identity and brand meaning (*brand responses*), and 4) transform these consumer responses to intense and long-term loyalty relationships between the consumer and the brand (*brand relationships*) (see Figure 2.2) (Keller, 2001).

Based on this process, Keller (2001) proposed the *Customer-Based Brand Equity (CBBE)* pyramid model, which has four levels and six building blocks (see Figure 2.3): in the first level at the bottom, *brand salience*, in the second level, *brand performance associations* and *brand imagery associations*, then in the third level, *consumer judgements* and *consumer feelings*, and finally at the top level *brand resonance*. As we will discuss further on, each layer corresponds to the aforementioned stages of brand development as well as to specific branding objectives which the organisation must achieve in order to reach the highest level, brand resonance, where an active and intense loyalty relationship between the consumer and the brand is created and maintained. Each layer, starting from the bottom, must be achieved in order to reach the pinnacle of the pyramid (Keller, 2001). Let us explore these four levels and six building blocks in more detail.

Brand salience (brand identity)

The first level of the CBBE pyramid model involves *brand salience*, which is consumers' awareness of the brand. In this stage, the firm must make consumers aware of the brand, and let them know it is part of a specific product or service category and/or is connected with a specific consumer need. This will enable the organisation to create a very strong *brand identity* and answer the consumer's question of 'who are you?' (Keller, 2001). Consumer awareness is all about the ability of the consumer to *recall* and/or *recognise* the brand. For instance, when launching a new soft drink, it is essential that the company makes consumers aware of the new product and clearly communicates, through suitable marketing communications activities, that the product is a soft drink and will satisfy their thirst. Of course, products do

DEVELOPING BRANDS

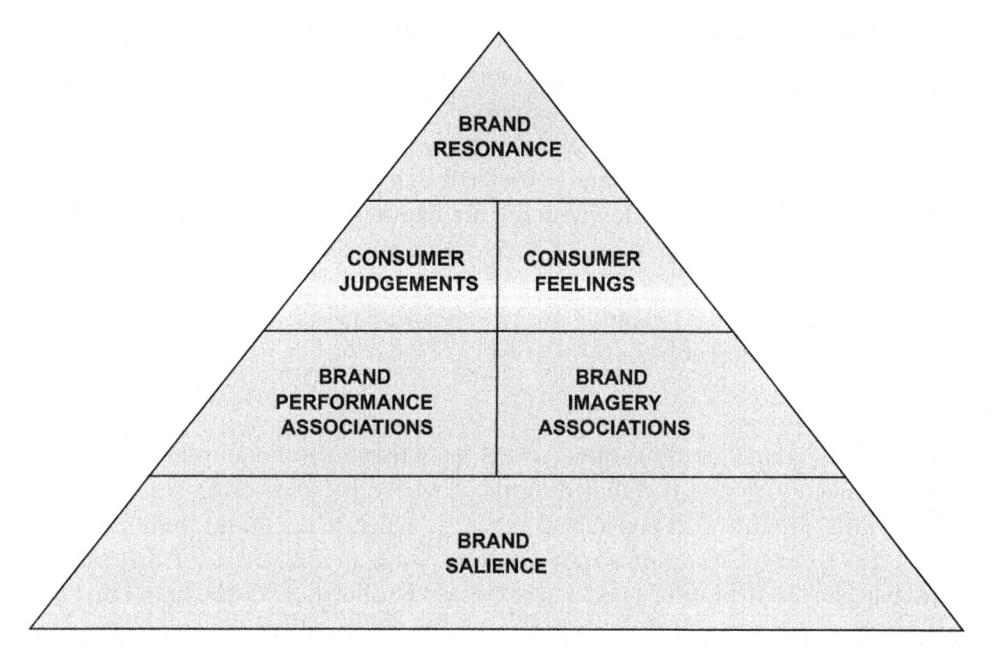

FIGURE 2.3 Customer-based brand equity pyramid model

not only satisfy consumers' physical needs, they can also satisfy their emotional and symbolic needs. For example, a firm seeking to launch a new brand of clothing for skaters or BMX bikers will want to make those consumers aware of the brand in the first place. It will also seek to demonstrate to them that the new brand is one which can satisfy not only their functional needs but also their symbolic needs for communicating a skater's or biker's identity and belonging to this specific social group.

Integrated marketing communications activities can help the organisation generate brand awareness. Such activities can include not only the traditional activities such as advertising, sales promotions, direct marketing, public relations and publicity, and personal selling, but also digital marketing activities. Initially the Internet and social media were seen by organisations as merely additional platforms for pursuing traditional strategies, however, in recent years, organisations have realised that digital marketing should be regarded as marketing communications activity in its own right and with its own key performance indicators. Gupta, Garg, and Sharma (2016) explain that in developed economies marketers strive for the right balance between traditional and digital media, while in emerging markets, things are slightly different.

> The digital fabric and reach in each emerging country vary, with China boasting of a permeated digital presence and India still in the formative years of digitalisation. The decision to utilise digital media, then, depends upon the reach and consumers targeted.
>
> (Gupta et al., 2016, p. 374)

Brand awareness is the starting point for building brand equity and it influences people's brand perceptions (in the second level of the model) and taste (Aaker & Joachimsthaler, 2009). Brand awareness can also affect consumer choice as demonstrated in the experimental study by Hoyer and Brown, which showed that in some cases people "who are aware of one brand in a choice set [might] choose the known brand even when it is lower in quality than other brands they have had the opportunity to sample" (1990, p. 147). As we mentioned earlier, generating brand awareness is about enabling the consumer to recall and/or recognise the brand. Brand recall and brand recognition are two distinct concepts and it is important to understand their difference.

Brand recall

Brand recall "relates to consumers' ability to retrieve the brand when given the product category, the needs fulfilled by the category, or some other type of probe as a cue…[It] requires that consumers' correctly generate the brand from memory" (Keller, 1993, p. 3). This means that if you were to ask an individual to name a brand of mobile phones, the top-of-mind answer would be able to name the brand that has the strongest salience in his/her mind, for example he/she might mention *Huawei* or *Samsung*. This is what we call *aided* brand recall because the consumer is provided a probe or cue such as a product category (mobile phones) or consumer need (telecommunication). The organisation should also seek to achieve *unaided* brand recall, where consumers are able to retrieve the brand from their memory without being provided a specific cue. For instance, if you were to ask an individual to name a brand, any brand, he/she might say *Apple*, *Nike*, or *Porsche*; these would be brands that enjoy the ultimate strength of brand salience, as they are top-of-mind without any probe or cue (Keller, 1993, 2001).

Brand recognition

Brand recognition is about the "consumers' ability to confirm prior exposure to the brand when given the brand as a cue…[It] requires that consumers correctly discriminate the brand as having been seen or heard previously" (Keller, 1993, p. 3). This means that consumers are able to recognise the brand name or other brand elements, e.g. the brand logo, colours, symbols, as something they have heard or seen before (and connect it with the right brand). Aaker (2010) suggests that recognition reflects familiarity with the brand generated from past exposure to the brand. Nevertheless, he emphasises that recognition does not automatically mean that the consumer can remember where he/she has seen the brand, why it is different from other brands, or even what the brand's product class is (Aaker, 2010). This does not mean, however, that brand recognition is unimportant. Quite the contrary, recognition in itself can lead to positive feelings, and a familiar brand will have an advantage over an unfamiliar one (Aaker, 2010), because "people like the familiar and are prepared to ascribe all sorts of good attitudes to items that are familiar to them" (Aaker & Joachimsthaler, 2009).

Brand recognition is particularly important for new or niche brands (Aaker, 1996) as the organisation relies on recognition for the successful launch of the new product, or the brand needs to be easily recognised by the eclectic set of targeted consumers. Brand recognition is also essential for successful product packaging because consumers need to be able to correctly recognise the packaging and therefore identify and purchase the product (Keller & Swaminathan, 2020). *Nike* has achieved global recognition, which means it no longer needs to include its brand name on its logo. The *Nike* swoosh has become an iconic symbol easily recognised around the world. Of course, brand recognition is not as demanding as brand recall because consumers are provided with the brand name or are exposed to a visual stimuli. Indeed, the question is how confident they are in recognising the brand element, and of course, whether or not they can match the brand element with the correct brand.

Branding objective: Depth and breadth of brand awareness

In the first stage of the CBBE pyramid model, the organisation's branding objective should be to create two dimensions of brand awareness: depth and breadth (Keller, 1993, 2001). *Depth* of brand awareness is about "how likely it is for a brand element will come to mind and the ease with which it does so" (Keller & Swaminathan, 2020, p. 108). This means that depth of brand awareness determines how easily the consumer can recall or recognise the brand element (Keller, 2001). *Breadth* of brand awareness is about the range of purchase and consumption situations in which the brand element will come to the consumer's mind (Keller, 2001; Keller & Swaminathan, 2020). A salient brand is one that has both depth and breadth of awareness, i.e. it is a brand that consumers not only can easily think of, but also think of in a range of different situations. For instance, *Sprite* is a soft drink consumers might be able to think of easily (depth), but also it is a product which consumers might think of in a variety of situations (breadth), such as when they want a drink to cool down, a drink to have with their meal, when watching TV, or when socialising with friends.

Brand performance and brand imagery associations (brand meaning)

The second level of the CBBE pyramid model involves *brand performance associations* and *brand imagery associations* (see Figure 2.3). In this stage, the organisation aims to create brand meaning by linking certain brand properties with a range of tangible and intangible brand associations in consumers' minds (see Figure 2.2), and seeks to answer the consumer's question of 'what are you?' (Keller, 2001). Creating a strong brand meaning means generating a positive brand image in consumers' minds (Keller, 2001). Brand image is the "perceptions about a brand as reflected by the brand associations held in consumer memory" (Keller, 1993, p. 3). However, this image will be unique for each individual depending on how the person interprets the brand. As Neumeier (2006) articulately emphasises:

A brand is a person's gut feeling about a product, service, or company…because we are all emotional, intuitive beings, despite out best efforts to be rational. It's a person's gut feeling, because in the end the brand is defined by individuals… Each person creates his or her own version of it. While companies can't control this process, they can influence it by communicating the qualities that make this product different than that product. When enough individuals arrive at the same gut feeling, a company can be said to have a brand.

(Neumeier, 2006, p. 2)

Culture influences the way an individual interprets the brand because culture acts as both "the 'lens' through which the individual views phenomena [and] the 'blueprint' of human activity, determining the co-ordinates of social action and productive activity, and specifying the behaviours and objects that issue from both" (McCracken, 1986, p. 72). An individual often uses other people, especially those who are similar to him/her, as a source of information for developing as well as evaluating his/her own beliefs about the world (Escalas & Bettman, 2005). However, as previously emphasised, meaning is dialogic (Morris, 2003), it is negotiated between organisations and consumers. Iconic brands connect with cultural shifts in society and deliver consumers ways to adapt to such shifts (Holt, 2004). Hence, "brands… serve as powerful repositories of meaning purposively and differentially employed [by consumers] in the substantiation, creation, and (re)production of concepts of self" (Fournier, 1998, p. 365). As Mark Batey, a leading brand consultant explains:

Meaning is at the heart of consumer behaviour, because meaning is at the heart of human behaviour. The millennia may have passed, but we are still hunters and gatherers – of meaning. Yet meaning is not some manufactured, concrete entity. Meaning is up for negotiation and interpretation, and the role of the individual in the creation of meaning is a very active one.

(Batey, 2014, p. 23)

The organisation should aim to create appropriate brand stimuli whence the consumer will generate his/her own brand meaning containing strong, unique, and favourable associations (Keller, 1993). The simplest way to understand the associations an individual has about a specific brand is to ask the open-ended question: 'what comes to your mind when you think of [Brand X]?' For instance, what comes to your mind when you think of *Mercedes-Benz*? Similarly, what comes to your mind when you think of *Absolut*? A consumer might mention a number of associations as illustrated in the spider diagrams in Figures 2.4 and 2.5. This is what we call a *free associations* task (Keller, 1993), which allows us to determine the consumer's *mental map* of brand associations that "reflect the structure of consumer memory on which CBBE is based" (French & Smith, 2013, p. 1358).

Extant literature on brand associations draws from the *Human Associative Memory* theory in cognitive psychology (Anderson & Bower, 1973; Srull & Wyer,

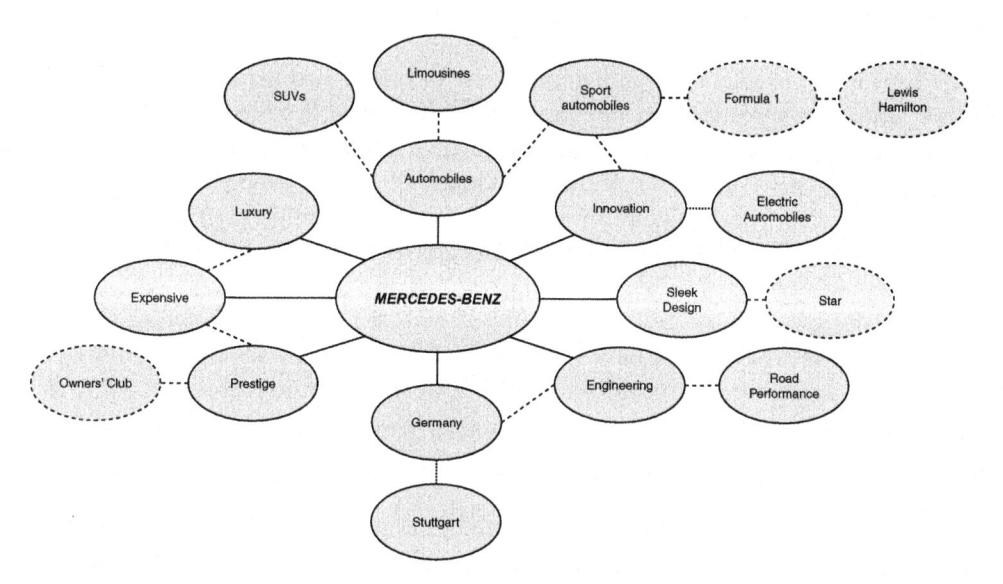

FIGURE 2.4 An example of a brand concept map for *Mercedes-Benz*

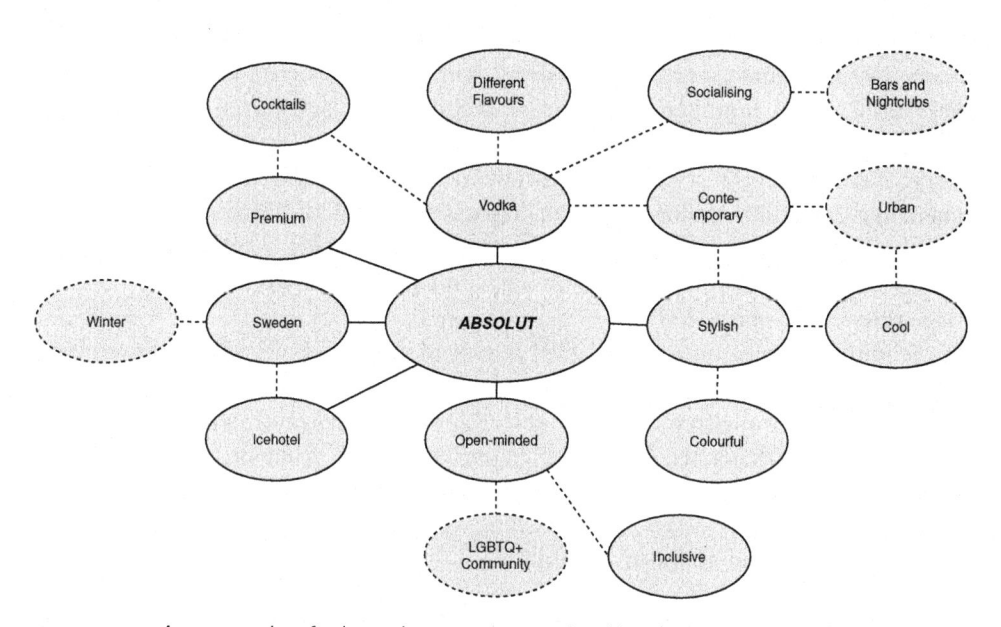

FIGURE 2.5 An example of a brand concept map for *Absolut*

1989) to explain how consumers develop *brand associations networks*. This theory postulates that brand knowledge is stored in a person's memory as individual pieces of brand information linked together to create a complex associative network of the brand (Anderson, 1983a; French & Smith, 2013; Teichert & Schöntag, 2010). Anderson (1983a) explains that there is an *activation* process whereby "one association stimulates the recall of another, linked association" (French & Smith, 2013, p. 1357) to enable an individual to recall brand information from memory. This activation spreads from one association to others, leading to a chain reaction (Anderson, 1983b; French and Smith, 2013). Based on the *Human Associative Memory* theory, John, Loken, Kim, and Monga (2006) developed the *brand concept mapping* approach which can illustrate consumer's complex network of brand associations where there are *first-order associations* directly linked with the brand (e.g. 'automobiles' or 'sleek design' in Figure 2.4, and 'open-minded' or 'stylish' in Figure 2.5), *second-order associations* linked with the first-order associations (e.g. 'Formula 1' or 'road performance' in Figure 2.4, and 'cocktails' or 'colourful' in Figure 2.5), and *tertiary associations* which are weak associations connected with the first-order or the second-order associations (e.g. 'owners' club' or 'Lewis Hamilton' in Figure 2.4, and 'LGBTQ+ community' or 'urban' in Figure 2.5) (French & Smith, 2013; John et al., 2006).

Specifically, with regards to the *strength* of brand associations, research studies have indicated that it "is a function of the number of associations, the strength of links between associations and the structure of the associative network, with those associations closest to the brand being the strongest" (French & Smith, 2013, pp. 1359–1360). Using *McDonald's* as the brand case for their study, French and Smith (2013) indicated that apart from the number of associations, the structure of these associations (number of first-order, second-order, and tertiary associations), how they are linked is also a very important element in measuring strength of brand associations. They developed a new measure of brand association strength where the *structural density* (type of associations and the links between them) is combined with *total number of associations* to provide a final metric of the strength of brand associations allowing comparisons between different mental maps (French & Smith, 2013).

Schnittka, Sattler, and Zenker (2012) extended John et al.'s (2006) brand concept mapping approach to examine the *favourability* of a brand association, "that is, an association's evaluative judgment and individual importance within a purchase situation" (Schnittka et al., 2012, p. 273), in more depth. They proposed the *brand association network value* (BANV), which includes information about strength and uniqueness of brand associations as articulated in extant literature whilst assimilating this with information about favourability (i.e. evaluative judgments and individual importance). BANV allows managers to distinguish between 'good' from 'bad' consumers' association networks as it provides a standardised method for calculating the overall favourability of a consumer's network (Schnittka et al., 2012).

Finally, the *uniqueness* of brand associations can be very beneficial for organisations because they make the consumers' decision-making process easier (Tversky, 1972), make it harder for new competitors to enter the market (Davidson, 1976), and increase distributors' interest in stocking the brand (Alpert, Kamins, & Graham, 1992): "Building perceived brand uniqueness is a useful and important strategy for maintaining and improving brand performance" (Romaniuk & Gaillard,

2007, p. 268). However, we have to be clear what we mean by a *unique association* because this is different to a *unique brand attribute*.

> Unique attributes are when only one brand has an attribute...and therefore associations with another brand is inaccurate. Unique associations are identified from the perspective of a single consumer, and are when a consumer only associates one brand with an attribute, regardless of whether other brands have it or not. It is a representation of what the consumer perceives rather than what the brand offers. This is the interpretation currently taken by most advertising campaigns that seek to build unique associations when communicating a brand position.
> (Romaniuk & Gaillard, 2007, p. 269)

Involving hundreds of consumers and ninety-four brands in eight markets, Romaniuk and Gaillard's (2007) quantitative study of the role of unique associations to brand equity, yielded some very interesting findings. Contrary to what Romaniuk and Gaillard had expected, their research indicated that 1) non-consumers of a brand have a higher share of unique associations for this brand than consumers of this brand, 2) consumers with a stronger preference for the brand did not have greater share of unique associations compared to consumers with a weaker preference, 3) larger brands (with higher market penetration, i.e. higher proportion of consumers who claim to use these brands)

> did not have a greater share of unique associations than smaller brands [, and] 4) the greater the number of brands in the market, the lower the level of uniqueness of brands within the market...due to the increasing number of competitors making it more likely that a brand will overlap with another brand on most qualities.
> (Romaniuk & Gaillard, 2007, p. 278)

These findings highlight that while uniqueness is important, its role is more nuanced than previously thought.

The implications for managers are that organisations have to first ensure that the brand is known for (product or service) category relevant characteristics before it is concerned about unique associations (Barwise & Meehan, 2004; Keller, Sternthal, & Tybout, 2002). Brand managers need to be careful because developing unique associations might work to the detriment of strengthening other attributes that connect with general (product or service) category benefits (Keller & Davey, 2001), which could make consumers uncertain about whether or not the brand can deliver primary (product or service) category needs, even when this brand is part of the consumers' consideration set (Barwise & Meehan, 2004). This of course does not mean that managers should not seek to develop unique associations. Rather, they should concentrate on making their brands *distinctive* rather than *differentiated*. A distinctive brand is one which can be easily identified in a muddled market because of its unique aesthetics trademarked and protected from competitors' imitation (more on brand identity and aesthetics in Chapter 3), essentially creating unique brand attributes instead of merely relying on unique associations in consumers' minds. Romaniuk and Gaillard explain that these "distinctive qualities, in themselves, do not add value to the consumer, in the sense of differentiation, but they provide easy and automatic identification of the brand through all of its consumer touchpoints" (2007, p. 281).

Combining strength, favourability, and uniqueness can lead to developing strong brand image (meaning) in the minds of the consumers, as an important step in the development of successful brand equity. These dimensions need to be created in this specific order, that is,

> it does not matter how unique a brand association is unless customers evaluate the association favourably, and it does not matter how desirable a brand association is unless it is sufficiently strong so that customers actually recall it and link it to the brand.
>
> (Keller, 2001, p. 12)

Keller (2001) has made a distinction between two types of brands associations in consumers' minds: brand performance associations and brand imagery associations. We will explore these two categories in more depth in the following subsections.

Brand performance associations

An individual who is aware of the brand will have a number of associations in his/her mind that relate to the manner in which the product or service seeks to satisfy his/her functional needs (Keller, 2001). *Brand performance associations* are related to the intrinsic properties of the brand; they are related to characteristics that are inherent in the product or service. In particular, these intrinsic brand properties include, first, the product's or service's *primary characteristics*, which are essential ingredients for the product to operate in the way it is supposed to, or for the service to deliver what is expected: "Hence they are related to a product's physical composition or a service's requirements" (Keller, 1993, p. 4). For example, a primary element for a mobile phone to operate is the microchip, which connects the phone to the network. For an airline service to deliver its primary purpose it needs to safely transport passengers to the selected destination – this is the bare minimum and most essential characteristic expected. There are also a number of *secondary features*, complementary to the primary characteristics, which enable the consumer to customise the product or make it more versatile (Keller & Swaminathan, 2020), for example, the colour of the mobile phone and its various accessories, or the aircraft's cabin design and the catering service on board.

Second, inherent brand properties include the product's reliability, durability, and serviceability. *Reliability* is about whether or not the product will perform consistently over time and from one purchase to the next. For example, when you buy a loaf of *Hovis* sliced bread, does it taste the same every time you buy it? Similarly, when you buy a new *Samsung* TV, you expect it to perform consistently over time. This takes us to the next point which is *durability*, i.e. how long the product is expected to last (its economic life). Durable products are supposed to last for a number of years; a laptop's economic life is at least three years. Finally, a product's *serviceability* is about how easily a product can be serviced if it needs to be repaired, so this includes "factors such as the speed, accuracy, and care of product delivery and installation; the promptness, courtesy, and helpfulness of customer service and training; the quality of repair service and the time involved" (Keller, 2001, p. 10). For example, when a firm purchases a new photocopier for its office, there will be a need for installation and some sort of instruction/guidance to future users. In addition, when necessary, the photocopier should be serviced and repaired promptly.

Third, intrinsic properties of the brand include the service effectiveness, efficiency, and empathy because the service interactions consumers have with brands often lead to performance-related associations in their minds (Keller, 2001). *Effectiveness* is about how well the brand meets consumers' service requirements, *efficiency* is about the manner of delivery of the service in relation to speed and responsiveness, and *empathy* is about whether or not the service-providing organisation is trusting, caring, and consumer-focused (Keller, 2001).

Fourth, the brand's inherent characteristics include its *style* and *design*. This relates to the product's or service's aesthetic characteristics. The product's size, shape, materials, and colours can influence its performance. Think about how the bottle design of sports drinks packaging, e.g. *Gatorade* or *Lucozade Sport*, is shaped in a way that allows easier grip and includes a lid for less spillage. Similarly, the aesthetics and layout of the company's premises can affect the service delivery and, consequently, consumers' experiences (see Chapters 3 and 5).

Finally, the product's or service's *price* can influence consumers' performance-related associations. We tend to use price as proxy for brand quality (Yoo, Donthu, & Lee, 2000), as we tend to make connections between price and quality. We usually think that the higher the price, the better the quality of the product or service. The price of the product or service is often determined by the product or service category to which it belongs. The organisation will have to make decisions about the brand's pricing policy and about any price discounts and their frequency (price volatility or variance). Naturally, you do not expect to see an up-scale brand discounted (or discounted often), as this would hurt value perceptions in consumers' minds. For instance, it is highly unlikely that you will find a *Hermès* bag or an *Oscar de la Renta* dress on sale. "The pricing strategy adopted for a brand can dictate how consumers categorise the price of the brand (e.g., low, medium, or high) and how firm or flexible that price is perceived to be (e.g. as frequently or infrequently discounted)" (Keller, 2001, p. 11). Generally speaking, Yoo et al. (2000) warn that despite potential short-term financial success, frequent use of price promotions can lead to consumers perceiving the brand as of low quality, which can corrode brand equity. Furthermore, "uniform pricing without price promotions is more desirable because it leads to consistency between the expected and the actual prices and implies high product quality. Instead of offering price promotions, managers should invest in advertising to develop brand equity" (Yoo et al., 2000, p. 207), as explained in more detail below.

Brand imagery associations

While brand performance associations are concerned with intrinsic properties of the brand, *brand imagery associations* are about its extrinsic properties, in relation to how the brand satisfies the consumers' psychological or social needs. These associations are abstract thoughts in consumers' minds, which derive not only from the consumers' direct experience with the brand, i.e. their use of the product or service, but also through their indirect experience with the brand. The ways the brand is depicted in advertising messages as well as brand messages based on face-to-face consumer interactions and online word-of-mouth contribute to the consumers' indirect experience of the brand leading to imagery associations (Keller, 1993, 2001): "Brand image is complicated, based on multiple experiences, facts, episodes, and exposures to brand information, and therefore takes a long time to develop. Advertising is a common way to develop, to shape, and to manage that image" (Yoo et al., 2000, p. 207).

These extrinsic brand properties include, first, *user profiles*, which include the associations consumers have about the demographic and psychographic characteristics of the actual or aspirational brand user (Keller, 2001). These associations might also relate to specific reference groups which are perceived as the brand's user audiences, e.g. skaters and *Vans* or *Supreme* products, 'preppie' university students and *Polo Ralph Lauren* or *Jack Wills*, or young fitness-conscious professional women and *Lululemon*, because consumers often form links between reference groups and the brands these groups use (Escalas & Bettman, 2005). Consequently, consumers develop connections with brands used by the reference groups they (want to) belong to (*in-groups*), and avoid connections with brands used by the *out-groups*, i.e. groups they do not (want to) belong (Escalas & Bettman, 2005).

Second, extrinsic brand properties can include associations about the *purchase and usage situations*, that is, abstract thoughts about the time, location, and context of typical purchase situation and consumption (i.e. occasions where the brand is usually purchased and consumed), as well as about the distribution channels through which the brand is made available, the specific stores it can be found at, and how easily it can be sourced. Careful consideration should be given to the *selection of stores* where the brand is made available because consumers use the image and reputation of the store as sources of inferences about brand quality (Yoo et al., 2000). In addition, *distribution intensity* leads to higher brand equity. However, seeking to achieve intensive distribution does not mean selling in any store regardless of its image; selected stores have to be suitable for creating the desired image in consumers' minds. Distribution intensity provides consumers convenience, speed and higher accessibility of service, which increases consumer satisfaction. This is also the case even for luxury brands for which marketers prefer using a limited number of stores for distribution (Yoo et al., 2000).

Third, imagery associations can include consumers' abstract thoughts about the brand's *personality* and *values*. In her seminal paper, Jennifer Aaker defines brand personality "as the set of human characteristics associated with a brand" (1997, p. 345), a construct which has symbolic or self-expressive purpose (Keller, 1993). Brand personality and values are discussed in more depth later in this chapter. Finally, extrinsic brand properties include associations about the *brand's history, heritage,* and *experiences*.

> These types of associations may involve distinctly personal experiences and episodes or be related to past behaviours and experiences of friends, family, or others. Consequently these types of associations may be fairly idiosyncratic, although they sometimes exhibit certain commonalities. Alternatively, these associations may be more public and broad-based and therefore will be shared to a larger degree. In either case, associations with history, heritage, and experiences involve more specific, concrete examples that transcend the generalisations that make up the usage imagery.
>
> (Keller, 2001, p. 12)

Consumers might have nostalgic associations and memories associated with the brand. In our post-modern society, these can be very powerful because of an aging population who is more prone to nostalgic feelings. Nostalgia as part of emotional branding will be discussed in more depth in Chapter 5.

Branding objective: Points-of-parity and points-of-difference associations

Based on the above, in the second stage of CBBE pyramid model, the organisation's branding objective should be to create *points-of-difference (POD) associations* and *points-of-parity (POP) associations*. These will provide appropriate stimuli which, upon interpretation by consumers, will lead to intended performance and imagery associations in their minds. POD associations are strong, favourable, and unique associations, that is, they are "attributes or benefits that consumers strongly associate with a brand, positively evaluate, and believe that they could not find to the same extent with a competitive brand" (Barwise & Meehan (2004), cited in Keller & Swaminathan, 2020, p. 82). In contrast, POP associations are those that the brand shares with other brands (Keller & Swaminathan, 2020). Creating successful POP and POD associations helps the organisation develop successful brand positioning as we will explore in more depth later.

Consumer judgements and consumer feelings (brand responses)

The third level of the CBBE pyramid model involves *consumer judgements* and *consumer feelings* (see Figure 2.3) in response to brand identity and brand meaning, established in levels 1 and 2. In this stage the organisation seeks to elicit consumers' rational and emotional reactions (*brand responses*) (see Figure 2.2), and to answer the consumer's question of 'what about you?' (Keller, 2001).

Consumer judgments

Consumer judgments derive from consumers bringing together their brand performance and brand imagery associations to develop their own opinions about the brand (Keller, 2001). Consumer judgments are consumers' rational reactions to the brand identity and brand meaning. In order of importance, there are four types of brand judgments we need to discuss. First, *brand quality* is perhaps the most important attitude consumers hold toward the brand and it is about the *perceived* quality of the brand in consumers' minds. Quality is a very subjective construct; a product or service which one person might regard as of high quality, another person might consider as substandard. Quality also influences an individual's perception of value and satisfaction (Keller, 2001). Despite the subjective nature of quality, it is an important prerequisite to successful brand development and management. This means that an organisation cannot develop and manage a successful brand unless, first and foremost, its product or service meets widely expected standards of quality. As Farquhar explains, "quality is the cornerstone of a strong brand. A firm must have a quality product [or service] that delivers superior performance to the consumer in order to achieve positive evaluation of the brand in the consumer's memory" (1989, p. 27).

Second, *brand credibility* is all about the question of whether or not the brand is considered credible in relation to three dimensions: 1) *brand expertise*, that is, whether or not the brand is perceived as competent, innovative, and a market leader, 2) *brand trustworthiness*, i.e. whether or not the brand is perceived as dependable and has the consumers' interests in mind, and 3) *brand likeability*, i.e. whether or not the brand is perceived as fun, interesting, and consumers feel it is worth spending time with the brand, that is, purchasing and consuming it (Keller, 2001). Third, *brand consideration* is also a very important type of brand judgement because consumers merely being aware of the brand cannot guarantee sales. Besides awareness, the brand needs to be part of the consumers' consideration set, which means that they would seriously consider purchasing and using the brand. Of course, this will depend on consumers' perception of how relevant, appropriate, and meaningful the brand is to them (Keller, 2001). Finally, *brand superiority* is about the extent to which consumers perceive the brand as unique and better than other brands in the same product or service category (Keller, 2001). This is fundamental because, as we have mentioned before, differentiation is one of the main objectives of branding.

Consumer feelings

Consumers are not only rational but also emotional decision-makers, thus they also react emotionally to brand identity and brand meaning: "Brand feelings relate to the social currency evoked by the brand" (Keller, 2001, p. 14). Therefore, the important questions here are 1) what feelings does the brand elicit in consumers' hearts?, and

2) how does the brand make consumers feel about themselves and their relationship with other people? (Keller, 2001). Drawing from Kahle, Poulos, and Sukhdial (1988), Keller (2001) indicates that there are six important types of brand-building feelings: 1) warmth – making consumers feel calm or peaceful, 2) fun – creating feelings of amusement, joy, and being light-hearted, playful, and cheerful, 3) excitement – feeling energised, cool, and sexy, 4) security – feeling safe, comfortable, reassured, 5) social approval – consumers feeling that other people "look favourably on their appearance [and] behaviour" (Keller, 2001, p. 14), and 6) self-respect – feeling pride, accomplishment, fulfilment, and generally feeling better about oneself.

Branding objective: Rational and emotional reactions

It is essential that the organisation generate positive rational and emotional consumer reactions to the brand identity and brand meaning. In particular, the organisation should aim to generate positive feelings in consumers' hearts because this will be an essential step for building a long-term relationship between brand and consumers. Richins (1997) developed a typology of sixteen consumption emotions, which were then organised on a perceptual matrix by Schmitt (1999) using two dimensions: inward–outward and positive–negative. Based on these dimensions, consumption emotions can be organised in four categories: 1) *inward positive emotions*, which include feelings of love, sentimentality, and warm-heartedness, hence consumers feel special and loyalty towards the brand, albeit not publicly expressing these feelings, 2) *outward positive emotions*, which involve consumers feeling pleased, excited, and enthusiastic, thus they are willing to spend money on the brand, praise, and recommend the brand to others, 3) *inward negative emotions*, which include feelings of frustration, irritation, and anger, leading to consumers' complaints and sabotage of the brand, and 4) *outward negative emotions* which involve feeling embarrassed, humiliated, and ashamed; these involve disastrous situations where consumers, as a result, would never return to the brand. Needless to say that organisations should seek to create positive inward and outward feelings in the hearts of their target consumers (Schmitt, 1999). Emotions and emotional branding are explored in more depth in Chapter 5.

Brand resonance (brand relationships)

The fourth and final level of the CBBE pyramid model involves *brand resonance* (see Figure 2.3). In this stage, the organisation seeks to transform the consumers' rational and emotional responses to intense long-term loyalty relationships with the brand (*brand relationships*) (see Figure 2.2), and aims to answer the consumer's question of 'what about you and me?' (Keller, 2001).

> Brand resonance refers to the nature of the relationship that customers have with the brand and the extent to which they feel that they are 'in synch' with the

brand. Brand resonance is characterised in terms of intensity or the depth of the psychological bond that customers have with the brand as well as the level of activity engendered by this loyalty.

(Keller, 2001, p. 15)

The level of activity can include the rate of consumers' repeat purchases, and the degree to which consumers seek out brand information, events, and other loyal consumers (Keller, 2001). There are four categories of brand resonance. First, *behavioural loyalty* is all about how many consumers buy the brand, how much they buy, and how often. In order for the organisation to generate profit, it is essential that target consumers buy the brand often, and where relevant (e.g. non-luxury items), they buy plenty of it. However, behavioural loyalty is not sufficient to build a long-term loyalty relationship between consumers and the brand because consumers might be buying the brand out of necessity, i.e. it might be the only one available, accessible, or affordable (Keller, 2001). Hence, second, consumers should feel *attitudinal attachment* toward the brand, that is, they feel the brand is something special which they love to buy and consume (Keller, 2001). Nonetheless, attitudinal attachment on its own is not sufficient either because a consumer might love the brand but this does not necessarily mean he/she turns affection to action; he/she might simply aspire to have the brand in the future. Evidently, an organisation ought to combine attitudinal attachment with behavioural loyalty so that its target consumers not only feel a personal connection with the brand but also purchase it often (and volumes of it – where appropriate).

Third, *sense of community* where the brand takes on a broader meaning, and loyal consumers form social relationships with each other leading to a *brand community*: "A brand community is a specialized, non-geographically bound community, based on a structured set of social relationships among admirers of a brand" (Muñiz Jr. & O'Guinn, 2001, p. 412). Finally, *active engagement* occurs when consumers evolve to brand ambassadors or evangelists. This is "the strongest affirmation of brand loyalty [where] customers are willing to invest time, energy, money, or other resources into the brand beyond those expended during purchase or consumption of the brand" (Keller, 2001, p. 15). Consumers as brand evangelists opt to receive regular brand information from the organisation (e.g. on their mobile phones), look for brand information themselves (e.g. on the brand's website or online blogs), discuss the brand with others on face-to-face or online basis, and encourage others to purchase the brand. Of course, strong attitudinal attachment and a sense of community are prerequisite for becoming actively engaged with the brand (Keller, 2001). As we will explore in Chapter 4, social media provide powerful platforms where active engagements can flourish, and bestow on each of us the power to become brand evangelists (Edelman, 2010; Kaplan & Haenlein, 2010; Mangold & Faulds, 2009).

Branding objective: Intense and active loyalty relationships
In relation to the top level of the CBBE pyramid model, the organisation's branding objective should be to establish a strong and active loyalty relationship between consumers and the brand. Fournier's (1998) exploratory study of consumer–brand

relationships generated seminal insights on the different types of relationships consumers can form with brands. She identified six facets of consumer–brand relationships. First, *love and passion* relationships, where consumers consider the brand as "irreplaceable and unique to the extent that separation anxiety [is] anticipated upon withdrawal" (Fournier, 1998, p. 364). In such consumer–brand relationships, feelings of love can include warmth and affection, passion, infatuation, and even selfish, obsessive dependency. Second, *self-connection* relationships, whereby the consumer feels that a brand can express a significant aspect of him/herself. Third, *interdependence* relationships, in which a certain level of interdependence joins consumers and the brand together. In such relationships, there are more frequent, more intense, and more diversified consumer–brand interactions leading to consumption rituals which foster and celebrate the relationship and endure over time even when there are low levels of affective involvement and intimacy in the relationship (Fournier, 1998). Fourth, *commitment* relationships, where consumers feel personal dedication to a brand which "fosters stability by implicating the self in relationship outcomes and by encouraging derogation of alternatives in the environment" (Fournier, 1998, p. 365). Fifth, *intimacy* relationships, where consumers develop intimate knowledge of the brand and feel that this intimacy is reciprocated by the brand. Finally, *brand partner quality* relationships, where consumers find in the brand the qualities they would want from a partner or a friend. These consumer–brand relationships make consumers feel that they are cared for, wanted, respected, and listened to, hence they can trust that the brand will behave in accordance with the established relationship rules (Fournier, 1998, Keller & Swaminathan, 2020).

While guaranteeing consumer satisfaction is an important step towards developing consumer loyalty with the brand, there are circumstances where this is not sufficient. Oliver (1999) sought to determine what portion of consumer loyalty with brands is a result of consumer satisfaction. He discovered that while satisfaction is a necessary step in forming loyalty, it "becomes less significant as loyalty begins to set through other mechanisms [which] include the roles of personal determinism ('fortitude') and social bonding at the institutional and personal level" (Oliver, 1999, p. 33). He explains that *fortitude* is "the degree to which the consumer fights off competitive overtures on the basis of his or her allegiance to the brand and not on the basis of marketer-generated information" (Oliver, 1999, p. 37). Nonetheless, there might be cases where these mechanisms – fortitude and social bonding, or even consumer loyalty – are not achievable, yet organisations should still strive for consumer satisfaction as a reasonable goal (Oliver, 1999).

BRAND POSITIONING

Developing the brand positioning concept

In mainstream marketing management theory, a product's *position* is defined as "the place the product occupies relative to competitors in consumers' minds" (Kotler, Armstrong, Wong, & Saunders, 2008, p. 157), on important attributes such as quality, price, and status. Perhaps readers are already familiar with positioning's role in *target marketing strategy*; positioning is the final step of the process often described as the segmentation–targeting–positioning (STP) process. To quickly remind the reader, in this process, the organisation recognises that it cannot serve the entire population, or at least it cannot serve it in the same way. Hence, it opts to divide the market in distinctive and well-defined *segments*; people within such segments share sociodemographic, psychographic, and behavioural characteristics. The onus is on the organisation to then decide which one or more segments it should *target*; for this it needs to evaluate the segments on the basis of how distinctive, accessible, actionable, measurable, and profitable they are. Upon decision of which segment(s) are to be targeted, the organisation will have to develop appropriate products or services which will satisfy the needs and desires of these segments, and *position* these offerings in the minds of the target consumers.

In comparison with (strategic) positioning explained above, *brand positioning*, in particular, concentrates on the process of developing or modifying consumers' perceptions about the brand (Fuchs & Diamantopoulos, 2010). It "involves establishing key brand associations in the minds of customers and other important constituents [internal and external stakeholders] to differentiate the brand and establish (to the extent possible) competitive superiority" (Keller & Lehmann, 2006, p. 740). In other words, Ries defines brand positioning as the "verbalisation of the empty hole your brand will be trying to fill" (2014, p. 5) and he advises organisations to develop a strong concept and associate this concept with the brand. In order for the organisation to develop successful brand positioning, the first step is to determine category membership and communicate it to its target audiences; this is all about developing its *competitive frame of reference*. In other words, the firm will have to decide on which product or service category the brand will compete in, and make consumers aware of this category membership (Keller & Swaminathan, 2020). A second step will include establishing successful POP associations and POD associations.

As explained earlier, POD associations are unique brand attributes or benefits consumers believe they cannot find in other brands (Barwise & Meehan (2004). There are two categories of POD associations: 1) *functional, performance-related POD associations* (which can lead to consumers' brand performance associations), and 2) *abstract, imagery-related POD associations* (which can lead to consumers' brand imagery associations). In contrast with POD associations, as we explained earlier, POP associations are those associations that the brand shares with other brands. There are three types of POP associations. First, *category POP associations*, which "are those associations that consumers view as being necessary to be a legitimate and credible offering with a certain product or service category…,[they are] necessary – but not necessarily sufficient – conditions for brand choice" (Keller, Apéria, & Georgson, 2012, p. 114), and change over time based on technological advances, legislation, and consumer trends. For example, for a smartphone to be considered a legitimate and credible offering within the smartphone product category, it must have phone and text capabilities, a camera, Internet connectivity, and access to smart phone applications (apps). Until relatively recently, these product characteristics were not considered a standard for a mobile phone. Second, *competitive POP associations* are

> those associations designed to negate competitors' points of difference…If, in the eyes of consumers, the brand association designed to be the competitor's point of difference…is as strongly held for the target brand as for competitor's brands *and* the target brand is able to establish another association as strong, favourable, and unique as part of its point of difference, then the target brand should be in a superior competitive position.
>
> (Keller et al., 2012, p. 114)

Figure 2.6 provides an illustration of a competitive POP association. Let's say a Brand X has a point-of-different association (e.g. unique drink taste) (POD1) and then a Brand Y creates the same association to negate Brand X's POD1 association, i.e. its drink has a similar taste. Then this is Brand Y's competitive point-of-parity association (POP1), as it is shared with Brand X and has also negated Brand X's POD1. Of course, Brand Y will create an extra point-of-difference association (its drink has less calories) to achieve differentiation, which is illustrated by POD2 in Figure 2.6.

The consumer electronics sector, including products such as mobile phones, is a good example of a market where competing brands such as *Apple*, *Samsung*, *Huawei*, and *Xiaomi*, continuously rely on category POP associations to legitimise their products as rightful parts of the sector, and on competitive POP associations to copy each other's product features and negate each other's point of difference

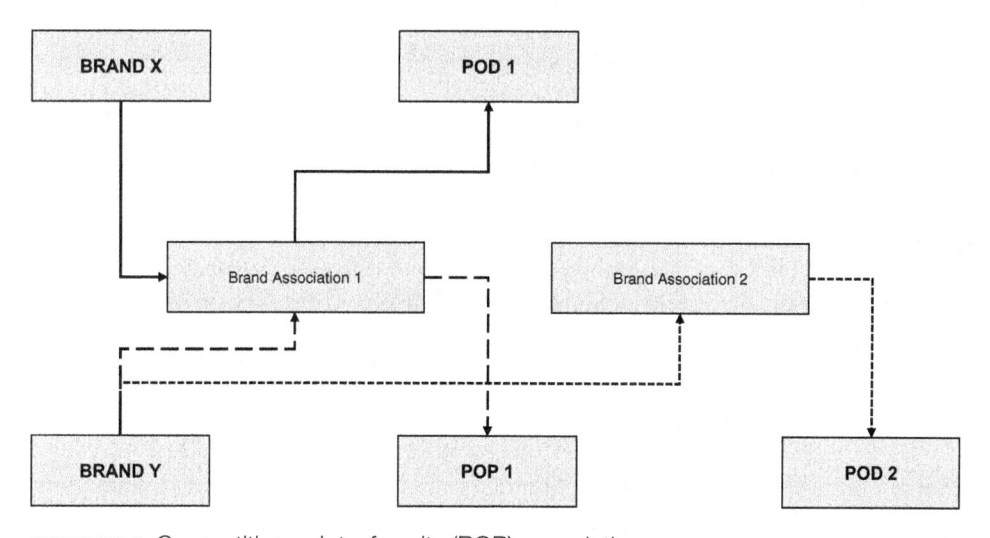

FIGURE 2.6 Competitive point-of-parity (POP) associations

associations. In addition, based on an infinite technological innovation progress, they constantly introduce new features to gain a competitive edge. Finally, a third type of POP associations is *correlational POP associations*, which are potentially negative associations generated from the brand having other, more positive associations. For instance, consumers might struggle to be persuaded that a brand is both inexpensive and of the highest quality (Keller & Swaminathan, 2020).

The above demonstrates that POP associations will eliminate any concerns consumers might have about possible disadvantages of the brand, while POD associations will convince consumers about the advantages of the brand against its competitors (Keller et al., 2012). Choosing POP associations and POD associations requires careful consideration and adhering to a number of criteria from both consumer and organisation perspectives. As far as the consumer perspective is concerned, the organisation must develop brand associations that meet the *desirability* criteria, which means that the associations would have to be 1) personally relevant to the target audiences, i.e. associations consumers view as important, 2) distinctive and superior, thus they create differentiation for the brand and communicate superiority in relation to competitors, and 3) believable, that is, consumers are convinced these associations are credible as they offer convincing reasons for selecting the brand over other options (Keller et al., 2012). With regard to the organisation perspective, the organisation must develop brand associations which meet the *deliverability* criteria, which means that the associations would have to be: 1) feasible, namely the organisation has the financial, human and intellectual resources to develop these associations within an appropriate time frame, 2) communicable, i.e. "there are current and future prospects of communicating information to create or strengthen the desired associations" (Keller et al., 2012, p. 125), and 3) sustainable, namely, the brand associations can be maintained over time, defended from competitive attacks, and reinforced over time (Keller et al., 2012).

Extant literature has identified a number of positioning bases that can form the core of an organisation's brand positioning strategy (Aaker & Shansby, 1982; Crawford, 1985; Keller, 1993; Vriens & ter Hofstede, 2000). Fuchs and Diamantopoulos (2010) grouped these in five overarching categories. First, *features* positioning whereby the firm emphasises objectively measurable and most often tangible features which are specific to the brand's product or service category in order to achieve competitive advantage, such as a hybrid engine in an automobile or face-recognition technology in a mobile phone. Second, *abstract attributes* positioning through which the organisation highlights intangible yet concrete attributes that are similar across different product or service categories, such as positioning the brand as a luxury one, e.g. *Issay Miyake*, or as a sporty brand, e.g. *Li-Ning*. Third, *direct functional benefits* positioning whereby the firm communicates the advantages of using the brand in terms of how it satisfies consumers' functional needs and provides problem solutions, for instance, how easy or convenient it is to use the product, e.g. *Smart* cars are especially suitable for highly congested urban areas. Fourth, *indirect experiential* or *symbolic benefits* positioning, which is designed to emphasise the ability of the brand to satisfy consumers' emotional and symbolic needs, for instance how the brand enables consumers to construct their identity and communicate it to others, e.g. *Abercrombie and Fitch* has been positioned as the quintessential Eastcoast Ivy League university student brand. Finally, *surrogate (user) positioning* which intends to create secondary associations related to intangible aspects of the brand (and *not* about features and benefits), which enable consumers to make their own conclusions (Fuchs & Diamantopoulos, 2010), e.g. the 'begin your own tradition' concept featured in all of the advertising messages of the luxury watch maker *Patek Philippe*.

Of course, it is important to recognise that an organisation can pursue a combination of the aforementioned positioning bases. However, a controversial issue in literature on brand positioning has been the fundamental question of which of these strategies is the best. In their empirical study, Fuchs and Diamantopoulos (2010) tested these strategies on three criteria: favourability, differentiation, and credibility. They discovered that "benefit-based positioning and surrogate (user) positioning generally outperform feature-based positioning strategies along the three effectiveness dimensions" (Fuchs & Diamantopoulos, 2010, p. 1763). However they also demonstrated that there was not one strategy that outperformed all the other strategies on all of these three dimensions (Fuchs & Diamantopoulos, 2010).

Developing the brand mantra

As we discussed earlier the free associations task ('what come to your mind when you think of [Brand X]?) is the simplest way to determine consumers' brand associations. This enables the brand marketer to develop consumers' mental maps of brand associations reflecting consumer knowledge. Once a brand evolves over time and expands to new categories, it is essential to define the set of *core brand associations* that represent the most important aspects of the brand. This can be achieved by bringing together all the associations consumers have, clustering them into categories based on how they are related, and then labelling each category with a descriptive tag (Keller at al., 2012). For example, the core brand associations for *Mercedes-Benz* can possibly include 'performance', 'status', 'origin', 'sport', and 'transport' (see Table 2.1), based on the example of brand associations illustrated in Figure 2.4, and the core brand associations for *Absolut* can perhaps include 'origin', 'quality', 'lifestyle', 'authenticity', and 'nightlife' (see Table 2.2), based on the example of brand associations illustrated in Figure 2.5, and generated by consumers' direct experience with the brand as well as its past advertising campaigns (e.g. *Absolut* 'Metropolis' and 'Kiss with Pride' advertising campaigns – see Images 2.1, 2.2, and 2.3).

Following this, brand marketers can synthesise these core brand associations to develop a brand mantra. *Brand mantras* are

> short three to five word phrases that capture the irrefutable essence or spirit of the brand positioning. Their purpose is to ensure that all employees within the

TABLE 2.1 Example of brand associations and core brand associations for *Mercedes-Benz*

Core brand associations

Performance	Status	Origin	Sport	Transport

Brand associations

Road performance	Luxury	Germany	Sport automobiles	Automobiles
Engineering	Expensive	Stuttgart	Formula 1	SUVs
Innovation	Prestige		Lewis Hamilton	Electric automobiles
Sleek design	Owners' Club			Limousines
	Star			

TABLE 2.2 Example of brand associations and core brand associations for *Absolut*

Core brand associations

Origin	Quality	Lifestyle	Authenticity	Nightlife

Brand associations

Sweden	Vodka	Open-minded	Contemporary	Bars and nightclubs
Winter	Premium	Inclusive	Urban	Cocktails
Icehotel	Different flavours	LGBTQ+ community	Stylish	Socialising
			Cool	
			Colourful	

TABLE 2.3 Example of brand mantras for *Mercedes-Benz* and *Absolut*

	Brand functions	Descriptive modifier	Emotional modifier
Mercedes-Benz	Engineering	Transport	Elegant
Absolut	Leisure	Beverage	Contemporary / Inclusive

organisation as well as external marketing partners understand what the brand most fundamentally is to represent with consumers so that they can adjust their actions accordingly.

(Keller, 1999, p. 45)

Brand mantras are important because they act as the heart and soul of the brand. They provide strategic and creative direction for the organisation in terms of what type of products or services to introduce under the brand, what sort of communications campaigns to pursue, and where the brand should be made available (Keller, 1999),

DEVELOPING BRANDS 47

IMAGE 2.1 *Absolut*'s 'Metropolis' advertising campaign (image courtesy of Absolut)

i.e. which physical stores and on which online platforms. Brand marketers can design brand mantras by bringing together three terms. First, the *brand functions* term, which provides a description of the product or service, experience, and benefits the brand provides to consumers. Second, the *descriptive modifier*, which "is a way to circumscribe the business functions term to further clarify its nature" (Keller, 1999, p. 48). Third, the *emotional modifier* provides further detail about how the brand delivers the benefits stated by the brand functions and the descriptive modifier, providing additional delineation and clarification (Keller, 1999). For instance, the brand

IMAGE 2.2 *Absolut*'s 'Metropolis' advertising campaign (image courtesy of Absolut)

mantra for *Mercedes-Benz* could potentially include words such as 'elegant, transport, engineering', and the brand mantra for *Absolut* could include words such as 'contemporary/inclusive, beverage, leisure' (see Table 2.3). As Keller emphasises, "for the brand mantra to be effective, no other brand should singularly excel in all three dimensions" (1999, p. 48). In addition, the brand mantra should capture the brand's POD associations, reinforce its POP associations, and define the brand's product or service category by setting boundaries and clarifying its uniqueness. It has to be short, vivid, and simple to be memorable, as well as meaningful and relevant to employees so it can inform, guide, and inspire them (Keller, 1999).

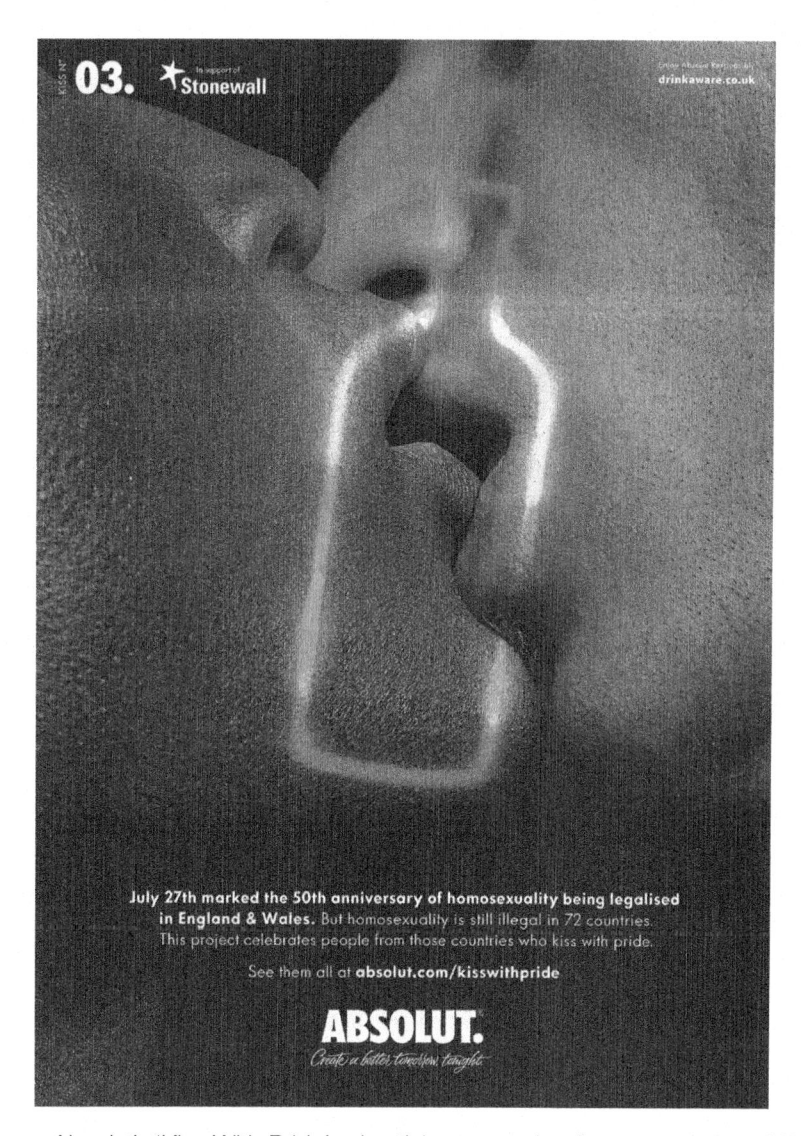

IMAGE 2.3 *Absolut*'s 'Kiss With Pride' advertising campaign (image courtesy of Absolut)

BRAND PERSONALITY AND BRAND VALUES

In our foregoing discussion, we mentioned that Jennifer Aaker has defined *brand personality* "as the set of human characteristics associated with a brand" (1997, p. 345), and that brand personality is a construct which has a symbolic or self-expressive purpose (Keller, 1993). In fact, brand personality is as important as human personality. We all choose our friends and acquaintances on the basis of their personality, that is, we strive to be associated with, and spend our time with, people whose personality matches with ours. Like human personality, brand personality is both distinctive and enduring (Aaker, 2010). In her seminal study, Aaker (1997) examined whether brand personality has any dimensions. She ascertained five personality dimensions, with each having a number of facets. These are: *sincerity* (down-to-earth, honest, wholesome, and cheerful), *excitement* (daring, spirited, imaginative, and up-to-date), *competence* (reliable, intelligent, and successful), *sophistication* (upper class and charming), and *ruggedness* (outdoorsy and tough). For example, one could say that *Dior* has a sophisticated personality, *Caterpillar* a rugged one, *IBM* is a competent brand, *Apple* is seen as an exciting brand, and *The Body Shop* as sincere. Of course one might argue that a brand's personality might include a combination of two or more dimensions, yet a single dimension could still be the most prominent.

Aaker (1997) also explored how these dimensions differ from the 'Big Five' human personality dimensions, i.e. extraversion, neuroticism, openness, conscientiousness, and agreeableness (Briggs, 1992), suggesting that

> although it could be argued that three brand personality dimensions relate to three of the "Big Five" human personality dimensions (i.e. Agreeableness and Sincerity both capture the idea of warmth and acceptance; Extraversion and Excitement both connote the notions of sociability, energy, and activity; Conscientiousness and Competence both encapsulate responsibility, dependability, and security), two dimensions (Sophistication and Ruggedness) differ from any of the "Big Five" of human personality (Briggs, 1992). This pattern suggests that brand personality dimensions might operate in different ways or influence consumer preference for different reasons. For example, whereas Sincerity, Excitement, and Competence tap an innate part of human personality, Sophistication and Ruggedness tap a dimension that individuals desire but do not necessarily have.
> (Aaker, 1997, p. 353)

Brand personality will be influenced by the set of values the brand upholds (de Chernatony, 1999), that is, the brand values. Akin to the parallels between brand personality and human personality, there are great similarities between the importance of human values and brand values. A value is defined as "the enduring belief that a specific mode of conduct or end-state of existence is personally or socially preferable to an opposite or converse mode of conduct or end-state of existence" (Rokeach, 1973, p. 5). Human values derive from culture, the society, its institutions, as well as an individual's personality (Rokeach, 1973). In any social setting, human values are significant because they can direct and influence people's behaviour, through their actions and judgments (Rokeach, 1968).

Equally, brand values provide strategic and creative direction for the organisation. From a consumer perspective, brand values are of great significance because consumers let the psychosocial differences between brands, that is, brand personalities and values, to influence their decision making (Antonides & van Raaij, 1998). Consumers look for brands whose values are well matched with the values they hold. The *self-congruity theory* (Johar & Sirgy, 1991) indicates that value congruity is all about the mental comparisons consumers conduct in order to determine how similar or dissimilar an entity's values are with their own values (Tuškej, Golob, & Podnar, 2013). Value congruity can positively influence a person's identification with the brand, and as a consequence, their commitment to the brand (Tuškej, Golob, & Podnar, 2013).

De Chernatony (2010) makes the distinction between *core* brand values and *peripheral* brand values. The former are those values which the brand will always support regardless of any changes in the environment, while the latter are those values which the brand considers secondary and can be updated according to environmental changes, or can even be removed from the brand's set of values. Hence, core values will have to be values which are credible, consistently achievable, and welcomed by the brand's target audiences, whereas peripheral values will be continuously augmented by the organisation on the basis of the changing conditions in market and society (Collins & Porras, 1996; de Chernatony, 2010): "This way the essence of the brand can be retained while still allowing it to evolve and adapt" (de Chernatony, Drury, & Segal-Horn, 2004).

CHAPTER REVIEW QUESTIONS

You can use the following questions to reflect on the material covered in Chapter 2:

1. Select a brand and ask your friends to explain to you what comes to their minds when they think of this brand.
2. Cluster these brand associations (Question 1) in specific categories and label these categories to determine the core brand associations.
3. Attempt to come up with the brand's mantra using the 'brand function, descriptive modifier, and emotional modifier' structure.
4. After consulting online information, explain whether or not this brand has achieved high levels of brand equity and if so, how. This can be carried out by explaining whether or not, and how, the brand has achieved each layer of the CBBE pyramid model.
5. Consider one of your favourite brands. How does this brand make you feel? Using Fournier's (1998) typology of brand relationships, how would you describe your relationship with this brand?

RECOMMENDED READING

1. Keller, K. L. (2001). *Building customer-based brand equity: A blueprint for creating strong brands* (pp. 3–27). Cambridge: Marketing Science Institute.
2. Keller, K. L. (2003). Brand synthesis: The multidimensionality of brand knowledge. *Journal of Consumer Research*, 29(4), 595–600.

3. Fournier, S. (1998). Consumers and their brands: Developing relationship theory in consumer research. *Journal of Consumer Research*, 24(4), 343–373.
4. Aaker, J. L. (1997). Dimensions of brand personality. *Journal of Marketing Research*, 34(3), 347–356.

CASE STUDY

Union: (Re)positioning a Slovenian icon

David Zappe
Marketing Director
Pivovarna Laško Union d.o.o, Slovenia

The *Union* brewery was initially founded in 1864 by the Kosler brothers in the capital city of what would later become the country of Slovenia. With 2 million inhabitants, Slovenia is one of the smaller countries of the European Union, but economically the most successful ex-communist country. Beer consumption is high at 82 litres per capita per year making it the 13th country in the world measured by that parameter.

The Slovenian beer market has been historically duopolistic with a strong and long impenetrable geographical divide: the *Union* brand ruled the centre and the South of the country, including the capital, whilst the *Laško* brand had a dominant position in the North and Northeast. Also, the brand imagery of the two brands couldn't be farther away: *Union* has been perceived as urban, cosmopolitan, and slightly feminine, while the *Laško* brand (coming from the picturesque small town of Laško) evoked associations to nature, simplicity, pride, and tradition.

After the *Laško* brewery took over the *Union* brewery in 2005, the frontiers started to blur but never disappeared. In 2018, alarm bells started to ring for the *Union* brand: whilst the brand had stable market share, the management couldn't but notice some warning signals jeopardizing the future value of the brand. Not only had its *Brand Health Tracking* shown a gradual decline in almost all brand health indicators, most of these indicators were massively inferior to the (in-house) competitor *Laško*: 32% of the beer drinking population considered themselves regular drinkers of *Laško*, while, only 22% for *Union*. In addition, 43% deemed that *Union* is 'worth its price' (54% for *Laško*), and a smaller number of consumer thought *Union* would be of 'high quality' or has an appealing taste (46% for both parameters for *Union* and 56% and 58%, for *Laško*, respectively).

Visual differentiation also emerged as a key issue of the brand: 'instantly recognisable' and 'attractive packaging' was the lowest among major brands in the market, and 10 to 15 percentage points below *Laško*. One of the reasons behind this lack of differentiation was also the deliberate strategy of the leading retailer of the country that designed their private label packaging in a way to resemble *Union* and made sure to position their product next to *Union* in store. The fact that for a while, this private label (retailer-owned) was produced in the *Union* brewery was also

IMAGE 2.4 *Union* and *Laško* products (image courtesy of Pivovarna Laško Union d.o.o.)

IMAGE 2.5 *Union*'s packaging (image courtesy of Pivovarna Laško Union d.o.o.)

common knowledge and blurred the line between *Union* and the private label. Focus groups discussion showed that the imagery of *Union* is much less clear than that of *Laško*; while the associations coming from the brand's urban roots have prevailed, consumers couldn't relate to the brand strongly. On the visual side, key elements were recognisable (red colour, dragon – the animal of Ljubljana city – and the typical font of the logo), but these didn't clearly lead to a positive attitude towards the brand. The role of the dragon wasn't clear either; it has been there in the background in the packaging design and the brand communication, but not markedly

IMAGE 2.6 Similarity of *Union*'s packaging with a private-label brand's packaging (image courtesy of Pivovarna Laško Union d.o.o.)

enough, unlike the ibex, the symbol of *Laško* and the national animal of Slovenia. It was clear the brand had strong PODs (e.g. the provenance from Ljubljana, leading to associations with the dragon) but those didn't clearly translate into a positive brand image. In addition, unsurprisingly, the evaluation of the brand communication lagged behind key competitors (advertising was deemed as good quality by 46% for *Union* in comparison with 61% for *Laško*, and advertising awareness was 37% in contrast with 54% for *Laško*).

When revising the positioning of *Union* with the aim to restore brand value, recreating the iconic brand design was paramount. The repositioning process started with a thorough analysis into available historical quantitative consumer data (brand health tracking, advertising tracking, penetration, market share, etc.) as well as qualitative studies (the aforementioned focus group discussions), next to a 'deep dive' into the history of the brand (the evolution of brand packaging design, line extensions, communication – TVCs, posters, print ads, and point-of-sale materials). An expert group consisting of the brand management team, research consultants, consumer and market intelligence and innovation teams, and a creative agency was tasked with drafting the new positioning via defining the core target, the consumer insight, the brand role, benefits (POPs and PODs) and proof points, brand personality, brand values, and ultimately the brand essence (a creative, simple expression of what the brand stands for, similar to the brand mantra).

It became clear early in the process that what sets *Union* apart from other brands is the notions of 'bonding' or 'unity' also expressed in the brand name. What stuck with consumers most historically, was the brand's slogan ('Here's to friends!' – '*Za prijatelje!*') used years ago. This also connected to an interesting consumer insight; many consumers expressed that they sometimes miss their friends, but because of their busy schedules, it can be hard to find the time for them). *Union* could play a role as the trigger to renew bonds with friends and family. The dragon, the symbol of the capital city also symbolises this unity of the citizens and serves as a patron to them. The renewal of the brand on that basis could start easily – as most of the times, the creative solution was framed around returning to the brand's roots, admitting proudly the provenance and heritage of the brand while talking to a contemporary audience. Step number one will be the renewal of the visual language starting with the most important consumer touch point, the packaging design of the brand. Following this, the brewery will design a creative campaign to introduce the revitalised product packaging of the *Union* brand to its target audience.

Questions for discussion

1. What are the POPs and PODs *Union* beer intends to create with its renewed positioning?
2. Using the three components of the brand mantra define the essence of *Union* beer.
3. Provide recommendations on how *Union* beer can improve its brand resonance (based on the Customer-Based Brand Equity (CBBE) pyramid model).

REFERENCES

Aaker, D. A. (1991). *Managing brand equity*. New York: Free Press.
Aaker, D. A. (1996). Measuring brand equity across products and markets. *California Management Review*, 38(3).
Aaker, D. A. (2010). *Building strong brands*. London: Simon and Schuster.
Aaker, D. A., & Joachimsthaler, E. (2009). *Brand leadership*. London: Simon and Schuster.

Aaker, D. A., & Shansby, J. G. (1982). Positioning your product. *Business Horizons*, 25(3), 56–62.

Aaker, J. L. (1997). Dimensions of brand personality. *Journal of Marketing Research*, 34(3), 347–356.

Alpert, F. H., Kamins, M. A., & Graham, J. L. (1992). An examination of reseller buyer attitudes toward order of brand entry. *Journal of Marketing*, 56(3), 25–37.

Anderson, J. R. (1983a). *The architecture of cognition*. Cambridge: Harvard University Press.

Anderson, J. R. (1983b). A spreading activation theory of memory. *Journal of Verbal Learning and Verbal Behavior*, 22(3), 261–295.

Anderson, J. R., & Bower, G. H. (1973). *Human associative memory*. Hillsdale: Erlbaum.

Antonides, G., & van Raaij, F. (1998). *Consumer behaviour: A European perspective*. Chichester: John Wiley & Sons.

Baalbaki, S., & Guzmán, F. (2016). Consumer-based brand equity. In F. Dall'Olmo Riley, J. Singh, & C. Blankson (eds), *The Routledge companion to contemporary brand management* (pp. 32–47). London: Routledge.

Barwise, P., & Meehan, S. (2004). *Simply better: Winning and keeping customers by delivering what matters most*. Cambridge: Harvard Business School Press.

Batey, M. (2014). Creating meaningful brands: How brands evolve from labels on products to icons of meaning. In K. Kompella (ed.), *The definitive book of branding* (pp. 22–41). London: Sage.

Briggs, S. R. (1992). Assessing the five-factor model of personality description. *Journal of Personality*, 60(2), 253–293.

Chaudhuri, A., & Holbrook, M. B. (2001). The chain of effects from brand trust and brand affect to brand performance: The role of brand loyalty. *Journal of Marketing*, 65(2), 81–93.

Christodoulides, G., & De Chernatony, L. (2010). Consumer-based brand equity conceptualization and measurement: A literature review. *International Journal of Research in Marketing*, 52(1), 43–66.

Collins, J. C., & Porras, J. I. (1996). Building your company's vision. *Harvard Business Review*, 74(5), 65.

Crawford, C. M. (1985). A new positioning topology. *Journal of Product Innovation Management*, 2(4), 243–253.

Davidson, J. H. (1976). Why most new consumer brands fail. *Harvard Business Review*, 54(2), 117–122.

de Chernatony, L. (1999). Brand management through narrowing the gap between brand identity and brand reputation. *Journal of Marketing Management*, 15(1–3), 157–179.

de Chernatony, L. (2010). *From brand vision to brand evaluation*. Oxford: Elsevier.

de Chernatony, L., Drury, S., & Segal-Horn, S. (2004). Identifying and sustaining services brands' values. *Journal of Marketing Communications*, 10(2), 73–93.

Edelman, D. (2010). Branding in the digital age: You're spending your money in all the wrong places. *Harvard Business Review*, 88(12), 62–69.

Erdem, T. (1998). An empirical analysis of umbrella branding. *Journal of Marketing Research*, 35(3), 339–351.

Escalas, J. E., & Bettman, J. R. (2005). Self-construal, reference groups, and brand meaning. *Journal of Consumer Research*, 32(3), 378–389.

Farquhar, P. H. (1989). Managing brand equity. *Marketing Research*, 1(3), 24–33.

Feldwick, P. (1996). Do we really need "brand equity"? *The Journal of Brand Management*, 21(2), 9–28.

Fournier, S. (1998). Consumers and their brands: Developing relationship theory in consumer research. *Journal of Consumer Research*, 24(4), 343–373.

French, A., & Smith, G. (2013). Measuring brand association strength: A consumer based brand equity approach. *European Journal of Marketing*, 47(8), 1356–1367.

Fuchs, C., & Diamantopoulos, A. (2010). Evaluating the effectiveness of brand-positioning strategies from a consumer perspective. *European Journal of Marketing*, 44(11/12), 1763–1786.

Gupta, S., Garg, S., & Sharma, K. (2016). Branding in emerging markets. In F. Dall'Olmo Riley, J. Singh, & C. Blankson (eds), *The Routledge companion to contemporary brand management* (pp. 366–377). London: Routledge.

Holt, D. B. (2004). *How brands become icons: The principles of cultural branding*. Cambridge: Harvard Business Press.

Hoyer, W. D., & Brown, S. P. (1990). Effects of brand awareness on choice for A common, repeat-purchase product. *Journal of Consumer Research*, 17(2), 141–148.

Johar, J. S., & Sirgy, M. J. (1991). Value-expressive versus utilitarian advertising appeals: When and why to use which appeal. *Journal of Advertising*, 20(3), 23–33.

John, D. R., Loken, B., Kim, K., & Monga, A. B. (2006). Brand concept maps: A methodology for identifying brand association networks. *Journal of Marketing Research*, 43(4), 549–563.

Kahle, L. R., & Poulos, B., & Sukhdial, A. (1988). Changes in social values in the United States during the past decade. *Journal of Advertising Research*, 28, 35–41.

Kaplan, A. M., & Haenlein, M. (2010). Users of the world, unite! The challenges and opportunities of social media. *Business Horizons*, 53(1), 59–68.

Keller, K. L. (1993). Conceptualizing, measuring, and managing customer-based brand equity. *Journal of Marketing*, 57(1), 1–22.

Keller, K. L. (1999). Brand mantras: Rationale, criteria and examples. *Journal of Marketing Management*, 15(1–3), 43–51.

Keller, K. L. (2001). *Building customer-based brand equity: A blueprint for creating strong brands* (pp. 3–27). Cambridge: Marketing Science Institute.

Keller, K. L. (2003). Brand synthesis: The multidimensionality of brand knowledge. *Journal of Consumer Research*, 29(4), 595–600.

Keller, K. L., Apéria, T., & Georgson, M. (2012). *Strategic brand management: A European perspective*. London: Pearson Education.

Keller, K. L., & Davey, K. K. (2001). Building customer-based brand equity. Advertising Research Foundation Workshop, October. New York: Advertising Research Foundation.

Keller, K. L., & Lehmann, D. R. (2006). Brands and branding: Research findings and future priorities. *Marketing Science*, 25(6), 740–759.

Keller, K. L., Sternthal, B., & Tybout, A. (2002). Three questions you need to ask about your brand. *Harvard Business Review*, 80(9), 80–89.

Keller, K. L., & Swaminathan, V. (2020). *Strategic brand management: Building, measuring, and managing brand equity* (5th edn). London: Pearson Education.

King, C., & Grace, D. (2009). Employee based brand equity: A third perspective. *Services Marketing Quarterly*, 30(2), 122–147.

Kotler, P., Armstrong, G., Wong, V., & Saunders, J. (2008). *Principles of marketing* (5th European edn). London: Pearson.

Lassar, W., Mittal, B., & Sharma, A. (1995). Measuring customer-based brand equity. *Journal of Consumer Marketing*, 12(4), 11–19.

Mangold, W. G., & Faulds, D. J. (2009). Social media: The new hybrid element of the promotion mix. *Business Horizons*, 52(4), 357–365.

McCracken, G. (1986). Culture and consumption: A theoretical account of the structure and movement of the cultural meaning of consumer goods. *Journal of Consumer Research*, 13(1), 71–84.

Morris, P. (2003). *The Bakhtin reader: Selected writings of Bakhtin, Medvedev, Voloshinov*. London: Arnold.

Muñiz Jr., A. M., & O'Guinn, T. C. (2001). Brand community. *Journal of Consumer Research*, 27(4), 412–432.
Neumeier, M. (2006). *The brand gap: How to bridge the distance between business strategy and design*. Berkeley: New Riders.
Oliver, R. L. (1999). Whence consumer loyalty? *Journal of Marketing*, 63(4 suppl1), 33–44.
Ries, A. (2014). The essence of positioning. In K. Kompella (ed.), *The definitive book of branding* (pp. 3–21). London: Sage.
Richins, M. L. (1997). Measuring emotions in the consumption experience. *Journal of Consumer Research*, 24(2), 127–146.
Rokeach, M. (1968). *Beliefs, attitudes and values: A theory of organization and change*. London: Jossey-Bass.
Rokeach, M. (1973). *The nature of human values*. New York: The Free Press.
Romaniuk, J., & Gaillard, E. (2007). The relationship between unique brand associations, brand usage and brand performance: Analysis across eight categories. *Journal of Marketing Management*, 23(3–4), 267–284.
Schmitt, B. H. (1999). *Experiential marketing: How to get customers to sense, feel, think, act, relate*. New York: The Free Press.
Schnittka, O., Sattler, H., & Zenker, S. (2012). Advanced brand concept maps: A new approach for evaluating the favorability of brand association networks. *International Journal of Research in Marketing*, 29(3), 265–274.
Srull, T. K., & Wyer, R. S. (1989). Person memory and judgment. *Psychological Review*, 96(1), 58.
Teichert, T. A., & Schöntag, K. (2010). Exploring consumer knowledge structures using associative network analysis. *Psychology & Marketing*, 27(4), 369–398.
Tuškej, U., Golob, U., & Podnar, K. (2013). The role of consumer–brand identification in building brand relationships. *Journal of Business Research*, 66(1), 53–59.
Tversky, A. (1972). Elimination by aspects: A theory of choice. *Psychological Review*, 79(4), 281.
Vriens, M., & ter Hofstede, F. (2000). Linking attribute, benefits, and consumer values. *Marketing Research*, 12(3), 4–10.
Winters, L. C. (1991). Brand equity measures: Some recent advances. *Marketing Research*, 3(4), 70.
Wood, L. (2000). Brands and brand equity: Definition and management. *Management Decision*, 38(9), 662–669.
Yoo, B., Donthu, N., & Lee, S. (2000). An examination of selected marketing mix elements and brand equity. *Journal of the Academy of Marketing Science*, 28(2), 195–211.

CHAPTER 3

Creating brand identity: Brand aesthetics and symbolism

CHAPTER AIMS AND LEARNING OUTCOMES

This chapter corresponds to the first stage of Keller and Swaminathan's (2020) *strategic brand management process*, i.e. identifying and developing brand plans (see Figure 3.1), and draws from extant literature in consumer psychology, consumer culture, sensory marketing, and design studies. Creating successful brand identities through brand aesthetics and symbolism contributes to an organisation's ability to effectively position its brand in the minds of the consumers, in relation to its competitors in the product or service category (unlike Keller and Swaminathan (2020) who argue that it is part of the second stage of the strategic brand management process): "Building customer-based brand equity requires the creation of a familiar brand that has favourable, strong, and unique brand associations. This can be done through the initial choice of the brand identities, such as the brand name, logo, or symbol…" (Keller, 1993, p. 9). A strong brand identity leads to higher brand equity as it contributes to creating deep and broad brand salience (and vice versa), articulates brand meaning, which consequently can elicit positive rational and emotional consumer responses, and build a strong relationship between consumers and the brand. In particular, this chapter aims to achieve the following:

1. Understand the brand identity development process by exploring the brand expressions–consumer impressions framework.
2. Explore the role of brand aesthetics and symbolism in developing successful brand identities.

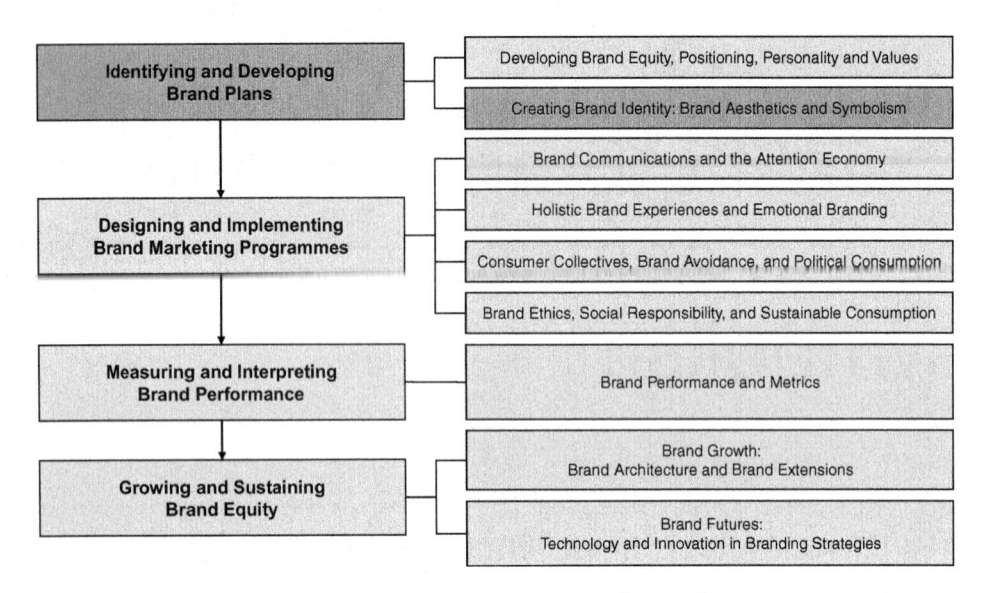

```
┌─────────────────────────┐     ┌──────────────────────────────────────────────────────┐
│ Identifying and Developing │────▶│ Developing Brand Equity, Positioning, Personality and Values │
│      Brand Plans         │     ├──────────────────────────────────────────────────────┤
└───────────┬─────────────┘     │ Creating Brand Identity: Brand Aesthetics and Symbolism │
            │                    └──────────────────────────────────────────────────────┘
            ▼
┌─────────────────────────┐     ┌──────────────────────────────────────────────────────┐
│                         │────▶│ Brand Communications and the Attention Economy        │
│ Designing and Implementing│     ├──────────────────────────────────────────────────────┤
│ Brand Marketing Programmes│────▶│ Holistic Brand Experiences and Emotional Branding    │
│                         │     ├──────────────────────────────────────────────────────┤
│                         │────▶│ Consumer Collectives, Brand Avoidance, and Political Consumption │
│                         │     ├──────────────────────────────────────────────────────┤
│                         │────▶│ Brand Ethics, Social Responsibility, and Sustainable Consumption │
└───────────┬─────────────┘     └──────────────────────────────────────────────────────┘
            ▼
┌─────────────────────────┐     ┌──────────────────────────────────────────────────────┐
│ Measuring and Interpreting│────▶│ Brand Performance and Metrics                        │
│   Brand Performance     │     └──────────────────────────────────────────────────────┘
└───────────┬─────────────┘
            ▼
┌─────────────────────────┐     ┌──────────────────────────────────────────────────────┐
│                         │────▶│ Brand Growth:                                        │
│ Growing and Sustaining  │     │ Brand Architecture and Brand Extensions              │
│     Brand Equity        │     ├──────────────────────────────────────────────────────┤
│                         │────▶│ Brand Futures:                                       │
│                         │     │ Technology and Innovation in Branding Strategies     │
└─────────────────────────┘     └──────────────────────────────────────────────────────┘
```

FIGURE 3.1 Strategic brand management process and book plan

BRAND IDENTITY DEVELOPMENT PROCESS

> Brand identity is tangible and appeals to the five senses [sight, sound, touch, taste, and smell]. You can see it, touch it, hold it, hear it, watch it move. Brand identity fuels recognition, amplifies differentiation, and makes big ideas and meaning accessible. Brand identity takes disparate elements and unifies them into whole systems.
>
> (Wheeler, 2013, p. 4)

As explained in Chapter 1, *brand identity* is all about an organisation's expressions and messages, which provide direction, purpose, and meaning for the brand (Aaker, 2010). Brand identity is about how a brand aims to identify itself to its stakeholders (Margulies, 1977; Nandan, 2005), whereas *brand image* is the perception of the brand by these stakeholders (Margulies, 1977). Christensen and Askegaard (2001) highlight the internal-external distinction between brand identity and brand image, and indicate that brand identity can be considered as belonging to the sender (firm), while the brand image to the receiver (consumer), in the communication process. Consumers receive the brand identity and process it to arrive to their own *brand image* in their minds (Dall'Olmo Riley, 2016). Thus, brand image "refers to the mental conceptions that the firm's multiple constituents (customers, employees, investors, and the public at large) hold of the firm based on its aesthetic output" (Schmitt,

Simonson, & Marcus, 1995, p. 83), and a consumer-generated holistic impression of the brand's position among its competitors (de Chernatony, 1999).

Schmitt and Simonson's (1997) *brand expressions–consumer impressions framework* outlines the essential steps for developing an effective brand identity through aesthetics and symbolism, leading to strong and positive impressions in consumers' minds.

Brand expressions

The first component of the framework is *brand expressions*. It is essential to remember that consumers do not have direct access to an organisation's culture, missions, strategies, and values, that is, the *private self* of the organisation. Instead, what consumers see is the *public face* of the organisation, which is all about the brand expressions manifested through the four elements of the identity mix (4Ps): properties, products, presentations, and publications (Schmitt & Simonson, 1997; Schmitt, Simonson, & Marcus, 1995). *Properties* include buildings, offices, retail spaces, and company vehicles, *products* involve the sensory aspects or attributes of the product or service, *presentations* include the surroundings elements of the product (e.g. packaging, labelling, and tags) or service (e.g. shopping bags, place settings, and the appearance of employees), and *publications* include promotional materials, advertising, business cards, and stationery (Schmitt & Simonson, 1997; Schmitt et al., 1995).

Schmitt and Simonson (1997) emphasise that brand marketers need to avoid or eliminate the *projection gap*, which occurs when "the private self of the organisation…[is] not adequately projected in the various identity elements that constitute the organisation's…public face" (Schmitt & Simonson, 1997, p. 72). As we will explore later, the identity elements (4Ps) have their own aesthetic elements that are created through primary elements, styles, and themes (Schmitt & Simonson, 1997). A significant question the organisation needs to address is the question of aesthetic consistency versus aesthetic variety, that is, "should the aesthetic elements of one identity element [i.e. its primary elements, styles, and themes] be repeated in other identity elements, or should they differ from one another?" (Schmitt & Simonson, 1997, p. 65).

Types of brand identities

There are three types of brand identities organisations can choose: (1) monolithic (or corporate) identity, (2) branded (or brand-based) identity, and (3) endorsed (or multiple-business) identity (Olins, 2008; Schmitt & Simonson, 1997; Wheeler, 2013). Let us explore the nature and characteristics of each type in more depth.

First, with a *monolithic (corporate) identity*, an organisation uses the same name, logo, signage, and aesthetics for all its departments and divisions and on all of its products and services, which means that the organisation *is* the brand (e.g. *Samsung, Yamaha, HSBC, Virgin,* and *HSBC*). Monolithic identities have many advantages including stronger uniformity and coherence for organisations. Each product or service within the organisation's portfolio is branded with the same name and brand elements and "everything within the organisation by way of promotion or product [/ service] supports everything else" (Olins, 2008, p. 47). In addition, having a monolithic identity, organisations can achieve greater visibility and a clearer positioning in consumers' minds (Olins, 2008). Nevertheless, there are two important disadvantages of this type of brand identity. First, when one part of the organisation gets in trouble, it affects everything else and the brand suffers (Olins, 2008). Think, for example, the *Volkswagen* emissions scandal and how the defects identified with its diesel cars affected the reputation of the entire firm. Second, there is a possibility that over time "the identity becomes amorphous: the company stands for anything – and nothing. Or the identity is tilted toward certain businesses" (Schmitt & Simonson, 1997, p. 67). If this happens then the organisation may choose to adopt another type of brand identity so it can redesign its brand expressions.

Second, in the case of a *branded (brand-based) identity*, the organisation is known by its name and (corporate) brand elements to suppliers and distributors, and by its brands to its consumers. Consider, for example, *Hellman's* mayonnaise (or *Best Foods* mayonnaise in Asia and Australia), *Knorr* soups, and *Persil* washing detergent. These are brands consumers purchase every day but they are owned and managed by one organisation, *Unilever*. Similarly, consumers know and trust *Gillette* razors, *Lenor* fabric conditioner, and *Herbal Essences* shampoo, which are products owned and managed by *Procter and Gamble (P&G)*. As Schmitt and Simonson observe, the "parent company is hardly known to consumers because its identity is not present in the marketplace" (1997, p. 67) (although it might feature on the back of the product's packaging).

Brand-based identities are created intentionally or through mergers and acquisitions and for a number of reasons. They enable firms to develop and manage multiple brands to appeal to different target segments with their own life cycle, distinct from that of the organisation. Olins explains that "the long-standing tradition of the fast-moving consumer goods [FMCGs] industry is that the consumer is readily influenced by basic and obvious symbolism…This somewhat naïve symbolism might

IMAGE 3.1 Procter and Gamble (P&G) logo

IMAGE 3.2 *Gillette* razors

seem to be inappropriate for a global, complex corporation" (2008, p. 51). There is also the possibility that brands of the same organisation compete in the same sector, so their integrity could be damaged in the minds of consumers if they were known to belong to the same firm, e.g. *Dior, Kenzo, Louis Vuitton,* and *Marc Jacobs* (are all owned by the *LVMH Group*).

Third, *endorsed (multiple-business) identity* is the hybrid of the previous two types, offering the best of both worlds where the organisation benefits from the brand identity and vice versa (Schmitt & Simonson, 1997). Organisations that use this type of brand identity usually have grown by acquisition and operate a multi-sector business; "they have often acquired competitors, suppliers, and customers, each with its own name, culture, tradition, and reputation amongst its own network of audiences" (Olins, 2008, p. 49). There might be cases where these organisations have acquired competitive ranges of products and thus face confusion among

IMAGE 3.3 *Lenor* fabric conditioner

consumers, suppliers, and their own employees. Their concern will be to "retain the goodwill associated with the brands…which they have acquired, but at the same time they want to superimpose their own management style, reward systems, attitudes, and sometimes name upon their subsidiaries" (Olins, 2008, p. 51). This means that while their portfolio is vast and they operate in many parts of the world where their product ranges and reputations vary, they want to demonstrate coherence and consistency instead of heterogeneity (Olins, 2010). However, this type of brand identity is not only suitable to acquisitions; for example, it is a very common type in the fashion industry, e.g. *Giorgio Armani*, *Emporio Armani*, and *Armani Exchange*, or *Dona Karan* and *DKNY* (Schmitt & Simonson, 1997).

Styles

As mentioned earlier, according to Schmitt and Simonson (1997), the identity elements have their own aesthetic elements that are created through primary elements, styles, and themes. *Primary elements* (explored later in more depth) include shapes, colours, and typefaces (vision), sounds (audition), materials and textures (haptics), and scents (gustatory and olfaction). When these primary elements are brought together they generate *style*. Schmitt and Simonson argue that "styles are composed of primary elements and can be analysed in terms of them" (1997, p. 85). Shapiro

IMAGE 3.4 *Herbal Essences* shampoo

defines style as "the constant form – and sometimes the constant elements and expression – in the art of an individual or a group" (1953, p. 287). Organisations integrate primary elements in order to achieve a holistic outcome. This also relates to Kotler's (1973) and Schmitt and Zarantonello's (2013) concept of *store atmospherics* where retailers bring together different primary elements to design a certain style for a retail store. From a branding perspective, style can be very powerful as it can: 1) create brand awareness and emotional and intellectual associations in individuals' hearts and minds, 2) differentiate products and services providing ways consumers can categorise them, 3) sub-categorise variations of products in product lines (by adopting different styles), 4) fine-tune the marketing mix across different target segments, and 5) beautify the environment creating pleasure and relaxation, reducing stress, and facilitating socialisation among individuals (Schmitt & Simonson, 1997).

One of the most significant "tasks of identity management through aesthetics, is to associate the organisation and its brands with a certain style" (Schmitt & Simonson, 1997, p. 85). In particular, organisations can harness the power of style to reposition an existing brand or develop a completely new brand. When the organisation seeks to reposition an existing brand, it can follow the *bottom-up* approach where, first, it needs to determine the primary elements that require an update, and

66 CREATING BRAND IDENTITY

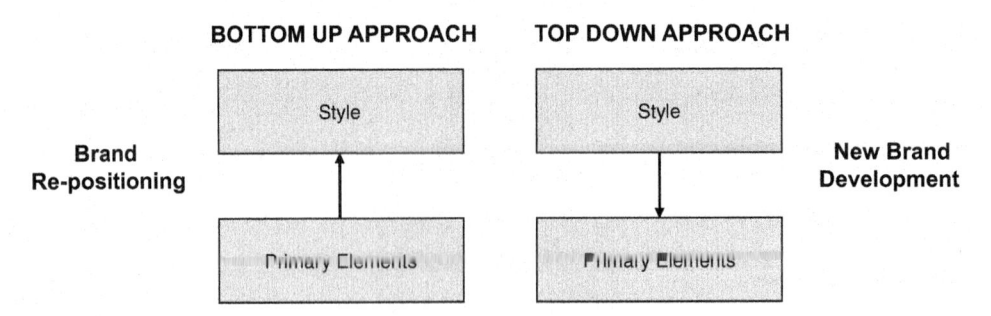

FIGURE 3.2 Managerial approaches to creating style

then determine how this will affect the brand style (see Figure 3.2). When the strategy includes developing a new brand, the firm can follow the *top-down* approach, which is strategic and systematic, where it first determines the style the new brand should have, and then it specifies the primary elements which, when brought together, will constitute this style (see Figure 3.2). Schmitt and Simonson (1997) identified four perceptual dimensions which can be used to evaluate styles: (1) *complexity*, i.e. how complex the brand style appears, with minimalism (e.g. *Giorgio Armani* or *Muji*) on the one end and ornamentalism on the other (e.g. *Versace* or *Shanghai Tang*), (2) *representation*, namely, whether the brand style represents reality (realism) or not (abstraction), (3) *movement*, that is, how dynamic does the brand style appear (dynamic vs. static), and (4) *potency*, i.e. how powerful and overwhelming the brand style should appear (loud and strong vs. soft and weak).

Organisations can choose to juxtapose different aesthetic elements in one or more identity elements (aesthetic variety), which can lead to asymmetry in style, similar to asymmetry in shape, and a more eclectic brand identity. For example, such an approach could be ideal for different product lines in the organisational portfolio. It is vital that brand styles are adapted over time to remain current and in line with consumers' preferences or to respond to changes in the competitive market environment. There might be instances where a style needs to be abandoned and replaced with another style when it has become dated (Schmitt & Simonson, 1997).

Themes

Style must be combined with themes in order to work effectively. Themes can concisely and directly communicate the brand mantra (see Chapter 2) (Schmitt & Simonson, 1997) and are messages that communicate brand content and meaning (Schmitt, 1999a; 1999b). "Themes provide mental anchors, reference points, and memory cues, [and] appear in the form of corporate and brand names, visual symbols, verbal slogans, jingles, general concepts, or in a combination of these theme elements to evoke sensory imagery" (Schmitt, 1999b, p. 107). Brand marketers create brand themes that act as signs and symbols to express brand characteristics and use themes as "prototypical expressions of an organisation's and/or brand's core values or mission" (Schmitt & Simonson, 1997, p. 124). They should also be used on a repeat basis, should be organised into a system of interrelated ideas to ensure consistency and to avoid confusion, and should be adapted over time if required (Schmitt & Simonson, 1997).

The organisation must address three strategic questions in relation to developing appropriate themes. First, it must decide which of the brand's characteristics must be portrayed, a decision that requires an analysis of the core elements in the firm's internal and external marketing environment (i.e. corporate mission, vision, objectives, core capabilities, brand characters and values, target consumer characteristics, and competitors' aesthetic strategies) (Schmitt & Simonson, 1997). Second, the organisation must determine the domains it can take rich thematic content from. This can include domains such as history, psychology, popular culture, fashion, philosophy, religion, politics, the physical world, and the arts (Schmitt & Simonson, 1997). Schroeder (2005) suggests that visual arts, in particular, can be a great source of inspiration for branding strategies. He studied the cases of three leading artists, Andy Warhol, Barbara Kruger, and Cindy Sherman, and argued that

> greater awareness of the connections between traditions and conventions of visual art and the production and consumption of images leads to enhanced ability to understand branding as a strategic signifying practice. Artists offer exemplary instances of image creation in the service of building a recognisable look, name, and style – a brand, in other words.
>
> (Schroeder, 2005, p. 1292)

The third question organisations must address is about how the themes should be presented to express the brand traits, that is, where the brand "themes should be embodied i.e. in names, symbols, slogans, narratives, concepts or combinations" (Schmitt & Simonson, 1997, p. 128). The firm must also make a decision on whether it should have one or multiple themes. One theme can be very powerful as it summarises its central positioning, whereas multiple themes can simultaneously represent different aspects of the brand. Determining the most effective approach will depend on the organisation's product line(s) and how uniform it wants to appear. Similarly, the organisation must choose between thematic isolation and thematic variation; the former creates strong associations, a global theme and powerful brand icons, while the latter provides the opportunity to micro-target specific consumer cultures. The general advice is that if there are no evident benefits for having thematic variation, i.e. the brand can be successful in being easily identified across different markets, then the organisation should maintain a single theme (Schmitt & Simonson, 1997). Like in the case of styles, the onus is on the firm to determine when a theme needs to be adapted or abandoned all together; updates may be necessary because of changes in consumer preferences, fashion trends, technology, and competition (Schmitt & Simonson, 1997).

Keller and Swaminathan (2020) expand Robertson's (1989) list of strategically desirable brand name characteristics to apply them on not only brand names but also on brand symbols and logos. They argue that the organisation must adhere to the following criteria when choosing brand elements (creating themes through names and symbols). First, the brand elements must be *memorable*, i.e. any brand name must be easy to comprehend, pronounce, and spell (Keller, 1993) and any symbols must be able to attract attention in order for all elements to be easy to recall and recognise. To improve this, organisations can use mnemonic factors, such as 'one-a-day', and vivid words to create rich imagery that is experiential or evaluative (Robertson, 1987). Second, they should be *meaningful*, that is, they must be descriptive and persuasive and they must contribute to the development of positive brand associations by explaining the product's or service's category, benefits, and qualities (Keller, 1993). However, the exception to this rule is *arbitrary* brand names that do not have an obvious tie-in to the company, e.g. *Apple* (consumer electronics) and *Orange* (telecommunications). Third, they ought to be *likeable*, i.e. they are rich in visual and verbal imagery, aesthetically pleasing, fun, and interesting. Fourth, they must be *transferable*, namely they can be applied on different products within a product category, or across different product categories, geographical locations, and cultures. Fifth, they should be *adaptable*, meaning they can be flexible and easily updated. Finally, they must be *protectable*, which means that they can be registered and legally protected; they should not infringe on other organisations' brand elements. For example, it would be impossible to register a new fast food restaurant business under the name *Burger King* (Keller & Swaminathan, 2020).

Keller (1993) recognises that it might be hard to choose names that are simple, familiar, *and* distinctive, because these criteria are not necessarily mutually compatible. For instance, extant literature indicates that words that are conventionally used in high frequency are easier to recall, whereas words that are not used frequently are easier to recognise (Gregg, 1976; Lynch & Srull, 1982). The responsibility lies with brand marketers to decide whether to highlight recall or recognition properties when selecting a brand name; they will have to consider "managerial properties concerning the extent of consumers' in-store processing for the product, [and] the nature of the competitive environment" (Keller, 1993, p. 9).

In order to discuss in more depth the development of themes through the creation of suitable visual symbols, we need to understand the concepts of semiotics and symbolism. Umberto Eco, the Italian philosopher, semiotician, and novelist, explains that

> *semiotics* is concerned with everything that can be *taken* as a sign. A sign is everything which can be taken as significantly substituting for something else. This something else does not necessarily have to exist or to actually be somewhere at the moment in which a sign stands in for it.
>
> (Eco, 1976, p. 7)

```
                    ┌─────────────────────────────────────────────┐
                    │                 Semantics                    │
                    │    Relationship between sign and object      │
                    └─────────────────────────────────────────────┘
┌──────────────┐    ┌─────────────────────────────────────────────┐
│ DIMENSIONS OF│───▶│                 Pragmatics                   │
│   SEMIOSIS   │    │  Relationship between sign and interpreter   │
└──────────────┘    └─────────────────────────────────────────────┘
                    ┌─────────────────────────────────────────────┐
                    │                 Syntactics                   │
                    │         Relationships between signs          │
                    └─────────────────────────────────────────────┘
```

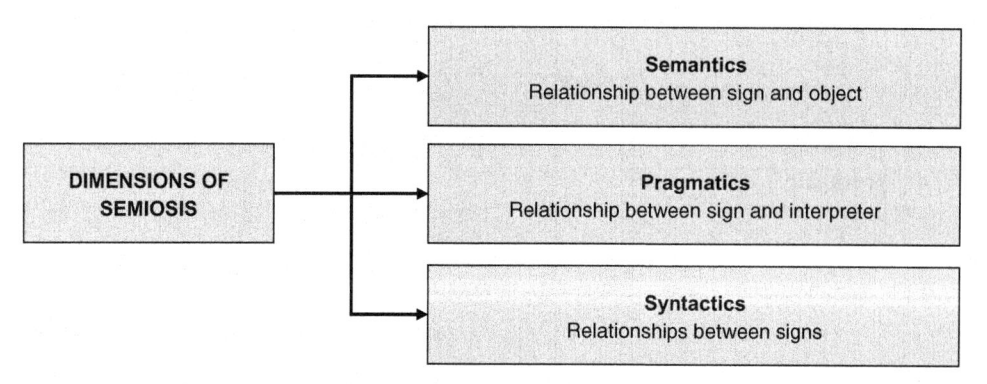

FIGURE 3.3 Dimensions of semiosis

According to Morris (1938) semiotics studies ordinary objects to the extent that these objects participate in *semiosis* because "something is a sign only because it is interpreted as a sign of something by some interpreter" (Morris, 1938, p. 4). Semiosis is "an action, or influence, which is, or involves, an operation of *three* subjects, such as sign, its object, and its interpretant, this tri-relative influence not being in any way resolvable into an action between pairs" (Peirce cited in Eco, 1986). This means that there are three components in the semiosis: The sign, the object (designatum), and the interpreter (Morris, 1938), and there are three dimensions of the semiosis: (1) *semantics*, the relationship between a sign and an object, (2) *pragmatics*, the relationship between a sign and the interpreter, and (3) *syntactics*, the relationships between signs (Morris, 1938) (see Figure 3.3). It is important to remember that things do not exist in isolation but in relation to other things. They derive their meaning through their relationships to each other and to the wider socio-cultural context: "All experience is mediated by signs, and communication depends on them. Semioticians study how meanings are made and how reality is represented (and indeed constructed) through signs and sign systems" (Chandler, 2017, p. 2).

Brand identity, and in particular, creating themes through symbols, is concerned with the semantic relationship between a sign (such as a brand logo or symbol) and an object (the product). A sign can be related to an object in three ways: 1) *iconic signs*, which are non-abstract signs that represent the object by drawing on a similarity of appearance, e.g. a photograph of a person represents the person because it resembles how he/she looks, 2) *indexical signs*, which refer to an object or event because of a connection or causal relationship with the object, for example, e.g. the tracks of a car after driving in the sand – the car *causes* the tracks in the sand, and 3) *symbolic signs*, which are related to an object on the basis of an agreement or convention, e.g. there is an agreement that the Union Jack represents the United Kingdom as a sovereign state (Antonides & Van Raij, 1998; Hall, 2012) (see Figure 3.4).

Organisations can develop symbolic signs that are matched with their brands. These symbolic signs can be legally registered (legal agreement) and can be repeated

```
                    ┌─────────────────────────────────────────┐
                    │            Iconic signs                 │
                    │   (Based on similarity of appearance)   │
                    └─────────────────────────────────────────┘
┌──────────────┐    ┌─────────────────────────────────────────────┐
│  SEMANTIC    │    │            Indexical signs                  │
│RELATIONSHIPS │───▶│ (Based on connection or causal relationship)│
└──────────────┘    └─────────────────────────────────────────────┘
                    ┌─────────────────────────────────────────┐
                    │           Symbolic signs                │
                    │   (Based on agreement or convention)    │
                    └─────────────────────────────────────────┘
```

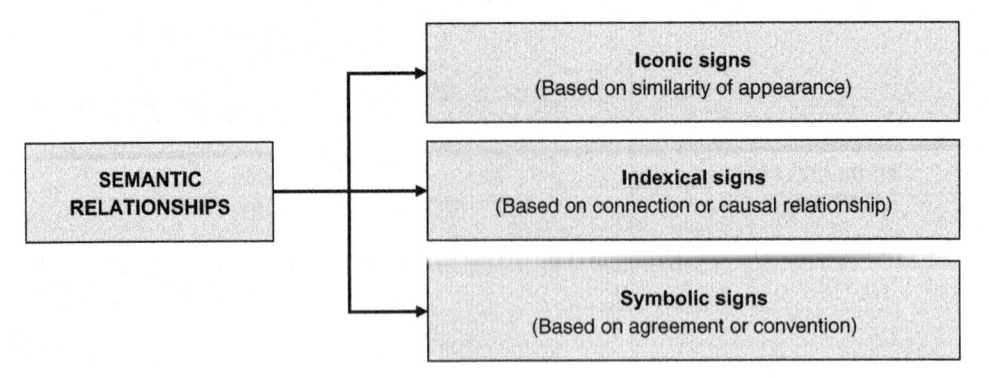

FIGURE 3.4 Types of semantic relationships

in brand communications (convention) over time so that they represent the brand. Firms need to be cautious when developing themes through symbols; when themes are successfully designed they can enhance brand evaluations, when inappropriate they can diminish these evaluations (Schmitt & Simonson, 1997). Brand marketers should resist the temptation of using (already) popular symbols because although they may generate attention, they seldom differentiate the brand. Organisations should be prepared to defend their symbolism because when successful it attracts imitation from competitors. Finally, symbolism is important for internal marketing purposes too because they can encourage employees' positive identification with the brand when these symbols are powerful and appropriate (Schmitt & Simonson, 1997).

Consumer impressions

The brand expressions explained above need to generate, through effective brand styles and themes, the desired impressions in target consumers' mind. Hence, it is essential at this stage to understand how individuals process information, i.e. brand expressions. This enables organisations to avoid or eliminate the *misinterpretation gap*, which occurs when target consumers misinterpret the brand expressions resulting to negative or unintended impressions in their minds (Schmitt & Simonson, 1997). It is widely recognised that consumers are active processors of messages; they can edit and interpret the primary elements, styles, and themes to form their own brand image. The interpretation of brand expressions is conscious and deliberate, due to interest in the brand or confusion with its messages (e.g. *Benetton*'s advertising posters in the 1990s), as well as unconscious.

Human beings engage in three processes to interpret information: integrations, inferences, and attitudes (Anderson, 1974). First, *integrations* are all about the process through which an individual integrates pieces of information to generate a coherent impression. It is important that firms understand the *centrality effect*, i.e. the fact that certain identity elements will have a central position in determining consumer impression; of course, which identity elements are central will vary depending on the brand, the individual, and the specific context. It is also essential that organisations understand the *primacy effect*, which is all about the suggestion that first impressions are stronger than latter ones. Second, *inferences* are all about the process individuals follow to make sense of something by filling in missing information. This process is of course based on individuals' previous experiences and common sense knowledge. Organisations should aim to create inferences that go in line with what their brands seek to achieve. Third, *attitudes* are individuals' effective evaluations of their own impressions. These evaluations can be positive, negative, or neutral. It is important to note that people have stronger and more intense evaluations to sensitive (to them) issues, and that direct experiences lead to more stable evaluations than indirect experiences, which usually lead to vague attitudes (Anderson, 1974; Schmitt & Simonson, 1997).

Consumers categorise the information they receive from organisations on the basis of six dimensions in order to arrive to their own impressions: 1) *time* – does the brand relate to the past, present or future?, 2) *space* – does the brand relate to urban environment or the countryside, East or West?, 3) *technology* – is the brand machine-made or hand-made?, 4) *authenticity* – is the brand authentic or derivative?, 5) *sophistication* – is the brand cheap or refined?, and 6) *scale* – is the brand grand or small-scale? (Schmitt & Simonson, 1997).

BRAND AESTHETICS

Design, aesthetics, and sensory marketing

One of the world's finest architects, Finland's Alvar Aalto, once stated that "beauty is the harmony of purpose and form". These words superbly resonate with the essence of *design*. Design is about the combination of function, i.e. purpose, and form which is directly connected with aesthetics. The business value of design was recently evidenced in a comprehensive study conducted by the management consultancy *McKinsey & Company*. Through the development of the *McKinsey Design Index*, which was used to assess organisations, the study emphasised that "good design is good business" (Sheppard cited in Moshakis, 2019) and proved that those organisations that invest in design successfully, improve their financial performance (Moshakis, 2019; Sheppard, Kouyoumjian, Sarrazin, & Dore, 2018).

In this section, we explore the concept of aesthetics and sensory marketing in more depth, providing a comprehensive discussion of primary elements, i.e. shapes, colours, typefaces, sounds, materials and textures, and scents. The term *aesthetics*, coined for the first time by the German philosopher Alexander Baumgarten in the eighteenth century, derives from the Greek verb *aesthanomai* (αισθάνομαι), meaning to perceive, and *aesthetikos* (αισθητικός), meaning sense perception (Patrick & Peracchio, 2010). Aesthetics refers to the philosophy of art and beauty (Taliaferro, 2012), and seeks to understand the effect of physical features on human experiences.

Aesthetics "produce a science of sensuous knowledge, in contrast with logic whose goal is truth" (Schmitt & Simonson, 1997, p. 18). Aesthetics appeal to humans' five senses: sight, sound, touch, taste and smell, generating sensations, which influence human perception, cognition and emotion, and ultimately judgment and behaviour (Biswas, Labrecque, Lehmann, & Markos, 2014a; Krishna, 2012).

In our post-modern society, we have witnessed an anesthetisation of everyday products and services (Featherstone, 1991); consumption has become symbolic, hedonic and aesthetic in nature, through which people have fun and pursue their feelings and fantasies (Holbrook & Hirschman, 1982). Drawing from Firat and Venkatesh (1995), Mazzalovo argues that in postmodern consumption,

> the realm of the senses...prevails over the world of ideas...Market awareness that the value of an object is not independent of its symbolic or imaginary dimension leads consumers to attribute more value to the aesthetic aspects of consumption experiences and forces marketers to "spectacularise" their offering and communication.
>
> (Mazzalovo, 2012, p. 23)

Organisations which harness the potential of aesthetics to develop a strong brand identity pursue what has often been called marketing aesthetics or sensory marketing. *Marketing aesthetics* is the "marketing of sensory experiences in corporate or brand output that contributes to the...brand's identity" (Schmitt & Simonson, 1997, p. 18). From a consumer psychology perspective, Krishna (2010, 2012) defines *sensory marketing* as the marketing that engages individuals' senses, and influences their perception, judgment, and ultimately behaviour. From a managerial perspective, she suggests that organisations can use sensory marketing to generate subconscious triggers which determine consumers' perceptions of the brand personality, as well as influence the perceived quality of abstract attributes such as the product's colour, shape, taste, or smell (Krishna, 2012). These triggers are sensory cues or stimuli which are associated with the visual, auditory, olfactory, haptic, and gustatory properties of an organisation's product or service. Elaborating Krishna's (2012) views further, Hultén (2015) highlights the marketing potential of sensory marketing in terms of positioning the brand in consumers' minds, and defines it as the

> service process that focuses on sensory strategies and stimuli with the goal of creating a multi-sensory brand experience, in supporting the individual's identity creation through the mind and the five senses to generate consumer value, consumer experiences, and brand [image].
>
> (Hultén, 2015, p. 106)

The main aim of sensory marketing is *sensory delight*. Brand marketers should not merely generate consumers' sensory arousal in response to (positive) stimuli;

consumer senses should not only be stimulated, but most importantly, they should be delighted (Schmitt, 1999), which means that organisations should deliver stimuli that their target consumers *like*, or even, *love*.

There are two concepts, in relation to sensory cues, which are important to understand because they both influence, but have distinctive roles in, the way individuals interpret the world. These are *sensations* and *perceptions* (Biswas, 2016). A sensation is when "the stimulus impinges upon the receptor cells of a sensory organ – it is biochemical (and neurological) in nature. Perception is the awareness or understanding of sensory information" (Krishna, 2012, p. 334). In other words, sensation is when our sensory organs gather 'raw' information and send it to our brains, while perception is the interpretation of these sensations (Biswas, 2016; Goldstein, 2013). There is also a certain *threshold* that "is the point at which a sensory cue / stimulus moves from being undetectable to being detectable to our sensory system" (Biswas, 2016, p. 219). Our perception then influences our cognition and emotion, and all these together affect our attitudes, learning and memory, and behaviour (Krishna, 2012) (see Figure 3.5).

The fact that perception influences attitude, behaviour and even memory, is widely accepted, however, there has been substantial scientific debate about whether "cognition is modally grounded, that is, [whether] our thoughts [are] stored in the modality in which they were perceived" (Krishna, 2012, p. 344). Some scholars argue that thought is a-modal, which means that cognition happens independent of perception. Yet, there are also those who believe that an individual's 1) *bodily state*, i.e. the unmoving physical condition that he/she is in, 2) *situated actions*, which are overt movements with certain associations developed over time (e.g. vertical or horizontal head movement for agreeing or disagreeing respectively), and 3) *mental simulations*, "whereby conceptual processing of sensory perceptions leads to neural activation of corresponding regions of the brain" (Krishna, 2012, p. 344), are used to generate the individual's cognitive activity (Barsalou, 2008; Krishna, 2012). The remaining of this section is organised on the basis of the five human senses as we examine their role in sensory marketing.

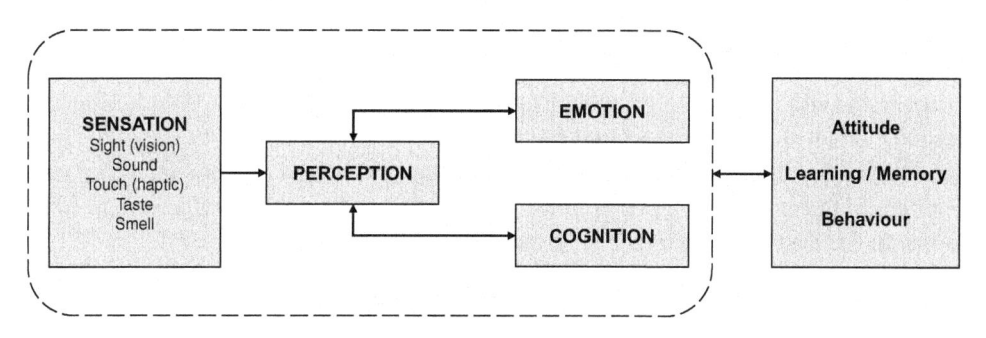

FIGURE 3.5 Conceptual framework of sensory marketing

Vision (Sight)

Perhaps an appropriate way to start our discussion of the human senses is by exploring the sense of *vision* first. This is because consumers usually encounter visual stimuli first, and more often than any other sensory cue (Biswas et al., 2014a). This explains the fact that brand marketers put significant emphasis on visual aspects of the brand, which are the most salient brand components to consumers. Over the years, "the advertising world has indulged and catered to our sense of sight ensuring optimal visual satisfaction" (Lindstrom, 2005, p. 84). The main task of human vision is to help an individual to identify differences in the surroundings and understand changes which might have occurred. An individual compares the image visually conveyed to his/her retina with his/her own past memories and experiences to determine any differences and changes in the environment (Hultén, 2015). This is natural since "our human senses are more attuned to danger detection than expectations of sensory delight" (Lindstrom, 2005, p. 84). In primitive societies, human senses helped tribal men and women navigate their way in the environment, and this is also the case in our post-modern society, of course with different kinds of challenges and 'assailants'.

The level of attention a person pays to a visual stimuli dictates the type of processing he/she engages in (e.g. non-conscious, heuristic, systematic etc.). The link between visual properties and attention is moderated by 1) contextual factors such as market norms and regulations, task complexity, and point of view, and 2) individual factors such as a person's visual ability, beliefs, culture, and goals (Raghubir, 2010). There are three primary elements associated with the sense of sight and these are shapes, colours, and typefaces, which feature in organisations' logos, advertising, product packaging, employee uniforms, spatial environments, websites, and social media presence. Let us explore these three primary elements in more depth.

Shapes

Shapes can be used for packaging a product or for the product itself, and can often imitate other objects (e.g. the simple drawing of a house). Shapes are very important in sensory marketing because if they are repeatedly paired with a brand, they can enable the organisation to build a strong, and global, brand identity. The identity can be global because shapes cross cultural boundaries with ease, which means that people tend to interpret shapes similarly regardless of their cultural background or country of origin (Schmitt & Simonson, 1997). Many global brands are strongly associated with the shape of their products (or packaging), for example, the triangular prism shape of *Toblerone* chocolate, or the iconic bottles of *Coca-Cola* and *Absolut* vodka. It is important to understand the key dimensions of shapes because they can influence people's perceptions. There are four dimensions which we need to understand: angularity, symmetry, proportion, and size.

First, *angularity* is all about the question of whether or not the shape includes angles (corners), with angular forms creating different associations than rounded forms. Angular shapes (e.g. triangles, squares, rectangles etc.) create mental

IMAGE 3.5 *Absolut* iconic bottle (image courtesy of Absolut)

associations of masculinity, dynamism and conflict, sharpness and abruption, whereas rounded shapes generate associations of harmony, softness, femininity, and continuity (Schmitt & Simonson, 1997). For example, if we have look at the shape of perfume bottles for men and women, we can see that the packaging of male aftershave products tend to have angular forms in contrast with women's products which tend to have more rounded-shaped packaging. Second, *symmetry* is defined as the "mirror identity of form or arrangement on the two sides of a dividing line (axis) or plane" (Schmitt & Simonson, 1997, p. 90). Humans tend to consider others attractive on the basis of the symmetry of their facial features. Therefore, symmetry increases the level of the shape's attractiveness, as it creates balance and order. Nevertheless, too much symmetry in a shape might be deemed boring, thus some asymmetry (lack of symmetry) can create a level of uniqueness and individuality, as some tension is needed to salvage the shape from monotony (Schmitt & Simonson, 1997).

Third, *proportion* also needs to be considered when designing the shape of the product or its packaging. Long angular and rectangular shapes extend vision and

IMAGE 3.6 *Absolut* 'Unique' special edition bottles (image courtesy of Absolut)

create domination, while short angular shapes are perceived as timid and humble. Round shapes are naturally symmetrical and "appear less powerful than oblong shapes, but they create perceptions of harmony, resonating with softness and perfection" (Schmitt & Simonson, 1997, p. 91).

Finally, with regards to *size*, large shapes (tall or wide) create mental associations of power and strength, whereas small shapes (short or thin) create associations of delicateness and weakness (Schmitt & Simonson, 1997). Size is the only dimension which can create different associations based on cultural and regional norms, for example, in Western societies, small is perceived as having little stature, whereas in Eastern societies, large size is often perceived as awkward and unwieldy (Schmitt & Simonson, 1997).

Colours
Colours are of outmost importance. They permeate brand identities and appear in all identity elements: properties, products, presentations, and publications. Laurie Pressman, Vice-President of the *Pantone Colour Institute* (www.pantone.com) emphasises that "nothing grabs our attention better than the thoughtful use of colour" (cited in Stocks, 2015, p. 107). Organisations can use a single distinctive colour or a colour palette to create their own terminologies and market their products or services. Colours can make the brand stand out, contributing to its differentiation, and can be used to separate product lines in subcategories. *Apple* has been very meticulous when choosing the colours of its products to ensure maximum differentiation;

the introduction of the *iMac* in 1998 in different colours made the product stand out from the banality of beige hardware products, and the introduction of the *iPod* in 2001 in white (with white earphones) made it distinctive and instantly recognised when the colour of most portable music players had been black or silver. Colours can be legally protected based on, for example, European Union legislation, or the "Lanham Act in the United States which protects product colours as trademarks" (Madden, Hewett, & Roth, 2000, p. 90), so the organisation can prohibit its direct competitors in the same product or service category from using the same colours in their identity, provided such a legal protection can be granted. Hugh Devlin, a legal advisor to the fashion and luxury industry, warns that "it is possible to register a colour as a trademark, but it's not easy…Generally, a colour will only be registrable if it can be shown to be very distinctive, and the brand can demonstrate its association" (cited in Stocks, 2015, p. 107). Examples of specific colours associated with luxury fashion brands include *Tiffany & Co*'s signature Robin's-egg blue, *Lanvin*'s blue (adopted in 2001), *Hermès* orange (adopted around 1952), and *Acne*'s pink (adopted in 2014) (Stocks, 2015).

It is important to remember that eighty per cent of an individual's response to colour is unconscious, according to Angela Wright, a colour psychologist (cited in Stocks, 2015). There are three dimensions of colours, saturation, brightness, and hue, which affect individuals' perceptions, and thus have to be explored in depth. First, *saturation* is all about chromatic purity, i.e. the colour's freedom from dilution with white. The more saturated the colour, the greater the impression that the object is moving. Second, *brightness*, that is, the colour's intensity or energy level, similar to music's loudness or amplitude, can influence a person's perception of how close or distant an object is; the brighter the colour, the greater the impression that the object is closer than it is. Third, *hue* is all about the colour's wavelength, which can create different colour shades. In particular, reds, oranges, and yellows are perceived as energetic and extroverted, while greens, blues, and purples are considered calmer and introverted (Mehta & Zhu, 2009; Schmitt & Simonson, 1997). There are also the so-called prestige colours, which include black and white, silver and gold. Black can be perceived as dark, mysterious, impure, and evil, while white as sunny, happy, pure, and innocent. Silver and gold create associations of brightness, luxury, and elegance, however, organisations ought to be careful when using these two colours because bad imitations can be perceived in the exact opposite way and create associations of cheapness. Finally, different colour combinations can create specific meaning such as country associations based on symbolism (Schmitt & Simonson, 1997), e.g. yellow and blue associated with Sweden or Ukraine, and orange associated with the Netherlands.

Despite the above generalisations, the organisation's colour strategy must be nuanced, as certain colours could mean different things in different countries. For example, green is associated with environmental consciousness and sustainability in the Western world, however, in Malaysia it symbolises death and disease (Belch & Belch, 2004). Madden et al. (2000) explored consumers' preferences of different colours and colour combinations across eight diverse cultures: Austria, Brazil, Canada, Colombia, Hong Kong, China (PRC), Taiwan, and the United States. They discovered that respondents from all countries liked blue, green, and white and the meanings of these colours were similar (with blue being the most liked colour). Contrastingly, although black and red were also well liked, their meanings differed from country to country (Madden et al., 2000). Aggregating the results together, they developed a spectrum of meaning: on the one end red, associated with attributes such as active, hot, and vibrant, and on the other end the blue-green-white cluster, associated with attributes such as calming, gentle, and peaceful (Madden et al., 2000).

In addition, there were differences in respondents' preferences of colour combinations across different cultures; in Taiwan and Hong Kong respondents matched colours they equally liked, in other countries responders matched colours with the same meaning (e.g. Austria and Colombia when pairing green), and in some other countries, colours were paired on the basis of their complementarity (different meanings) (e.g. Canada and PRC when pairing green) (Madden et al., 2000). Colour combinations were also explored by Deng, Hui, and Hutchinson (2010) in their study of the *NikeiD* online configurator, which allows consumers to customise their *Nike* shoes. They discovered that, first, people focus more on hue and saturation than the lightness of colours, second, they like to combine relatively close or exactly matching colours apart from when they want to emphasise a "signature product component by using a contrastive colour, [and] third, …the total number of colours used in the average design was smaller than would be expected…" (Deng et al., 2010, p. 476). Based on the above, it becomes apparent that

> simply taking the colour(s) of a particular logo, package, or product design from one market to other markets should not be done without thorough understanding of how colours and colour combinations are perceived in each location…Managers must acknowledge that the meanings associated with some colours maybe be pancultural, regional, or unique to a given culture.
> (Madden et al., 2000, p. 102)

Typefaces

Typefaces (fonts) are a primary element composed of other elements: shapes, colours, and materials, which need to be considered separately and together. There are a seemingly endless variety of typefaces, and typographers are continuously designing new typefaces that can be found on brand logos, stationery, print and broadcast advertising, product packaging, and publicity and product display materials. Successful typography can increase brand recognition because "brand logos can often be recognised from the type alone" (Hyndman, 2016, p. 16). As previously discussed, vision helps us to identify differences and changes in the environment (Hultén, 2015), and our brains as 'pattern-matching machines' compare what we look at to things we have seen before and have catalogued in our minds.

With familiar logos we do not even need to read the words to know what they say because we recognise these logos by their shape (Hyndman, 2016) (e.g. the *Coca-Cola* or *Google* logos). Consumers easily notice alterations of typographic style when the new typeface does not match with consumes' values, for example, *Gap* had to scrap the re-design of its logo and return to its original *Spire* typeface following consumer protests (Hyndman, 2016).

The most important characteristic of typefaces is that they can add representational qualities to words that already have their own meaning (Schmitt & Simonson, 1997). People use words to construct sentences and communicate with others; writing these words with a certain typeface can add to the words' meaning. Hand-written-like typefaces are perceived as low-key, people-oriented, and unthreatening. Capital letters create associations of authority and aggressiveness, in contrast with low-case letters, which are perceived as daring and understated (Schmitt & Simonson, 1997). Table 3.1 provides a summary of vision and its characteristics.

Audition (Sound)

The second sense whose role in aesthetics we must explore is *audition*, i.e. the sense of sound. From a physiology perceptive,

> through the stereocilia in the ears and the auditory nerve, a person's sense of sound conveys the sounds that the brain then can interpret and give meaning to the environment and the surroundings. For several millennia, people have used sound to shape their identity and find meaning in life in different societal cultures. In this context, music and voices have been an important element in creating a better understanding and perception of reality in humans from birth.
> (Hultén, 2015, p. 113)

In sensory marketing, sounds are an important primary element because they can create or enhance a brand identity (Schmitt & Simonson, 1997). Auditory strategies can include jingles, sounds made when pronouncing brand names, distinctive sounds produced by using the product, voiceovers and music in advertising, and background music in retail and other premises (as an identity enhancer) (Biswas, 2016; Schmitt & Simonson, 1997). Sound can be a flexible device in sensory marketing because it has inherent variability and it is easy to change, however, it is important to remember that its effects depend on the impressions that consumers have (Schmitt & Simonson, 1997).

Jingles are melodic messages that accompany a brand logo or advert. They can create a distinctive brand identity, and if repeated, can become salient, easily recognised, and remembered by consumers through associative learning, even when the brand name is not displayed, influencing brand evaluations (Biswas, 2016). Classic examples of jingles include *Intel*'s sound when a computer gets switched on,

TABLE 3.1 Visual sense and its characteristics

Visual sense	Dimensions	Associations
Shapes	***Angularity***	
	Angular shapes	Masculinity, dynamism, conflict, sharpness, and abruption
	Rounded shapes	Harmony, softness, femininity, and continuity
	Symmetry	
	Symmetrical	Attractiveness, balance, and order
	Asymmetrical	Uniqueness, individuality, and save from monotony
	Proportion	
	Long angular and oblong shapes	Extend vision and create domination
	Short angular shapes	Timid and humble
	Round shapes	Less powerful, soft, and perfect
	Size	
	Large shapes (tall or wide)	Powerful and strong
	Small shapes (short or thin)	Delicate and weak
Colours	***Saturation***	The more saturated the colour, the greater the impression that the object is moving
	Brightness	The brighter the colour, the greater the impression that the object is closer than it is
	Hues	
	Red, orange, and yellow	Energetic, extroverted, active, hot, and vibrant
	Green, blue, and purple	Calming, extroverted, gentle, and peaceful
	Black	Dark, mysterious, impure, and evil
	White	Sunny, happy, pure and innocent
	Silver and gold	Brightness, luxury, and elegance
Typefaces	Hand-written-like	Low key, people-oriented and unthreatening
	Capital letters	Authority and aggressiveness
	Low-case letters	Daring and understated

Source: Based on Schmitt & Simonson (1997).

the *McDonald's* 'I'm lovin it' jingle, and *MGM*'s lion roar, which has been associated with the brand since 1928 (Biswas, 2016).

Krishna states "[w]hen we hear the sound of a word, we attach meaning to it" (2012, p. 341). The phonetics of the brand name, that is, the way the brand is named and the sound made when pronouncing the name (Biswas, 2016), can influence consumers' inferences about the attributes of the product or service, and general brand evaluations (Yorkston & Menon, 2004). Apart from the actual definition of a word, its mere sound can carry meaning (Lowrey & Shrum, 2007). Many scholars have explored the effects of sound symbolism on people's memory and perceptions. For example, Vanden Bergh, Collins, Schultz, and Adler discovered that words which begin with *plosives*, i.e. stop consonants such as /p/ and /d/, "are more frequently recalled and recognised" (1984, p. 835), for instance *Pepsi* and *Pantene Pro-V*. In addition, Klink (2000) determined that the /i/ vowel sound can create notions of something being lighter, thinner, and softer. Contrastingly, according to Newman (1933) and Sapir (1929), "long, back vowels sounds such as /a/ in father and /o/ in bought, are associated with larger objects" (Meyers-Levy, Bublitz, & Peracchio, 2010, p. 139).

Other scholars have explored distinctive sounds produced by using products, for example, the sound food makes when bitten can influence taste perceptions of freshness (e.g. potato crisps, celery, and crackers) (Zampini & Spence, 2004). Thus, brands can incorporate "auditory elements as embedded features in their products" (Biswas, 2016), for instance, deodorant spray makers invest a lot of money to find the optimal spray sound (Biswas et al., 2014a). Lowrey and Shrum (2007) determined that when a brand name sounds congruent with what consumers expect, brand evaluations are positive.

> Other aspects of brand names also can evoke desired attributes or other positive connotations. For example, because *FedEx* stands for *Federal Express* [the American courier delivery company], consumers may associate the abbreviated Ex in the brand name with ideas of speed, which has positive connotations for this service company.
>
> (Meyers-Levy et al., 2010, p. 141)

Any incongruency with consumer expectations can bring negative results as it was evident with the introduction of the more efficient V6 hybrid engines in Formula 1 in 2014, which generated criticism from fans of the sport because the engines sounded significantly different and quieter to what they used to; after all, Formula 1 is a spectacle besides a technology-driven sport. In response to spectators' feedback and in line with their expectations, future engine changes planned for 2021 will include reduced costs, and louder sound (Formula 1, 2017).

Advertising voiceovers can create different tonalities and accents influencing recognisability, and creating favourable associations, emotions, and brand evaluations (Schmitt & Simonson, 1997). For example, the advertising of *Dolmio*, the Mars-owned instant tomato sauce brand, always features the *Dolmio puppets* conversing with an Italian accent in order to create in consumers' minds brand associations with Italy despite the fact that the product is manufactured elsewhere. *Music* in radio, TV, and Internet advertising can work as a peripheral persuasion cue, generating emotions that can influence a consumer's attitude towards the advert or brand (Park & Young, 1986).

Finally, *ambient background music* in retail outlets, supermarkets, hotels, bars and restaurants, and office receptions, can influence consumers' mood, the time they spend in a place, the perception of the time they have spent, and money they spend (Krishna, 2012). Background music creates a micro-activity (Burrows, 1990) in people's hearts, influencing their emotions. The music in a store can affect the pace of shopping, with slower-tempo music leading to slower pace but more purchases (Milliman, 1982). Consider, for instance, the difference between the music likely to be played in a luxury boutique (e.g. *Valentino*) and a fast-fashion clothing store (e.g. *H&M*); the former is likely to play slower-paced background music so that consumers enjoy the ambience and slowly browse through the merchandise, while the latter more up-beat music to hurry people to make quick choices. In addition, drawing from Yalch and Spangenberg (2000) and Kellaris and Kent (1992), Krishna explains that enjoying the background music makes consumers "feel they have spent less time shopping relative to the actual amount of time they have spent in the store" (2012, p. 341). It is important to note that an organisation's auditory strategy does not only include adding sound to the service process (e.g. in a retail store), but also making sure that any sound considered unpleasant or disturbing to consumers, i.e. negative cues which can contradict or distract from the main theme of the experience, are eliminated (Hultén, 2015; Pine II & Gilmore, 1999; 2011). Table 3.2 provides a summary of audition and its characteristics.

Haptics (Touch)

Haptics, the sense of touch, is the first sense the human embryo develops in the womb, and the last sense a person loses with age (Krishna, 2012). Based on his

TABLE 3.2 Auditory sense and its characteristics

Auditory sense	Contribution
Jingles	Melodic messages that accompany a brand logo or advert can increase brand recall and recognition through associative learning and influence brand evaluation.
Brand name phonetics	The way the brand is named and the sound made when pronouncing the name can influence consumers' inferences and brand evaluation.
Sounds produced by using the product	Distinctive sounds produced by using products can influence taste perceptions (e.g. perceptions of freshness) and brand evaluation.
Voiceovers and music in advertising	Tonalities and accents used in advertising voiceovers can create associations, and influence brand recognition and evaluation. Music in advertising as peripheral persuasion cue can influence consumer brand attitudes.
Background music	Ambient music used in retail outlets, supermarkets, hotels, bars and restaurants, and office receptions can influence mood, time spent in a place, perception of time spent, and money spent.

theory of aesthesis (sensation), Aristotle considered touch as the highest in the hierarchy of senses (Krishna, 2012), which can mediate all senses even vision (Siegel, 1970). Hence, the rest of the senses simply add to the insight gained through touch. Aristotle believed that touch can provide a true understanding of the intrinsic nature of an object, and that there is a strong connection between touch and the cosmos because sexual stimulation works through the sense of touch (Krishna, 2012).

Our kinesthetic system allows each of us to experience objects and people through physical contact. Our bodies are full of receptors which enable us to feel, through touch, mechanical pressure on our skin (Hultén, 2015). Based on haptic inputs, we are able to gather information about four properties of objects around us: their texture, hardness, temperature, and weight (Klatzky & Lederman, 2002). In their 'need-for-touch' scale, Peck and Childers (2003) determined two dimensions which could be considered as two types of human touch: instrumental and autotelic. *Instrumental* need for touch is functional, it has an objective, which is generally to purchase a product, thus, this is about touch as a means to an end. On the other hand, *autotelic* need for touch is about compulsive touch or hedonic touch (Peck and Childers, 2003), i.e. "touch as an end in itself" (Peck, 2010, p. 20). Based on observations of consumers' behaviour, Peck (2010) proposed a taxonomy of touch where consumers touch to 1) purchase, i.e. pick up a product and there is no additional product information intentionally extracted (instrumental), 2) obtain non-haptic product information related to the other four senses (instrumental), 3) obtain haptic information on the texture, hardness, temperature, and weight of the product (instrumental), and 4) generally explore, the hedonic touch for fun and sensory experience (autotelic) (Peck, 2010). Indeed, generally speaking, consumers touch products to understand them better. For instance, observe your behaviour next time you go shopping for clothes, it is very likely that you will touch the clothes you want to try on, not merely to pick them up but in order to get a 'feel' for their fabric and texture.

Organisations can follow a tactile approach to develop a brand identity, which allows consumers to experience the product or service through the sense of touch. The primary elements associated with this sense are *materials and textures* found in print communications, product or service design, packaging, office exteriors and interiors, and company uniforms. Humans usually interpret materials and textures in relation to their strength, warmth, and naturalness. Different materials create different associations in consumers' minds; inorganic materials such as marble, glass, and metal are perceived as cold and hard, in contrast with organic materials such as wood and leather which are associated with softness and warmth (Schmitt & Simonson, 1997). The textures of certain materials can be great sources of sensations for consumers and they create a certain 'feel' for the product. Rough textures are perceived as 'outdoorsy' whereas polished textures are more indoor-oriented (Schmitt & Simonson, 1997). Most importantly, "these types of associations apply equally to the materials themselves and to pictures and drawings of the materials or their patterns, which can be used in all sorts of marketing communications (advertising, packaging, or product design)" (Schmitt & Simonson, 1997, p. 103).

TABLE 3.3 Haptic sense and its characteristics

Haptic sense	Dimensions	Associations
Materials	Inorganic materials (marble, glass, and metal)	Cold and hard
	Organic materials (wood and leather)	Softness and warmth
Textures	Rough textures	Outdoor oriented
	Polished textures	Indoor-oriented
Oral	Hard or rough vs. soft or smooth	Food with hard or rough oral haptic properties are perceived as healthier options

Source: Partly based on Schmitt & Simonson (1997).

Besides manual haptics, i.e. touching by hand, Biswas, Szocs, Krishna, and Lehmann (2014b) explored *oral haptics*, i.e. touch felt through the mouth. Oral haptics are particularly important in the case of food and beverage products, because "in most Western societies, people tend to use cutlery to eat food, [thus] the haptic cues related to food items are often orally evaluated without any manual haptic input" (Biswas, 2016, p. 223). Biswas et al. (2014b) discovered that food with hard or rough (in comparison with soft or smooth) oral haptic properties are perceived as healthier options. They also discovered that oral haptics can influence consumption behaviour and argue that brands and consumer health advocates should focus on such oral haptic cues.

> For instance, food with soft (vs hard) haptic properties are eaten in a greater volume when consumers are eating in mindless contexts (such as eating while watching TV) but the effects reverse in the context of mindful eating, such as when consumers pay attention to calorie information in foods.
>
> (Biswas, 2016, p. 223)

Table 3.3 provides a summary of haptics and its characteristics.

Gustatory (Taste)

Closely related to oral haptics discussed above is the *gustatory* human sense, simply known as *taste*, which is usually associated with food- and beverage-related products but it can also apply on other products such as toothpaste and mouthwash, and even edible underwear and flavoured condoms (Biswas, 2016). From a physiology perspective, Hultén (2015) explains that

> the sense of taste and the chemical receptor system allows a person to use the taste organs in the oral cavity to experience the gastronomic tastes, the so-called

inner taste. Thanks to the taste buds...scattered on the tongue, palate, and throat, a taste experience can be achieved. In each taste bud there are several kinds of taste cells, which means that an individual taste bud is sensitive to several different flavours.

(Hultén, 2015, p. 117)

The sensory system can evaluate five different tastes: sweet, salty, bitter, sour, and umami (savoury) (Biswas, 2016; Hultén, 2015; Krishna, 2012). As the above quote explains, contrary to popular belief that different parts of the tongue pick up one of these tastes, "in fact, there is uniform distribution of taste across the different tongue buds and areas of the tongue" (Biswas, 2016, p. 224). It is important to emphasise that the olfactory and the visual senses significantly affect taste evaluation (Biswas, 2016), which means that an individual can find it difficult to distinguish between receptive sensory contributions (Hultén, 2015). If either olfactory or visual inputs are restricted, perceptions or even ability of taste can change. Consider for instance the situation where having a cold restricts your ability to *smell* your dinner; it is very likely that you are equally unable to *taste* it. Smell significantly influences taste because our nose is very close to our mouth (Krishna & Elder, 2010), which enables us to smell the food when it is outside our mouth (called *orthonasal*) and when we are actually chewing the food in our mouth (called *retronasal*) (Rozin, 1982). This is also the reason that when we eat something we think we will not like the taste of, we pinch our nose to block the air passageway and inhibit our ability to smell (Krishna & Elder, 2010). Hoegg and Alba (2007) discovered that changing the colour of a drink can change people's perception of its taste even when the actual taste has not been changed, and Herz's (2008) study indicated that consumers cannot distinguish between the taste of potato and apple, *Coke* and *Sprite*, or red wine and coffee, when their visual and olfactory inputs are inhibited. This is explained by the fact that people can only detect five distinct tastes, and as a result what a person considers 'tasty' "may have nothing to do with the 'taste' sense, but may be largely dependent on the other senses" (Krishna, 2012, p. 342).

External factors such as physical attributes, brand name, product information about ingredients and nutrition, product packaging, and advertising can influence taste (Krishna, 2012) because general ambiguity of product experience results in greater susceptibility to external influences (Hoch & Ha, 1986). In particular, when it comes to advertising, adverts which put an emphasis on multiple sensations of taste, touch, and smell, can lead to better taste perception than adverts which emphasise taste alone, because of sensory stimulation (Elder & Krishna, 2010; Krishna, 2012). As previously explained, sound can also affect the sense of taste. Zampini and Spence (2004) discovered that changing the loudness and frequency of sound can influence perceptions of freshness (e.g. of potato crisps). Similarly, haptics, i.e. touch, can influence taste and Krishna and Morrin (2008) indicated that the haptic quality of glasses can influence taste perception of the beverage consumed. Other research studies have examined the influence of brand names on perceived beer characteristics (Allison

TABLE 3.4. Gustatory sense and its characteristics

Gustatory sense	Contribution
Taste and smell	Smell can influence taste because of the proximity of nose to mouth (orthonasal and retronasal).
Taste and colour	Changing colour of a drink can influence perception of its taste even if taste has not been changed.
Taste and other external factors	Physical attributes (e.g. sound when eating food), brand names, product information (ingredients and nutrition), product packaging, and advertising can influence taste.
Outer taste	Connection between physical taste and aesthetics – contribution of beauty to physical and emotional satisfaction and quality of life.

& Uhl, 1964), on taste preferences (Hoegg & Alba, 2007), as well as the influence of food ingredients on taste where it was identified that people assume that food categorised as unhealthy tastes better than healthy food (Raghunathan, Naylor, & Hoyer, 2006).

Hultén brings together all the points from our discussion above to explain the power of taste with the following:

> Taste experience is often expressed through stimuli such as presentation, environment, and knowledge to contribute to a taste experience both in a service environment as well as for products and services. Even interactions with other senses regrading stimuli such as design, scent, sound, texture, and weight contribute to a culinary experience, which is based on synergy. Then a taste experience is often an expression of the individual's total sensory experience.
>
> (Hultén, 2015, p. 118)

Table 3.4 provides a summary of gustatory and its characteristics.

Olfaction (Smell)

As previously emphasised, the sense of smell strongly influences our sense of taste. In fact, *olfaction* is considered one of our strongest senses because of its close connection with memory and emotion. Scents are ubiquitous, they are everywhere and it is difficult to control them.

> Thanks to the olfactory receptors in the nostrils, scent that is inhaled can be forwarded to the olfactory centre in the brain. It is then that we perceive a scent as pleasant or unpleasant, which can affect an individual on an emotional level.
>
> (Hultén, 2015, p. 115)

The sense of smell can influence human judgement and behaviour (Krishna, 2012; Krishna, Lwin, & Morrin, 2010; Morrin & Ratneshwar, 2003). Scientists and scholars have identified many biological or anatomical reasons which explain "why scent-encoded information may last for longer stretches of time versus information encoded along with other sensory cues" (Krishna, 2012, p. 338). The main reason for this is the physical and neural proximity of olfaction and memory systems in the human body; the olfactory nerve is very close to the amygdala and the hippocampus, which play a vital role in emotion and emotional memory (Cahill, Babinsky, Markowitsch, & McGaugh, 1995; Eichenbaum, 1996), meaning that any olfactory information has direct connection to memory (Krishna, 2012). The power of the human olfactory system is strongly evidenced by Bushdid, Magnasco, Vosshall, and Keller's (2014) study published in *Science*, the leading scientific journal. They explain that

> on the basis of the results of psychophysical testing, we calculated that humans can discriminate at least 1 trillion olfactory stimuli. This is far more than previous estimates of distinguishable olfactory stimuli. It demonstrates that the human olfactory system, with its hundreds of different olfactory receptors, far outperforms the other senses in the number of physically different stimuli it can discriminate.
>
> (Bushdid et al., 2014, p. 1370)

Studies in the recognition of smells have revealed that people have the ability to recognise scents they have come across before and that their ability to do so reduces minimally over time (Engen, Kuisma, & Eimas, 1973; Engen & Ross, 1973; Zucco, 2003). Olfactory cues can also "evoke auto-biographical memories, or memories of events that have taken place long ago" (Krishna, 2012, p. 339). Undoubtedly, smells can make us think of past events or other people, and can generate emotions such as nostalgia (Belk, 1990). We have all "felt our emotions stirred by the faint smell on an article of clothing left behind by a loved one (the individuality of which was probably determined, in part, by a particular brand of detergent)" (Gobé, 2010, p. 99). In addition, ambient scents can increase recall and recognition of brands consumers have encountered in the past (Morrin & Ratneshwar, 2003) and product-embedded scents increase memory of associated information (Krishna et al., 2010).

There are seven categories of scents: minty, floral, ethereal, musky, resinous, foul, and acrid (Schmitt & Simonson, 1997). People evaluate and learn about smells on the basis of the verbal labels they attach to them: "We typically describe smells not necessarily in terms of their own properties but by comparing them to other things that the smell evokes in memory" (Schmitt & Simonson, 1997, p. 104). Certain smells are universally appealing and some universally offensive. However, Morrin argues that scent preferences are learned and "not innate or hardwired…[thus] if you experience a particular scent while a pleasant activity or event occurs, you will likely end up liking the scent for the rest of your life" (2010, p. 78). Cinnamon- or piney-based smells are associated with winter, while fruity and floral smells are associated with spring. The latter are smells generally preferred by women, whereas males tend to prefer woody and spicy smells (Schmitt & Simonson, 1997). Olfactory cues tend to be more influential for women than men because they have "lower threshold points for scent detection than men and [they] rely on olfactory cues to gather information to a greater extent than men do. Hence…brands targeted towards women tend to have greater degree of olfactory cues embedded" (Biswas, 2016, p. 224).

A decade and a half ago, Lindstrom was astonished to find out that "99 percent of all brand communication…is focused on our two senses: what we hear and see. In sharp contrast, 75 per cent of our emotions are generated by what we in fact smell" (2005, p. 85). Indeed, in the past, many brands have focussed on the sense of smell to a lesser extent than the other senses, especially human vision. This can be explained by the fact that although humans can identify a trillion olfactory stimuli, they are not as good at describing smells as they are at describing visual stimuli (Krishna, 2012). In general, people find it hard to label scents, which is a phenomenon called 'tip-of-the-nose' effect (Lawless & Engen, 1977) and take ten times longer to detect a scent in the surroundings than a visual object (450 milliseconds instead of 45 milliseconds) (Hertz & Engen, 1996). However, organisations are gradually paying more attention to the olfactory aspects of their brands, as they recognise the great potential of scents in creating successful brand identities and generating brand recall and recognition (Hultén, 2015). Scents can also be used to enhance a brand identity and in this case they act in a very subtle way like background music. Pleasant scents can enhance consumers' brand evaluations, however, perceived congruency between the scent and the product or service is required to generate these results. Similarly, under certain conditions, scents can increase consumer spending (Morrin, 2010). Apart from scent congruency, other moderating factors of the connection between scents and brand evaluation and consumer behaviour can include impulsivity and age (Morrin, 2010). Brand marketers can develop legally protected signature scents for their brands in order to create a specific emotion or perception in people's hearts and minds (Hultén, 2015; Schmitt & Simonson, 1997). Examples include retailers

TABLE 3.5 Olfactory sense and its characteristics

Olfactory sense	Dimensions	Associations
General	Piney- and cinnamon-based smells	Winter
	Fruity and floral smells	Spring
Gender differences	Woody and spicy smells	Preferred by men
	Fruity and floral smells	Preferred by women

Source: Partly based on Schmitt & Simonson (1997).
Note: Women have higher scent detection and rely more on olfactory cues than men.

such as *Victoria's Secret*, *Abercrombie and Fitch*, and *Bloomingdale's*, hotel brands such as *Ritz Carlton* and *Westin*, and airlines such as *Singapore Airlines* and *British Airways*, which all use ambient signature scents in their stores, their lobbies and rooms, and their cabins, respectively (Biswas, 2016). Table 3.5 provides a summary of olfaction and its characteristics.

CHAPTER REVIEW QUESTIONS

You can use the following questions to reflect on the material covered in Chapter 3:

1. Discuss the main drivers for identity management. In your opinion, which of these is the most important driver and why?
2. Explain the 4Ps of the identity elements mix. In your opinion, which is the most important element and why?
3. Choose a logo and analyse it based on the primary elements of shapes, colours, and typefaces.
4. Choose a brand and discuss its sensory marketing strategy (across all five senses: sight, sound, touch, taste, and smell).

RECOMMENDED READING

1. Krishna, A. (2012). An integrative review of sensory marketing: Engaging the senses to affect perception, judgment and behavior. *Journal of Consumer Psychology*, 22(3), 332–351.
2. Biswas, D. (2016). Sensory aspects of branding. In F. Dall'Olmo Riley, J. Singh, & C. Blankson (eds), *The Routledge companion to contemporary brand management* (pp. 218–227). London: Routledge.
3. Chapters 3–6 from Schmitt, B. H., & Simonson, A. (1997). *Marketing aesthetics: The strategic management of brands, identity, and image*. New York: Simon and Schuster.

CASE STUDY

The Lakes Distillery

David Shanks
Director of Strategy & Copy
D8

> "It was a moment of magic, a revelation so unexpected that I stood transfixed… I had seen landscapes of rural beauty pictured in the local art gallery, but here was no painted canvas; this was real. This was truth."
>
> Alfred Wainwright

The Lake District has long been a crucible for creativity, a place in which the imagination can flourish, and it's no different for Dhavall Gandhi. *The Lakes Distillery*'s whisky maker takes his inspiration from the UNESCO World Heritage Site where a state-of-the-art distillery has been built meticulously within a 160-year-old farmstead on the banks of the River Derwent.

In 2018, D8 was tasked with developing a new brand identity for *The Lakes Distillery* in keeping with its ambition to become one of the world's leading luxury single malt whisky makers. We delved deep into the distillery's background and carried out competitor and sector research, culminating in a brand workshop with the leadership team. The output of this was a new brand framework, resetting the brand in line with the company's ambitious commercial objectives. The brand framework provided the foundations of the new brand positioning; the unique Lakes Distillery story.

The Lakes Distillery story
Whisky making in its highest form is a dance between science and art, control and creativity. It necessitates being sensitive to how the climate affects the conversation between oak and air and spirit, and flowing new ideas around this frame. Dhavall works across what seem to be two very different disciplines, that of the artist, and the man of science. *The Lakes Distillery* practices holistic whisky making, with the whisky maker at the helm throughout the journey through the distillery. His single-minded focus at every stage provides continuity of character; an assurance that every flavour possibility is achieved. Under Dhavall's guidance, the Lakes' fermentation process is pushed up to 96 hours, twice the industry average, to create the desired complexity and depth of flavour. Distillation is also slow and long; the more contact the alcohol vapour has with the copper still, the more fruitier and vibrant the resulting spirit will be. As with his unique spirit creation, Dhavall's expertise in sherry casks has shaped whisky making at the Lakes, where, contrary to most contemporary distilleries' use of ex-bourbon casks, 80–90% of the spirit is filled into different types of ex-sherry cask. Made from American, Spanish, or French oak, in different sizes, the casks are seasoned with Oloroso as well as Pedro Ximenez, Cream, and Fino. This sets the Lakes apart.

Dhavall knows each cask intimately; how the flavours are evolving and then how they can be blended with others to complement, enhance, deepen, broaden, or contrast. They nudge against each other, some excited, some sulky, some diffident, the heavy and the light. It takes time, so the final hand-selected casks are allowed to marry together for up to a year before bottling, significantly longer than other whisky. This creates depth, roundness, and harmony, the final touch which makes it the Lakes whisky.

This cannot be done by computer or tick list. This is active involvement. This is the art of blending. Blending is what we do unconsciously every day. We do it when we add milk or sugar to our tea or coffee, which themselves are blends. Blending makes things taste better. It is dynamic, it is creative, and expressive. It is also personal. At the Lakes, blending is a creative expression of ideas, emotions, and feelings through the language of whisky. It comes from the heart. The story is at the heart of the distillery; the distillery is at the heart of the story. We sought to capture this duality in the key message of *The Lakes Distillery* communications, which is simultaneously underpinned and inspired by the brand framework:

"The nature of our art is whisky, the inspiration of our art is nature." The Lakes Distillery

Developing a brand framework

The 26 nineteenth-century quatrefoils – four leaf symbols – engraved in the original Victorian stonework on which *The Lakes Distillery* has been established have come to represent the company's founding beliefs. The significance and use varies across time, from ancient Mayan monuments to Gothic Europe modern superstitions in association with the 'four-leaf clover'. In the case of *The Lakes Distillery*, we drew on the ancient Celtic symbol representing faith, hope, luck, and love to establish the company's founding beliefs. It made sense to establish these beliefs as the cornerstone of the brand framework, on which we built values, personality, and tone of voice. All of these had to simultaneously dovetail with, and encompass, the new Lakes Distillery brand essence, the barometer at the heart of the brand that all brand, marketing and even strategic commercial decisions can be measured against.

The internally facing essence – Inspirational Luxury – is both a description of the company and its people (as a group of people, they inspire each other; as a brand they inspire the world) as well as a rallying call (encouraging workers to make the company aspirations a reality by behaving like a luxury brand). We developed a consumer-facing brand purpose to appeal to adventurers everywhere – a broad but well-defined range of target consumers, including whisky connoisseurs and novices alike – who could be tempted to try English whisky; something new from an unexpected and unusual source.

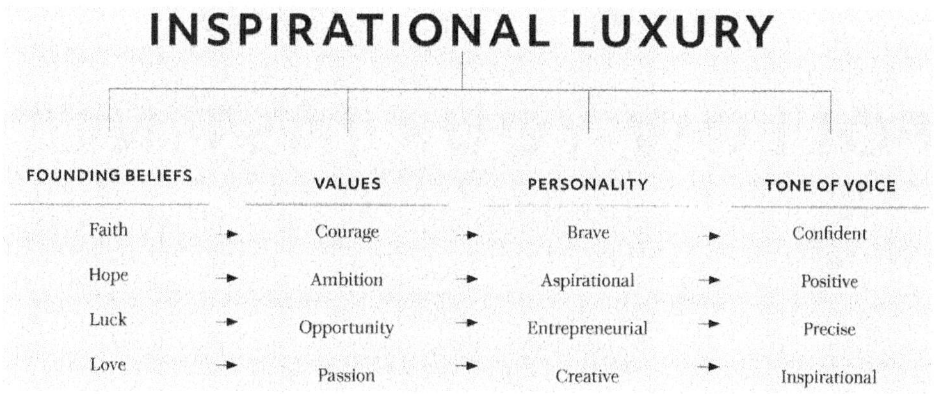

INSPIRATIONAL LUXURY

FOUNDING BELIEFS	VALUES	PERSONALITY	TONE OF VOICE
Faith →	Courage →	Brave →	Confident
Hope →	Ambition →	Aspirational →	Positive
Luck →	Opportunity →	Entrepreneurial →	Precise
Love →	Passion →	Creative →	Inspirational

IMAGE 3.7 *The Lakes Distillery* brand essence (image courtesy of The Lakes Distillery)

The visual identity
The brand framework was the catalyst for the development of a new visual identity with the brand essence of inspirational luxury at its heart. When developing the identity we established three core design principles in keeping with the brand framework.

Modern craft
The Lakes Distillery may be based in a beautifully restored Victorian farmstead, but it is not a distillery or brand that lives in the past. Being handmade, bespoke, or crafted with passion, expertise, and precision doesn't mean rustic (below right and left). Their whisky maker, Dhavall Gandhi, practices a clinical precision working in laboratory-like conditions, using modern, groundbreaking equipment, techniques, and approaches.

True luxury never shouts
Our brand essence "Inspirational Luxury" can be found in the attention to detail that has been painstakingly adhered to in everything we do, from the restoration of our distillery to the precise finishing of our packaging.

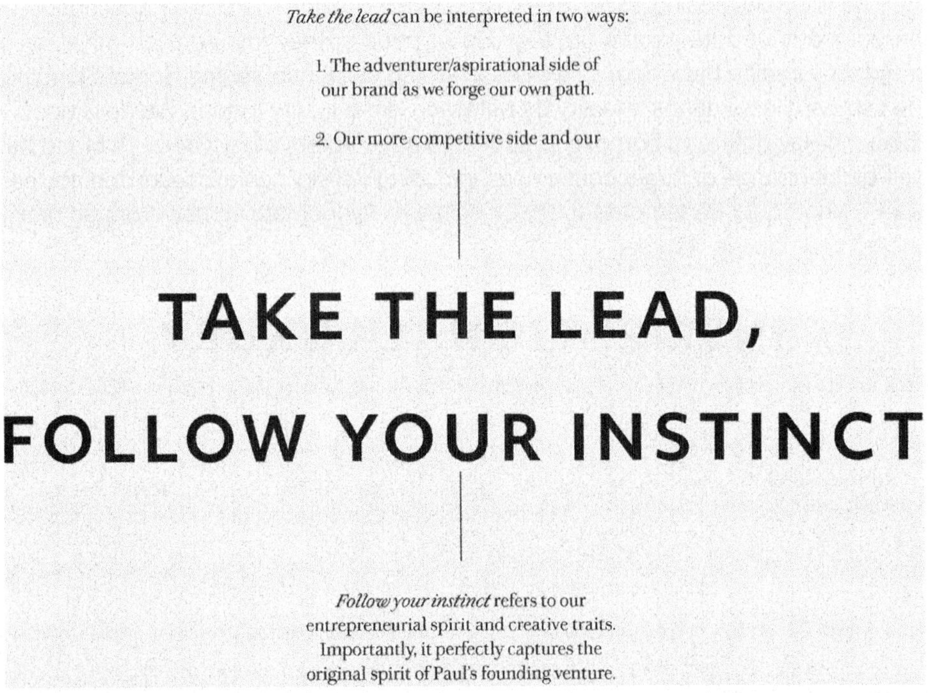

Take the lead can be interpreted in two ways:

1. The adventurer/aspirational side of our brand as we forge our own path.

2. Our more competitive side and our

TAKE THE LEAD, FOLLOW YOUR INSTINCT

Follow your instinct refers to our entrepreneurial spirit and creative traits. Importantly, it perfectly captures the original spirit of Paul's founding venture.

IMAGE 3.8 *The Lakes Distillery* brand purpose (image courtesy of The Lakes Distillery)

A lightness of touch

The Lakes Distillery world-class whisky making adheres to the Scotch Whisky Association's strict guidelines. But it is not a traditional Single Malt Scotch Whisky so they don't need to look like one. The Lake District is a place of immensely diverse beauty and the inspiration for much of the distillery's unique approach to whisky making. Its captivating landscape is reflected in a rich colour palette across

Post rebrand

IMAGE 3.9 *The Lakes Distillery* re-brand packaging (image courtesy of The Lakes Distillery)

The Quatrefoil Collection

IMAGE 3.10 *The Lakes Distillery* – The Quatrefoil Collection (image courtesy of The Lakes Distillery)

94 CREATING BRAND IDENTITY

IMAGE 3.11 *The Lakes Distillery* – The Quatrefoil Collection (image courtesy of The Lakes Distillery)

IMAGE 3.12 *The Lakes Distillery* guidelines and toolkit (image courtesy of The Lakes Distillery)

packaging and communications, providing an antidote to the typically dark visual coding of many Single Malt Scotch Whisky brands.

We developed the visual identity to consist of multiple assets, which, when used together as a system, communicate a well-established, focused brand. This included: primary logos, wordmarque logos, infinity foil logos, roundel, colour palette, quatrefoil pattern, landscape illustration, typefaces, tone of voice, brand purpose, whisky maker's sign-off, and image library. The coherent global activation of the brand, from product packing to digital, to experiential tourism to point of sale, is fundamental to the development of a world-class luxury Single Malt Whisky brand.

Detailed guidelines and toolkits have been created for *The Lakes Distillery* to activate the brand framework, architecture, and visual identity consistently and effectively, enabling the distillery to build lasting consumer relationships worldwide and, most importantly, make its vision a reality.

Questions for discussion

1. How would you describe *The Lakes Distillery* brand positioning?
2. What type of brand identity has D8 developed for *The Lakes Distillery* brand (i.e. monolithic, branded, or endorsed identity)?
3. Discuss the primary elements D8 has brought together to create *The Lakes Distillery* brand aesthetics and their likely consumer associations (i.e. shapes, colours, typefaces, sounds, scents, materials, and textures).
4. How would you describe the likely consumer impressions of *The Lakes Distillery* brand identity on the basis of the six dimensions (i.e. time, space, technology, sophistication, and scale)?

REFERENCES

Aaker, D. A. (2010). *Building strong brands*. London: Simon and Schuster.
Allison, R. I., & Uhl, K. P. (1964). Influence of beer brand identification on taste perception. *Journal of Marketing Research*, 1(3), 36–39.
Anderson, J. R. (1974). *Language, memory, and thought*. Hillsdale: Erlbaum.
Antonides, G., & van Raaij, W. F. (1998). *Consumer behaviour: A European perspective*. Hoboken: John Wiley & Sons Ltd.
Barsalou, L. W. (2008). Grounded cognition. *Annual Review of Psychology*, 59(1), 617–645.
Belch, G. E., & Belch, M. A. (2004). *Introduction to advertising and promotion management: An integrated marketing communications perspective* (3rd edn). Chicago: Richard D. Irwin Inc.
Biswas, D. (2016). Sensory aspects of branding. In F. Dall'Olmo Riley, J. Singh, & C. Blankson (eds), *The Routledge companion to contemporary brand management* (pp. 218–227). London: Routledge.
Biswas, D., Labrecque, L. I., Lehmann, D. R., & Markos, E. (2014a). Making choices while smelling, tasting, and listening: The role of sensory (dis)similarity when sequentially sampling products. *Journal of Marketing*, 78(1), 112–126.
Biswas, D., Szocs, C., Krishna, A., & Lehmann, D. R. (2014b). Something to chew on: The effects of oral haptics on mastication, orosensory perception, and calorie estimation. *Journal of Consumer Research*, 41(2), 261–273.
Burrows, D. L. (1990). *Sound, speech, and music*. Amherst: The University of Massachusetts Press.
Belk, R. W. (1990). The role of possessions in constructing and maintaining a sense of past. *Advances in Consumer Research*, 17, 669–676.
Bushdid, C., Magnasco, M. O., Vosshall, L. B., & Keller, A. (2014). Humans can discriminate more than 1 trillion olfactory stimuli. *Science*, 343(6177), 1370–1372.

Cahill, L., Babinsky, R., Markowitsch, H. J., & McGaugh, J. L. (1995). The amygdala and emotional memory. *Nature, 377*(6547), 295–296.
Chandler, D. (2017). *Semiotics: The basics* (3rd edn). London: Routledge.
Christensen, L. T., & Askegaard, S. (2001). Corporate identity and corporate image revisited: A semiotic perspective. *European Journal of Marketing, 35*(3/4), 292–315.
Dall'Olmo Riley, F. (2016). Brand definitions and conceptualizations. In F. Dall'Olmo Riley, J. Singh, & C. Blankson (eds), *The Routledge companion to contemporary brand management* (pp. 3–12). London: Routledge.
de Chernatony, L. (1999). Brand management through narrowing the gap between brand identity and brand reputation. *Journal of Marketing Management, 15*(1–3), 157–179.
Deng, X., Hui, S. K., & Hutchinson, J. W. (2010). Consumer preferences for color combinations: An empirical analysis of similarity-based color relationships. *Journal of Consumer Psychology, 20*(4), 476–484.
Eco, U. (1976). *A theory of semiotics* (Vol. 217). Bloomington: Indiana University Press.
Eco, U. (1986). *Semiotics and the philosophy of language* (Vol. 398). Bloomington: Indiana University Press.
Eichenbaum, H. (1996). Olfactory perception and memory. In R. Llinás & P. Churchland (eds), *The mind-brain continuum: Sensory processes* (pp. 173–202). Cambridge: MIT Press.
Elder, R. S., & Krishna, A. (2010). The effects of advertising copy on sensory thoughts and perceived taste. *Journal of Consumer Research, 36*(5), 748–756.
Engen, T., Kuisma, J. E., & Eimas, P. D. (1973). Short-term memory of odors. *Journal of Experimental Psychology, 99*(2), 222.
Engen, T., & Ross, B. M. (1973). Long-term memory of odors with and without verbal descriptions. *Journal of Experimental Psychology, 100*(2), 221.
Featherstone, M. (1991). *Consumer culture and postmodernism*. London: Sage.
Firat, A. F., & Venkatesh, A. (1995). Liberatory postmodernism and the reenchantment of consumption. *Journal of Consumer Research, 22*(3), 239–267.
Formula 1 (2017). FIA and Formula 1 set out clear direction for 2021 F1 power units. Available at: www.formula1.com/en/latest/article.fia-andformula-1-set-out-clear-direction-for-2021-f1-power-units.rw0M1YhrSCEK4miu2cc8a.html) [accessed on 7 August 2019].
Gobé, M. (2010). *Emotional branding: The new paradigm for connecting brands to people*. New York: Allworth Press.
Goldstein, E. B. (2009). *Sensation and perception*. Belmont: Wadsworth Cengage Learning.
Gregg, V. (1976). Word frequency, recognition and recall. In J. Brown (ed.), *Recall and recognition*. London: John Wiley & Sons, Inc.
Herz, R. S. (2007). *The scent of desire: Discovering our enigmatic sense of smell*. New York: William Morrow.
Herz, R. S., & Engen, T. (1996). Odor memory: Review and analysis. *Psychonomic Bulletin & Review, 3*(3), 300–313.
Hoch, S. J., & Ha, Y. W. (1986). Consumer learning: Advertising and the ambiguity of product experience. *Journal of Consumer Research, 13*(2), 221–233.
Hoegg, J., & Alba, J. W. (2007). Taste perception: More than meets the tongue. *Journal of Consumer Research, 33*(4), 490–498.
Holbrook, M. B., & Hirschman, E. C. (1982). The experiential aspects of consumption: Consumer fantasies, feelings, and fun. *Journal of Consumer Research, 9*(2), 132–140.
Hultén, B. (2015). *Sensory marketing: Theoretical and empirical grounds*. London: Routledge.
Hall, S. (2012). *This means this, this means that: A user's guide to semiotics* (2nd edn). London: Laurence King Publishing.
Hyndman, S. (2016). *Why fonts matter*. London: Penguin Random House.

Kellaris, J. J., & Kent, R. J. (1992). The influence of music on consumers' temporal perceptions: Does time fly when you're having fun? *Journal of Consumer Psychology,* 1(4), 365–376.

Keller, K. L. (1993). Conceptualizing, measuring, and managing customer-based brand equity. *Journal of Marketing,* 57(1), 1–22.

Keller, K. L., & Swaminathan, V. (2020). *Strategic brand management: Building, measuring, and managing brand equity* (5th edn). London: Pearson Education.

Klatzky, R. L., & Lederman, S. J. (2002). "Touch" in experimental psychology. In A. F. Healy and R. W. Proctor (eds), *Handbook of psychology* (Vol. 4.) (pp. 147–176). New York: Wiley.

Klink, R. R. (2000). Creating brand names with meaning: The use of sound symbolism. *Marketing Letters,* 11(1), 5–20.

Kotler, P. (1973). Atmospherics as a marketing tool. *Journal of Retailing,* 49(4), 48–64.

Krishna, A. (ed.) (2010). *Sensory marketing: Research on the sensuality of products.* London: Routledge.

Krishna, A. (2012). An integrative review of sensory marketing: Engaging the senses to affect perception, judgment and behavior. *Journal of Consumer Psychology,* 22(3), 332–351.

Krishna, A., & Elder, R. S. (2010). The gist of gustation: An exploration of taste, food, and consumption. In A. Krishna (ed.), *Sensory marketing: Research on the sensuality of products.* London: Routledge.

Krishna, A., Lwin, M. O., & Morrin, M. (2010). Product scent and memory. *Journal of Consumer Research,* 37(1), 57–67.

Krishna, A., & Morrin, M. (2007). Does touch affect taste? The perceptual transfer of product container haptic cues. *Journal of Consumer Research,* 34(6), 807–818.

Lawless, H., & Engen, T. (1977). Associations to odors: Interference, mnemonics, and verbal labeling. *Journal of Experimental Psychology: Human Learning and Memory,* 3(1), 52–59.

Lindstrom, M. (2005). Broad sensory branding. *Journal of Product & Brand Management,* 14(2), 84–87.

Lowrey, T. M., & Shrum, L. J. (2007). Phonetic symbolism and brand name preference. *Journal of Consumer Research,* 34(3), 406–414.

Lynch Jr., J. G., & Srull, T. K. (1982). Memory and attentional factors in consumer choice: Concepts and research methods. *Journal of Consumer Research,* 9(1), 18–37.

Madden, T. J., Hewett, K., & Roth, M. S. (2000). Managing images in different cultures: A cross-national study of color meanings and preferences. *Journal of International Marketing,* 8(4), 90–107.

Margulies, W. P. (1977). Make most of your corporate identity. *Harvard Business Review,* 55(4), 66–74.

Mazzalovo, G. (2012). *Brand aesthetics.* Basingstoke: Palgrave Macmillan.

Mehta, R., & Zhu, R. J. (2009). Blue or red? Exploring the effect of color on cognitive task performances. *Science,* 323(5918), 1226–1229.

Meyers-Levy J., Bublitz M. G., & Peracchio L. A. (2010). The sounds of the marketplace: The role of audition in marketing. In A. Krishna (ed.), *Sensory marketing: Research on the sensuality of products* (pp. 137–156). New York: Routledge.

Milliman, R. E. (1982). Using background music to affect the behavior of supermarket shoppers. *Journal of Marketing,* 46(3), 86–91.

Morrin, M. (2010). Scent marketing: An overview. In A. Krishna (ed.), *Sensory marketing: Research on the sensuality of products* (pp. 75–86). New York: Routledge.

Morrin, M., & Ratneshwar, S. (2003). Does it make sense to use scents to enhance brand memory? *Journal of Marketing Research,* 40(1), 10–25.

Morris, C. W. (1938). Foundations of the theory of signs. In *International encyclopedia of unified science* (pp. 1–59). Chicago: The University of Chicago Press.
Moshakis, A. (2019). Design values. *Wallpaper* (Issue 241, April).
Nandan, S. (2005). An exploration of the brand identity–brand image linkage: A communications perspective. *Journal of Brand Management, 12*(4), 264–278.
Olins, W. (2008). *Wally Olins: The brand handbook*. London: Thames & Hudson.
Olins, W., & Selame, E. (1998). *The corporate identity audit: A set of objective measurement tools for your company's image and reputation*. Uster-Zürich: Strategic Directions Publications.
Park, C. W., & Young, S. M. (1986). Consumer response to television commercials: The impact of involvement and background music on brand attitude formation. *Journal of Marketing Research, 23*(1), 11–24.
Patrick, V. M., & Peracchio, L. A. (2010). "Curating" the JCP special issue on aesthetics in consumer psychology: An introduction to the aesthetics issue. *Journal of Consumer Psychology, 20*(4), 393–397.
Peck, J. (2010). Does touch matter? Insights from haptic research in marketing. In A. Krishna (ed.). *Sensory marketing: Research on the sensuality of products* (pp. 17–31). London: Routledge.
Peck, J., & Childers, T. L. (2003). Individual differences in haptic information processing: The "need for touch" scale. *Journal of Consumer Research, 30*(3), 430–442.
Pine II, B. J., & Gilmore, J. H. (1999). *The experience economy: Work is theatre & every business a stage*. Cambridge: Harvard Business Press.
Pine II, B. J., & Gilmore, J. H. (2011). *The experience economy* (revised edn). Cambridge: Harvard Business Press.
Raghubir, P. (2010) Visual perception: An overview. In A. Krishna (ed.), *Sensory marketing: Research on the sensuality of products* (pp. 201–217). New York: Routledge.
Raghunathan, R., Naylor, R. W., & Hoyer, W. D. (2006). The unhealthy=tasty intuition and its effects on taste inferences, enjoyment, and choice of food products. *Journal of Marketing, 70*(4), 170–184.
Robertson, K. R. (1987). Recall and recognition effects of brand name imagery. *Psychology & Marketing, 4*(1), 3-15.
Robertson, K. R. (1989). Strategically desirable brand name characteristics. *Journal of Consumer Marketing, 6*(4), 61–71.
Rozin, P. (1982). "Taste–smell confusions" and the duality of the olfactory sense. *Perception & Psychophysics, 31*(4), 397–401.
Schmitt, B. (1999a). Experiential marketing. *Journal of Marketing Management, 15*(1-3), 53–67.
Schmitt, B. H. (1999b). *Experiential marketing: How to get customers to sense, feel, think, act, relate*. New York: The Free Press.
Schmitt, B. H, & Simonson, A. (1997). *Marketing aesthetics: The strategic management of brands, identity, and image*. New York: Simon and Schuster.
Schmitt, B. H., Simonson, A., & Marcus, J. (1995). Managing corporate image and identity. *Long Range Planning, 28*(5), 82–92.
Schmitt, B. H., & Zarantonello, L. (2013). Consumer experience and experiential marketing: A critical review. In N. K. Malhotra (ed.), *Review of Marketing Research* (Vol. 10) (pp. 25–61). London: Emerald Publishing.
Schroeder, J. E. (2005). The artist and the brand. *European Journal of Marketing, 39*(11/12), 1291-1305.
Sheppard, B., Kouyoumjian, G., Sarrazin, H., & Dore, F. (2018). *The business value of design*. McKinsey & Company.

Siegel, R. E. (1970). *Galen on sense perception. His doctrines, observations and experiments on vision, hearing, smell, taste and pain, and their historical sources*. Basel and New York: Karger.

Stocks, C. (2015). Hues talking: Why so many fashion brands are on the spectrum. *Wallpaper* (Issue 192, March).

Taliaferro, C. (2012). *Aesthetics: A beginner's guide*. London: Oneworld Publications.

Vanden Bergh, B. G., Collins, J., Schultz, M., & Adler, K. (1984). Sound advice on brand names. *Journalism Quarterly*, 61(4), 835–840.

Wheeler, A. (2013). *Designing brand identity: An essential guide for the whole branding team*. Hoboken: John Wiley & Sons.

Yalch, R. F., & Spangenberg, E. R. (2000). The effects of music in a retail setting on real and perceived shopping times. *Journal of Business Research*, 49(2), 139-147.

Yorkston, E., & Menon, G. (2004). A sound idea: Phonetic effects of brand names on consumer judgments. *Journal of Consumer Research*, 31(1), 43–51.

Zampini, M., & Spence, C. (2004). The role of auditory cues in modulating the perceived crispness and staleness of potato chips. *Journal of Sensory Studies*, 19(5), 347–363.

Zucco, G. M. (2003). Anomalies in cognition: Olfactory memory. *European Psychologist*, 8(2), 77.

CHAPTER 4

Brand communications and the attention economy

CHAPTER AIMS AND LEARNING OUTCOMES

This chapter corresponds to the second stage of Keller and Swaminathan's (2020) *strategic brand management process*, i.e. designing and implementing brand marketing programmes (see Figure 4.1), and explores brand communications by bringing together managerial, cultural, and critical perspectives. More specifically, it aims to achieve the following:

1. Review the characteristics of brand communications options and media platforms available to organisations (with a particular focus on digital communications and media).
2. Explore how these influence consumer decision-making and contribute to brand equity development.
3. Understand how organisations can plan effective brand integrated marketing communications (IMC) programmes.
4. Critically discuss the implications of social media for consumer culture through the concepts of digital consumption, co-creation, and the (over)democratisation of marketing.
5. Critically consider the role of social media in the wider society by exploring ethical issues related to self-branding and hyper-narcissism in the attention economy.

BRAND COMMUNICATIONS OPTIONS AND THEIR CONTRIBUTIONS

The role of brand communications

When there is a gap between the consumers' *current brand knowledge* (determined by conducting free associations exercises) and the desired brand knowledge (the optimal POPs and PODs and the brand mantra), organisations need to pursue a

```
┌─────────────────────────┐    ┌──────────────────────────────────────────────────┐
│  Identifying and Developing │───┤  Developing Brand Equity, Positioning, Personality and Values │
│       Brand Plans       │    ├──────────────────────────────────────────────────┤
└───────────┬─────────────┘    │  Creating Brand Identity: Brand Aesthetics and Symbolism      │
            │                  └──────────────────────────────────────────────────┘
            ▼
┌─────────────────────────┐    ┌──────────────────────────────────────────────────┐
│                         │───┤  Brand Communications and the Attention Economy  │
│ Designing and Implementing │    ├──────────────────────────────────────────────────┤
│ Brand Marketing Programmes │───┤  Holistic Brand Experiences and Emotional Branding │
│                         │    ├──────────────────────────────────────────────────┤
└───────────┬─────────────┘    │  Consumer Collectives, Brand Avoidance, and Political Consumption │
            │                  ├──────────────────────────────────────────────────┤
            │                  │  Brand Ethics, Social Responsibility, and Sustainable Consumption │
            ▼                  └──────────────────────────────────────────────────┘
┌─────────────────────────┐    ┌──────────────────────────────────────────────────┐
│ Measuring and Interpreting │───┤          Brand Performance and Metrics           │
│    Brand Performance    │    └──────────────────────────────────────────────────┘
└───────────┬─────────────┘
            │
            ▼
┌─────────────────────────┐    ┌──────────────────────────────────────────────────┐
│                         │───┤               Brand Growth:                      │
│  Growing and Sustaining │    │     Brand Architecture and Brand Extensions      │
│      Brand Equity       │    ├──────────────────────────────────────────────────┤
│                         │───┤              Brand Futures:                      │
│                         │    │  Technology and Innovation in Branding Strategies │
└─────────────────────────┘    └──────────────────────────────────────────────────┘
```

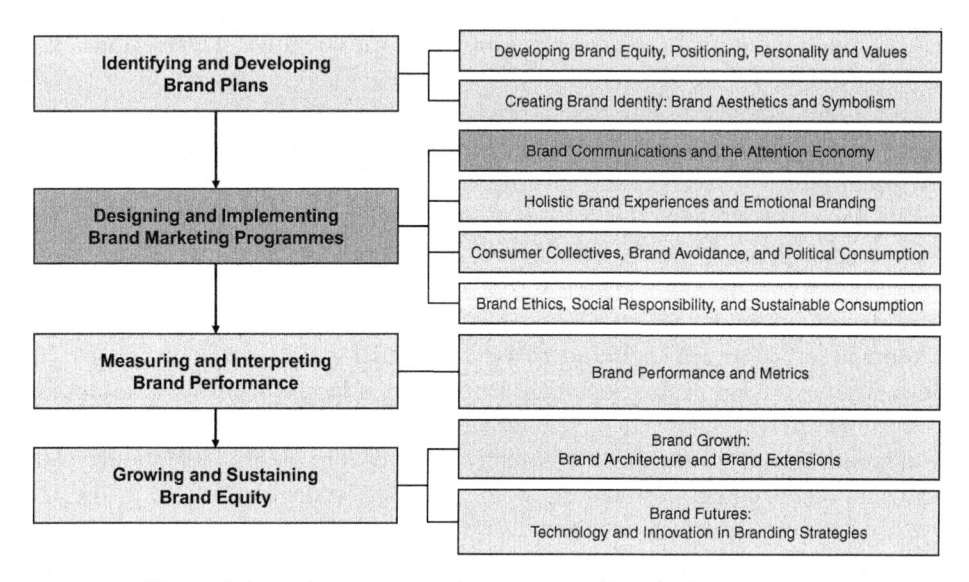

FIGURE 4.1 Strategic brand management process and book plan

brand integrated marketing communications (IMC) strategy to transform target consumers' knowledge from its current to the desired state (Keller & Swaminathan, 2020). Brand communications enable the organisation to "inform, persuade, incite, and remind consumers" (Keller, 2001a, p. 823) about its brand. An organisation can provide detailed information about its product or service by demonstrating how and why the product or service is used, who the typical consumer of the product or service is, and when and where he/she uses it. It can offer incentives to generate product or service trial and usage, and can communicate messages about itself and about what its brand stands for (Keller, 2001a). Organisations can also associate their brands with specific attributes such as people, places, experiences, or other constructs. This allows them to "transcend the physical nature of their products or the technical specifications of their services to imbue products and services with additional meaning and value" (Keller, 2001a, p. 823). Generally speaking, brand communications contribute to brand equity development as explored in our ensuing discussion.

Keller (2001a) highlighted the importance of integrating various communications activities effectively; he argues for a holistic approach which ensures all activities fit together so that the 'whole' is much bigger than the 'sum of its parts'. Based on this premise, he explained that IMC programmes use "multiple communications options where the design and execution of any communication option reflects the nature and content of other communication options that also makes up the communications programme" (Keller, 2001a, p. 825). In consumer behaviour studies, conventional models of the *consumer decision-making* (CDM) process suggest that consumers move through three stages to arrive at a purchase: the cognitive, the emotional, and the behavioural, stages (the buyer-readiness stages). This process reflects a typical 'learn-feel-do' sequence in purchasing products or services where consumers become aware of a brand and develop their own brand knowledge (cognitive), then they develop a liking, preference, and positive conviction about the brand (emotional), and finally, they purchase the organisation's offering (behavioural) (hierarchy of effects model) (Belch & Belch, 2012; Darley, 2016).

Edelman (2010) has challenged this process, as well as the 'funnel metaphor', which assumes that consumers systematically narrow down their choices to ultimately decide which brand to buy. Instead he argues that consumers go through an extended evaluation stage where they add and subtract a number of brands and after purchase they "remain aggressively engaged, publicly promoting or assailing the products they've bought, collaborating in the brands' development, and challenging and shaping their meaning" (Edelman, 2010, p. 63). He proposed a more iterative consumer decision-making process which involves four stages: 1) considering a set of alternatives, 2) evaluating these brands, 3) buying a brand (making a decision and purchasing), and then 4) enjoying, advocating, and bonding with the brand chosen (Edelman, 2010). We will be referring to these processes when discussing the influence of different communications options and media to consumer decision-making.

Traditional brand communications options

This section provides a concise review of traditional and online brand communications options available to organisations and explores how they contribute to different stages in the aforementioned consumer decision-making processes. We focus primarily on advertising and on online brand communications options.

Advertising

Advertising is perhaps the most well known and most traditional of all communications options, and is defined as the "paid form of non-personal presentation and promotion of ideas, goods, or services by an identified sponsor" (Keller & Swaminathan, 2020, p. 218). Advertising works on both cognitive and emotional levels as it can create new, and reinforce existing, mental associations, and generate positive emotions about the brand. The power of advertising can be found in its ability to dramatize the brand through creative use of motion, colour, print, and sound (Darley, 2016; Keller, Apéria, & Georgson, 2012). Undoubtedly, it can be difficult to predict and/or quantify the effectiveness of advertising due to the fact that there can be a plethora of factors influencing consumer judgement and behaviour: "The question of how advertising affects consumer behaviour represents one of the most complex and intriguing aspects of understanding in marketing" (Meenaghan, 1995, p. 28). However, financial results typically indicate that those organisations which invest in their advertising, manage to maintain or increase their market share on a continuous basis (Keller & Swaminathan, 2020).

McCracken (1986) argues that there is a strong relationship between culture and consumption and that cultural meaning is transferred from the culturally constituted world to consumer goods and then from consumer goods to individual consumers. He believes that

> advertising [can work] as a potential method for meaning transfer by bringing the consumer good and a representation of the culturally constituted world together within the frame of a particular advertisement…[and] when this symbolic equivalence is successfully established, the viewer/reader attributes to the consumer good certain properties s/he knows exist in the culturally constituted world. The known properties of the culturally constituted world thus come to reside in the unknown properties of the consumer good and the transfer of meaning from world to good is accomplished.
>
> (McCracken, 1986, p. 74)

Advertising has multiple purposes. It can aim to inform, persuade, excite, and remind (Durgee, 1988), and can contribute to the early stages of the CDM process whereby consumers consider different brand options, increasing consumer awareness, and fostering comprehension and brand acceptance (Darley, 2016).

Sales promotions

In contrast with advertising, which provides consumers with reasons to buy a product or service, *sales promotions* provide incentives to do so. Sales promotions are "temporary and tangible monetary or nonmonetary incentives intended to have a direct impact on consumer behaviour" (Chandon, Wansink, & Laurent, 2000, p. 65), manifested as product/service trial and usage (Keller & Swaminathan, 2020), e.g. 'two-for-one' or '25% off' offers. From a branding perspective, sales promotions can attract consumers' attention and create a sense of urgency among target audiences. They can contribute to getting consumers to experience, advocate, and bond with the brand, as well as generating awareness and brand acceptance in the CDM process (Darley, 2016). However, organisations need to use sales promotions with caution and in moderation. Too many offers might discredit the brand and reduce its perceived quality in the minds of consumers who potentially interpret such tactics as desperate and opportunistic.

Direct marketing and personal selling

With *direct marketing*, organisations can reach consumers on a direct basis in order to generate a response or a commercial transaction (Belch & Belch, 2012; Darley, 2016). It requires developing a consumer database (including socio-demographic and psychographic information and purchase history), which enables sending out messages tailored to an individual consumer's preferences and behavioural characteristics (Darley, 2016). Direct marketing contributes to the latter stages of the CDM process whereby consumers get to purchase the product or service.

In comparison with other options, *personal selling* is not a mediated form of communication but involves personal face-to-face interactions with existing or prospective consumers for the purpose of answering consumer questions and getting purchase orders. The onus is on the salesperson to make such interactions memorable, to develop strong relationships with buyers and to find the best solution for them. Personal selling contributes to the latter stages of the CDM process and is most appropriate in cases where the product or service is expensive, complex, and risky, as well as in markets where there are fewer and larger buyers (Darley, 2016).

Public relations and publicity

Finally, *public relations* (PR) is "a distinctive management function which helps establish and maintain mutual lines of communication, understanding, acceptance, and cooperation between an organisation and its publics" (Harlow, 1976, p. 36), and develop and maintain organisational reputation (Roberts-Bowman, 2016). PR's purposes can be achieved by the organisation developing and maintaining strong media relations to get stories covered, lobbying governments and other institutions on public affairs, and organising and sponsoring events. PR can generate *publicity* which, in contrast with advertising, is all about messages that are not paid or run by the organisation (Darley, 2016). PR and publicity can contribute to building brand equity by generating a buzz for the brand before the start of a media campaign, introducing a product or service without the need for advertising, developing a strong image in the minds of existing and prospective consumers (hence contributing to the early stages of the CDM process), and building relationships with them. Figure 4.2 illustrates the contributions of traditional communications options to consumer decision-making.

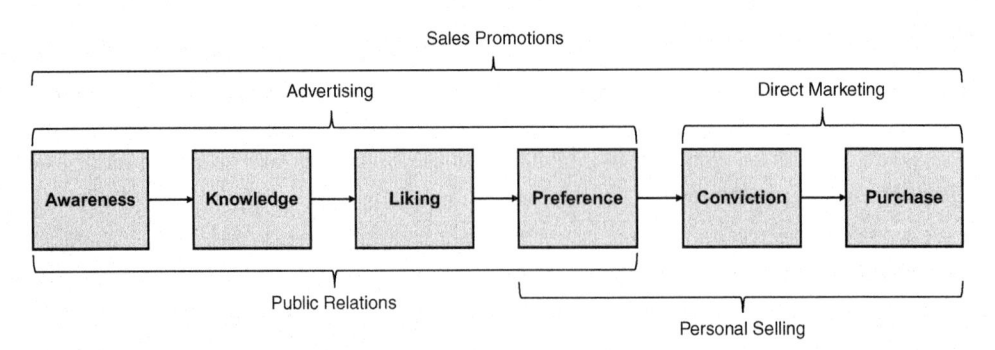

FIGURE 4.2 Traditional communications options and their contributions to consumer decision-making

Online brand communications options

The Internet has revolutionised the ways organisations communicate with their target audiences, challenging traditional communications strategies (Edelman, 2010). In this section we discuss the online brand communications options available to organisations.

Mobile marketing

Mobile marketing includes marketing activities "conducted through a ubiquitous network to which consumers are constantly connected using a personal mobile device" (Kaplan, 2011, p.130). By deconstructing this definition, we identify three conditions in mobile marketing. First, consumers have access to a *ubiquitous network*, which is a combination of different networks. Moving between these networks takes place in a smooth and invisible way, e.g. moving from your home Wi-Fi to 3G/4G network without noticing it. Second, consumers have *constant access* to this network. This condition is rather trivial because nowadays most people never go anywhere without their phones and they make the conscious decision of keeping their devices constantly connected. Third, mobile marketing requires the use of a personal mobile device such as a mobile phone; this device is *personal* because most often it can only be accessed by one individual, thus it is not shared with anyone else (Kaplan, 2011).

Mobile marketing activities can be classified on the basis of two variables. First, the *degree of consumer knowledge*, which is about whether or not the consumer intentionally or unintentionally reveals information about him/herself to the organisation, that is, whether or not the organisation has information about who has been reached (Kaplan, 2011). Second, the *trigger of communication*, which is concerned with the question of who, consumer or organisation, initiates the mobile marketing activity, i.e. whether or not the consumer opts to receive the message or this is pushed to the consumer by the organisation. Hence, Kaplan (2011) makes the distinction between *push* communications initiated by the organisation, and *pull* communications initiated by the consumer. Combining the aforesaid variables leads to different types of mobile marketing (Kaplan, 2011). A significant part of mobile marketing that is growing fast is *in-app advertising*, which enables organisations to target audiences with the right content at the right time, engaging with consumers without being interruptive and irritating (Darley, 2016). In general, mobile marketing contributes to CDM process by increasing brand awareness, and it is most appropriate in Edelman's (2010) experience, advocate and bond stages, turning passive audiences to active loyal consumers (Darley, 2016).

Social media and influencer marketing

Social media have revolutionised the way organisations engage with consumers, and should be explored both as a communications option and as a platform upon which other options can be pursued. Social media are the "group of Internet-based applications that build on the ideological and technological foundations of Web 2.0, and that allow the creation and exchange of user generated content" (Kaplan & Haenlein, 2010, p. 61). This definition includes two more terms which require explaining: *Web 2.0* is the platform "whereby content and applications are no longer created and published by individuals, but instead are continuously modified by all users in a participatory and collaborative fashion" (Kaplan & Haenlein, 2010, p. 61), and *user generated content* describes "various forms of media content that are publicly available and created by end-users" (Kaplan & Haenlein, 2010, p. 61). Social media, as an overarching term, describes digital socio-technical systems including "email discussion forums, blogs, microblogs, texting, chat, social networking sites [e.g. *Facebook, Twitter, Instagram, LinkedIn, Snapchat*], wikis [e.g. *Wikipedia*], photo [e.g. *Flickr*] and video sharing sites [e.g. *YouTube*], review sites, and multi-player gaming communities [e.g. *Second Life*]" (Hansen, Sneiderman, & Smith, 2010, p. 12).

Social media can be used as a communications option to achieve interactions between the organisation and its target consumers (B2C); such interactions can take place on the organisation's own social media pages or on those controlled by individual consumers or other organisations (the distinction between these different types of media platforms will be explored later) (Mangold & Faulds, 2009). Most importantly, social media enable interactions among consumers (C2C) whereby consumers share information about brands and shape their meaning (Edelman, 2010). This leads to an extended, magnified version of word-of-mouth (WOM); what would normally take place on a face-to-face basis (sharing experiences with up to ten people), happens online and to a much greater extent (sharing them with hundreds of people). Thus, Mangold and Faulds (2009) argue that social media is a hybrid element of the communications mix

> because it combines characteristics of traditional IMC tools (companies talking to customers) with a highly magnified form of word-of-mouth (customers talking to one another) whereby marketing managers cannot control the content and frequency of such information. Social media is also a hybrid in that it springs from mixed technology and media origins that enable instantaneous, real-time communication, and utilizes multi-media formats (audio and visual presentations) and numerous delivery platforms...with global reach capabilities.
> (Mangold & Faulds, 2009, p. 359)

This means that social media challenge the traditional communications paradigm which stipulated that the organisation develops an IMC strategy and dictates the content, frequency, and timing of the message, as well as the media used to transmit this message. Any information which flows out with the paradigm's boundaries is limited to face-to-face WOM with minimal influence because of constrained dissemination of information (Mangold & Faulds, 2009; Mayzlin, 2006). Instead, in a new communications paradigm, the organisations' control of the content, timing, and frequency of the message has been grinded down due to the fact that conversations about brands can also take place on consumers' own social media platforms, which organisations cannot restrict or control. Of course, organisations can use their own social media pages, along with traditional communications options, to pursue what Keller (2009) describes as *interactive marketing communications*, whereby they can communicate their own messages to target audiences and can receive feedback from them, allowing better understanding between parties. But most importantly, information about the brand is also created by consumers themselves *in the market place*, on consumers' social media pages (on a C2C basis) (Mangold & Faulds, 2009). Therefore, the fundamental difference is that there are now two sources of brand information: the organisation and the consumer. Social media provide consumers with greater control over media consumption and have become the main information source for individuals because they are perceived as much more trustworthy than organisation-sponsored traditional advertising. Undoubtedly, many consumers nowadays use social media to gather brand information, generate their own brand information, evaluate their options, and make purchasing decisions (Mangold & Faulds, 2009).

Over time, many consumers who engage with social media on a daily basis to write comments about brands, co-constructing their meaning, become social media bloggers acquiring themselves a large number of followers (most of) who they have never met in person. These individuals are now called social media *influencers* because of their power to influence the opinion of others e.g. *Kim Kardashian, Caroline Daur, Steve Cook, Lauren Simpson, Rachel Brathen (yoga_girl* on *Instagram*), and *Camilla Akerberg* to name a few. They often blog about different topics such as health, fitness, sports, fashion etc., as well as about personal issues, and often achieve micro-celebrity or celebrity status. In response, Kumar and Mirchandani (2012) urge organisations to engage with such influencers and outline a seven-step process to pursuing *influencers marketing* communications: 1) monitor online activity to identify conversations about the brand and gather useful information about people's online behaviour, 2) identify potential influencers who can spread positive brand messages, 3) determine the factors shared by influential individuals online, 4) locate those prospective influencers who have interests similar to the brand campaign, 5) recruit those potential influencers to discuss the brand online, 6) provide them with incentives to disseminate positive WOM about the brand, and 7) generate benefits from a more effective social media campaign (Kumar & Mirchandani, 2012).

However, providing influencers with incentives (e.g. free products or access to services) can raise questions about the transparency of such activities which connects with the issue of authenticity of social media influencers' support for the brand (Khamis, Ang, & Welling, 2017). One could question the authenticity of influencers because of the lack of transparency and passion (personal interest) in their posts. Increasing the *transparency* of posts is being addressed, to an extent, by regulators in many countries seeking to determine rules which force influencers to disclose when their *Instagram* content is sponsored by organisations (including #ad, #advertisement, #sponsored in image captions). For example, in response to South African advertisers' often reckless approach to regulation, the country's Advertising Regulatory Board has laid down new rules for influencers (Schimmel, 2019). However, *passion* is a more subjective construct, and requires an honest fit between brands and the influencer's interests, style, image, and editorial content (Audrezet, De Kerviler, & Moulard, 2020). To achieve *absolute authenticity*, transparency needs to be combined with high levels of passion (Audrezet et al., 2020).

Social media have transformed the way consumers engage with brands and have challenged the status quo in many different sectors such as the fashion industry. One example of such transformation is how social media are reshaping fashion shows (Mower, 2016). In the digital landscape, set designers have a key role to play as they need to ensure the catwalk is arranged in a way that provides the audience unique smartphone vantage points to facilitate smartphone action (taking and uploading images on social media) where "every iPhone-armed influencer [has] something a little different to feed their followers" (Mower, 2016, p. 148). Yet as fashion houses still have to provide space for professional photographers to get cleaner shots, the fashion show has become more multifaceted as it "has to be many things to many people" (Mower, 2016, p. 148). We have moved to a post-catwalk generation where the Internet and social media act as both a point of contact and a point of sale and offer a powerful arena where a new generation of fashion brands, e.g. *Vetements*, *Marques'Almeida*, and *Wanda Nylon*, can blossom (Fury, 2017). Skilled use of social media and influencers can contribute to all stages of the CDM process allowing for powerful dissemination of brand messages and imagery to a global audience and encouraging consumers to purchase; it has been observed that "online shopping seems to lead to more adventurous buying" (Fury, 2017, p. 94).

Search engine optimisation (SEO) and pay-per-click (PPC) advertising

Search engine optimisation (SEO) is concerned with "optimising search engines, understanding key performance indicators, and using web analytics, aimed at redirecting apposite traffic to the concerned organisational/business webpages" (Kapoor, Dwivedi, & Piercy, 2016, p. 183). This means that organisations need to employ experts who will optimise the content featured on the brand's webpages to take advantage of search engines' regularly updated algorithms so that these webpages feature higher up on the search results pages to drive more traffic to the brand's online environments.

On the other hand, with *pay-per-click* (PPC) advertising a webpage owner "also known as the web publisher, allows business to advertise products/services on the owner's page; each time a visitor on the publisher's webpage clicks on that advertisement, the business will pay a certain amount to the publisher" (Kapoor et al., 2016, p. 183), e.g. the *Adwords* function on *Google* search engine results pages whereby businesses will pay *Google* every time viewers click on their sponsored links. PPC adverts tend to show at different corners of the results page in contrast with 'organic'

BRAND COMMUNICATIONS & THE ATTENTION ECONOMY

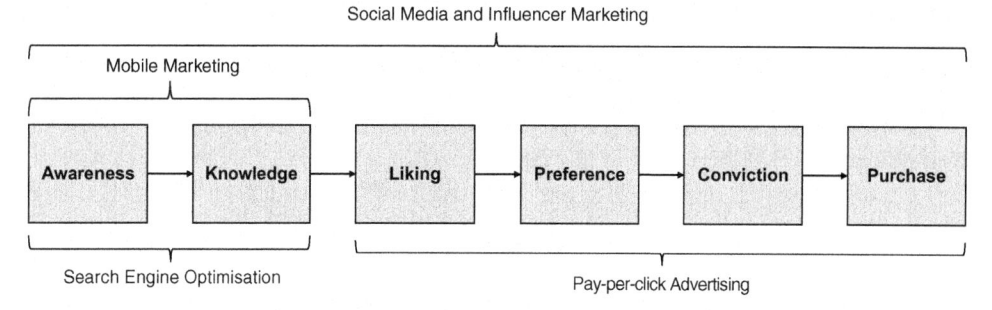

FIGURE 4.3 Digital communications options and their contributions to consumer decision-making

results (Kapoor et al., 2016). There are three beneficiaries in a PPC advert context: the search engine (web publisher), the advertiser (the organisation/brand), and the consumer. The advantages of PPC advertising include 1) the fact that viewers of these adverts are personally interested in them because they used one of their keywords, 2) the potential for localising PPC adverts, 3) the ability to increase brand visibility, and 4) ease of scheduling and measuring results (Kapoor et al., 2016). On the other hand, the disadvantages of PPC advertising include 1) click fraud where an automated program or human intervention manipulates number of clicks, 2) poor positioning of the adverts, 3) limited conversion rates as not every single click converts to a sale, 4) the rise of the prices of certain keywords or keyphrases, 5) 'piggybacking', whereby advertisers use competitors' brand names in their keywords, and 6) "web users' lack of trust in the legitimacy of the advertisement featured online" (Kapoor et al., 2016, p. 185). SEO contributes to the awareness and knowledge stages of the CDM process, while PPC advertising contributes to the latter stages of the process because it can direct consumers to the brand website where a commercial transaction can take place. Figure 4.3 illustrates the contributions of digital communications options to consumer decision-making.

Contributions to consumer-based brand equity

The organisation's IMC strategy, which combines offline and online brand communications options, can positively influence every part of the customer-based brand equity pyramid model (Keller, 2001b) (see Chapter 2). It can improve the depth and breadth of brand awareness, create crucial POPs and PODs against competitors, influence attitude formation, generate positive feelings, and facilitate brand attachment through frequent encounters and ways to provide feedback (Keller, 2001a). An effective IMC strategy is crucial to strategic brand management as it reinforces the interface between the brand identity strategy and customer-based brand equity (Madhavaram, Badrinarayanan, & McDonald, 2005). The brand identity strategy (as explored in Chapter 3) should form the foundation for the organisation's holistic IMC strategy in order to develop and maintain brand equity: "Clearly and consistently communicating the brand identity to other brand stewards...leads to stronger consumer-based brand equity. An ideal outcome of such a strategy would be [that] a consumer-held brand image...is congruent with the strategist's intended brand identity" (Madhavaram et al., 2005, p. 70).

Brand stewards include internal and external constituent groups who are responsible for communicating the brand to its internal and external publics (de Chernatony, 1999). Thus, brand stewards include the organisation's salesforce and brand ambassadors who deal with existing and prospective consumers, as well as marketing and creative agencies hired by the organisation to develop and deliver its marketing and design strategy (Madhavaram et al., 2005). If brand stewards have a thorough and consistent understanding of the brand identity strategy, they will be able to plan an IMC programme that delivers this strategy. Needless to say that the organisation must take into consideration market environment information including feedback from current and potential consumers, competitors, and the rest of its publics, when planning its IMC strategy (Madhavaram et al., 2005).

TRADITIONAL AND DIGITAL MEDIA PLATFORMS

"Two inescapable features of contemporary society are the wide availability of media texts and technologies, and the organisation of life around various forms of market exchange" (Iqani, 2018, p. 275). In this section we provide an overview of the traditional and digital media platforms organisations can take advantage of to transmit their messages and pursue the aforementioned communications options.

Traditional media platforms

Television
Television is the most common platform through which consumers become informed of products or services, and it has significant influence upon branding strategies (Darley, 2016). Television advertising combines sight, sound, and motion to create vivid and powerful messages which inform about product or service features and benefits, generate excitement about the company's offering, and demonstrate its use to a wide audience. Television advertising messages can explain what the brand can do and how it can do it, and can dramatically portray brand user and usage imagery, brand personality, and brand intangible characteristics (Darley, 2016; Keller & Swaminathan, 2020) (see Chapter 2). Of course, organisations need to mitigate potential disadvantages of television advertising. First, it is important that the creative elements of the television advert do not distract from the intended brand message. Second, in our time there is an abundance of advertising messages which leads to information clutter, hence consumers might ignore, forget, or even avoid advertising messages because they have more control on what information

they consume and how. Third, television advertising can be very expensive to produce and place, especially during prime time (e.g. 6–10:30pm in the United Kingdom). There has been an increase on the costs of advertising while the share of audience is getting smaller (Keller & Swaminathan, 2020). However there are still events which can enable huge audience reach e.g. the *Olympic Games*, the *Eurovision Song Contest*, and the *Super Bowl* which "is the single biggest event in America's ad calendar, bringing a guaranteed audience of 100m on TV and tens of thousands more online…[However] with a single 30-second slot [costing] an average of $5.235 million [in 2018]" (Eleftheriou-Smith, 2019, p. 18), it is a very expensive affair. Despite their enormous cost, many brands including established players such as *Pepsi*, *Burger King*, and *Doritos*, as well as young brands such as *Bumble*, *Expensify*, and *Bubly*, sought to communicate messages during the 2019 *Super Bowl* commercial break. Two brands managed to stand out: *Bubly* showed singer Micheal Bublé discovering how the brand's name is pronounced, and *Burger King* aired a 45-second vintage film featuring, pop artist Andy Warhol eating its iconic *Whopper* (Eleftheriou-Smith, 2019).

Eleftheriou-Smith explains that "[d]espite innovations within digital advertising…brands still choose to invest in big TV show finals and sports matches. Just because traditional media may not return immediate tracking results, what it delivers over time shows that it still pays" (2019, p. 18). Important national football matches, such as Brazil playing Argentina, are Latin America's *Super Bowl* equivalent. In addition, elections can also offer big advert events in Latin America as demonstrated by *Coca-Cola* running an advert with the 'We are closer than you think' campaign message. This message taped into Argentinian's habit of getting into each other's personal space and was in response to divisions felt in the country as a result of the election campaign (Eleftheriou-Smith, 2019).

When designing or evaluating a television advertising campaign, it is vital that the organisation defines the message and creative strategies. The *message strategy* is the scientific aspect of the campaign and determines the positioning the advertising campaign intends to create (including the desirable and deliverable POPs and PODs) (see Chapter 2). The *creative strategy* defines the creative way the campaign delivers this positioning and is the artistic aspect of the campaign. Organisations have two routes in regards with the creative strategy. First, the *informational route*, which achieves benefit elaboration, explains how the product or service provides solutions to problems, articulates how the product or service works, compares it with those of the competitors, and delivers testimonials to support the brand message. For example, a *Sensodyne* toothpaste television advert usually explains product use and benefits, and features a dental expert to add clinical gravitas to the brand message. Second, *the transformational route* whereby organisations communicate typical or aspirational user and usage imagery, and articulate brand personality and values. The main purpose is to demonstrate how the consumer will be intellectually and socially transformed by using the product or service (Keller et al., 2012; Meenaghan, 1995; Rossiter & Percy, 1987).

Irrespective of which route organisations follow, it is likely that they will combine it with a *motivational approach* which may include using popular music, humour, sex appeal, and social effects to grab viewers' attention. However, it is important that these effects do not distract from, but support, the message strategy (Keller & Swaminathan, 2020) and adhere to ethical values. In particular, regarding sex appeal, brands need to avoid hyper-sexualisation and promote gender equality. In the past *Skol*, the Brazilian beer brand, had run competitions to find the most beautiful model to lead their campaign, sticking to the notion that sex sells. However, over the last ten years, the brand has stopped featuring hyper-sexualised adverts in which women are objectified, first because of the need to stand out from other brands (which were also pursuing hyper-sexualised strategies). As many of its old adverts were still available on the Internet, old consumer perceptions were difficult to change. So the brand commissioned illustrators who reimagined its previous campaigns; these artists not only covered the female models in the old posters, but also presented them

> in a range of empowering scenarios. Instead of bikinis, they sported slogan tees; lone girls acquired friends and were shown having fun on their own terms. Consumers were also encouraged to report places where "old" images cropped up, so *Skol* could "reposter" them.
>
> (Cudderford-Jones, 2019, p. 42)

The campaign was a huge success with millions of organic views and millions of people reached, re-addressing the relationship of the brand with its audiences (Cudderford-Jones, 2019).

Radio

Radio is a very pervasive medium with many people around the world listening to the radio on a daily basis. It provides flexibility to advertisers because radio advertising messages are relatively (compared to television) inexpensive to produce and place. It can offer greater locality, which means that organisations can produce local adverts and place them on local radio stations targeting audiences in close vicinity. The main disadvantage of radio advertising messages is that they lack visuals and only appeal to people's auditory sense (Keller & Swaminathan, 2020). Yet radio can tap into listeners' imagination because it "has the capability to stage a 'theatre of the mind' and to create an enabling environment that allows listeners to become part of the scene" (Darley, 2016, p. 208). Another disadvantage relates to the fact that people often listen to the radio without paying attention, thus they passively process the information transmitted (Keller & Swaminathan, 2020). David Ogilvy, the advertising guru, has argued that in order for radio advertising to be effective, it is important that the message identifies the brand early in the commercial and it identifies it often. It should also promise the listener a benefit of using the product or service early in the message, and repeat this promise often (Ogilvy, 1983).

Print media

Print media include newspapers and magazines. Many iconic newspapers such as *The Washington Post* and *The Times*, or magazines such as *The Economist*, and *Vogue* have been around for decades. One of the main advantages of print advertising is that it is self-paced in nature, which means that readers can process the message in their own time, hence organisations can provide thorough information about their offerings. Most importantly newspapers or magazines can add associations beyond those created by the advertising message itself because, over the years, these publications have developed their own brand personality and associations (Keller et al., 2012). For example, placing a *Dior* advert in *Vogue* could add associations of glamour and sophistication to the message, while placing an *American Express* advert in the *Economist* could add associations of competence and professionalism, because these publications have been customarily associated with these attributes.

Magazine adverts, in particular, have the power to build imagery about brand user and usage situations. Newspaper adverts are timely and pervasive; they can be placed over night and can appear in the following day's issue, thus can deliver on local advertising needs. A disadvantage of print advertising is its static nature which makes it a challenge for advertisers who wish to create dynamic presentations or demonstrations. Print is also a passive medium which means that readers might flick through the pages without paying attention to adverts hence not necessarily processing these messages in the way they have been intended to. Newspaper adverts often have poor reproduction quality and a very short-life span because readers throw away daily newspapers after one or two days (Keller et al., 2012). In contrast, magazines have a relatively longer shelf life (Darley, 2016) and consumers might collect magazines they have a subscription to. Burton and Purvis (1991) argue that effective print advertising require a clear message that features a benefit in the headline. Print adverts have to be easy to read and interpret, and the organisation and/or brand easily and clearly identified. Print adverts ought to achieve a level of consistency and coherence, i.e. the visual elements must support the textual headline, and the rest of the copy has to support the visual elements and the headline (Burton & Purvis, 1991).

Digital media platforms

Organisations have numerous digital platforms that they can harness to communicate their brand messages. Edelman (2010) indicates three types of media platforms which can be applied to digital media: paid, owned, and earned media. *Paid media* are those media the organisation commissions to transmit its messages in exchange of money, e.g. paying *Google* a fee for every click on sponsored links, or paying a billboard company to place brand posters in prime locations. *Owned media* are those platforms the organisation owns and has control over. For instance, a firm can maintain its own websites and social media profiles where it can feature its advertising messages. It is important that the brand's website is "adaptable to the use of different screen resolutions in order to preserve both the layout and the display of product information" (Darley, 2016, p. 206). *Earned media* are "customer-created channels such as communities of [brand] enthusiasts" (Edelman, 2010, p. 66) and fan pages. For example, *Ferrero*, the organisation which owns *Nutella*, the sweetened hazelnut cocoa spread, can commission TV and radio stations to transmit messages in exchange of a fee (paid media) and can regularly update the brand's website and social media pages (owned media). But the firm has to look beyond the media platforms it controls. *Nutella* enthusiasts have developed webpages on which they share recipes for baking cookies using the spread (earned media). While the organisation cannot control these media platforms, it should have "the people and technology required to create and manage content for a profusion of channels and to monitor or participate in them" (Edelman, 2010, p. 66).

Drawing from theories in media research, Short, Williams, and Christie's (1976) *social presence* theory can help us understand the media aspect of social media in more depth. This theory indicates that media differ on the degree of social presence they achieve, i.e. the acoustic, visual, and physical contact achieved between communicating parties; the higher the social presence, the greater the social influence communicating parties have on each other (Kaplan & Haenlein, 2010; Short et al., 1976). Social presence is determined by the *level of intimacy*, i.e. whether interpersonal or mediated, and the *immediacy* of the medium, whether *synchronous* or *asynchronous*. Synchronous interactions occur at the same time, e.g. face-to-face interactions, whereas asynchronous "presume a staccato pattern of interaction, spread out over [time]" (Hansen et al., 2010, p. 14), e.g. e-mail conversations. Social presence is lower for mediated interactions but higher for synchronous interactions. Despite social media involving mediated interactions, their high level of immediacy (synchronous interactions) increase social presence achieved. Strongly associated with social presence theory is Daft and Lengel's (1986) *media richness* concept, which argues that media differ on the basis of the amount of information they can transmit in a given time interval; some media can be more effective in reducing ambiguity and uncertainty between communicating parties than others (Kaplan & Haenlein, 2010). Digital media can improve brand IMC strategies because they provide easier and constant access to real-time consumer data leading to deeper consumer insights (more on this in Chapter 10), more effective data-driven planning, automated cross-media integration, and connections with even more stakeholders (Mulhern, 2009).

PLANNING AND IMPLEMENTING BRAND IMC PROGRAMMES

The organisation must manage its IMC in a holistic manner to achieve its strategic objectives (Kitchen, Brignell, Li, & Jones, 2004). A solid IMC strategy requires employing multiple communications options and designing them in a way that they work together in a coherent manner. This means that firms need to define the effects each communications option has in isolation and the effects it has in combination (Keller, 2001a). On a micro level, there is a set of four factors that affect the effectiveness of marketing communications, portrayed by Keller (2001a) as the *marketing communication tetrahedron* (see Figure 4.4). The four constituent factors in this framework are: consumer, situation, communication, and consumer response. The general premise of the marketing communication tetrahedron is that

> studying the effects of individual marketing communications requires understanding how different types of consumers, under different processing circumstances, exposed to different types of communications, respond to different brand- or communication-related tasks or measures.
>
> (Keller, 2001a, p. 827)

As far as the *consumer* factor is concerned, beyond the socio-demographic (e.g. gender, age, and race), psychographic (e.g. interests and attitudes towards self and possessions), and behavioural (product usage, frequency, and brand loyalty) characteristics which can undoubtedly influence a consumer's response to brand communications, there are three more dimensions which we must take into consideration. First, the consumers' prior amount and nature of knowledge, i.e. what and how much they know about 1) the product or service category, 2) the organisation

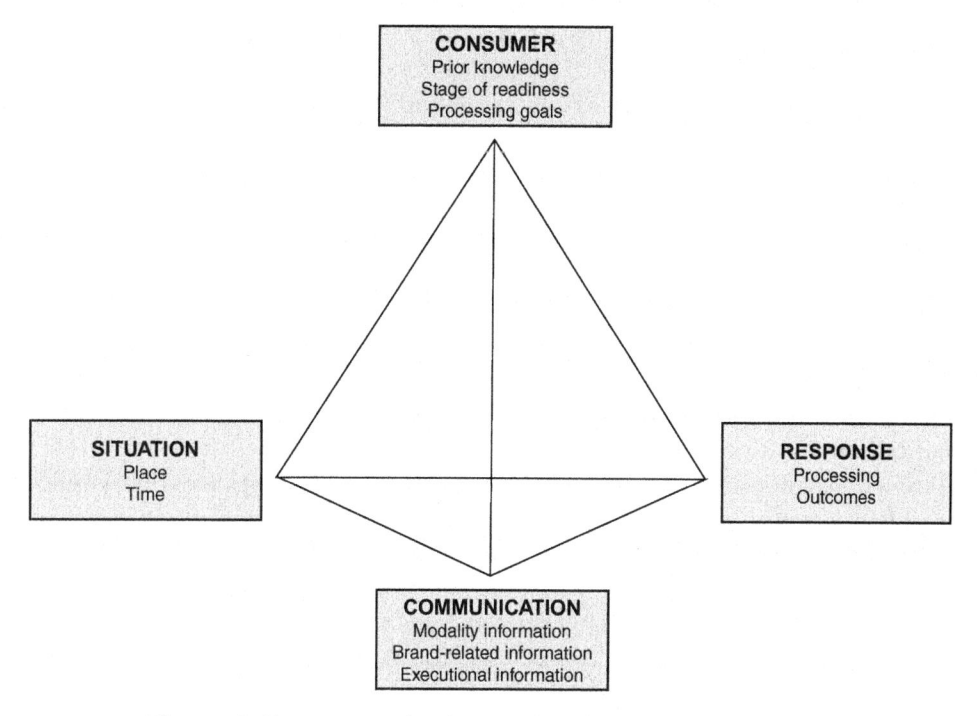

FIGURE 4.4 The marketing communication tetrahedron

behind the product or service, and 3) the brand and its past communications. Second, the consumers' "goals or stage of readiness with respect to the brand or product category at the time at which they are exposed to the marketing communication" (Keller, 2001a, p. 827) which can vary in terms of their urgency and the informational and memory requirements (Alba, Hutchinson, & Lynch, 1990). Third, what consumers want to get out of the specific brand communication, that is, whether they want to gather information about the brand or want to assess it, "or, instead...[they] want to attend to more executional, non-brand-related information (e.g. because they do not want to make a purchase in the category or do not view the marketed brand as a viable candidate)" (Keller, 2001a, p. 827).

The *communication* factor is about the dimensions of the communications option under consideration, including the number (whether it includes sight, sound, motion, spoken or written text) and nature (whether it is static, dynamic, interactive, or customised) of the modalities it involves, brand-related information (the message strategy – what it says about the brand), and executional information (the creative strategy – how it is said). The *consumer response* factor focuses on the temporal or permanent changes of the consumer's state as a result of the brand communication. Consumer responses can differ in terms of the processing involved, which can lead to cognitive or emotional responses with varied levels of abstraction, evaluative nature (negative, positive, or neutral), and relationship to the brand. They can also differ on the basis of outcomes measured by 1) recall and recognition of the messages (memory), 2) consumer perceptions, attitudes, and intentions (judgement), and 3) choice preferences and quantity and frequency of subsequent purchases (behavioural) (Keller, 2001a).

Finally, the *situation* factor is concerned with external issues related to place and time, which may influence consumers and the effectiveness of the brand communication by facilitating or hindering consumer processing. These include "exposure location, the extent and nature of competing stimuli (advertising or otherwise) at communication exposure, the amount of time lag involved with measurements of response or outcomes, [and] the type of retrieval conditions present during these measurements" (Keller, 2001a, p. 829). It is evident that the main argument of the marketing communication tetrahedron is that the effectiveness of a brand communication is very contextual, and that the consumer's response to any communication activity is a nuanced outcome of the interplay of multiple factors as discussed above.

On a macro level, Keller (2001a, 2016) argues that there are six criteria which organisations must consider when planning an IMC programme: 1) *coverage*, i.e. proportion of the audience reached by each communications option in the IMC programme and how much overlap exists among these communications options, 2) *contribution*, that is, the main effects of the communications option, its inherent ability "to create the desired response and communication effects from consumers in the absence of exposure to any other communication option" (Keller, 2001a, p. 832), 3) *commonality*, which is about whether the communications options share meaning and reinforce similar associations, 4) *complementarity*, which is concerned with different associations created by different communications options and the linkages among them, 5) *robustness* or *conformability*, i.e. whether or not a communications option can perform well with different consumer groups which is considered on the basis of achieving its intended result irrespective of consumers' past communication experience, 6) *cross-effects*, which is about "the extent to which communications options are designed to explicitly work together...and enhanced communication effects emerge as the result of exposure by consumers to both options" (Keller, 2016, p. 292), and 7) *cost*, which of course, will have to be taken into consideration to effectively plan an IMC strategy (Keller, 2001a, 2016).

Organisations need to bear in mind that when they successfully plan and design each communications option, it can play an important and unique role in generating desired consumer responses and meeting organisational objectives. Hence, there are not intrinsic differences across communications options in relation to contribution and complementarity. Nevertheless, based on the audiences they can speak to, they can differ in terms of their breadth and depth of coverage. In addition, depending on the number of modalities employed, they can vary in terms of commonality and robustness. Essentially, "the more modalities available with a communications type, the greater its potential commonality and robustness" (Keller, 2001a, p. 837).

Planning an effective IMC programme requires organisations to consider the following: 1) target audiences, 2) communications objectives (inform, persuade, excite, or remind), 3) product or service characteristics, 4) the stage the brand is at in its lifecycle, 5) the size of the overall budget, and 6) the size of competitors' budget and their media strategy (Keller et al., 2012). Organisations need to consider their priorities and find effective ways to reconcile the following trade-offs in their IMC programmes:

> 1) Commonality and complementarity will often be inversely related as the more it is the case that various marketing communication options emphasize the same brand attribute or benefit, all else equal, the less they can be effectively emphasizing other attributes and benefits. 2) Robustness and complementarity will also often be inversely related: The more a marketing communication program maximizes complementarity in content, the less critical is the robustness of any communication option. In other words, the more a communication program accounts for differences in consumers across communication options, the less necessary it is that any one communication is designed to appeal to different consumer groups. 3) Commonality and robustness, on the other hand, do not share an obvious relationship, as it may be possible, for example, to develop a sufficiently abstract message (e.g. 'brand is contemporary') that can be effectively reinforced across multiple communication types (e.g. advertising, interactive, sponsorship, promotions, etc.).
>
> (Keller, 2001a, p. 837)

Organisations need to understand that there is not a singularly most effective communications programme because different communications options can generate similar effects. However, every context is idiosyncratic; the onus is on the firm to assemble an IMC strategy which ensures that the whole is greater than the sum of its parts. In order to achieve this, there must be a thorough understanding of what the organisation is trying to achieve, the audiences it intends to target, and the market it operates in. This highlights the importance of carrying out consumer and market research when planning an IMC strategy, as well as during the implementation process, to allow for refinements based on real-time feedback from the various publics reached by the IMC programme.

SOCIAL MEDIA AND THE (OVER)DEMOCRATISATION OF MARKETING

Digital consumer culture and the connected self

> It is arguably impossible to understand or analyse human condition in almost any context, be it at the local, national or global scales, without engaging to some extent with either the media or consumer culture. [In fact], it is impossible to study one without the other.
>
> (Iqani, 2018, p. 275)

This statement applies equally to social media which consumers use on a daily basis to engage with family, friends, colleagues, and others, for work and for leisure, to stay informed and to inform others of their thoughts, preferences, and actions. Social media have been very successful because human beings are social creatures; they have the inherent need to communicate with each other (Smith & Zook, 2011) and the

> desire to feel accepted, to fit in, and to belong. Web 2.0 fosters a sense of community through virtual connections among like-minded people and enables the search for and celebration of micro-targeted niche groups to which people can easily belong.
>
> (Fournier & Avery, 2011, p. 195)

Social media communications like any other communication "require two actors: 1) a *sender* who is willing to share information and 2) a *receiver* who is willing to listen to it" (Kaplan, 2011, p. 4). It is important to understand the reasons a person might wish to share information with others on social media, and the concepts of self-presentation and self-disclosure can provide an explanation. According to *self-presentation*, in any social interaction, individuals want to control and influence the impressions they create in other peoples' minds (Goffman, 1959; Kaplan, 2011; Kaplan & Haenlein, 2010) in order to create an image which is consistent with their personal identity, and to gain rewards such as making a good impression on important others. As argued by philosophers Alexander Bard and Jan Söderqvist, "we are obsessed with being seen and validated by the world around us…We are born exhibitionists, [and] we insist on attention from an audience" (2018, p. 195). With regards to consumption, one might want to engage with a brand (e.g. *Balenciaga*, the fashionable luxury clothes and accessories maker) on social media in order to create an image of being trendy and eclectic. Usually this is achieved through *self-disclosure*, which is the "conscious or unconscious revelation of personal information (e.g., thoughts, feelings, likes, dislikes) that is consistent with the image one would like to create" (Kaplan & Haenlein, 2010, p. 62).

In addition, the *impulsiveness theory* can provide another reason why one might want to share information on social media. This theory suggests that people face a continuous struggle between exerting long-term control and giving into short-term temptations (Ainslie, 1975; Hoch & Lowewenstein, 1991; Kaplan, 2011), hence, they might share status updates in the same way that they would impulsively buy a chocolate bar at the supermarket check-out, despite the fact that it is not congruent with their plan to have a healthy diet. In general, people's motivations to publish their experiences on opinion platforms (electronic WOM) include "social benefits, economic incentives, concern for others, and extraversion/self-enhancement" (Hennig-Thurau, Gwinner, Walsh, & Gremler, 2004, p. 50).

It is equally important to explore why people are willing to read and react to the information communicated to them on social media. Regular status updates can help the receivers achieve *ambient awareness*, which is "awareness created through regular and constant reception, and/or exchange of information fragments through social media" (Kaplan, 2011, p. 4). This means that receiving small snippets of information on a regular and continuous basis, e.g. the locations a person has been to during the day, and the brands he/she has consumed (e.g. food, drinks, clothes, make-up etc.), might say more about this person than a two-page email (Kaplan, 2011). In short, people are curious (or nosey) about what other people do, and social media feeds to their curiosity in an uninterrupted and effortless way.

Much of the content consumers share online involves brands they own, use, or aspire to have. Consumer online conversations can benefit the brand because its messages can spread more easily and at faster pace, consumers can feel stronger connections with the brand, and organisations can gather more information about consumer preferences. However, as we will explore later, organisations cannot control or dictate these conversations (Fournier & Avery, 2011; Smith & Zook, 2011). Instead, firms should facilitate, participate, and monitor online discussions, engaging with consumers while respecting the rules and norms as determined by social media users. Brand employees who engage in consumer discussions must reveal their affiliation to ensure and retain transparency. According to Pentina, Guilloux, and Micu the "low ability to control consumer-generated content can be perilous for brand image, [and] this issue is particularly salient for luxury brands, characterised by precise…positioning based on exclusivity, uniqueness and association with high society" (2018, p. 55). In their recent exploratory study with luxury consumers, they sought to identify social media engagement behaviours in the context of luxury brands. Their results determined a typology of online behaviour types that varied in terms of

> 1) the intended engagement audience (the brand, other social media users,…or both), 2) intensity of applied effort and creativity…, 3) content creation medium utilized (textual, visual, or hybrid), 4) dominant motivational drivers (singular or combined, intrinsic or extrinsic), and differences and similarities among social media platforms.
> (Pentina et al., 2018, p. 64)

Starting from the lowest in terms of level of engagement effort and creativity required, these types of online behaviour are: 1) simply following or liking the brand online, 2) commenting on brand's posts and ads, 3) liking, tagging, and sharing the brand's posts, 4) mentioning friends in comments on the brand's social media pages, 5) tagging brand names and using fashion-related hashtags, 6) publishing photos of the brand's products, 7) publishing photos of oneself with the brand, 8) explicitly soliciting comments to brand selfies, 9) initiating and maintaining brand-related conversations in personal social networks, 10) publishing multimedia shopping stories, and 11) modifying the branded product or suggesting new interpretation of its use and image (Pentina et al., 2018). This last behaviour is the highest in terms of the level of applied effort and creativity required, and it involves both the brand and other brand enthusiasts. The motivation behind this online behaviour is both intrinsic and extrinsic and those consumers who engage in such behaviour perceive

> the brand not only as a reciprocal social entity but also as a legitimate member of their personal social networks. The expansion of engagement audiences to include both other brand users and the brand itself may testify to increasing self–brand identification and perception of the brand as an extension of the self.
> (Pentina et al., 2018, p. 64)

The above statement echoes Belk's (1988) influential concept of the extended self, which is as profoundly relevant in the Internet Age (Belk, 2013) as it was in pre-digital consumer culture. Belk (1988) asserted that the *extended self* includes a person's body, internal processes, ideas, and experiences, as well as the people, places, and objects to which a person feels attached (the last three are the most clearly extended). He argued that it is a "fact of modern life that we learn, define, and remind ourselves of who we are by our possessions" (Belk, 1988, p. 160) and emphasised the symbolic importance of daily consumption especially in relation to collections, pets, money, organ donation, gift-giving, and product disposition and disuse (Belk, 1988, 2013). The acute changes the Internet and social media have brought to consumer culture – influencing all aspects of human life: our daily routines, hobbies, plans, and desires – called for an update to the concept of the extended self. We have become what Llamas and Belk (2013) describe as *homo connectus*, wired and wireless creatures who are always logged on because of our fear of missing out (FOMO). In his theoretical update, Belk (2013) explains that

> the concept of the extended self…is alive and well in the digital world, but there are a number of differences. There are many new possessions and technologies through which we present and extend our self, and they operate quite differently than in predigital days. They also create different ways through which we can meet, interact with, and extend our aggregate selves through other people while experiencing a transcendent sense that we are part of something bigger than us alone.
>
> (Belk, 2013, p. 494)

Co-creation and collective brand narratives

Undoubtedly, social media have revolutionised consumer–brand relationships because of their sheer power and the profound changes they have brought in consumer culture. Social media have opened up new channels of communication that organisations can harness to facilitate discussions among brand marketers, opinion formers, and consumers. Such discussions can take place within the firm's official digital space but also out with this online space, most often among consumers without the influence or even the knowledge of organisations. In the digital age, the flow of marketing information is no longer controlled by organisations; it is consumers who have the power to control discussions, block any interruption, and use social media as their means to search for information, find products and services, and share their experiences with hundreds of other people (Smith & Zook, 2011). This means that marketing, as an organisational function, has become democratised because of the Internet and social media. Social media enable organisations to establish and maintain strong relationships with their target consumers. This, of course, resonates with the *relationship marketing* paradigm which postulates that it is more cost-efficient for the firm to develop and preserve relationships with existing customers than constantly trying to acquire new ones. As Grönroos argued, marketing seeks to "establish, maintain and enhance long-term customer relationships at a profit, so that the objectives of the parties involved are met" (1990, p. 138). However, the important difference is that the Internet and social media have empowered consumers, elevating the consumer–brand relationship to a partnership of *equals*.

Nowadays, organisations need to view consumers as active brand stakeholders and invite them to engage in collaborative co-creation at a higher level, in order to design and develop new products and services with them. Enlightened organisations are those that find novel ways to encourage and facilitate consumer engagement, which can lead to higher brand loyalty. The ideal consumer is one who becomes a brand evangelist and, beyond merely spending time and money to purchase and use the brand, shares his/her experiences with others and invites them to join the brand fold. The onus is on organisations to identify those consumers with a potential to evolve to brand evangelists in order to move them up the *strategic ladder of engagement*; these consumers do not only provide ratings and write reviews, but also take part in discussions, and ultimately co-develop with the organisation new ideas, adverts, brands, and products which they subsequently consume (see Figure 4.5) (Smith & Zook, 2011). Hence, organisations can transform their consumers to *prosumers*, that is, a producer-consumer hybrid (see Chapter 8 in Lalaounis, 2017, for more on the concept of prosumption).

Consumers no longer need an invitation or a nudge to engage in the current digital landscape. Because of social media, the power has shifted from marketers to consumers; marketers can neither determine the brand message, alone, nor can they control its reach, timing, and frequency. Brand messages are co-created with consumers and other stakeholders. Fournier and Avery (2011) call this emergent landscape *open source branding*, which involves "participatory, collaborative, and socially linked behaviours whereby consumers serve as creators and disseminators of the branded content" (Fournier & Avery, 2011, p. 194). The notion of co-creation does not only relate to objects but also to interpretation and the production of meaning and content (Ind & Coates, 2013). Meaning is dialogic (Morris, 2003); it is socially constructed as the result of continuous debate among individuals as interpreters of cultural phenomena. Organisations can instigate and generate brand narratives which

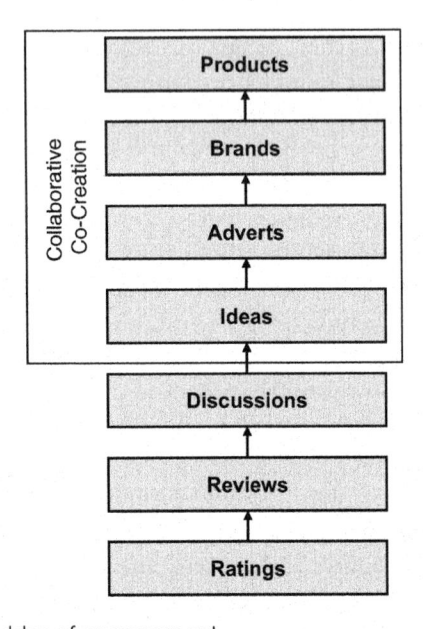

FIGURE 4.5 Strategic ladder of engagement

aim to create and strengthen consumers' relationship with the brand by providing a theme for conversations between consumers and firms…and among consumers themselves. Such conversations enable consumers to integrate their own brand-related experiences and thoughts into the brand story.

(Gensler, Völckner, Liu-Thompkins, & Wiertz, 2013, p. 242)

This means that consumers embrace, interpret and morph firm-generated stories into their own evolving brand narratives shared on social media on a real-time basis. Consumer culture theorists have challenged the conventional brand management paradigm, which argues that brands are owned and controlled by organisations and can be developed in the minds of consumers through diligently planned and implemented brand marketing strategies (Gensler et al., 2013). Based on a postmodern view of the marketplace, they view brands as a "repository of meanings for consumers to use in living their own lives" (Allen, Fournier, & Miller, 2008, p. 782) and consumers (and all other stakeholders) as "active co-creators of these brand meanings" (Gensler et al., 2013, p. 243). Consumers' brand stories are dynamic; they add to the organisation's intended brand meaning but also challenge the brand identity communicated by the organisation. This means that "a brand's meaning emerges… between the collective sharing of what the brand means to all of its stakeholders and the active and often conflictual negotiation of such meanings" (Cayla & Arnould, 2008, p. 100). To achieve brand success, organisations must coordinate their own narratives with consumer-generated brand stories.

Fournier and Avery (2011) argue that we live in the age of social collectivism, transparency, criticism, and parody, which are the four overarching themes enabled by the Internet and social media (see Figure 4.6). *Social collectivism* stems from the desire to communicate and share our stories online thanks to our very nature as social creatures. Barack Obama's 2008 presidential campaign focused

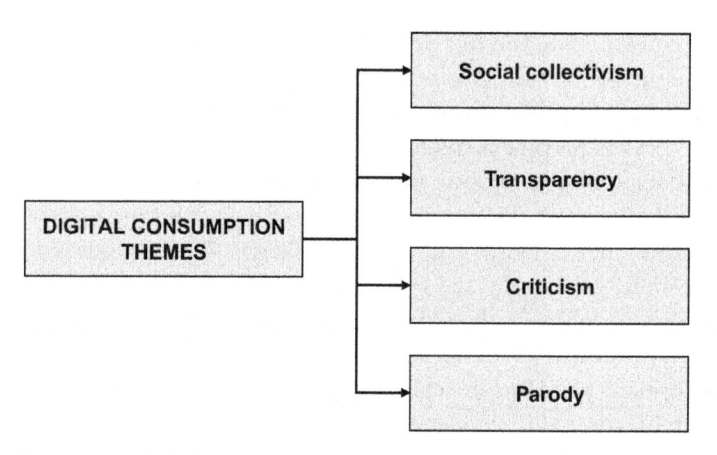

FIGURE 4.6 Themes in digital consumption landscape

on the power of the collective to generate support for him and the *Democratic Party* and to keep voters informed (Fournier & Avery, 2011). Fast forward few years, Donald Trump took this approach to a dangerous extreme. Trump's 2016 presidential "campaign was conducted to a revolutionary unprecedented extent in…slogans, claims, pledges, attacks and rebuttals on Twitter. A reality TV star, he intuitively understood the power of communicating in shocking, sensational headlines" (Peston, 2017, p. 58).

The Internet has also brought *transparency* because consumers now have convenient access to information; like 'part-time journalists', they can easily uncover the truth behind the news and can expose organisations' malpractices (Fournier & Avery, 2011). However, it is not as easy as we might want to think, anymore. We have seen the rise of *fake news* about celebrities, brands, organisations, politicians, and political parties, that is, false stories which are "liked, shared and retweeted with the self-reinforcing momentum of the hysterical mob, [and are] then read, watched and taken as truth by gazillions of people" (Peston, 2017, p. 63). The fake news phenomenon makes distinguishing facts from 'alternative facts' an endeavour which requires skill and time. Ordinary people now doubt everything and everyone, and conspiracy theories are now shared and repeated like (the digital world's equivalent of) folk tales. There is a threat that

> future elections may not be battles of ideas but contests to scrape the Internet for precious details about our hopes, fears and vulnerabilities, so that tailored messages can be sent to us that we find irresistible. It will be a war to find out who each of us thinks we truly are.
>
> (Peston, 2017, p. 101)

Transparency can lead to *criticism* because online consumers have the power to be "ardent brand arbiters and commentators, providing authoritative judgment and critique of companies and brands" (Fournier & Avery, 2011, p. 200). This criticism can be constructive, forcing organisations to improve their practices and be more transparent about their decisions. Criticism can also take a more humorous approach with *parody*, where consumers spend time spoofing, i.e. parodying people and brands. This has become a trendy hobby among consumers, and brands can be a great theme for spoofing because of their cultural richness. In fact, being a target of parody can be a sign of the brand's cultural resonance (Fournier & Avery, 2011). However, unrestricted criticism can get destructive, especially when it maliciously directed at people, as seen by the recent rise of aggression on social media. One could argue that social media have led to over-democratisation where people abuse the freedom to post or write online anything they like; this has become an anathema when inappropriate words or uncensored images lead to self-harm or even suicide. In his *National Geographic* article, Agustín Fuentes, an evolutionary anthropology professor explains that anonymity and the lack of face-to-face interaction on social media platforms remove a crucial part of the equation of human sociality...On social media, where the troll is remote and anonymous, even the best intentioned individual challenge may devolve into a shouting match.

(Fuentes, 2018, p. 20)

But social media can also be used to nurture positive campaigns as evidenced by the #metoo and the #BlackLivesMatter campaigns which have highlighted important social issues and have inspired many people around the world.

Fournier and Avery (2011) identified three principal strategies adopted by organisations in order to cope with the aforesaid cultural phenomena. First, "the *path of least resistance* [which] involves ceding control of the brand to consumers, bowing to social media pressure" (Fournier & Avery, 2011, pp. 194–195), which one could argue is an unavoidable strategy given the strength of the social collectivism phenomenon. *Nutella* and *Coca-Cola* have been successful in this strategy as they acknowledged consumers rightful claims over the ownership of their *Facebook* profile pages and relinquished brand control, leading to good citizenship credentials which can benefit brand equity immensely. Second, *playing their game* requires from the brand

being where the action is happening on social media, and fitting in seamlessly with what is happening there. This approach requires mastery of the nuanced principles, styles, and mechanisms governing the new cultural environment such that the brand can dilute its inherent intrusiveness on the people's web.

(Fournier & Avery, 2011, p. 195)

This can involve *hijacking* whereby brand marketers can harness consumer-created brand messages for the benefit of the brand. *Harley-Davidson* took notice of skateboarder Heath Kirchart's summer tour video *Emerica: The wild ride* uploaded on *YouTube* and two years later the company officially sponsored his tours (Fournier & Avery, 2011). Similarly, *Gatorade* engages in *active listening* with its 24-hour social media centre, to monitor online conversations and intervene when there is an opportunity. The third strategy adopted by organisations in order to cope in the digital landscape is *leveraging Web 2.0 interconnectedness* with which organisations get consumers to 'play the brand's game' by feeding "into their evolving habits... This strategy strives to tip the power back to marketing by providing fodder to get consumers to work on behalf of the brand" (Fournier & Avery, 2011, p. 195). For example, *Groupon*'s offers are only valid if enough people sign up to them, this encourages people to spread the message on their social networks to generate the numbers required (Fournier & Avery, 2011).

Regardless of the strategy pursued, the general advice is that organisations should create engaging content which people are willing to listen to and share with other people on their networks, leading to a viral effect. It is not only about being differentiated as a brand, it is about creating cultural resonance with meanings which consumers want. Brands should "create resonant cultural conversations..., branded artefacts, social rituals, and cultural icons which issue invitations to their own parties rather than waiting patiently for consumer hosts to invite the brand in" (Fournier & Avery, 2011, p. 205).

SOCIAL MEDIA, HYPER-NARCISSISM, AND THE ATTENTION ECONOMY

Nowadays the digital landscape provides consumers with an abundance of choices; brands from all over the world can efficiently communicate their messages in real time and successfully market their products and services with less effort and expenditure. Indeed, there is a myriad of brands seeking to target consumers who are now "distracted, dispersed,...privatised" (Khamis et al., 2017, p. 195), impatient, and demanding audiences. Scholars advocate that we now live in the *attention economy* (Bard & Söderqvist, 2018; Brody, 2001; Fairchild, 2007; Khamis et al., 2017; Marwick, 2015), where organisations vie for the consumers' attention in a market which assigns "value according to something's capacity to attract 'eyeballs' in a media-saturated, information-rich world" (Marwick, 2015, p. 138). This competition gradually becomes even fiercer because "we humans have in a short period of time become worse at focusing our attention during long-term, uninterrupted information gathering, since we have become accustomed to and dependent upon constantly being distracted by something completely different" (Bard & Söderqvist, 2018, p. 193).

Many of the attention-getting techniques used by organisations are now pursued by individual users in order to increase their own popularity and build their own self-brands. Peters (1997) argued that "we are CEOs of our own companies: Me Inc...Our most important job is to be head marketer for the brand called You" (Peters, 1997, p. 83). The main premise of *self-branding* is that, similar to branding products or services, one can brand him/herself. By developing a distinct identity which leads to desired images in the minds of important others, one can achieve commercial gains and increase his/her own social and cultural capital (Khamis et al., 2017). Of course, branding requires consistency, which is difficult to achieve when trying to market oneself because "consistency requires vigilance, authenticity, and the absence of unexpected hurdles that would require amendments or negotiation, all of which are extremely difficult for humans to ensure" (Khamis et al., 2017, p. 193). Despite this, self-branding is a very dominant concept in a network society made of individuals hungry for attention and fame. According to Khamis et al. (2017) there are three reasons for this: 1) social media promises fame to ordinary people, encouraging micro-celebrity practices, 2) our individualistic culture encourages self-branding and promises rewards, 3) many social media *influencers* become commercially successful and their practices can be replicated by anyone who has a social media profile.

Influencers develop their own fan clubs (their followers) and stand out in the attention economy through their photos, captions, tweets, and messages, which are then liked, shared, and commented (by their followers) consolidating the influencers' self-brands (Khamis et al., 2017). Social media offer excellent platforms where ordinary people can become micro-celebrities, competing to get noticed, and building their own brand. Micro-celebrities develop digital profiles where they constantly reveal personal information to generate attention and increase online status (Marwick, 2015). "[There] is the vacuous hunt for attention for attention's own sake, a kind of grinding quest for affirmation on autopilot" (Bard & Söderqvist, 2018, p. 138).

In particular, *Instagram* has become paramount to building successful and visually appealing self-brands. Nowadays, attention-craving individuals seek to achieve *instafame*, "the condition of having a relatively great number of followers on the app" (Marwick, 2015, p. 137). Nowadays, regular people seek to build their own self-brand by frantically sharing photos of the places they go to, the food they eat, and the clothes and accessories they buy. Yet most of the photos posted on social media are *selfies* where the focal subject is not places, objects, or other people, but the person him/herself (who is also the photo-taker) (Kedzior, Allen, & Schroeder, 2016). Selfies are now a genre of photography which has its own visual conventions and clichés, e.g. 'myspace angle', i.e. taking a selfie from above to make oneself look thinner, or 'duckface', that is, the pursed lips facial expression spluttered all over social media. "Selfies…have [also] become…a resource for brand management campaigns – as epitomized during the 2014 *Academy Awards* when host Ellen DeGeneres' seemingly spontaneous group selfie was later revealed to be a planned promotion for *Samsung* smartphones" (Kedzior et al., 2016, p. 1768).

Scholars argue that the desire for instafame and for achieving a micro-celebrity status, by competing for high numbers of followers, likes, and comments (Marwick, 2015), is creating a *narcistic society*. We are slowly moving to epidemic levels of *self-obsession* because of our desire to be successful in self-branding: "Young people in particular appear convinced that good looks, good living and conspicuous consumption warrant adoration and emulation" (Khamis et al., 2017, p. 199). The branded self becomes a commodity to be marketed on social media, getting people hooked on continuously promoting themselves online and maintaining online relationships which have been reduced to mere transactions (e.g. 'like for like', 'follow for follow' etc.). The greatest irony is that while we are all busy talking and sharing incessantly on social media, seldom anyone is actually *listening*, and this is to the detriment of our personal relationships and the society in general.

> Everyone sees himself as an artist of sorts, but the audience attention for all these amateur productions de facto is non-existent; we are talking about productions that to all intents and purposes completely lack value…The last thing a logical person wants to give their valuable *attention* to is after all another person's desperate *hyper-narcissism*.
>
> (Bard & Söderqvist, 2018, p. 186)

CHAPTER REVIEW QUESTIONS

You can use the following questions to reflect on the material covered in Chapter 4:

1. How do traditional and online brand communications options influence consumer decision-making? How do they contribute to brand equity development?
2. Choose a brand you are familiar with and explore its social media activities.
3. Discuss the advantages and disadvantages of the traditional and digital media platforms available to organisations.
4. What are the essential criteria an organisation must consider when planning a brand IMC strategy?
5. Discuss the emerging cultural phenomena in the digital landscape and explain the three strategies organisations can use to cope with these phenomena.
6. What are the ethical issues associated with the concepts of self-branding and the attention economy?

RECOMMENDED READING

1. Keller, K. L. (2001a). Mastering the marketing communications mix: Micro and macro perspectives on integrated marketing communication programs. *Journal of Marketing Management, 17*, 819–847.
2. Hansen, D. L., Shneiderman, B., Smith, M. A., & Himelboim, I. (2010). Social media: New technologies of collaboration. In *Analyzing social media networks with NodeXL*: Insights from a connected world (pp. 11–29). Cambridge: Morgan Kaufmann.
3. Belk, R. W. (2013). Extended self in a digital world. *Journal of Consumer Research, 40*(3), 477–500.
4. Fournier, S., & Avery, J. (2011). The uninvited brand. *Business Horizons, 54*(3), 193–207.

CASE STUDY

Burberry and 'brand heat' strategy

Dr. Nina Van Volkinburg
Lecturer in Fashion Marketing
London College of Fashion, University of the Arts London, London, UK

Representative of British character and synonymous with the trench coat, the global luxury fashion house *Burberry* is celebrated for its creativity, innovation, and design. Founded in 1856 by a 21-year-old Thomas Burberry, a former draper's apprentice, *Burberry* originally supplied outdoor attire, but has since evolved to distribute ready to wear, fashion accessories, fragrances, sunglasses, and cosmetics. Globally, the brand employs nearly 10,000 people and is the only luxury fashion brand in the FTSE 100. For the year ending 30 March 2019, the company reported a revenue of £2.72 billion, -1% at constant exchange rates, and an adjusted operating profit of £438 million, flat on the same basis compared with the year before. However, the second quarter of 2019 saw a stronger performance with a 4% increase in sales, with shares up 14% (its best performance in a decade). The surge boosted *Burberry*'s stock market value by more than £1 billion to £9.4 billion. Notably, the company was listed as 96th on *Interbrand*'s Best Global Brands 2019 rankings, a 4% increase from 2018, whilst competitors including *Louis Vuitton* (part of the LVMH group) was placed at 17th (+14%) and *Gucci* (part of the Kering group) was placed at 33rd (+23%).

Since 2017, the company has undergone a series of transformations, most notably with the departure of its longstanding Creative Director and CEO Christopher Bailey and the subsequent arrivals of Riccardo Tisci, overtaking the position of Creative Director and Marco Gobbetti as Chief Executive. The appointment of Tisci, who presented his first collection for the brand in September 2018 at London Fashion Week, initially came as a shock within the fashion industry, as the Italian was renowned for his rebellious, gothic, and 'street' aesthetic; the antithesis of *Burberry*'s polished roots in British tradition. His designs however, won over many critics and customers, providing a sharp and edgy revamp to *Burberry*'s classic designs. During Tisci's previous tenure at *Burberry*-rival *Givenchy*, he introduced casual t-shirts, sweatshirts, and sneakers into the luxury vocabulary, appealing to, and arguably moulding, the *hypebeast* demographic defined as typically a man, who keeps up with fashion trends, particularly in streetwear, for the purpose of making a social statement. Through his influence on youth culture, Tisci himself is a celebrity, acquiring 2.5 million *Instagram* followers and often shares photos of himself with friends including Kim Kardashian and Madonna to his audience. Next to bringing in Tisci and his streetwear-driven aesthetic, the brand has repositioned itself to be firmly within the luxury segment, raising the quality and prices for core items in categories such as leather goods, and closing up to 10% of its global stores. Additionally, it has redefined its branding strategy resulting in, what Gobbetti refers to as *brand heat*. He used this term to explain the strategy of the brand pulling in substantial interest from a variety of stakeholders generating cultural traction, where *Burberry* plays a central role in pop-culture and has become a desirable target of discussion amongst trend-setters and early adopters.

The first example of *Burberry*'s redefined branding strategy was the introduction of its new 'TB' monogram, based on the initials of the brand's founder, born from a collaboration with the graphic designer Peter Saville. Prior to the monogram's release, *Burberry* shared images of email correspondences between Tisci and Saville across its social media platforms giving the audience an insight as to how the collaboration unfolded. The monogram of interlocking "Ts" and "Bs" was transformed into a new print, complimenting the fashion house's iconic check pattern, and was not only splashed across print advertisements, but was brought to life, for example, on the giant, inflatable *Thomas Burberry* bears, which appeared in New York, Shanghai, and London. Additionally, the monogram was wrapped around various landmarks and major *Burberry* stores across the world, encouraging consumers to share pictures of the spotted monogram on their own platforms via the hashtags #thomasburberrybear and #thomasburberrymonogram. The brand also modernised its traditional typeface, adopting a bold minimalist *Sans Serif Helvetica* font, sparking both outrage and excitement amongst consumers.

Secondly, *Burberry* has adopted a direct-to-consumer 'drop' model, where it has launched product releases on the 17th of each month exclusively through the brand's social media channels including *Instagram*, *WeChat*, *Line*, and *Kakao*. Products including socks, t-shirts, and hoodies are only on sale across the platforms for 24 hours, however, they are often sold out much sooner. For example, a pair of black leather gloves sold out within 20 minutes on *WeChat*.

A final example of *Burberry* creating brand heat is its implementation of user-generated content across social media. By using the hashtag #burberrygeneration, users are invited to style, wear, photograph themselves in *Burberry* products, and finally upload their images to their own social media platforms such as *Instagram*. Here, users not only endorse *Burberry* and their own personal brands to their followers, but they may also be featured on *Burberry*'s own social media accounts. Users, many also considered to be social media influencers, who are chosen to be featured on *Burberry*'s social media accounts might not necessarily have big followings, however, they provide a unique visual perspective, underlining the notion that the brand can be relevant for anyone and any taste. Influencers, or consumers, thus contribute and shape the content and the aesthetic of the luxury brand, appealing to a wide variety of demographics and cultures leading a degree of relatability for other consumers. The notion of appealing to diverse consumers through user generated content, is also reflected in the brand's latest advertising campaign featuring supermodel Gigi Hadid and shot by Nick Knight. Here, Hadid poses as four different characters: the girl, the boy, the lady, and the gentleman, suggesting *Burberry* quenches both conservative (e.g. knee length skirts and headscarves) and street style (e.g. hoodies, bum bags, sneakers) tastes.

Despite gaining momentum as a leading global brand, *Burberry* operates in a volatile and hyper competitive industry faced with a host of challenges. Firstly, social media continues to influence consumer demand, and brings the constant threat of small emerging brands. Secondly, footfall in the physical retail environment continues to decline. Thirdly, due to the rise of artificial intelligence, value chains are being disrupted and design, curation, and assortment are more reliant on data science. Lastly, sustainability and transparency continue to be dominant concerns for consumers and companies about how to reduce their impact on the environment. It was only in 2017, when *Burberry* was accused of burning £28.6 million worth of unsold goods, including accessories and perfume. Whether *Burberry*, under the leadership of Tisci and Gobbetti, will be able to rely on its brand heat in order to succeed in a turbulent and uncertain macro-environment, remains to be seen.

References

Cochrane, L. (2019). In the trenches: Riccardo Tisci on his new era at Burberry. *The Guardian* [accessed 28 October 2019]

Sandle, P. (2019). Burberry Profit Steady Awaiting New Collections in Stores. *The Business of Fashion* [accessed 28 October 2019]

Questions for discussion

1) Whilst *Burberry* targets a variety of customers, is there a risk of "when you speak to everyone, you speak to no one"?
2) As a global brand, what are the dangers of working with influencers and attempting to harness user-generated content?
3) Is it necessary to have a large social media following today, to be appointed as a creative director (or hold a position of power) for a global brand?
4) How does immediate communication via social media and direct-to-consumer 'drops' influence consumers' perception of luxury?
5) What are the positive and genitive implications of obtaining rapid brand heat?

REFERENCES

Ainslie, G. (1975). Specious reward: A behavioral theory of impulsiveness and impulse control. *Psychological Bulletin*, 82(4), 463.

Alba, J. W., & Hutchinson, J. W. (1987). Dimensions of consumer expertise. *Journal of Consumer Research*, 13(4), 411–454.

Alba, J. W., Hutchinson, W. J., & Lynch Jr., J. G. (1990). Memory and decision-making. In T. S. Robertson & H. H. Kassarjian (eds), *Handbook of consumer theory and research*. Englewood Cliffs: Prentice-Hall.

Allen, C. T., Fournier, S., & Miller, F. (2008). Brands and their meaning makers. In C. Haugtvedt, P. Herr, & F. Kardes (eds), *Handbook of consumer psychology* (pp. 781–822). London: Routledge.

Audrezet, A., De Kerviler, G., & Moulard, J. G. (2020). Authenticity under threat: When social media influencers need to go beyond self-presentation. *Journal of Business Research*, 117: 557–569.

Bard, A., & Söderqvist, J. (2018). *Digital libido: Sex, power and violence in the network society*. Stockholm: Futurica Media.

Belch, G. E., & Belch, M. A. (2012). *Advertising and promotion*. New York: McGraw-Hill/Irwin.

Belk, R. W. (1988). Possessions and the extended self. *Journal of Consumer Research*, 15(2), 139–168.

Belk, R. W. (2013). Extended self in a digital world. *Journal of Consumer Research*, 40(3), 477–500.

Brody, E. W. (2001). The "attention" economy. *Public Relations Quarterly*, 46(3), 18.

Burton, P. W., & Purvis, S. C. (1991). *Which ad pulled best?* (9th edn). New York: McGraw-Hill/Irwin.

Cayla, J., & Arnould, E. J. (2008). A cultural approach to branding in the global marketplace. *Journal of International Marketing, 16*(4), 86–112.

Chandon, P., Wansink, B., & Laurent, G. (2000). A benefit congruency framework of sales promotion effectiveness. *Journal of Marketing, 64*(4), 65–81.

Cudderford-Jones, M. (2019). How sex lost its sparkle: The Brazilian beer brand defying stereotypes. *Catalyst, 2,* 42–44.

Daft, R. L., & Lengel, R. H. (1986). Organizational information requirements, media richness and structural design. *Management Science, 32*(5), 554–571.

Darley, W. K. (2016). Brand building via integrated marketing communications. In F. Dall'Olmo Riley, J. Singh, & C. Blankson (eds), *The Routledge companion to contemporary brand management* (pp. 201–217). London: Routledge.

de Chernatony, L. (1999). Brand management through narrowing the gap between brand identity and brand reputation. *Journal of Marketing Management, 15*(1–3), 157–179.

Durgee, J. F. (1988). Understanding brand personality. *Journal of Consumer Marketing, 5*(3), 21–25.

Edelman, D. C. (2010). Branding in the digital age. *Harvard Business Review, 88*(12), 62–69.

Eleftheriou-Smith, L. (2019). Make a splash: Advertisers pin their hopes on primetime. *Catalyst, 2,* 16–21.

Fairchild, C. (2007). Building the authentic celebrity: The "Idol" phenomenon in the attention economy. *Popular Music and Society, 30*(3), 355–375.

Fournier, S., & Avery, J. (2011). The uninvited brand. *Business Horizons, 54*(3), 193–207.

Fuentes, A. (2018). Are we as awful as we act online? *National Geographic,* 17–20 August.

Fury, A. (2017). Rebel sell: A new breed of fashion designer is making it big by breaking all the rules. *Wallpaper, 216,* 93–94.

Gensler, S., Völckner, F., Liu-Thompkins, Y., & Wiertz, C. (2013). Managing brands in the social media environment. *Journal of Interactive Marketing, 27*(4), 242–256.

Goffman, E. (1959). *The presentation of self in everyday life.* New York: Doubleday Anchor Books.

Grönroos, C. (1990). *Service management and marketing: Managing the moments of truth in service competitions.* Lexington: Lexington Books.

Hansen, D. L., Shneiderman, B., Smith, M. A., & Himelboim, I. (2010). Social media: New technologies of collaboration. In *Analyzing social media networks with NodeXL: Insights from a connected world* (pp. 11–29). Cambridge: Morgan Kaufmann.

Harlow, R. F. (1976). Building a public relations definition. *Public Relations Review, 2*(4), 34–42.

Hennig-Thurau, T., Gwinner, K. P., Walsh, G., & Gremler, D. D. (2004). Electronic word-of-mouth via consumer-opinion platforms: What motivates consumers to articulate themselves on the internet? *Journal of Interactive Marketing, 18*(1), 38–52.

Hoch, S. J., & Loewenstein, G. F. (1991). Time-inconsistent preferences and consumer self-control. *Journal of Consumer Research, 17*(4), 492–507.

Iqani, M. (2018). Consumer culture and the media. In O. Kravets, P. Maclaran, S. Miles, & A. Venkatesh (eds), *The Sage handbook of consumer culture* (pp. 275–289). London: Sage.

Ind, N., & Coates, N. (2013). The meanings of co-creation. *European Business Review, 25*(1), 86–95.

Kaplan, A. M. (2011). If you love something, let it go mobile: Mobile marketing and mobile social media 4x4. *Business Horizons, 55*(2), 129–139.

Kaplan, A. M., & Haenlein, M. (2010). Users of the world, unite! The challenges and opportunities of social media. *Business Horizons, 53*(1), 59–68.

Kapoor, K. K., Dwivedi, Y. K., & Piercy, N. C. (2016). Pay-per-click advertising: A literature review. *The Marketing Review, 16*(2), 183–202.

Kedzior, R., Allen, D. E., & Schroeder, J. (2016). The selfie phenomenon–consumer identities in the social media marketplace. *European Journal of Marketing*, 50(9/10), 1767–1772.

Keller, K. L. (2001a). Mastering the marketing communications mix: Micro and macro perspectives on integrated marketing communication programs. *Journal of Marketing Management*, 17, 819–847.

Keller, K. L. (2001b). *Building customer-based brand equity: A blueprint for creating strong brands* (pp. 3–27). Cambridge: Marketing Science Institute.

Keller, K. L. (2003). Brand synthesis: The multidimensionality of brand knowledge. *Journal of Consumer Research*, 29(4), 595–600.

Keller, K. L. (2009). Building strong brands in a modern marketing communications environment. *Journal of Marketing Communications*, 15(2–3), 139–155.

Keller, K. L. (2016). Unlocking the power of integrated marketing communications: How integrated is your IMC program? *Journal of Advertising*, 45(3), 286–301.

Keller, K. L., Apéria, T., & Georgson, M. (2012). *Strategic brand management: A European perspective*. London: Pearson Education.

Keller, K. L., & Swaminathan, V. (2020). *Strategic brand management: Building, measuring, and managing brand equity* (5th edn). London: Pearson Education.

Khamis, S., Ang, L., & Welling, R. (2017). Self-branding, "micro-celebrity" and the rise of social media influencers. *Celebrity Studies*, 8(2), 191–208.

Kitchen, P. J., Brignell, J., Li, T., & Jones, G. S. (2004). The emergence of IMC: A theoretical perspective. *Journal of Advertising Research*, 44(1), 19–30.

Kumar, V., & Mirchandani, R. (2012). Increasing the ROI of social media marketing. *MIT Sloan Management Review*, 54(1), 55–61.

Lalaounis, S. T. (2017). *Design management: Organisation and marketing perspectives*. London: Routledge.

Llamas, R., & Belk, R. W. (2013). Living in a digital world. In R. W. Belk & R. Llamas (eds), *The Routledge companion to digital consumption* (pp. 3–12). London: Routledge.

Madhavaram, S., Badrinarayanan, V., & McDonald, R. E. (2005). Integrated marketing communication (IMC) and brand identity as critical components of brand equity strategy: A conceptual framework and research propositions. *Journal of Advertising*, 34(4), 69–80.

Mangold, W. G., & Faulds, D. J. (2009). Social media: The new hybrid element of the promotion mix. *Business Horizons*, 52(4), 357–365.

Marwick, A. E. (2015). Instafame: Luxury selfies in the attention economy. *Public Culture*, 27(1/75), 137–160.

Mayzlin, D. (2006). Promotional chat on the Internet. *Marketing Science*, 25(2), 155–163.

McCracken, G. (1986). Culture and consumption: A theoretical account of the structure and movement of the cultural meaning of consumer goods. *Journal of Consumer Research*, 13(1), 71–84.

Meenaghan, T. (1995). The role of advertising in brand image development. *Journal of Product & Brand Management*, 4(4), 23–34.

Morris, P. (2003). *The Bakhtin reader: Selected writings of Bakhtin, Medvedev, and Voloshinov*. London: Arnold.

Mower, S. (2016). Parade's end: Social media is reshaping the fashion show and set design is key to its future. *Wallpaper*, 210, 147–148.

Mulhern, F. (2009). Integrated marketing communications: From media channels to digital connectivity. *Journal of Marketing Communications*, 15(2–3), 85–101.

Ogilvy, D. (1983). *Ogilvy on advertising*. New York: Vintage Books.

Pentina, I., Guilloux, V., & Micu, A. C. (2018). Exploring social media engagement behaviors in the context of luxury brands. *Journal of Advertising*, 47(1), 55–69.

Peston, R. (2017). *WTF: What have we done? Why did it happen? How do we take back control?* London: Hachette.

Peters, T. (1997). The brand called you. *Fast Company, 10*(10), 83–90.

Roberts-Bowman, S. (2016). What is public relations? In A. Theaker (ed.), *The public relations handbook*. London: Routledge.

Rossiter, J. R., & Percy, L. (1987). *Advertising and promotion management*. London: McGraw-Hill.

Schimmel, G. (2019). A ruling influence: South Africa's advertising regulator lays down some ground rules for influencer marketing. *Catalyst, 2*, 32–33.

Short, J., Williams, E., & Christie, B. (1976). *The social psychology of telecommunications*. Hoboken: John Wiley & Sons.

Smith, P. R., & Zook, Z. (2011). *Marketing communications: Integrating offline and online with social media*. Philadelphia: Kogan Page.

CHAPTER 5
Holistic brand experiences and emotional branding

CHAPTER AIMS AND LEARNING OUTCOMES

This chapter corresponds to the second stage of Keller and Swaminathan's (2020) *strategic brand management process*, i.e. designing and implementing brand marketing programmes (see Figure 5.1), and explores branding and consumption from an experiential perspective. In particular, it aims to achieve the following:

1. Provide an understanding of human experiences and discuss experiential perspectives of consumption.
2. Examine the application of the human experiences construct in branding through an exploration of the concepts of the experience economy and experiential marketing.
3. Discuss ways organisations can pursue emotional branding by harnessing the complex human emotion of nostalgia in their brand marketing.
4. Provide a discussion of retro branding and understand its contribution to the development and management of brand meaning.

HOLISTIC BRAND EXPERIENCES

Understanding experiences

The term *experience* can be understood in a number of different ways.

> It is both a noun and a verb and it is used variously to convey the process itself, participating in the activity, the affect or way in which an object, thought or emotion is felt through the senses or the mind, and even the outcome of an experience by way of a skill or learning...
> (Tynan & McKechnie, 2009, pp. 502–503)

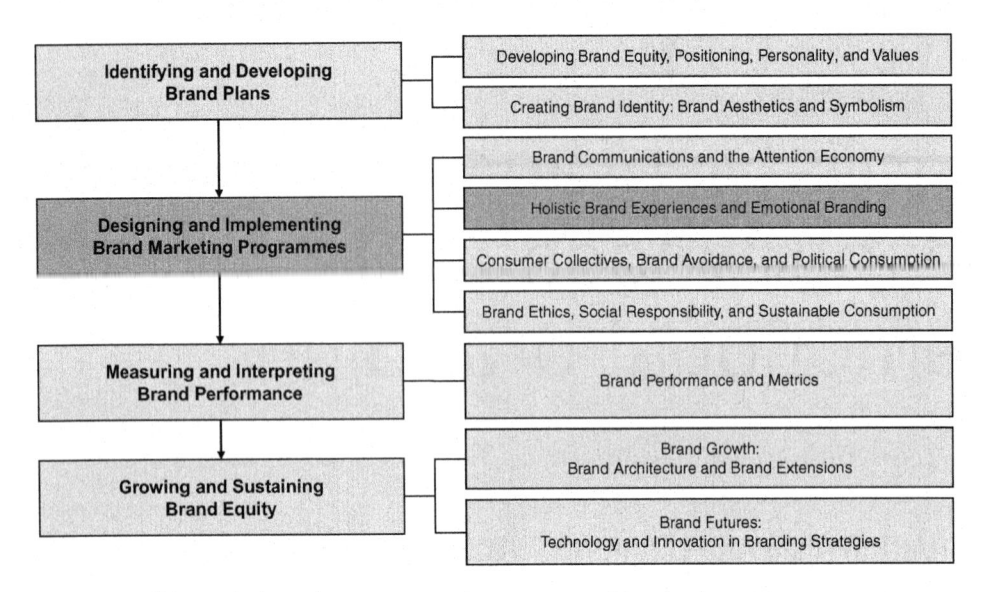

FIGURE 5.1 Strategic brand management process and book plan

It is important to recognise that human experiences are *phenomenal* because a person can never have the same experience twice, and two people can never have the same experience (Coxon, 2015; Pine II & Gilmore, 1998). As Coxon explains, "[e]ven if two people share the same event in close proximity, each of those people will always experience the event to some degree uniquely" (2015, p. 17). It is imperative to state that the subjectivity of experiences means that organisations cannot create experiences *per se*; what they create are experiential stimuli, platforms or contexts which "consumers mobilise to realise their own experiences" (Carù & Cova, 2012, p. 165).

The plethora of ways the concept of experience can be understood has resulted in different interpretations and conceptualisations of experiences in marketing literature, including product experiences, shopping and service experiences, and consumption experiences. *Product experiences* occur when consumers search and evaluate products; these can be direct experiences deriving from physical contact with the product or indirect experiences when the "product is presented virtually or in an advertisement" (Brakus, Schmitt, & Zarantonello, 2009, p. 53). *Shopping and service experiences* result from consumers' interactions with a store's physical environment and personnel, it is thus about how store atmospherics and staff behaviour influence consumers' experiences. *Consumption experiences* are multidimensional experiences occurring when consumers use products with hedonic dimensions (Holbrook & Hirschman, 1982). Finally, *brand experiences* are the "subjective, internal consumer responses (sensations, feelings, and cognitions) and behavioural responses evoked by brand-related stimuli [which make up brand identities]" (Brakus et al., 2009,

p. 53). Thus, brand experiences derive from consumer–brand interactions at various touchpoints (Schmitt & Zarantonello, 2013). An individual's brand experience is always the result of the interaction between the brand and the individual's frame of mind. Of course, one could argue that the phenomenal nature of consumers' experiences makes brand marketers' goal of designing identical brand experiences for each consumer an impossible task. Indeed, brand marketers should aim to create consumers' brand experiences which are as consistent as possible across all individuals within the same target audience.

Experiential view on consumption

Consumer behaviour "is the fascinating and endlessly complex result of a multifaceted interaction between organism and environment" (Holbrook & Hirschman, 1982, p. 139). Humans and things are *entangled* in relationships of dependence, that is, humans (over)depend on things to achieve tasks and make progress, but also things depend on humans for their development and maintenance (Hodder, 2012). The environment can shape people's behaviour and, in return, they can shape the environment through their own actions. An orderly well-designed physical space can generate positive feelings, foster appropriate behaviour, and improve social welfare. Reciprocally, people can influence the environment by conserving nature while constantly making improvements on human-made spaces (see Chapter 7 in Lalaounis, 2017 for more on the concept of entanglement and human experiences).

Holbrook and Hirschman (1982) challenged the information processing model which viewed consumers as merely logical problem-solving decision-makers. They determined an experiential view of consumption, which centres on the pursuit of fantasies, feelings, and fun (3Fs) and is "a primarily subjective state of consciousness with a variety of symbolic meanings, hedonic responses, and aesthetic criteria" (Holbrook & Hirschman, 1982, p. 132). Their framework (see Figure 5.2) suggests that *environmental inputs* such as products, stimulus properties, and communication content, and *consumer inputs* such as resources

> are processed by an *intervening response system* (cognition-affect-behaviour) that generates output consequences which, when appraised against criteria, result in a learning feedback loop. Individual differences, search activity, type of involvement, and task definition affect the criteria by which output consequences are evaluated.
>
> (Holbrook & Hirschman, 1982, p. 132)

The experiential view of consumption concentrates on the symbolic meanings of high-involvement *products*, on the multisensory properties of *stimulus*, and on the syntactic aspects of the *communication content*. The information-processing view of consumption has emphasised the semantic aspects of message content; as we explored in Chapter 3, semantics is about the relationship between a sign and an

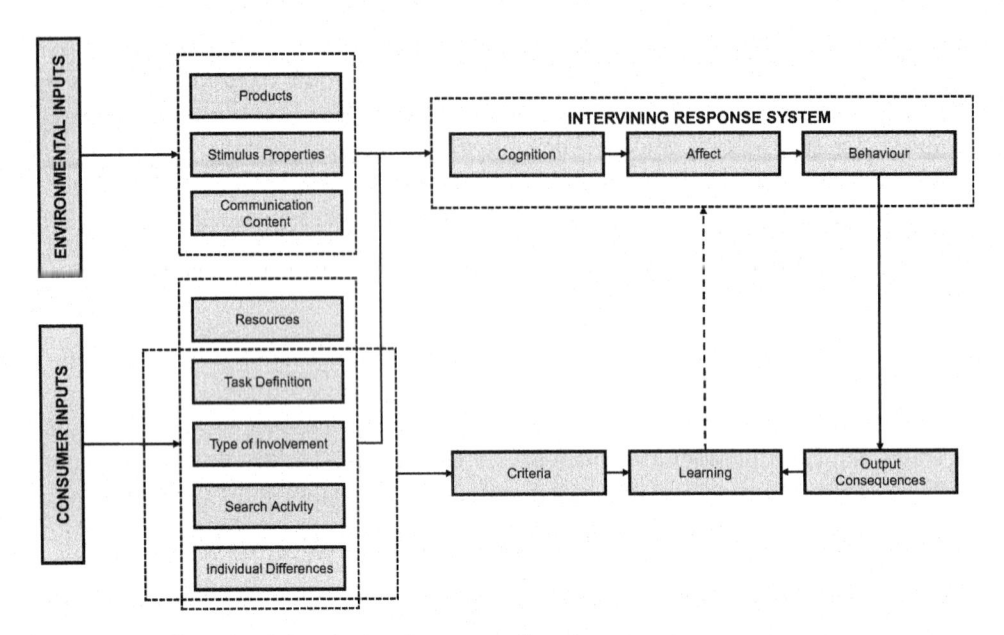

FIGURE 5.2 Experiential aspects of consumption framework

object (Morris, 1939). Instead, the experiential view focuses on the message syntax (the relationships between signs) which can directly impact hedonic responses, e.g. people's emotional responses to music, drawing, and other art forms (Holbrook & Hirschman, 1982). In addition, it focuses on *resources* including not only the monetary cost but also the consumers' allocation of time, as well as on consumer *tasks*, which seek immediate pleasure or gratification, in accordance with Sigmund Freud's *pleasure principle* (Hilgard, 1962). The experiential view on consumption brings attention to the *type of involvement* (cognitive vs. sensory arousal) instead of the degree of consumer involvement (low vs. high), to *search activity* as an exploratory behaviour instead of as merely information acquisition, and to individual differences that go beyond economic, socio-demographic, and psychographic characteristics to include sensation seeking, creativity, religious worldview, perceived time pressure, and engagement with leisure activities (Holbrook & Hirschman, 1982).

With regards to *cognition*, the focus is on subconscious and private cognitive processes, while *affect* includes not only attitudes and preferences (like vs. dislike) but also emotions and feelings. The experiential view recognises that *behaviour* transcends merely purchasing a product; "one's purchase decision is obviously only a small component in the constellation of events involved in the overall consumption experience" (Holbrook & Hirschman, 1982, p. 137), that is, incorporating a product or service in one's daily life. The output consequences of consumption, besides the functional benefits, include hedonic value manifested "in the fun that a consumer derives from a product, the enjoyment that it offers, and the resulting feeling of pleasure that it evokes" (Holbrook & Hirschman, 1982, p. 138). Echoing Howard and Sheth's (1969) traditional model of buyer behaviour, the experiential view of consumption framework indicates

> that learning effects exert a strong impact on future components of the intervening response system...[see Figure 5.2]. [Besides] operant conditioning or instrumental learning, where satisfaction with the purchase serves to reinforce future behavioural responses in the form of repeat purchases...A second principle, contiguity...suggests that sensations, imagery, feelings, pleasures, and other symbolic or hedonic components which are frequently paired together in experience tend to become mutually evocative [respondent conditioning]. [Thus] though satisfaction certainly constitutes one important experiential component – the stream of associations that occur during consumption (imagery, daydreams, emotions) may be equally important experiential aspects of consumer behaviour.
> (Holbrook & Hirschman, 1982, p. 138)

Vargo and Lusch's (2004, 2008) seminal work on the *service-dominant logic* in marketing integrated the notions of goods and services and moved marketing thought and practice in a new direction. It emphasised that consumers co-create value by participating in value-creation networks (Baron & Harris, 2008; Tynan & McKechnie, 2009). Vargo and Lusch (2008) stated that goods are a distribution mechanism for service provision. They argued that the common denominator of exchanges is not goods as previous marketing theories posited, but the application of knowledge and skills (Vargo & Lusch, 2004). They believe that "knowledge and skills can be transferred 1) directly, 2) through education or training, or 3) indirectly by embedding them in objects" (Vargo & Lusch, 2004, p. 9). This means that products are *appliances* that are embodiments of knowledge and skills, e.g. a razor can be the embodiment of shaving skills once performed by trained barbers. These appliances can be considered platforms for fulfilling higher-order needs and desires (Rifkin, 2001), artefacts "around which customers have experiences" (Prahalad & Ramaswamy, 2000, p. 84), and means for achieving emotions such as security, happiness, and accomplishment (Gutman, 1982): "People often purchase goods because owning them, displaying them, and experiencing them...provide satisfaction beyond those associated with the basic functions of the product" (Vargo & Lusch, 2004, p. 9). Value is always uniquely and phenomenologically (experientially) determined by the beneficiary. This means that the "value [co-created] is idiosyncratic, *experiential*, contextual, and meaning laden" (Vargo & Lusch, 2008, p. 7).

The experience economy

Progress of economic value: From commodities to personal experiences

Twenty years ago, US-based brand consultants B. Joseph Pine II and James H. Gilmore, published their seminal work on a new form of economy – the *experience economy* (Pine II & Gilmore, 1998, 1999, 2011). Their main thesis was that post-modern

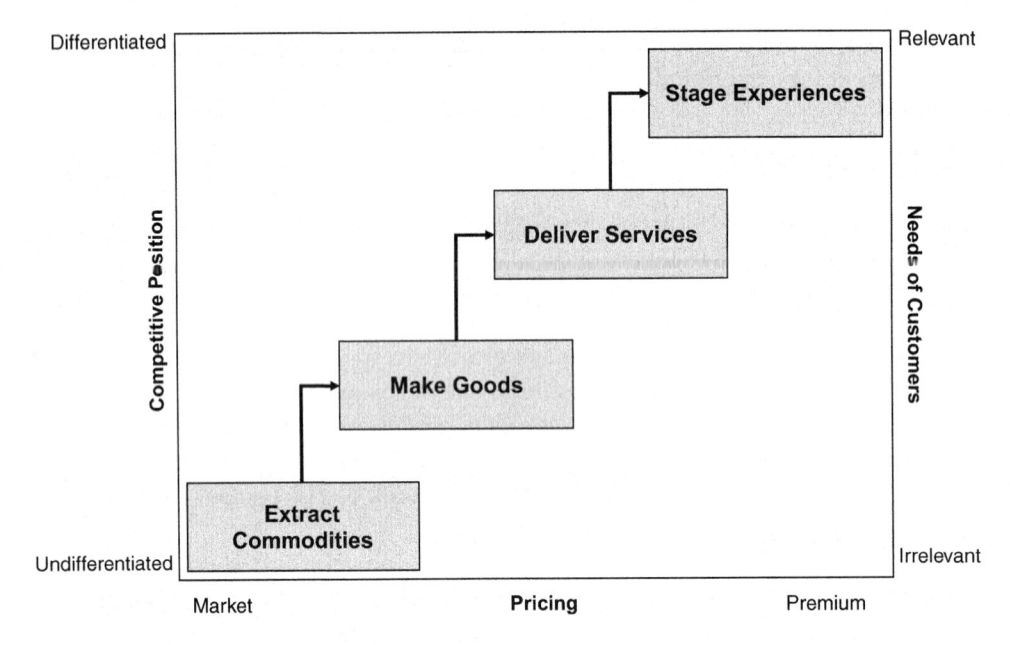

FIGURE 5.3 Progress of economic value

economy has evolved from services to an experience economy, where the new economic offering is memorable personal experiences. They argued that an "experience is not an amorphous construct; it is as real an offering as any service, good, or commodity" (Pine II & Gilmore, 1998, p. 98). This emerging paradigm involves organisations deliberately designing and staging experiences in exchange for a fee. Such experiences occur when an organisation intentionally uses its services as the stage and its goods as props to connect with individual consumers on an emotional, physical, intellectual, and at times, even a spiritual level (Pine II & Gilmore, 1999, 2011).

Pine II and Gilmore (1998, 1999, 2011) explain that economic value has progressed from the agrarian economy where there was an exchange of undifferentiated commodities, irrelevant to consumer needs with their value based on the market, to the industrial economy, and then to the services economy. Eventually we find ourselves in the experience economy where organisations stage differentiated, personally relevant experiences for which they charge a premium price because of their distinctive value. While commodities were fungible (mutually interchangeable), goods were tangible, and services were intangible, experiences are extremely personal and memorable (Pine II & Gilmore, 1998, 1999, 2011) (see Figure 5.3). The organisation, as the experience stager, no longer offers goods or services; it markets personal experiences created within the consumer (Pine II & Gilmore, 1998, 1999, 2011).

Four realms of experiences
In order to identify the types of experiences organisations can stage, we must understand two dimensions that can be used to define four realms of experiences. The first

dimension is the *consumer participation* in the experience, which is about whether the consumer participates in the activity or event that generates the experience, in an active or passive way. On the one hand, a*ctive participation* occurs when consumers play a key role, and on the other hand, *passive participation* happens when consumers do not affect the activity or event. The second dimension is "the *connection*, or environmental relationship, that unites customers with the event" (Pine II & Gilmore, 1998, p. 101). On the one hand, with *absorption* the event or performance occupies "a person's attention by bringing the experience into the mind from a distance" (Pine II & Gilmore, 2011, p. 46) which means that the experience 'goes into' the consumer, and, on the other hand, with *immersion* the consumer becomes "physically (or virtually) a part of the experience itself" (Pine II & Gilmore, 2011, p. 46), which means that the consumer 'goes into' the experience.

Combining these two dimensions in a matrix generates the four realms of experiences (see Figure 5.4). First, with *entertainment* experiences (passive-absorptive) consumers participate passively and have an absorptive connection with the event that yields the experience, e.g. when they watch their favourite sitcom on television or on *Netflix*, or attend a concert of their favourite music band. Second, *educational* experiences (active-absorptive) include a more active participation yet the connection is still absorptive because the experience goes into the consumer, e.g. attending a university lecture where "students are still more outside the event than immersed in the action" (Pine II & Gilmore, 1998, p. 102) yet they can participate by asking and answering questions. Third, *escapist* experiences (active-immersive), which "can teach just as well as educational events can, or amuse just as well as entertainment, but they involve greater customer immersion" (Pine II & Gilmore, 1998, p. 102), e.g. when sky-diving, consumers immerse themselves in the activity

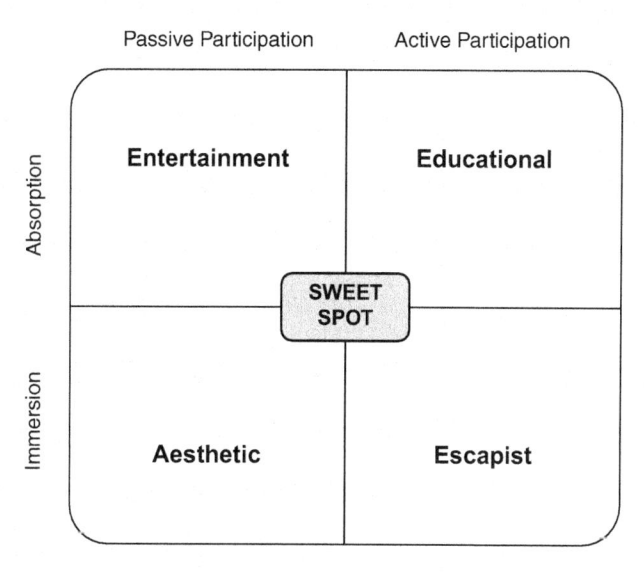

FIGURE 5.4 The four realms of experiences

and play an active role in it. Fourth, *aesthetic* experiences (passive-immersive) where consumers are immersed in the event or activity but they have little or no influence on it, e.g. visiting an art gallery, consumers can immerse themselves in the art exhibited but they cannot have an effect on it (Pine II & Gilmore, 1998).

Ideally, organisations should seek to create experiences that incorporate aspects of all realms; Pine II and Gilmore (1998) call the point where they all meet the *sweet spot*. Perhaps, a vivid example of staging experiences, which achieve the combination of these realms, is *Nike Town*. Based on an ethnographic study, Peñaloza (1998) explains that *Nike Town* is a hybrid experiential consumption institution, which combines

> qualities of a commercial store with those of a *non*-commercial museum [emphasis in the original]…When juxtaposed with the qualities of a museum, the store experience changes from touching and buying/not buying to emphasizing a way of looking and valuing its contents, which further enhances the spectacle. Analogously, when juxtaposed with the qualities of a store, the museum experience blends not touching or owning the objects with being able to do both, hence evoking desire and facilitating its satisfaction by means of an imaginative remuneration or purchase.
>
> (Peñaloza, 1998, p. 388)

Despite the popularity of concept of the experience economy, it has attracted some criticism from other scholars. Pine II and Gilmore (1998) have stressed that the difference between the experience economy and the (previous) service economy is mainly qualitative. However, Raghunathan (2008) argues that

> the thesis that experiential offerings are qualitatively different from those that came before is…untenable…because there is no well-accepted set of (necessary and sufficient) conditions that can be applied to assess whether a consumption offering is an exceptional service or a great experience…The difference between experiences and services may, therefore, potentially be a matter of degree – staging a memorable experience may involve going the extra mile or being more creative than when delivering a great service – which points to a quantitative (rather than a qualitative) difference.
>
> (Raghunathan, 2008, p. 138)

In addition, Gupta and Vajic (2000) warn that if the staging of experiences is executed in a superficial manner to add entertainment value, the value will wear off once the novelty is gone, and what remains might be a hollow core. Most importantly, Schmitt (2011) argues that Pine II and Gilmore's (1998, 1999, 2011) conceptualisation of experiences as events or 'event-like' economic offerings reduces the scope of the experience economy to merely a small part of most economies. He posits that rather than entering a new economic stage, it may be more appropriate to view business attention to experiences as a new way of marketing products and services, and even consumer commodities (such as salt, pepper, or produce). The experiential value would then not exist in the commodities, products or services per se, but in the marketing of these items.

(Schmitt, 2011, p. 15)

The above reflects the fundamental difference between the concepts of the experience economy and experiential marketing (discussed in the following section). Finally, according to Holbrook (2000), Pine II and Gilmore's (1999) "energy and breadth of focus [in their investigation of the] topic...[is] both admirable and refreshing" (Holbrook, 2000. p. 179) yet their conceptualisation of progression of economic value is rather problematic. Pine II and Gilmore's (1999) thesis encourages brand marketers to "think of all products as experiences staged for guests – even in cases of experiential products for which this viewpoint might be counterproductive (such as education, medical services, clinical social work, or the penal system)" (Holbrook, 2000. p. 180). Furthermore, this conceptualisation disagrees with Holbrook and Hirschman's (1982) experiential view on consumption, which advocates the maxim that "*all* products involve goods that perform services to provide consumption experiences. This conflation of goods-services-and-experiences applies...to every sort of experiential consumption...In other words, *every* consumption event provides some form of experience(s) [emphases in the original]" (Holbrook, 2000, p. 180). Holbrook (2000) agrees with Pine II and Gilmore's (1999) argument that the *sweet spot*, which incorporates all four realms of experiences, will create a captivating experience, but he views their advising organisations to charge a fee for what used to be free as absurd because, for example, brand marketers cannot and should not charge customers a fee for entering a store and browsing through merchandise (Holbrook, 2000).

Experiential marketing

Columbia University professor, Bernd Schmitt (1999a, 1999b) introduced the concept of *experiential marketing* and explained that

> today, customers take functional features and benefits, product quality, and a positive brand image as a given. What they want is products, communications, and marketing campaigns that dazzle their senses, touch their hearts, and stimulate their minds. They want products, communications, and campaigns that they can relate to and that they can incorporate into their lifestyles.

(Schmitt, 1999b, p. 22)

Holbrook (2000) agrees with the above statement but disagrees with the way it is formulated. He argues that it is not consumers who have changed, instead it is brand marketers who have changed and revised their understanding of consumers. The latter have always wanted and valued consumption experiences, it is simply that brand marketers had failed in the past to recognise this and harness the potential of experiences.

Schmitt (1999a, 1999b) argued that unlike traditional marketing, experiential marketing 1) recognises that consumers are not only rational but also emotional decision-makers, 2) shifts the focus from functional features and benefits to experiences, 3) does not narrowly define product category and competition, and 4) considers every situation as idiosyncratic, which means that methods and tools for collecting consumer information are eclectic, diverse, and multifaceted. Experiential marketers seldom only consider direct competitors; instead they view the product as part of a consumption experience within a specific social context. This experience can involve other products, and experiential marketers seek to make synergies between their brands and these products (even when these are their competitors' products). A *Rimel London* mascara is part of an individual's make-up experience involving numerous other products situated within the cultural context of socially accepted (or expected) beauty look.

It is evident that the concept of the experience economy, which states that organisations seek to market (stage) experiences as their economic offering (Pine II & Gilmore, 1998, 1999, 2011) is different to experiential marketing, which is concerned with organisations marketing products and services in an experiential way (Schmitt, 1999a, 1999b). The experiential marketing paradigm suggests that it is during the process of experientially marketing products or services where experiences emerge. The experience economy focuses on experiences marketed as the core offering, in contrast with experiential marketing, which concentrates on the process.

The experiential marketing concept has two main components. First, the strategic experiential modules (SEMs), which form its strategic underpinning and are essentially the five types of experiences organisations can create for their target audiences; these include sense, feel, think, act, and relate experiences. Second, the experience providers (ExPros), which are the "implementation tools of experiential marketing" (Schmitt 1999a, p. 62). Our experiences are mediated by the things around us; this means that organisations can influence human experiences through their brands' properties, products, presentations, and publications (Schmitt & Simonson, 1997). Experience providers include: 1) communications, 2) visual and verbal identity, 3) products (and services), 4) co-branding activities (events, sponsorship, and product placement), 5) spatial environments, 6) websites and electronic media, and 7) people. We can draw parallels between the five SEMs and Holbrook and Hirschman's (1982) conceptualisation of fantasies, feelings and fun.

> *Fantasies* [include] all aspects of experientially oriented cognitions...which encompass [the] sense and think [SEMs] – especially with respect to [the] emphasis on sensory and aesthetic elements and on thoughts consistent with convergent,

divergent, directional, and associative ideation. *Feelings* [emphasise] the various consumption-related affects [connecting with]...the hedonic, pleasure-seeking aspects of moods, emotions, or other affective responses [feel SEM]. *Fun* [refers] to various play- or leisure-oriented aspects of behaviour [act SEM].

(Holbrook, 2000, p. 182)

Let us now explore these five types of experiences (SEMs) in more depth.

Sense experiences

Building on our extensive discussion of aesthetics and sensory marketing in Chapter 3, *sense* experiences appeal to the five human senses: sight, sound, touch, taste, and smell, and have three strategic objectives: differentiation, motivation, and value provision (Hultén, 2015; Schmitt, 1999a, 1999b). They lead to "aesthetic pleasure, excitement, beauty, and satisfaction through sensory stimulation [and delight]" (Schmitt, 1999b, p. 99). Sense experiences can act as a *differentiator* when they are executed in an unusual way, so that they go beyond what target consumers have been accustomed to. Sense experiences can act as a *motivator* when they can motivate consumers to purchase and use the product or service, and as a *value-provider* when they generate added value for the consumer, which of course requires that the organisation understands the kind of sense experiences its target audience desire.

These objectives are not mutually exclusive, quite the contrary. Schmitt (1999b) proposes the stimuli–processes–consequences (S-P-C) model which combines three stages to achieve the highest sensory impact. The first stage relates to the differentiator objective and involves the organisation deciding on which *stimuli* are the most appropriate. The human brain is more interested in stimuli that are vivid (attention-getting), salient (which stands out), and meaningful, i.e. it is relevant to what is already known. The second stage relates to the motivator objective, and determines how to create these experiences, i.e. the *process*, thus making decisions about which modalities to combine (which senses to target), which experience providers to use to deliver these, and how to organise these across time and space. The third stage relates to the value-provider objective and is about the consequences of the sensory stimulation and delight; the fundamental question here is whether the organisation intends to create an experience which aims to please (pleasing beauty) (e.g. *Singapore Airlines* or *Starbucks*), excite (e.g. *Nike* or *Apple* stores), or both (Schmitt, 1999b).

Feel experiences

Schmitt states "*[f]eel* marketing is the strategy and implementation of attaching affect to the company and brand via experience providers. [This] requires a clear understanding of how to create feeling during the consumption experience" (1999b, p. 118). Face-to-face interactions are the strongest cause of feelings in consumption situations. Consumers are pleasure-seekers; they want to feel good. This means that feelings and emotions are extremely important to human nature and people try to avoid whatever makes them feel bad. Emotional experiences range from moods to strong emotions. *Moods* are unspecific, which means that individuals sometimes cannot identify the cause of their mood states. Contrastingly, emotions are more intense and humans can identify their cause such as objects (products), agents (people, and institutions), and events (things that happen). There are two types of emotions: basic and complex emotions. Basic emotions include feeling happy, sad, angry, and excited, while complex emotions are combinations of basic emotions, e.g. nostalgia. Emotional branding, and in particular nostalgia, will be discussed in more depth in the second part of this chapter. *British Airways* has incorporated feelings of nostalgia and pride in its advertising messages to harness its heritage and make connections with its brand slogan, 'To Fly. To Serve'.

Think experiences

Think experiences seek to engage consumers in creative thinking, attracting their acute attention, and building intriguing long-lasting relationships with the brand. Engaging consumers in elaborative thinking can result in the consumer re-evaluating the brand. A classic example of a think advertising campaign include *Apple*'s 'Think Different' campaign (in response to *IBM*'s 'Think' campaign) aired in 1997, which featured inspirational people of the twentieth century, including Albert Einstein, Maria Callas, Richard Branson, and others; geniuses who challenged the status quo and changed the world. Gobé (2009) warns that urging people to think differently and creatively cannot work effectively if the product and/or brand is not innovative and does not trigger such creative endeavours. Commenting on *Apple*'s 'Think Different' campaign, he articulately explains this point with the following:

> While the advertising was arresting and original, I personally could not equate something so profound as the larger-than-life personalities of Martin Luther King and Gandhi with a commercial brand. It felt to me like desperation at its best (or worst), from an advertising perspective – no product news to communicate, nothing else to say. Then came the iMac, and suddenly, 'Think Different' made sense, I could see just *how* [emphasis in the original] Apple was thinking differently about technology! The motto was validated by the product – an innovative, well designed, relevant one. The association between the advertising and the product was vivid, evident, and real.
>
> (Gobé, 2009, pp. 119–20)

It is well established that any creative endeavour requires both convergent and divergent thinking. These two types of thinking form two different modes of cognitive operation. *Convergent thinking* is about narrowing one's mental focus, concentrating in order to converge on a solution, whereas *divergent thinking* is about broadening one's mental focus, expanding to different directions to come up with new and different ideas (Guilford, 1950). Divergent thinking requires cognitive fluency, flexibility, originality, and elaboration and is vital for creativity. Nevertheless, both convergent and divergent thinking are essential in the creative process and must go hand in hand (Woodman, Sawyer, & Griffin, 1993). Schmitt (1999b) suggests that different kind of campaigns will target a different type of thinking. *Directional* think campaigns involve convergent thinking because they "spell out precisely what or how customers are supposed to think about the options put in front of them" (Schmitt, 1999b, p. 146). In contrast, *associative* think campaigns involve divergent thinking as they "make prominent use of more abstract, generic concepts as well as diffused visual imagery" (Schmitt, 1999b, p. 146).

Schmitt (1999b) provides his own recipe for creating successful think campaigns, including three objectives: surprise, intrigue, and provoke. *Surprise* requires the brand to visually, verbally, or conceptually depart from a common expectation so consumers get more than, or something different to, what they asked, leading to their delight. *Intrigue* targets individuals' curiosity, puzzling, fascinating, or challenging their ingenuity and deeply held assumptions. Social advertising campaigns seek to raise awareness about social issues such as domestic abuse, and challenge the social stigma associated with reporting such behaviours. *Provoke* involves campaigns which

> can stimulate discussion, create controversy – or shock, depending on [organisational] intentions and the intended target group. Provocations may appear irreverent and aggressive, and they can be risky if they go overboard, i.e. if they exceed good taste or violate morality.
>
> (Schmitt, 1999b, p. 152)

An example that serves as the epitome of provocative think campaigns going overboard is past *United Colors of Benetton*'s advertising. Although intriguing at their best, many of the print adverts were exceedingly provocative if not desperate for attention. Gobé argues "these moralistic ads, steeped in pedagogy, are more of a ploy to get their brand attention than a sincere attempt to either make a statement or build brand awareness" (2009, p. 237). He explains that the reason these campaigns failed was that they did not attempt to make the necessary connections with the product or people of *Benneton*, leading to market underperformance in the United States. Gobé (2009) claims that "provocation is not a business strategy, just a short-term tactic to claim the spotlight…Brands need to clearly express humanistic solution messages in line with their consumers' concerns and demonstrate that they are sensitive and supportive of the consumers' values" (Gobé, 2009, p. 236). Evidently, the use of provocation in brand marketing should be pursued with caution and moderation. Similarly, engaging consumers in convergent and divergent thinking should be planned carefully by brand marketers, as too much convergent thinking can be dangerous because it might make consumers 'overthink' the experience, while divergent thinking requires knowledge and should be avoided unless the consumer has the necessary knowledge about the area/topic of the experiential campaign. Brand marketers should have a clear understanding of the type and level of consumer knowledge so they make an informed decision on whether to target divergent thinking or not. Ultimately, it is very important that the campaign appeals to an appropriate thinking frame in light of the idiosyncrasies of the brand (Schmitt, 1999b).

Act experiences

According to (Schmitt, 1999b), *act* experiences enhance a person's life by positively influencing his/her bodily experiences, lifestyles, and interactions with other people; act experiences can also demonstrate to consumers an alternative way of doing things. As far as bodily experiences are concerned, by nature the human body produces sensations and perceptions of the outside environment (through the five senses discussed in Chapter 3) and is a rich source of experiences. The marketing of bodily experiences relies on developing appropriate products, stimulation, and atmosphere. However, it is important to note that in some cultures, body functions are considered a taboo as they relate to personal and private activities such as body washing, sexuality, disease, and substance addiction, hence it is imperative that brand marketers consider local and regional cultural values when designing bodily experiences. The general suggestion is that organisations should "locate [their] marketing close to a place where physical desires are most likely to arise…, [to] not only create an experience but simultaneously reinforce it" (Schmitt, 1999b, p. 164).

Lifestyle is "a person's pattern of living in the world as expressed in the person's activities, interests, and opinions" (Kotler, 1994, p. 182). Nowadays consumption is meaning-based as individuals consume not only to satisfy their functional needs, but also their emotional, social, and symbolic needs. People seek brands they can incorporate into their lifestyles and help them construct, maintain, and communicate their identity (Belk, 1988). Brand marketers need to stay in tune with lifestyle trends, and ideally drive these trends, creating brands that become part of target audience's daily life, providing appropriate lifestyle experiences (Schmitt, 1999b). A great example of a lifestyle brand that encourages physical experiences is *Nike*, which has become part of many people's way of life and often drives consumer trends. From its 'Just do it' slogan to campaigns such as 'Achieve your greatness', *Nike* has always encouraged people to take on physical activity and pursue a healthy and active lifestyle.

Finally, act experiences can involve one's interactions with other people. Naturally a person is not only influenced by his/her own beliefs, attitudes, and intentions, but also by social norms and the beliefs of reference groups. The physical and social behaviour of the interacting parties will influence the interaction experiences. Organisations need to create physical environments that facilitate appropriate perceptions and interactions. With continuous advances of customer service technology, an important strategic question organisations face is whether to automate or personate, that is, whether services are delivered by machines, or by humans, maintaining face-to-face interactions between employees and customers. For example, financial services organisations can offer both; automated services, with cash automatic withdrawal and deposit machines, and in-person services, with employees at their local branches (Schmitt, 1999b).

Relate experiences

Relate experiences go beyond sensations, moods and emotions, cognitions, actions, and interactions generated by sensory, feel, think, and act experiences respectively, to create a relationship between the individual self and the broader socio-cultural context the brand reflects (Schmitt, 1999b). Relate experiences "imply a connection with other people, other social groups (occupational, ethnic, or lifestyle, for example) or a broader, more abstract social entity such as a nation, society or culture" (Schmitt, 1999b, p. 171). Relate experiences often contain aspects of, and can lead to, the other four types of experiences. Nevertheless, the main objective of relate experiences is fostering and maintaining consumer relationships with the social meaning of the brand (Schmitt, 1999b). Consumer possessions "become a summary representation of these…abstract social entities in a variety of consumption contexts" (Schmitt, 1999b, pp. 172–173). This echoes Belk's (1988) concept of the *extended self* as he explained that

> we cannot hope to understand consumer behaviour without first gaining some understanding of the meanings that consumers attach to possessions. A key to understanding what possessions mean is recognising that, knowingly or unknowingly, intentionally or unintentionally, we regard our possessions as part of ourselves.
>
> (Belk, 1988, p. 139)

Relate experiences can harness the power of *social influence*; social psychology indicates that a person's thoughts and behaviour can be influenced by face-to-face interactions, known as *actual presence*, and by *imagined* or *implicit presence*, which involves people's belief that "they can change their identity or membership in a reference group by purchasing a certain brand" (Schmitt, 1999b, p. 175). Relate experiences can enable an individual to connect with other people, social groups, and cultures through the brand. They can capitalise on people's need to belong and to find meaning through *social categorisation* and *social identity*. People tend to describe themselves or be described by others in terms of social categories.

> These individual and complex categories are often not merely descriptive but become 'prototypical' or stereotypical images that are used by showing certain user types in relate communications campaigns. Prototypes serve an important function for individuals: they provide them with a sense of social identity. Social identity is defined as the part of the individual's self-concept, which is affected by the knowledge of membership in a social group.
>
> (Schmitt, 1999b, p. 175)

Relate experiences can also be based on kin relations, that is, one's relations with family, relatives, and other loved ones. A good example of a brand which builds its entire ethos on the love of kin which comes naturally, and on the notion of family heritage, is *Patek Philippe*, the Swiss luxury watchmaker whose slogan claims that "[y]ou never actually own a Patek Philippe, you merely look after it for the next generation. Begin your *own* tradition [emphasis in the original]" (www.patek.com). Apart from kinship, social relationships can be formed with other people in a more generalised or abstract way through *social roles* such as a woman feeling affinity with other women in general (Schmitt, 1999b).

However, relate experiences that harness social roles depend on *cultural values*, hence, they have to take into consideration local cultural norms to be successful. A typical dichotomy used to describe cross-cultural differences is the individualism versus collectivism distinction. *Individualism* is associated with Western cultures and puts emphasis on an independent view of the self, shows preference for personal goals, focuses on needs and rights, and on rational analysis of relations. In contrast, *collectivism* is associated with Eastern cultures; "members of collectivist societies… describe themselves as part of groups [interdependent view of the self], subordinate personal to group goals, [focus on obligations and duties, and]…derive strong attachments from belonging to a group" (Schmitt, 1999b, p. 180), emphasising the importance of developing and keeping relations. This means that messages of self-reliance, assertiveness and differentiation from others will suit better individualist consumers, whereas messages about how to assimilate oneself with a reference group will appeal to collectivist consumers. According to Hofstede, Hofstede, and Minkov (2010) besides *individualism–collectivism*, other dimensions based on which we can analyse cultural values include *power distance* (strength of social hierarchy), *masculinity–femininity*, *uncertainty avoidance*, *long-term orientation*, and *indulgence–restraint*. Unquestionably, relate experiential marketing strategies will have to be tailored to the characteristics of each cultural context targeted by the organisation.

Thorough knowledge of reference group norms is a prerequisite for developing powerful relate experiences. When seeking to harness social categorisation in their experiential marketing strategies, brand marketers should do the following:

> 1)…create or allude to a certain social category X, 2)…get customers to apply the label 'I am X', 3)…persuade them that labelling themselves as 'part of X' provides a positive experience, and 4)…show them that they can create this positive experience by consuming a certain brand.
>
> (Schmitt, 1999b, p. 184)

Finally, relate experiences can harness the power of *brand communities* (explored in the next chapter). Brand communities emphasise not only the relationship between the consumer and the brand, but also the multiple relationships of one consumer-enthusiast of the brand with other consumers-enthusiasts of the same brand (Muñiz Jr. & O'Guinn, 2001). Consumers create shared brand experiences and can take the brand in directions different to what brand marketers intend to. In summary, "the key challenge of relate experiences is the selection of the right reference group and reference appeal that creates a differentiating social identity for customers by celebrating the group or culture that customers want to be part of" (Schmitt, 1999b, pp. 188–189).

Brand experiences, satisfaction, and loyalty

Brakus et al. (2009) recognised the need to identify the dimensions of brand experience in similar fashion that Aaker (1997) identified the five dimensions of brand personality. Their extensive research study led to a typology of four dimensions: *sensory*, *affective*, *behavioural*, and *intellectual*. Readers will notice that while these dimensions reflect four of the aforementioned SEMs (sense, feel, think, and act), relate is not included. Although there was a *social* dimension in Brakus et al.'s (2009) initial model, their empirical results led them to drop this dimension in the final configuration of their typology. Their study also tested whether brand experience impacts consumer satisfaction and loyalty directly, and indirectly through brand personality as an associative concept (see Figure 5.5). They explained their results with the following:

> Notably, there are differential effects of brand experience and brand personality on satisfaction and loyalty. The direct effect of experience on loyalty…is higher than the direct effect of experience on satisfaction…; however, the direct effect of brand personality on loyalty…is lower than the direct effect of brand personality on satisfaction…Thus, brand experience seems to be a stronger predictor of actual buying behaviour than brand personality, which in turn is a better predictor of satisfaction. This result may be related to the very nature of experience. If a brand stimulates the senses, makes the person feel good, and engages the mind and body, a stimulation seeking organism may strive to receive such stimulation again. In contrast, the private nature of experiences may make them less malleable and less subject to situational influences than the more social and self-expressive brand personalities.
>
> (Brakus et al., 2009, p. 65)

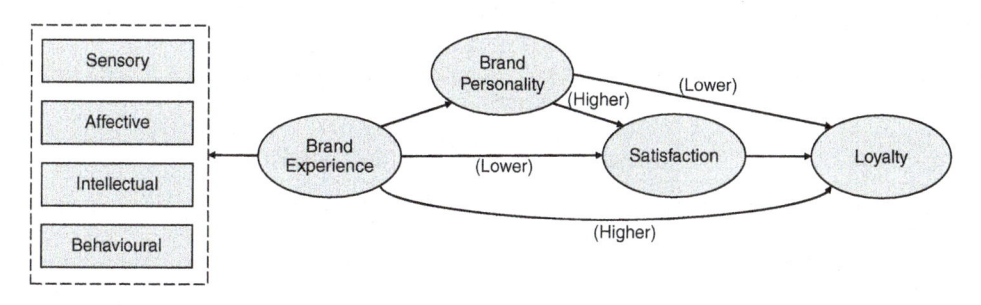

FIGURE 5.5 Impact of brand experience on consumer satisfaction and loyalty

EMOTIONAL BRANDING: NOSTALGIA AND RETRO BRANDING

Consumption emotions

"Emotional branding is the conduit [i.e. channel] by which people connect subliminally with companies and their products in an emotionally profound way" (Gobé, 2009, p. xxix). Attaching appropriate emotion to the brand can be a successful brand marketing strategy because humans are emotional decision-makers and "we all respond emotionally to our life experiences and we naturally project emotional values onto the objects around us" (Gobé, 2009, p. xxix). Individuals often develop as strong relationships with their possessions as with other people, and their love for objects can frequently be a substitute for challenging emotional relationships with people (Heilbrunn, 2018).

As mentioned earlier, face-to-face interactions with organisational employees are the strongest cause of feelings in consumption situations. Thus, it is essential to discuss at this stage the variety of emotions that a consumer may feel during purchase and consumption. In her seminal study, Richins (1997) determined the *Consumption Emotions Set* (CES), an extensive list of positive and negative emotions which occur in consumption situations (see Table 5.1). Schmitt (1999b) distilled and organised these consumption emotions on a useful matrix using two dimensions: inward–outward and positive–negative (see Table 5.2). Inward feelings are emotions you

TABLE 5.1 Consumption emotions set

anger	envy	optimism	eagerness	impatient
discontent	loneliness	joy	relief	longing
worry	romantic love	excitement	awed	nostalgic
sadness	love	surprise	carefree	rotective
fear	peacefulness	guilt	comforted	wishful
shame	contentment	pride	helpless	

Source: Based on Richins (1997).

TABLE 5.2 Typology of consumption emotions

	Inward	Outward
POSITIVE	Warm-hearted	Pleased
	Sentimental	Excited
	Loving	Enthusiastic
NEGATIVE	Frustrated	Embarrassed
	Irritated	Ashamed
	Angry	Humiliated

Source: Based on Schmitt (1999b).

are likely to keep to yourself, whereas outward feelings as those you are likely to express and show to others. In his arrangement, *inward-positive* emotions include feeling warm-hearted, sentimental, and loving, these feelings "make you feel special; you are likely to show understated customer loyalty (but without outward publicity)" (Schmitt, 1999b, p. 133). *Outward-positive* emotions involve feeling pleased, excited, and enthusiastic which make consumers praise, spend more, and make recommendations to others. Contrastingly, *inward-negative* emotions include feeling frustrated, irritated, and angry, making consumers more likely to complain about, or sabotage, the brand and the organisation. *Outward-negative* emotions involve feeling embarrassed, humiliated, and ashamed, and in such situations consumers will never go back to the brand (see Table 5.2). Needless to say that organisations must avoid negative- inward and outward emotions; failing to create positive emotions among your target audiences hinders brand development strategy as the two upper layers of the Customer-Based Brand Equity (CBBE) pyramid model (Keller, 2001) (brand judgements and feelings, and brand resonance) cannot be successfully achieved, therefore the organisation cannot reach the highest level of brand loyalty and achieve strong brand equity (Keller & Swaminathan, 2020).

Defining nostalgia

Nostalgia is a human emotion brand marketers have increasingly been exploring over the last two decades as part of 'feel' experiential strategy because people live longer and the world's population is ageing (Schmitt, 1999b). Etymologically, the word nostalgia comes from the Greek *nostos* (νόστος) which means 'to return home or to one's native land' and *algos* (ἄλγος) which means 'pain, suffering or grief' (Daniels, 1985; Hofer, 1934). Therefore, nostalgia is all about the yearning we often feel for an earlier period in our lives coupled with the harsh realisation that a return to the past or to a distant situation is not possible. It is a complex and bittersweet emotion that combines basic positive emotions of "warmth, joy, and affection…[deriving from] the pleasant memory of the past…, with a sense of loss associated with the realisation that the past cannot be recreated" (Holak & Havlena, 1998, p. 222). Hence, nostalgia can be placed between inward and outward positive emotions with a hint of negative emotions, which proves its complexity. Brand marketers seeking to infuse nostalgia in their experiential marketing strategy must make sure that any links with a past memory is combined with reducing the sense of loss associated with the nostalgic feeling (Holak & Havlena, 1998). Some studies on nostalgia (e.g. Batcho (1995) and Holbrook & Schindler (2003)) have indicated that people "generally associate more positive than negative feelings with the past when asked about nostalgia" (Loveland, Smeesters, & Mandel, 2010, p. 394). Nostalgia is a uniquely private emotion, because what is nostalgic for one person might leave everyone else indifferent (Davis, 1979). Hence, nostalgia is defined as

> a preference (general liking, positive attitude or favourable effect) towards experiences associated with objects (people, places or things) that were more

common (popular, fashionable or widely circulated) when one was younger (in early adulthood, in adolescence, in childhood or even before birth).

(Holbrook & Schindler, 2003, p. 108)

The above statement raises the question of whether or not one can be nostalgic for a period or situations he/she has not lived through; certainly it seems that Holbrook and Schindler (2003) think that we can have a yearning for people, places, or things that predate our life span. Many could dismiss this as an impossible thought, yet some scholars support this argument (Davis, 1979; Havlena & Holak, 1991). When a "generation both privately and collectively reminisces about its adolescence, these memories become, in essence, a new experience for the next generation" (Havlena & Holak, 1991, p. 326). As today's youth reaches middle age their nostalgic thoughts will also contain some of their parents' nostalgic memories (Davis, 1979) and when they become elderly they will repeat their own, their parents', and even their grandparents' nostalgic stories. As we will explore later, this can help organisations develop (communal) nostalgia-based messages.

Nostalgia: A multidimensional phenomenon

Over the years, nostalgia has been explored as a medical, a historical, a psychological, and a sociological phenomenon. Hofer (1934) was the first to explore nostalgia and described it as a *clinical* condition with psychophysical symptoms where the mind affects the body. As a *historical* phenomenon, nostalgia has often appeared in literature and poetry referring to one's feeling of homesickness, for instance, Odysseus' yearning to go back to Ithaca, his island-kingdom, in Homer's epic *Odyssey*. From a *psychological* perspective, nostalgia has been described as one's desire to return to his/her mother's womb (Havlena & Holak, 1991): "Freud (1906) illustrates perhaps more simply the 'message of nostalgia': the desire to return to a hidden home, to monuments concocted of our wanderings through the half-forgotten memories of another time, festooned and elaborated by our present fantasies" (Daniels, 1985, p. 379). Nostalgic feelings bring to the fore memories of the past, however, these memories may be distorted generating a more positive picture of the past than what reality would indicate (Davis, 1979).

More recent perspectives on nostalgia have of course questioned the pathological nature of nostalgia and have explored the phenomenon from a *sociological* perspective. Scholarly work in the last thirty years demonstrates a 'de-psychologisation' of nostalgia due to the increasing mobility of post-modern society where people are less attached to a particular location reframing what homesickness means when referring to nostalgic emotions. A sociological perspective elevates the value of nostalgia in society. Nostalgia is considered a way for people to preserve their identity when faced with major life transitions which operate as discontinuities in their life cycles (Havlena & Holak, 1991). Such life transitions can include when one moves "from childhood...[to] adolescence to adulthood...[or] from single life to married life" (Havlena & Holak, 1991, p. 325); it is very likely that most of us have felt nostalgic feelings when going through such changes in our lives. Of course, the propensity to have nostalgic feelings fluctuates over one's lifetime.

> Not all past experiences and eras are equally likely to evoke nostalgic feelings. Nostalgia for adolescence and early adulthood [such as one's university student years] appears to be stronger than for any other period...'Nostalgia-proneness' has been hypothesised to peak as individuals move into middle age and during the 'retirement' years.
>
> (Havlena & Holak, 1991, p. 325)

Belk believes that nostalgia can "be prompted by an object, a scene, a smell, or strain of music" (1990, p. 670). In an exploratory study including the collection of consumers' (participants') introspective vignettes, essays and stereographic photographs, Holbrook and Schindler (2003) identified ten different, yet overlapping, *categories* of objects with potential for developing nostalgic bonding (see Table 5.3).

TABLE 5.3 Categories of nostalgic objects

Categories	Characteristics
Sensory experiences	Objects associated with pleasurable sensory experiences from one's youth (e.g. perfumes or food).
Homeland	Objects related to a distant location (e.g. one's homeland).
Rites of passage	Objects associated with transitional moments.
Friendships and loved ones	Cherished objects from the past which signify close relationships with family, friends, and other loved ones, as well as objects which represent eras gone yet unforgotten.
Gifts of love	Valued objects presented as gifts by loved ones which act as tangible symbols of human affection.
Security	"[O]bjects linked with aspects of continuity valued as tokens of security among otherwise troubled familial or other interpersonal relationships" (Holbrook & Schindler, 2003, p. 117).
Breaking away	Objects associated with freedom to travel (e.g. a bike, a souvenir, or an old atlas).
Arts and entertainment	Objects which allow owners to travel not in physical terms but to achieve a spiritual sense of freedom (e.g. books, musical recordings, and music players).
Performance and competence	Objects used as tools in one's own trade (e.g. a hairdresser's first pair of professional scissors, or a medical doctor's first stethoscope).
Creativity	"Objects from the past associated with artistic creativity...and with musical prowess" (Holbrook & Schindler, 2003, p. 120) (e.g. old musical instruments).

Source: Based on Holbrook & Schindler (2003).

Orders and types of nostalgia

According to Davis (1979), there are three orders or levels of nostalgic experiences: simple, reflexive, and interpreted nostalgia. First, *simple nostalgia* is related to regular yearning to return to the past because of the basic belief (or misconception) that things were much better then. Second, *reflexive nostalgia* occurs when people "question or analyse the past rather than sentimentalise it, [asking] 'what is it really that way?'" (Havlena & Holak, 1991, p. 326). Third, with *interpreted nostalgia*, instead of critically analysing the past (as in reflexive nostalgia), one deeply analyses the nostalgic response itself by asking "questions concerning its sources, typical character, significance, and psychological purpose. 'Why am I feeling nostalgic?'" (Davis, 1979, p. 24). Organisations should seek to create the first level of nostalgic experiences, simple nostalgia, and avoid the other two. Brand messages should not encourage a critical examination of the past (reflexive nostalgia) and/or a critical interpretation of one's nostalgic feelings (interpreted nostalgia) as both would reduce the power of nostalgia due to a mental consideration of negative information.

Davis (1979) has also identified two types of nostalgia: personal and communal nostalgia. *Personal nostalgia* is associated with a person's own life cycle; as already explained, as individuals progress in their lives, they are prone to reflect on their adolescence and early adulthood. In contrast, *communal nostalgia* "occurs at a societal level in the wake of epochal changes precipitated by wars, revolutions, invasions, economic dislocations, or environmental catastrophes" (Brown, Kozinets, & Sherry Jr., 2003a, p. 20). Chaotic times can lead to an increase of communal nostalgia (Davis, 1979). Great examples from history include the 1960s social turmoil, which fostered the nostalgia boom of the 1970s, the fall of the Berlin Wall, and the collapse of the Soviet Union in the 1990s, which led to the rise of retro products (Brown et al., 2003a; Leadbeater, 2002). Other, more recent examples, include the 9/11 catastrophic events in 2001, the ongoing (at the time of writing) Syrian civil war leading to mass dislocations of people, the 2008 global economic crisis which has subsequently led to a rise of nationalistic rhetoric in the United States (e.g. Trump's 'make America great again') and in the United Kingdom (e.g. Brexit's 'bring back control'), and the 2020 Covid-19 pandemic. Successful experiential (feel) marketing strategies can intertwine personal and communal nostalgia because "long established brands can evoke not only former epochs but also former selves. Old brands serve to bind consumers to their pasts and to the communities that shared those brands" (Brown et al., 2003a, p. 20). As brands are often associated with certain events, for instance the old *Volkswagen Beatle*'s connections with the 'flower-power' of the 1970s, the associations of these events can become associations of the brand too (Brown et al., 2003a).

As discussed earlier, some scholars have argued that people can not only feel nostalgic feelings towards events and eras which occurred in their lifetime, but also towards those which they have not personally experienced. On that basis, organisations often develop messages with "references to the past in the marketplace [reaching] back to periods within the consumer's own experience – possible ranging from ten to seventy years – and to eras that predate the consumer's lifespan" (Havlena & Holak, 1991, p. 327). This brings us to the distinction between nostalgic messages and nostalgia-based messages. *Nostalgic messages* are 'true' nostalgic messages which rely on an individual's own memories and experience and enable him/her to re-experience parts of his/her past. Thus, these messages harness personal nostalgia. In contrast, *nostalgia-based messages* allow people "to experience the collective past of the society vicariously [i.e. secondhandedly] through fantasy" (Havlena & Holak, 1991, p. 327), which means they capitalise on communal nostalgia. For example, the *Jack Daniel's* 'Maybe' advertising campaign is a nostalgia-based message which sought to make consumers yearn for the slow way of living in traditional Tennessee countryside (where this whisky is made), despite the fact it is very unlikely that these target audiences have ever experienced life in the south-eastern US state to be *personally* nostalgic about it.

Retro marketing

Many organisations pursue nostalgic experiential strategies leading to the rise of retro marketing. Brown (1999) has discussed the reasons for the success of retro marketing strategies on a micro and macro level. From a *micro perspective*, current organisations seek to capitalise on their brands' heritage, which enhances differentiation and adds a competitive advantage (Brown, 1999). Think, for example, how *Volkswagen* capitalises on the strong heritage of its *Golf* model, with multiple successful product generations over the years. In other cases, some organisations in trouble are inclined to revive successful marketing strategies from the past, although this does not mean that by following a retro marketing strategy the organisation is desperate or that it admits marketing defeat: "On the contrary, retro is a very successful way of softening the hard sell. Rip-offs don't seem quite so rapacious when they are seen through the rose-tinted, soft-focus lens of nostalgia" (Brown, 1999, p. 367). In addition, as we live longer and the world's population is ageing, we are more prone to retrospection and brand marketers respond to our demands. Finally, retro marketing can create the sense of community often missing in the busy lives of city dwellers.

From a *macro* perspective, retro marketing is a successful marketing strategy because our world is going through political, economic, and even constitutional turmoil and transformation, which makes people more likely to feel communal nostalgia (Brown, 1999; Brown et al., 2003a; Davis, 1979). In addition, retro is characteristic of post-modern society, which looks for a touch of cheek, irony, and quirkiness. There is also a widespread societal concern about climate change, which leads to society's increasing conviction that we must restore, protect, and conserve the past (Brown, 1999). Rapid technological changes accentuate people's desire for a less stressful lifestyle. In a globalised world, the more multinational an organisation becomes, the more it is inclined to remind consumers about its contributions to the community on the local level. Finally, nowadays it is impossible for brands to be radical with their aesthetic styling as "everything has already been done and dusted, and all that remains is to mix, match and play with the pieces of the past" (Brown, 1999, p. 369). For example, this is evident by today's clothing fashion trends, which are seldom disruptive; instead, they tend to juxtapose different stylistic elements of bygone eras.

Brown (1999) claims that retro marketing is an amorphous concept due to a lack of an agreed definition, but he argues that there are three different types of it: repro, retro, and repro-retro. First, *repro* marketing

> pertains to reproducing the old…as it was, albeit meanings may have changed in the meantime…It is the least demanding from an organisational resources standpoint [and]…a fairly low cost way of emphasising the distinguished lineage of a product or service, whilst intimating that the company doesn't take itself too seriously. Old ads, after all, are inherently amusing, especially those that boast the 'latest' technology or new and improved reformulations of then futuristic (now Palaeozoic) product.
>
> (Brown, 1999, p. 365)

An example of repro is the TV series *Mad Men*, a historically authentic programme depicting life in a 1960s New York-based advertising agency. Second, following the *retro* approach, organisations can combine old and new, usually old aesthetics and styling with new technology. This an approach followed by many car manufacturers with models such as the *Volkswagen Beatle*, the *Fiat 500*, and the new *Mini*. *Nokia* recently re-introduced its iconic *3310* model maintaining original aesthetic features while incorporating current technology. In film, a recent example is the critically acclaimed movie *La La Land*, which combined contemporary characteristics with 1950s aesthetics and the 1930s single-take filming approach. Finally, *repro-retro* is "an even more superlative twist in the retro tale. In classic postmodern fashion, repro-retro comprises revived revivals, nostalgia for nostalgia itself and state-of-the-art reproductions of past state-of-the-art reproductions of the past" (Brown, 1999, p. 366). Hence, repro-retro is a re-production of something which traded on nostalgia in the first place. For example, the stage production of the film *Grease* is a revival of the 1970s original which was set in the 1950s (Brown, 1999).

Retro branding

Retro branding is defined as "the revival or re-launch of a product or service brand from a prior historical period, which is usually but not always updated to contemporary standards of performance, functioning or taste" (Brown et al., 2003a, p. 20). Retro brands represent a conceptual conundrum for organisations because while consumers look for authentic and unique brands and decry imitation (Aaker, 1997; Person, Snelders, Karjalainen, & Schoormans, 2007), our post-modern market is saturated with popular retro brands which are essentially 'updated imitations' (Brown et al., 2003a). This raises the vital question of what constitutes the source of retro branding's success.

Criteria for brand revival
Brown, Kozinets, and Sherry Jr. (2003b) determined six important traits that a brand must have if it is to be successfully resurrected. They articulately explain these traits with the following:

> [First,] *dormancy* is the ante to get into the game…The brand must reside in collective memory but remain undisturbed by current marketing attention. [Second,] *iconicity* is central to the brand's appeal. The brand must have been salient during a specific developmental (or transitional) stage for a particular generation or cohort. [Third,] *evocativeness* animates the retro brand. The brand must be capable of summoning vivid experience from collective memory, and of encouraging consumers to embroider that experience with contemporary relevance. [Fourth,] *utopianism* is perhaps the hallmark of the retro-brand. The brand must be capable of mobilising an Elysian vision, of engendering a longing for an idealised past that is satisfied through consumption. [Fifth,] *solidarity* is an important unifying quality of the retro-brand. Whether as extreme as a cargo cult or as moderate as fictive kinship, the brand must inspire among its users the sense of belonging to a community. *Perfectibility* is the final trait a retro-brand encompasses. The brand must be indefinitely updateable, both technologically and ideologically, to assure its perpetual relevance to consumers who are constantly revising their own identities.
>
> (Brown et al., 2003b, p. 143)

The 4As of retro branding
Drawing from theories of Walter Benjamin (1973, 1985, 1999), the renowned literary critic, Brown et al. (2003a) determined four conceptual elements of retro branding (4As): allegory, arcadia, aura, and antinomy. In their seminal paper they explored these with the case of two prominent retro brands: the new *Volkswagen Beatle* (examined in this section) and the *Star Wars: Episode I – The Phantom Menace* film (refer to Brown et al. (2003a) for analysis of this case). The 4As typology can provide brand marketers with guidance in their effort to develop and market retro brands as well as manage their meaning.

First, brand *allegory* are symbolic brand stories and narratives which are dynamic because they are morphed and adapted to popular tastes and trends (Stern, 1988). Using "the reception discourse surrounding retro-marketed products, or those products that combine qualities of old and new, [we can] study the links among brand meanings, brand heritage, and the morality tales that consumers tell one another" (Brown et al., 2003a, p. 21). In the case of the new *Volkswagen Beatle*, Brown et al. explain that the "old Beatle and [the] new Beatle share personalities, origins, names and values forming a brand allegory that is moral, functional, and yet prone to individualisation through consumer storytelling" (2003a, p. 23). Second, brand *arcadia* (denoting a perfect world and named after a Greek region known for its astounding beauty) is all about an idealised brand community which is vital for the brand's appeal. Retro-brands can evoke a "utopian sense of past worlds and communities…This sense of the past as a special, magical place…is festooned with the latest technological magic" (Brown et al., 2003a, p. 21). An examination of retro brands' idealised communities enable brand marketers to make links between brand meanings, consumer communities, and bygone times. The new *Volkswagen Beatle* enjoys a strong "reference to flower power [and the] romanticized, upbeat, optimistic…attitude associated with the Sixties…[overlooking] *Volkswagen Beetle*'s Nazi propaganda past…[and] the turmoil of the Sixties" (Brown et al., 2003a, p. 23).

Brand *aura* relates to the importance of authenticity found in all works of artistic expression. Achieving differentiation through authenticity is an undisputed canon in contemporary branding and uniqueness is vital for building a strong brand identity (Keller, 1993). The core brand values constitute what Kelly (1998) describes as the *brand essence*, which is associated with authenticity as it is made of unique brand elements (Brown et al., 2003a). While respecting the brand's historical continuity, *Volkswagen*'s brand managers sought to animate

> the *New Beetle* with the same brand essence as the original. [They] attempted to rebuild the…brand essence and the physical vehicle by piecing it together from pop culture and retro references. They tried to make the car an 'original' again, refashioning it to read as both old-fashioned and new-fangled, simultaneously retro and techno.
>
> (Brown et al., 2003a, p. 24)

They achieved this by maintaining the core brand values while altering some of the new car model's physical properties (Brown et al., 2003a). Finally, brand *antinomy* is about the intrinsic paradoxes found in retro brands, which include "the simultaneous presence of old and new, tradition and technology, primitivism and progress, same and different" (Brown et al., 2003a, p. 21). Old aesthetics often help consumers accept and learn how to consume technology (Mick & Fournier, 1998). The new *Volkswagen Beatle* exhibits many irresolvable tensions as it combines old and new elements by juxtaposing "a Third Reich history with a worker's utopia, the rebellious American Sixties, flower-power hippies, and the middle-class ethos of contemporary American consumers" (Brown et al., 2003a, p. 25).

Building on the above discussion, we must try to understand the reasons for the enduring consumer appeal of retro brands. First, from an organisation perspective, a retro brand can combine technology with imitating old aesthetics, allowing the organisation to eradicate the advantage of first-movers in the market, while capitalising on the consumer trust and loyalty toward the old brand. Second, from a consumer and societal perspective, as we have already discussed, communal nostalgia rises during epochal changes and global events that change the course of history (Brown et al.,

2003a; Davis, 1979). However, managing retro brands is a complex pursuit and not merely a case of re-using an old advertising campaign, bringing back a delisted brand, or bragging about the organisation's history and heritage. Retro brands have the power of uniting fans to develop brand communities which are different to other brand communities due to their moral and utopian shared consciousness (Brown et al., 2003a; Muñiz Jr. & O'Guinn, 2001).

> A retro brand is a powerful totem that regathers its loyal users into a contemporary clan. Members of the clan share an affinity that situates them in a common experience of belonging, both to a brand community…and to a particular era and its ethos.
>
> (Brown et al., 2003a, p. 29)

In addition to the criteria determined by Brown et al. (2003b) (i.e. dormancy, iconicity, evocativeness, utopianism, solidarity, and perfectibility), in order for a delisted brand to qualify for revival it must also have the four conceptual elements explained above (4As).

Scholars in consumer culture theory consider brands as symbolic constructs and marketing as the management of brand meaning based on the experiential nature of consumer–brand relations harnessing consumers' creativity (Brown et al., 2003a; Fournier, 1998; Hirschman & Holbrook, 1982; Holbrook & Hirschman, 1982; Peñaloza, 2000). Consumers are recognised as meaning and brand essence co-creators. Brown et al.'s (2003a) seminal study determined that the 4As of retro branding facilitate the management of brand meaning: allegory serves as the plot, arcadia as the setting, aura as the character, and antinomy animates these three elements to spur the paradoxical nature of the retro brand: "Consumers draw holistically from their lived experiences with products, history, mass media and one another, as well as marketing sources, for the meanings they ascribe to brands" (Brown et al., 2003a, p. 30). Consumers combine their own experiences with the historical associations of retro brands to preserve and evolve the plot, the brand allegory, which nowadays can be shared globally and instantaneously because of the Internet and social media. The brand communities forming around retro brands serve as the setting "in which [brand] stories take place…[places where]…cohorts of consumers are nostalgic together and can idealise similar versions of utopia" (Brown et al., 2003a, p. 30). Consumers use these settings to render the brand with core moral values, character, and identity. Finally, the way antinomy animates the three other dimensions is eloquently explained by Brown et al. (2003a) with the following (see Figure 5.6):

> Antinomy, the final element of our 4As abbreviation, is perhaps most important of all, for brand paradox brings the cultural complexity necessary to animate each of the other dimensions. The brand is both alive and not alive, a thing and a personality, a subject and an object: This is the paradoxical kernel of brand meaning. The story is both truth and fiction, composed of clever persuasions and

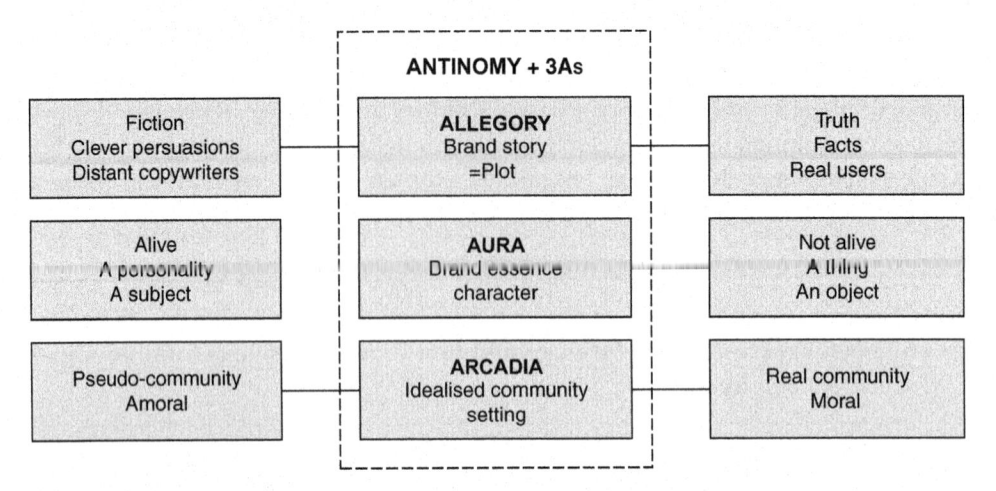

	ANTINOMY + 3As	
Fiction Clever persuasions Distant copywriters	ALLEGORY Brand story =Plot	Truth Facts Real users
Alive A personality A subject	AURA Brand essence character	Not alive A thing An object
Pseudo-community Amoral	ARCADIA Idealised community setting	Real community Moral

FIGURE 5.6 Retro brand antinomy: Animating brand allegory, aura, and arcadia

facts, devised by distant copywriters and real users. This is the central conundrum of brand story and consumer–marketer co-dependence. The idealized community is both a real community and a pseudo-community, moral and amoral, in thrall to a commercial creation and a rebellious uprising, dependent and independent, a gathering of both angry activists and covetous consumers.

(Brown et al., 2003a, pp. 30–31)

This inherent paradox is the source of the creative pull of retro brands which make them enormously attractive to consumers around the world, combining "the benefits of uniqueness, newness, and exclusivity (with its hints of higher functionality, class, styling, and premium prices) with oldness, familiarity, recognition, trust, and loyalty" (Brown et al, 2003a, p. 31).

CHAPTER REVIEW QUESTIONS

You can use the following questions to reflect on the material covered in Chapter 5:

1. What makes human experiences phenomenal and what makes consumption experiential?
2. Explain the four realms of experiences and provide your own examples.
3. What are the differences between traditional marketing and experiential marketing?
4. Discuss the main components of the experiential marketing concept.
5. Explain the different types of nostalgia and the common triggers of nostalgia.
6. What are the different types of retro-marketing? Provide your own examples for each type.

7. Discuss the 4As of retro branding typology and its contribution to brand meaning management.

RECOMMENDED READING

1. Holbrook, M. B., & Hirschman, E. C. (1982). The experiential aspects of consumption: Consumer fantasies, feelings, and fun. *Journal of Consumer Research*, 9(2), 132–140.
2. Schmitt, B. H. (1999a). Experiential marketing. *Journal of Marketing Management*, 15(1–3), 53–67.
3. Pine II, B. J., & Gilmore, J. H. (1998). Welcome to the experience economy: As goods and services become commoditised, the customer experiences that companies create will matter most. *Harvard Business Review*, 76, 97–105.
4. Brown, S., Kozinets, R. V., & Sherry Jr., J. F. (2003a). Teaching old brands new tricks: Retro branding and the revival of brand meaning. *Journal of Marketing*, 67(3), 19–33.

CASE STUDY

Building the YO! brand: From kaiten belts to multi-format experiences

Victoria Mathers
Restaurant Brand & Marketing Business Partner
YO!

In 1997, *YO!* turned the restaurant world on its head being the first to bring the excitement of the Japanese 'kaiten' conveyor belt to the UK, educating the British public on a new exciting way to dine out. Fast forward 20+ years and they have a global restaurant business as well as a retail proposition and a *YO! To Go* take-out sushi range.

This iconic brand changed their name from *YO! Sushi* to *YO!* in 2016 to reflect the breadth of the menu as it moved from serving just sushi to a broader range of Japanese cuisine, as well as diversifying from its traditional kaiten belt restaurants to a range of new products and formats. In a time of epochal change *YO!* is working with partners to develop new technology to evolve its kaiten belt dining experience, keeping the experience fresh for the 2020s and beyond. Additionally, *YO!* are looking at ways to develop new products for this ever-changing world and how they bring the *YO!* experience to guests even when they are not dining in through its social media strategy.

There is great emotion associated with the brand; the experience drives a feeling of happiness through being fun. It's essential to keep the essence of *YO!* at the heart of everything new the brand develops. The brand embraces and capitalises on its heritage as it evolves its brand proposition for new markets and generations.

YO! restaurants have a truly unique proposition centred around the kaiten belt where guests are more actively involved in the dining experience than other restaurants due to how you eat being very different from a traditional restaurant

IMAGE 5.1 *YO!* logo (image courtesy of YO!)

IMAGE 5.2 *YO!* kaiten belt (image courtesy of YO!)

setting. The experience of watching the colourful plates spinning round the belt itself as the guest decides what to grab is fun and allows diners to customise their meal almost like a Japanese pick 'n' mix. *YO!* delivers each guest an individual experience as it allows you to select lots of small dishes from the conveyor itself or, by pushing a buzzer, to order hot dishes from a team member. The environment encourages grazing so how you eat is a very different experience to a standard restaurant where you order at least your starter and main which are then brought to you. At *YO!*, as soon as guests sit down they can start tucking in, so at *YO!* you eat what you want when you want it, and normal restaurant rules do not apply here!

At *YO!* guests' involvement is greater than most restaurants as they are involved in the excitement of the experience as soon as they walk in. Whether it's watching for your favourite dish to come around the belt, the temptation of trying something new, selecting your own dish, pressing the buzzer for the waiter, or using the self-service water taps, guests' involvement and interaction is central to the experience.

Moreover, the role the chefs play is unique as they are the focal point of the experience with guests sitting around the kitchen, watching the chefs work away in the vibrant bustling open kitchen. It's the chefs, not traditional waiters, who pass the dishes directly to diners from the kitchen, and this reinforces the importance of cooking delicious fresh food which is at the heart of the *YO!* experience.

Although the theatrical nature of the *YO!* restaurant experience is what makes it so unique it has to be supported with delicious product (food and drink) and intuitive service, or the experience would fall flat which is why *YO!* are continuously looking at ways to drive excitement through their products as well as the experience itself. In summary, immersing guests in the dining experience enables the brand to ignite their five senses and set the scene from the start; by playing on trend lively music, watching the theatre of the open kitchen and belt, salivating at the smell of

IMAGE 5.3 *YO!* food (image courtesy of YO!)

delicious food being prepared in the open kitchen, grabbing the plates from the belt, or enjoying delicious flavoursome food – the *YO!* experience encapsulates it all.

The beauty of the *YO!* concept is that it fulfils different guests' needs in different markets and it's exceptionally flexible to different guest occasions. It's perfect not only for single time-strapped diners on the move in transport hubs, or shoppers searching for a quick pit stop, but it also works as a destination restaurant in many locations where families and groups of friends love dining around the belt because it's a really fun, different way to dine out.

Capitalising on the experience economy, *YO!* have developed sushi masterclasses extending the in-restaurant experience past traditional dining. There are adult Sushi Schools and Mini Ninja classes for children where guests can learn how to make the brand's most popular sushi dishes and enjoy their creations after. These classes are fun for friends, corporate events, and parties, further extending the occasions where guests can enjoy *YO!*. Moreover, the classes are a brilliant way to introduce new people to *YO!*. They further immerse guests in the *YO!* experience as they make them feel the brand shares its secrets, recipes, and skills which helps build brand consumer trust. Likewise, as sushi is hard to replicate at home and as an extension to Sushi Schools, *YO!* have developed their own Sushi Making kit which guests can buy to recreate their *YO!* favourites at home.

IMAGE 5.4 *YO!* restaurant experience (image courtesy of YO!)

YO! is now not only a dine-in restaurant brand as it has extended into different retail formats with a range of products available to pick up instore and at mainstream supermarkets. The launch of YO! To Go, initially within the restaurants and now within supermarket kiosks, offered a way to adapt to ever changing consumer needs as the 'grab & go' and delivery economy grew. With the YO! To Go sub-brand the company increased the number of occasions guests could enjoy YO!. More so, the guest experience of YO! has changed as people now eat the food away from the belt, at their desks and at home, leading the brand to focus on developing what the at-home brand experience is. Something as simple as forgetting chopsticks in a YO! To Go order can completely change the brand experience for the guest by them needing to use a fork instead. When you have limited chances to communicate the brand dining experience away from the instore-theatre of the belt, every little detail which tells the story of Japanese dining must be transferred to the guest at home. This extends to the development of the YO! at home retail range which includes sauces, snacks, ready meals, and gifting. The brand has also integrated on the back of the product packaging a link to recipes on the YO! website to help guests use the products to recreate their favourite dishes at home.

Both within the restaurant and retail setting it is important to ensure all touchpoints communicate the brand experience. Extending across all digital channels, menus, packaging, and point of sale materials, YO! brings the brand experience to life by maintaining consistency through all touchpoints and communications. Utilising social media channels to bring the YO! multi-channel experience together is essential to their success. Examples include showcasing the fun and uniqueness of the belt dining experience to sharing recipes guests can recreate at home. Social media and monthly newsletters are integral to communicating the consumer occasions to enjoy YO! and how YO! has a format and experience for every guest occasion.

Increasing the opportunities and occasions to enjoy YO! is instrumental for building a successful multi-format brand way beyond the kaiten belt, and for achieving the highest level of resonance with guests.

Questions for discussion

1. Which experience realm does the YO! brand experience belong to?
2. Which strategic experiential module(s) (SEMs) have YO! aimed to create?
3. During a time of epochal change what opportunities are there for YO! to deliver brand experience through nostalgia?

REFERENCES

Aaker, J. L. (1997). Dimensions of brand personality. *Journal of Marketing Research*, 34(3), 347–356.

Baron, S., & Harris, K. (2008). Consumers as resource integrators. *Journal of Marketing Management*, 24(1–2), 113–130.

Batcho, K. I. (1995). Nostalgia: A psychological perspective. *Perceptual and Motor Skills*, 80(1), 131–143.

Belk, R. W. (1988). Possessions and the extended self. *Journal of Consumer Research*, 15(2), 139–168.

Belk, R. W. (1990). The role of possessions in constructing and maintaining a sense of past. *Advances in Consumer Research*, 17, 669–676.

Benjamin, W. (1973). Theses on the philosophy of history. In *Illuminations*. H. Zohn (trans.) (pp. 245–255). London: Verso.

Benjamin, W. (1985). *One-way street and other writings*. E. Jephcott & K. Shorter (trans.). London: Verso.

Benjamin, W. (1999). *The arcades project*. H. Eiland & K. McLaughlin (trans.). Cambridge: Belknap.

Brakus, J. J., Schmitt, B. H., & Zarantonello, L. (2009). Brand experience: What is it? How is it measured? Does it affect loyalty? *Journal of Marketing*, 73(3), 52–68.

Brown, S. (1999). Retro-marketing: Yesterday's tomorrows, today! *Marketing Intelligence & Planning*, 17(7), 363–376.

Brown, S., Hirschman, E.C., & Maclaran, P. (2000). Presenting the past: On marketing's re-production orientation. In S. Brown, & A. Patterson (eds), *Imagining marketing: art, aesthetics, and the avant-garde* (pp. 145–191). London: Routledge.

Brown, S., Kozinets, R. V., & Sherry Jr., J. F. (2003a). Teaching old brands new tricks: Retro branding and the revival of brand meaning. *Journal of Marketing*, 67(3), 19–33.

Brown, S., Kozinets, R. V., & Sherry, J. F. (2003b). Sell me the old, old story: Retromarketing management and the art of brand revival. *Journal of Customer Behaviour*, 2(2), 133–147.

Carù, A., & Cova, B. (2012). Experiencing consumption: Appropriating and marketing experiences. In L. Peñaloza, N. Toulouse, & L. M. Viskonti (eds), *Marketing management: A cultural perspective* (pp. 164–177). London: Routledge.

Coxon I. (2015). Fundamental aspects of human experience: A phenomeno(logical) explanation. In P. Benz (ed.), *Experience design: Concepts and case studies*. London: Bloomsbury.

Daniels, E. B. (1985). Nostalgia and hidden meaning. *American Image*, 42(4), 371–383.

Davis, F. (1979). *Yearning for yesterday: A sociology of nostalgia*. New York: The Free Press.

Fournier, S. (1998). Consumers and their brands: Developing relationship theory in consumer research. *Journal of Consumer Research*, 24(4), 343–373.

Freud, S. (1959). Delusions and dreams in Jensen's Gradiva. In *The standard edition of the complete psychological works of Sigmund Freud, Volume IX (1906–1908): Jensen's 'Gradiva' and other works* (pp. 1–96). London: The Hogarth Press and the Institute of Psychoanalyis.

Gobé, M. (2009). *Emotional branding: The new paradigm for connecting brands to people*. New York: Allworth Press.

Guildford, J. P. (1950). Creativity. *American Psychologist*, 14, 205–208.

Gupta, S., & Vajic, M. (2000). The contextual and dialectical nature of experiences. In J. A. Fitzsimmons & M. J. Fitzsimmons (eds), *New service development: Creating memorable experiences* (pp. 33–51). London: Sage.

Gutman, J. (1982). A means-end chain model based on consumer categorization processes. *Journal of Marketing*, 46(2), 60–72.

Havlena, W. J., & Holak, S. L. (1991). The good old days: Observations on nostalgia and its role in consumer behavior. *Advances in Consumer Research*, 18, 323–329.

Heilbrunn B. (2018). Objects: From signs to design. In O. Kravets, P. Maclaran, S. Miles, & A. Venkatesh (eds), *The Sage handbook of consumer culture* (pp. 404–423). London: Sage.

Hilgard, E. R. (1962). Impulsive versus realistic thinking: An examination of the distinction between primary and secondary processes in thought. *Psychological Bulletin*, 59(6), 477-488.

Hirschman, E. C., & Holbrook, M. B. (1982). Hedonic consumption: Emerging concepts, methods and propositions. *Journal of Marketing*, 46(3), 92-101.

Hodder, I. (2012). *Entangled: An archaeology of the relationships between humans and things*. Chichester: John Wiley & Sons.

Hofer, J. (1934). Medical dissertation on nostalgia. (C. K. Anspach, Trans.). *Bulletin of the History of Medicine*, 2 (pp. 376–391). (original work published 1688).

Hofstede, G., Hofstede, G. J., & Minkov, M. (2010). *Cultures and organizations: Software of the mind* (3rd edn). New York: Mcgraw-Hill.

Holak, S. L., & Havlena, W. J. (1998). Feelings, fantasies, and memories: An examination of the emotional components of nostalgia. *Journal of Business Research*, 42(3), 217-226.

Holbrook, M. B. (2000). The millennial consumer in the texts of our times: Experience and entertainment. *Journal of Macromarketing*, 20(2), 178-192.

Holbrook, M. B., & Hirschman, E. C. (1982). The experiential aspects of consumption: Consumer fantasies, feelings, and fun. *Journal of Consumer Research*, 9(2), 132-140.

Holbrook, M. B., & Schindler, R. M. (2003). Nostalgic bonding: Exploring the role of nostalgia in the consumption experience. *Journal of Consumer Behaviour*, 3(2), 107-127.

Howard, J. A., & Sheth, J. N. (1969). The theory of buyer behaviour. The Wiley Marketing Series. New York: Wiley.

Hultén, B. (2015). *Sensory marketing: Theoretical and empirical grounds*. London: Routledge.

Keller, K. L. (1993). Conceptualizing, measuring, and managing customer-based brand equity. *Journal of Marketing*, 57(1), 1-22.

Keller, K. L. (2001). *Building customer-based brand equity: A blueprint for creating strong brands* (pp. 3–27). Cambridge: Marketing Science Institute.

Keller, K. L., & Swaminathan, V. (2020). *Strategic brand management: Building, measuring, and managing brand equity* (5th edn). London: Pearson Education.

Kelly, T. (1998). Brand essence—Making our brands last longer. *Journal of Brand Management*, 5(6), 390-391.

Kotler, P. (1994). *Marketing management* (8th edn). Englewood Cliffs: Prentice Hall.

Lalaounis, S. T. (2017). *Design management: Organisation and marketing perspectives*. London: Routledge.

Leadbeater, C. (2002). *Up the down escalator: Why the global pessimists are wrong*. New York: Penguin.

Loveland, K. E., Smeesters, D., & Mandel, N. (2010). Still preoccupied with 1995: The need to belong and preference for nostalgic products. *Journal of Consumer Research*, 37(3), 393-408.

Mick, D. G., & Fournier, S. (1998). Paradoxes of technology: Consumer cognizance, emotions, and coping strategies. *Journal of Consumer Research*, 25(2), 123-143.

Morris, C. W. (1939). Esthetics and the theory of signs. *The Journal of Unified Science (Erkenntnis)*, 8, 131-150.

Muñiz Jr., A. M., & O'Guinn, T. C. (2001). Brand community. *Journal of Consumer Research*, 27(4), 412-432.

Peñaloza, L. (1998). Just doing it: A visual ethnographic study of spectacular consumption behavior at Nike Town. *Consumption, Markets and Culture*, 2(4), 337-400.

Peñaloza, L. (2000). The commodification of the American West: Marketers' production of cultural meanings at the trade show. *Journal of Marketing*, 64(4), 82-109.

Person, O., Snelders, D., Karjalainen, T. M., & Schoormans, J. (2007). Complementing intuition: Insights on styling as a strategic tool. *Journal of Marketing Management*, 23(9–10), 901-916.

Pine II, B. J., & Gilmore, J. H. (1998). Welcome to the experience economy: As goods and services become commoditised, the customer experiences that companies create will matter most. *Harvard Business Review*, 76, 97–105.

Pine II, B. J., & Gilmore, J. H. (1999). *The experience economy: Work is theatre & every business a stage*. Cambridge: Harvard Business Press.

Pine II, B. J., & Gilmore, J. H. (2011). *The experience economy* (revised edn). Cambridge: Harvard Business Press.

Prahalad, C. K., & Ramaswamy, V. (2000). Co-opting customer competence. *Harvard Business Review*, 78(1), 79–91.

Raghunathan, R. (2008), Some issues concerning the concept of experiential marketing. In B. H. Schmitt & D. L. Rogers (eds), *Handbook of brand and experience management* (pp. 132–143). Cheltenham: Edward Elgar Publishing.

Rifkin, J. (2001). *The age of access: The new culture of hypercapitalism: Where all of life is paid-for experience*. New York: Putnam.

Richins, M. L. (1997). Measuring emotions in the consumption experience. *Journal of Consumer Research*, 24(2), 127–146.

Schmitt, B. H. (1999a). Experiential marketing. *Journal of Marketing Management*, 15(1–3), 53–67.

Schmitt, B. H. (1999b). *Experiential marketing: How to get customers to sense, feel, think, act, relate*. New York: Free Press.

Schmitt, B. H. (2011). *Experience marketing: Concepts, frameworks and consumer insights* (Vol. 5, No. 2). Boston: Now Publishers.

Schmitt, B. H., & Simonson, A. (1997). *Marketing aesthetics: The strategic management of brands, identity, and image*. New York: The Free Press.

Schmitt, B. H., & Zarantonello, L. (2013). Consumer experience and experiential marketing: A critical review. In N. K. Malhotra (ed.), *Review of marketing research* (Vol. 10) (pp. 25–61). London: Emerald Publishing.

Stern, B. B. (1988). Medieval allegory: Roots of advertising strategy for the mass market. *Journal of Marketing*, 52(3), 84–94.

Tynan, C., & McKechnie, S. (2009). Experience marketing: A review and reassessment. *Journal of Marketing Management*, 25(5–6), 501–517.

Vargo, S. L., & Lusch, R. F. (2004). Evolving to a new dominant logic for marketing. *Journal of Marketing*, 68(1), 1–17.

Vargo, S. L., & Lusch, R. F. (2008). Service-dominant logic: Continuing the evolution. *Journal of the Academy of Marketing Science*, 36(1), 1–10.

Woodman, R. W., Sawyer, J. E., & Griffin, R. W. (1993). Toward a theory of organizational creativity. *Academy of Management Review*, 18(2), 293–321.

CHAPTER 6

Consumer collectives, brand avoidance, and political consumption

CHAPTER AIMS AND LEARNING OUTCOMES

This chapter corresponds to the second stage of Keller and Swaminathan's (2020) *strategic brand management process*, i.e. designing and implementing brand marketing programmes (see Figure 6.1), and explores branding and consumption from a sociological perspective. More specifically, it aims to achieve the following:

1. Understand the collectivist and constructivist aspects of consumption.
2. Explore the characteristics of the four types of communities of consumption (consumer collectives) and understand their differences and similarities.
3. Discuss the branding implications of the four types of communities of consumption.
4. Understand the phenomena of brand avoidance and anti-consumption.
5. Discuss the different types of political consumption.

COLLECTIVIST AND CONSTRUCTIVIST ASPECTS OF CONSUMPTION

While in the previous chapter, we adopted an experiential view on consumption, this chapter explores the collective and constructive aspects of consumption (Cova & Dalli, 2018) drawing from sociology, anthropology, and consumer culture theory. Consumption can be considered a *collective* phenomenon where groups of people are the unit of analysis. Human life is social and consumers are not "sealed off and separated from their experiential worlds" (Cova & Dalli, 2018, p. 236). Consumers participate in networks of social relations, i.e. collectives, which are capable of their own agency and act as intermediaries between individuals and organisations and markets (Cova, 1997; Cova & Dalli, 2018; Schouten & McAlexander, 1995).

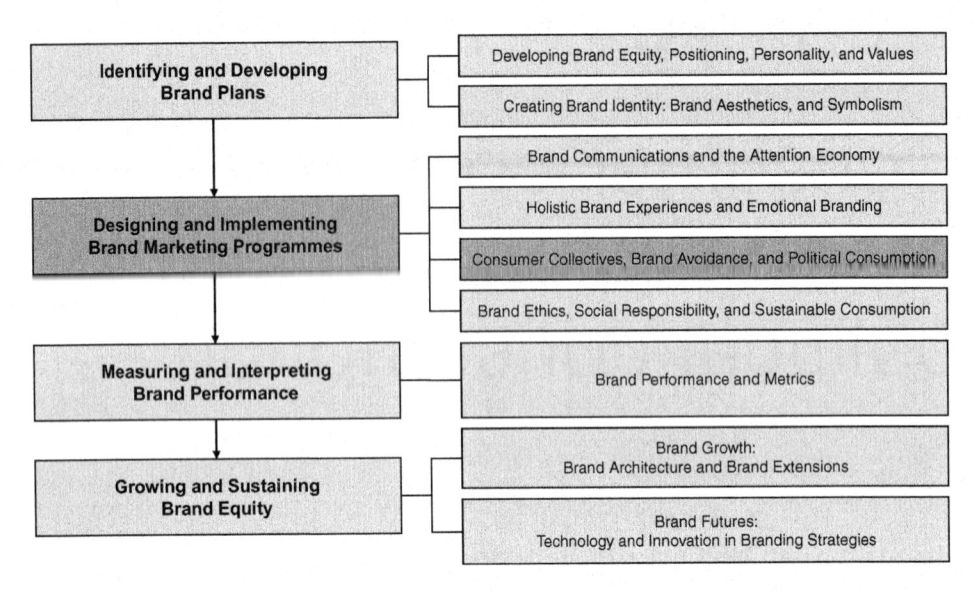

```
┌─────────────────────────┐   ┌──────────────────────────────────────────────────────────┐
│ Identifying and Developing │──┤ Developing Brand Equity, Positioning, Personality, and Values │
│    Brand Plans           │   ├──────────────────────────────────────────────────────────┤
└─────────────────────────┘   │ Creating Brand Identity: Brand Aesthetics, and Symbolism │
            │                 └──────────────────────────────────────────────────────────┘
            ▼
┌─────────────────────────┐   ┌──────────────────────────────────────────────────────────┐
│                          │──┤ Brand Communications and the Attention Economy          │
│                          │   ├──────────────────────────────────────────────────────────┤
│ Designing and Implementing│──┤ Holistic Brand Experiences and Emotional Branding       │
│ Brand Marketing Programmes│   ├──────────────────────────────────────────────────────────┤
│                          │──┤ Consumer Collectives, Brand Avoidance, and Political Consumption │
│                          │   ├──────────────────────────────────────────────────────────┤
│                          │──┤ Brand Ethics, Social Responsibility, and Sustainable Consumption │
└─────────────────────────┘   └──────────────────────────────────────────────────────────┘
            │
            ▼
┌─────────────────────────┐   ┌──────────────────────────────────────────────────────────┐
│ Measuring and Interpreting│──┤ Brand Performance and Metrics                           │
│   Brand Performance      │   └──────────────────────────────────────────────────────────┘
└─────────────────────────┘
            │
            ▼
┌─────────────────────────┐   ┌──────────────────────────────────────────────────────────┐
│                          │──┤ Brand Growth:                                           │
│ Growing and Sustaining   │   │ Brand Architecture and Brand Extensions                 │
│   Brand Equity           │   ├──────────────────────────────────────────────────────────┤
│                          │──┤ Brand Futures:                                          │
│                          │   │ Technology and Innovation in Branding Strategies        │
└─────────────────────────┘   └──────────────────────────────────────────────────────────┘
```

FIGURE 6.1 Strategic brand management process and book plan

Nowadays, the importance of this collective dimension is undoubted as there is an abundance of resources and platforms upon which consumers can communicate and interact with each other, on a face-to-face basis as well as on the Internet and social media (Cova & Dalli, 2018). In addition, consumption can be viewed as a *constructive* act whereby consumers add value to the organisation's offerings by customising products and services (material value), by taking part in socio-cultural interactions "in which...brands are enriched through comments, reviews and discourses [(immaterial value), and by constructing] the social network in which and through which these offerings are actually channelled: without the social networks the market alone...should not effectively work" (Cova & Dalli, 2018, p. 235).

The consumer culture, which followed from the Industrial Revolution, led to the emergence of consumption communities which Boorstin described as "invisible new communities...created and preserved by how and what [individuals] consumed" (1974, p. 89). Consumption communities are crucial to the success of brand development strategies because they can carry and circulate value, can undermine marketing campaigns, or raise them to new success levels (Canniford, 2011a). There are four types of consumption communities: 1) subcultures of consumption, 2) brand communities, 3) consumer tribes, and 4) brand publics (see Figure 6.2).

We must explore each kind separately while discussing their similarities and nuanced differences (see Table 6.1). Cova and Dalli (2018) argue that their similarities

COLLECTIVES, AVOIDANCE, & CONSUMPTION 173

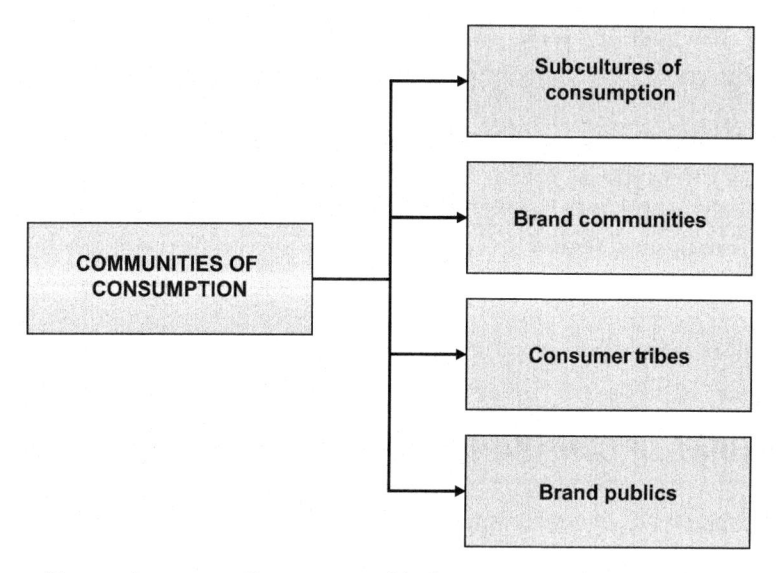

FIGURE 6.2 Types of consumption communities

TABLE 6.1 Types of consumption communities – similarities and differences.

	Subcultures of consumption	Consumer tribes	Brand communities	Brand publics
Locus	Activity	Linking value	Brand	Mediation through social media
Power structure	Hierarchy of core members	Diffuse, democratic, hybrid network	Hierarchy of core members and brand managers	Diffuse, democratic, hybrid network
Purposes	Sociality and response to alienation	Sociality and passion	Brand use and sociality	Visibility and publicity
Time Span	Long-term	Transient	Long-term	Short term and ephemeral
Structure	Slow to change	Fluid and fast-moving	Slow to change	Fluid and fast-moving
Social position	Marginalised	Mobile	Mainstreamed	Mobile and mainstreamed

Sources: Adapted from Canniford (2011), and based on Arvidsson & Caliandro (2016).

are greater than their differences but such categorisation is essential because it allows brand marketers to differentiate consumption communities on the basis of

> three main traits: 1) the strength of the ties that bind people (from strong to fluid), 2) the type of interaction (from long-established rituals to ephemeral experiences); and 3) the object of their shared passion (a product, service, brand, or consumption activity).
> (Cova & Dalli, 2018, p. 237)

Let us explore these types of consumption communities in more depth.

SUBCULTURES OF CONSUMPTION

Defining subcultures of consumption

In sociological terms, *subcultures* are viewed as subversions of dominant institutions such as family and the market, which develop their own "marginal forms of value and status around alternative social ties" (Canniford, 2011a, p. 593). When such subversions or deviations relate to consumer culture, we talk about *subcultures of consumption*, in which individuals challenge the mainstream and the mundane to liberate themselves from authority and constraints, and behave in an anti-establishment, and often unpredictable, manner (Canniford, 2011a). In their seminal paper, Schouten and McAlexander (1995) explored subcultures of consumption by drawing from a three-year ethnographic fieldwork with *Harley-Davidson* motorcycle owners. They defined a subculture of consumption as

> a distinctive subgroup of society that self-selects on the basis of a shared commitment to a particular product class, brand, or consumption activity. Other characteristics of a subculture of consumption include an identifiable, hierarchical social structure; a unique ethos, or set of shared beliefs and values; and unique jargons, rituals, and modes of symbolic expression.
> (Schouten & McAlexander, 1995, p. 43)

Within subcultures, we can find members who enjoy high-status and act as opinion leaders for the collective. A subculture finds cultural meanings in certain products or activities, which are expressed as "unique, homologous styles or ideologies of consumption" (Schouten & McAlexander, 1995, p. 43). These styles are often shared or copied by larger audiences in the periphery to the core subculture, and can eventually become commercialised for the masses. The scope and influence of subcultures is enormous because they transcend national, cultural, demographic, racial, ethnic, and class differences (Schouten & McAlexander, 1995). Subcultures of consumption are ubiquitous in our post-modern society and can include any social group that is brought together by shared consumption values and behaviours. In consumer culture, people define themselves

> in terms of activities, objects, and relationships that give their lives meaning. It is... consumer goods...that substantiate their place in the social world. It is through objects that they can relate to other people and make judgments about shared values and interests. Through consumption activities they form relationships that allow them to share meaning and mutual support. Those relationships and activities are governed by ideologies of consumption. Around those ideologies of consumption consumers constitute their own categories, and those categories define subcultures of consumption.
> (Schouten & McAlexander, 1995, p. 59)

Characteristics of subcultures of consumption

Deconstructing the definition of subcultures of consumption, we can identify four important characteristics (see Figure 6.3). First, a subculture of consumption has a certain *structure*. A subculture of consumption emerges when individuals identify with objects or consumption activities and, through these, with other individuals. A certain ethos and set of values direct consumption patterns and "the structure of the subculture, which governs social interactions within it...[and] is a direct reflection of the commitment of individuals to the ethos" (Schouten & McAlexander, 1995, p. 48). The hierarchical social structure of a subculture is constructed on the basis of the relative statuses of its members. As subcultures are often consisted of

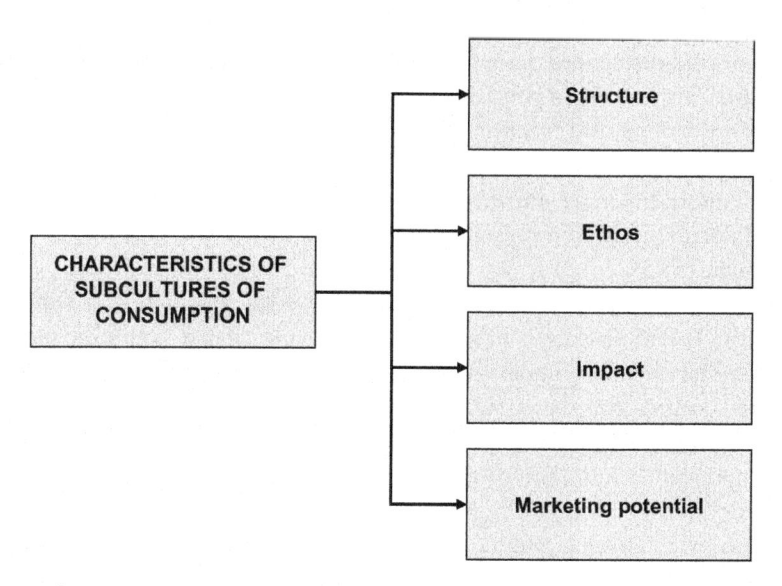

FIGURE 6.3 Characteristics of subcultures of consumption

separate groups, such structures can be complex systems. 'Outlaw bikers' (the hard core members), 'trinity road riders' (born-again Christians), 'dykes on bikes' (lesbian motorcycle enthusiasts) are examples of groups found in the *Harley-Davidson* motorcycle owners' subculture (Schouten & McAlexander, 1995). Schouten and McAlexander identify that "[w]ithin-group status is a function of an individual's commitment to the group's ideology of consumption. Across-group status is based on each group's judgments of the other group's authenticity as representatives of the subculture" (1995, p. 50). We can organise subculture members in three broad categories: 1) the *hard-core members* who act as the opinion leaders, 2) *less-committed members* who are essential because they provide material support and worship the hard-core members, and 3) the *aspirants* who act as the audience and convey their envy which justify the subculture members' (1 and 2) actions and efforts (Schouten & McAlexander, 1995).

Second, a subculture of consumption has its own *ethos* which relates to the expression and maintenance of its underlying values which are accepted by subculture members to a varying extent. These values are articulated in the usage of certain brands. The way these values are expressed through symbolic consumption "may reflect [the] cultural and socioeconomic idiosyncrasies of the subgroups" (Schouten & McAlexander, 1995, p. 55) found in the subculture. Members often become extremely committed to key brands consumed by the subculture, and with their missionary-like behaviour they add to the brands' iconicity and popularity (Schouten & McAlexander, 1995).

Third, the *impact* of subcultures of consumption is manifested by the *transformation* of consumers' own selves. In order to join a subculture, individuals must enter at the bottom of the hierarchy and go through a process of socialisation, which requires their transformation through "an evolution of motives for involvement and a deepening of commitment to the subculture and its ethos" (Schouten & McAlexander, 1995, p. 56). This process of socialisation starts with individuals experimenting with personas, conforming and imitating the required performances, and assessing their effectiveness in relation to relevant and evolving audiences. As individuals commit increasingly more time and effort to the subculture, they internalise the subculture's values and norms, and can eventually achieve hard-core member status (Schouten & McAlexander, 1995).

Finally, it is essential to understand the *marketing potential* of a subculture of consumption. Brand marketers must engage a subculture in a symbiotic manner and seek to serve its needs by understanding its structure and ethos. Besides providing the required brands for the subculture's functioning, organisations must also aid "the socialisation of new members, facilitate communications within the subculture, and sponsor events that provide havens for the activities of the subculture" (Schouten & McAlexander, 1995, p. 59). This can lead to greater profitability for the organisation by generating greater publicity for the brand, receiving consumer feedback (which the organisation can swiftly act on), and achieving greater consumer loyalty. However, any organisational effort to make the subculture more accessible to mainstream consumers must avoid alienating hard-core members, which would corrupt the subculture and dilute its original appeal (Schouten & McAlexander, 1995). It is important to bear in mind that subcultures of consumption can be unpredictable and tricky which can hinder brand marketers' attempts to assemble them (Canniford, 2011a; Holt, 2004).

BRAND COMMUNITIES

Defining brand communities

The second type of consumption communities, brand communities, have attracted most of attention from scholars and brand marketers because they are seen as the ideal locus of value co-creation (Schau, Muñiz Jr., & Arnould, 2009) between organisations and brand enthusiasts: "On a sociological level, brand communities herald new forms of collectives emerging in contemporary society: rather than communities creating symbols, they form around symbols" (Cova & Dalli, 2018, p. 238). The important element of a brand community is that they coalesce around a specific brand, hence, they can be a perfect brand marketing strategy for organisations. As explained in Chapter 5, a successful experiential marketing strategy can harness the power of brand communities by fostering strong relate experiences among targeted consumers (Schmitt, 1999). A *brand community* is defined as

> a specialized, non-geographically bound community, based on a structured set of social relationships among admirers of a brand. It is specialized because at its centre is a branded good or service. Like other communities, it is marked by a shared consciousness, rituals and traditions, and a sense of moral responsibility. Each of these qualities is, however, situated within a commercial and mass-mediated ethos, and has its own particular expression. Brand communities are participants in the brand's larger social construction and play a vital role in the brand's ultimate legacy.
>
> (Muñiz Jr. & O'Guinn, 2001, p. 412)

With a brand community, a brand can act as the social glue that bounds people together (Avery, 2012). A brand community enables a consumer to connect with the brand, *and* with other consumers. In general, brand communities, as social entities, are ardent manifestations of the central place brands have in consumers' daily lives (Muñiz Jr. & O'Guinn, 2001).

A key question is whether brand communities are different to subcultures of consumption, and if so, how. In Schouten and McAlexander's (1995) study, the *Harley-Davidson* motorcycle riders' connection with one another provides the basis for a significant part of their understanding of the brand and this understanding becomes an *actual way of life*. Subcultures of consumption have some similarities with brand communities such as a shared ethos, patterns of acculturation, and hierarchies of status, however they have some important differences too. First, subcultures of consumption are characterised by marginality and an outlaw ethos that is not a characteristic of brand communities which can be considered as *mainstream*. Perhaps subcultures of consumption could be viewed as brand communities, which have become somehow peculiar and unusual (Muñiz Jr. & O'Guinn, 2001). Second, unlike subcultures of consumption where a brand has "a socially fixed meaning… brand communities [have] an active interpretive function, with brand meaning being socially negotiated, rather than delivered unaltered from context to context, consumer to consumer" (Muñiz Jr. & O'Guinn, 2001, p. 414). Third, Schouten and McAlexander (1995) emphasise the importance of the transformation of the self at the expense of collective identities; contrastingly, brand communities have a more social constructivist character where collective identities are very important (Muñiz Jr. & O'Guinn, 2001). Finally, subcultures of consumption tend to define cultural symbols in a way that is different to the meanings attached to them by the (mainstream) majority. In contrast, "brand communities do not typically reject aspects of the surrounding culture's ideology. They embrace them" (Muñiz Jr. & O'Guinn, 2001, p. 414).

Characteristics of brand communities

Based on an ethnographic study of three brand communities: *Ford Bonco* (automobiles), *Saab* (automobiles), and *Macintosh* (computers), Muñiz Jr. & O'Guinn (2001) determined three important characteristics of brand communities (Figure 6.4). First, a brand community has a *consciousness of kind* as members feel stronger connections toward one another; a feeling of 'we-ness'. This consciousness of kind has a more commercial ethos than other communities, and transcends geographic boundaries: "Members also frequently note a critical demarcation between

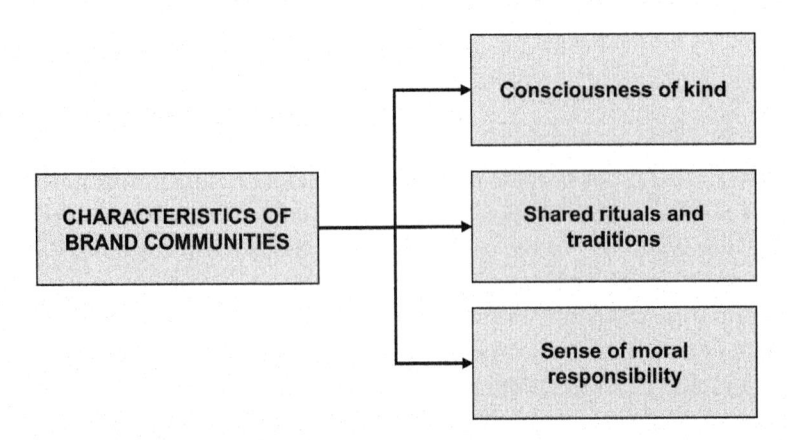

FIGURE 6.4 Characteristics of brand communities

users of their brand and users of other brands [which]...sets them apart from others and makes them similar to one another" (Muñiz Jr. & O'Guinn, 2001, p. 418). In addition, members are keen to distinguish between those who are true devotees to the brand and those who are simply opportunistic. Hence, *legitimacy*, is the process with which community members determine who is a true member and who is not. Brand communities are open to new members who are truly passionate about the brand and its culture and history; anyone who attempts to use the brand for the wrong reasons is not conferred to the required legitimacy (Muñiz Jr. & O'Guinn, 2001). Consciousness of kind is also maintained by *oppositional brand loyalty*, that is, "the opposition to competing brands...[which delineates] what the brand is not, and who the brand community members are not" (Muñiz Jr. & O'Guinn, 2001, p. 420).

Second, a brand community has its own *shared rituals and traditions*, based on shared experiences with the brand, which reproduce and transmit meaning within the community and beyond. When an individual knows the community's rituals and traditions, he/she is able to celebrate the brand's history and acquire cultural capital within the brand community (Bourdieu, 1984; Holt, 1998) because such knowledge "demonstrates one's expertise, secure membership status, and commitment to a larger community" (Muñiz Jr. & O'Guinn, 2001, p. 422). Cultural capital reinforces distinctions between social groups on the basis of taste and consumption patterns (Townley, 2015). Members tend to engage in storytelling, sharing brand stories based on common brand experiences, which adds vitality to the brand community and preserves it. Members actively engage in the social construction of brand meaning, thus, they influence the brand itself (Muñiz Jr. & O'Guinn, 2001).

Third, a brand community has a *sense of moral responsibility*, that is, "a sense of duty to the community as a whole, and to individual members of the community" (Muñiz Jr. & O'Guinn, 2001, p. 424), which generates collective action and provides cohesion for the social group. These subtle and contextualised moral systems achieve two tasks, they 1) enable the integration and retention of community members warranting the brand community's survival, and 2) assist members in the proper use of the brand. The latter involves helping fellow members "repair the product or solve problems with it [drawing from]...specialised knowledge acquired through several years of using the brand" (Muñiz Jr. & O'Guinn, 2001, p. 425). It also involves sharing information about the brand, such as ways to protect the product, enhance its use, or promotional materials. Information shared by community members lacks commercial self-interest, thus is deemed more useful than any information provided by brand marketers (Muñiz Jr. & O'Guinn, 2001). Brand communities can be considered communities of limited liability (Jannowitz, 1952); members voluntarily participate in them and can withdraw from them at any time. The sense of moral responsibility found in brand communities is limited and specialised, yet it is still important and legitimate (Muñiz Jr. & O'Guinn, 2001).

Fostering brand communities

The above discussion demonstrates the enormous scope and potential brand communities offer organisations seeking to achieve strong brand equity. However, we must bear in mind that organisations cannot *create* brand communities, as they cannot force a brand consumer-enthusiast to form strong relationships with other brand consumers-enthusiasts. Instead, organisations can *foster* brand communities and encourage such relationships among brand admirers, hence they can provide consumers the opportunity to construct their own brand communities and modify the products, services, or brands as they wish (Schau, Muñiz Jr., & Arnould, 2009).

Brand community practices

Schau et al. (2009) indicated how brand community practices create value and determined the practices organisations should encourage facilitating the creation of brand communities. They arranged these practices in four overarching categories. First, *social networking* practices demonstrate the similarities among community members and their expectations, and include *welcoming*, *empathising*, and *governing*. These practices evolve over time and move beyond brand boundaries, which means that Schau et al. (2009) challenge Muñiz Jr. & O'Guinn's (2001) view of brand communities as communities of limited liability. Social networking practices sustained over a long period of time can transfigure brand communities beyond limited liability because they can enable friendships to grow beyond the boundaries of the brand and even when members have dispossessed themselves of the brand (Schau et al., 2009).

Second, *impression management* practices have "an external, outward focus on creating favourable impressions of the brand, brand enthusiasts, and the brand community in the social universe beyond the brand community" (Schau et al., 2009, p. 34) and include *evangelising* and *justifying*. Third, *community engagement* practices strengthen the engagement of members with the brand community, and highlight and maintain the brand community's heterogeneity in terms of distinctions among members and subsets of the brand community. These practices are *documenting*, *badging*, *milestoning*, and *staking*, and endow members with social capital, i.e. durable networks of inter-personal relationships based on mutual acquaintance and recognition (Bourdieu, 1986). Finally, *brand use* practices "are specifically related to improved or enhanced use of the focal brand" (Schau et al., 2009, p. 35) and include *customising*, *grooming*, and *commoditising* (see Table 6.2. for description of each brand community practice).

Schau et al. (2009) explain that all these brand community

> practices have a common 'anatomy' and varied 'physiology' evincing discursive knowledge, or explicit procedures for doing; know-how and tacit elements, or taken-for-granted knowledge of worthy projects; and affective commitments to brand-centred practices, as well as intra- and inter-thematic linkages. [These]

TABLE 6.2 Brand community practices

Category	Practice	Description
Social networking	*Welcoming*	Greeting new members, beckoning them into the fold, and assisting in their brand learning and community socialisation. Welcoming can also be negatively valenced, as in discouraging participation in the brand community and/or a specific practice.
	Empathising	Lending emotional and/or physical support to other members, including support for brand-related trials (e.g. product failure, customising) and/or for non-brand-related life issue (e.g. illness, death, job). Empathising can be divisive if the emotional support is in regard to intragroup conflict.
	Governing	Articulating the behavioural expectations within the brand community.
Impression management	*Evangelising*	Sharing the brand 'good news', inspiring others to use, and preaching from the mountaintop. It may involve negative comparisons with other competing brands. Evangelising can be negative (annoying, off-putting) if extreme.
	Justifying	Deploying rationales generally for devoting time and effort to the brand and collectively to outsiders and marginal members in the boundary. May include debate and jokes about obsessive-compulsive brand-directed behaviour.
Community engagement	*Staking*	Recognizing variance within the brand community membership. Marking intragroup distinction and similarity.
	Milestoning	Milestoning refers to the practice of noting seminal events in brand ownership and consumption.
	Badging	Badging is the practice of translating milestones into symbols.
	Documenting	Detailing the brand relationship journey in a narrative way. The narrative is often anchored by and peppered with milestones…
Brand use	*Grooming*	Caring for the brand…or systematising optimal use patterns…
	Customising	Modifying the brand to suit group-level or individual needs. This includes all efforts to change the factory specs of the product to enhance performance. Includes fan fiction/fan art in the case of intangible products.
	Commoditising	Distancing/approaching the marketplace. A valenced behaviour regarding marketplace. May be directed at other members (e.g., you should sell/should not sell that). May be directed at the firm through explicit link or through presumed monitoring of the site (e.g., you should fix this/do this/change this).

Source: Schau, Muñiz Jr., & Arnould (2009).

practices evidence remarkable consistency in a range of product category classifications. Practices foster consumption opportunities and create value for both consumers and marketers.

(Schau et al., 2009, p. 40)

Schau et al.'s (2009) study provides three important theoretical contributions. They demonstrate that 1) value can be generated by the collective performing of these practices, 2) giving consumers (some) control of the brand can lead to higher consumer engagement and greater brand equity, and 3) organisations can generate added value by utilising brand enthusiasts as operant resources, which according to Vargo & Lusch (2004), involve skills and knowledge. In order to foster the creation of brand communities, organisations can carry out seeding practices whereby they encourage or sponsor social networking practices to develop and maintain the community and stimulate further co-creation. As Schau et al. suggest, "[a]gents of the marketer could initiate basic practices in a brand-centred forum, documenting any modifications they make" (2009, p. 41) and external after-sales providers can be motivated to provide numerous brand-centred customising, grooming, and documenting practices. These providers should act with transparency disclosing to brand enthusiasts their affiliation with the organisation, allowing marketers to be kept informed in the process. Finally, marketers can "foster community engagement by encouraging the interacting practices to promote engagement...Combined with badging as part of documenting brand use, milestoning leads to increased community engagement" (Schau et al., 2009, p. 41).

Pools, webs, and hubs

As mentioned above, it is imperative that organisations cede control of their brands to consumers-enthusiasts if they want to harness the great potential of brand communities. Indeed as Fournier and Lee emphasise, "brand communities generate more value when members control them – and when companies create conditions in which communities can thrive" (2009, p. 105). They provided practical guidance for organisations about how to engineer brand communities in the right way, drawing from their work with the *Harley-Davidson* brand. Organisations must pursue community strategies that combine three forms of community affiliation: pools, webs, and hubs. *Pools* include members who are tied together by shared goals or values such as political parties, e.g. the UK's *Conservative* and *Labour* parties, or *Apple* enthusiasts. Mainstream marketing management practices has always involved identifying and consistently communicating a set of values that bind a consumer with the brand in an emotional way. However, although important, this is not sufficient as it does not necessarily mean that the consumer develops interpersonal relationships with other consumers of the brand.

That is the why organisations must develop *webs* that include affiliations "based on strong one-to-one connections...[and] are the strongest and most stable form of community because [members] are bound by many and varied relationships"

(Fournier & Lee, 2009, p. 108). This type of affiliation involves Schau et al.'s (2009) aforementioned social networking practices, which organisations should encourage or sponsor in order to foster a brand community. Social media can provide a platform for developing these webs, but these can also be formed offline, for example,

> [the] Harley Davidson Museum…builds webs of interpersonal connections through features such as walls around the campus decorated with large, custom-inscribed stainless-steel rivets commissioned by individuals or groups. As museum visitors read the inscriptions on the rivets, they reflect on the stories and people behind them. People who meet at the rivet walls soon find themselves comparing interesting inscriptions, and before long they're engaged in conversation, planning to stay in touch and perhaps even share a ride someday. Through rivet walls and other means of fostering interpersonal connections, the museum strengthens the *Harley-Davidson* brand pool by building webs within it.
> (Fournier & Lee, 2009, p. 108)

Finally, with *hubs*, people are brought together by their admiration for a central figure, for example Michael Jordan (*Nike*), Elon Musk (*Tesla*), Heath Kirchart (*Harley-Davidson*), and in the past, the late Steve Jobs (*Apple*). Hubs can help a community gain new members whose values are congruent with the community's values. They can generate or strengthen a brand pool, and "must be bonded to the community through webs" (Fournier & Lee, 2009, p. 108). In fact, it is crucial that all pools, webs, and hubs are combined in a mutually reinforcing system to establish a stable community (Fournier & Lee, 2009).

Brandfests: Achieving greater integration in brand communities

We have already discussed that an important element of brand communities is their ability to empower members to connect with the brand *and* with other members. Thus, instead of merely dyadic relationships (consumer–brand), brand communities involve *triadic* social constellations (consumer–brand–consumer) (Muñiz Jr. & O'Guinn, 2001). McAlexander, Schouten, and Koenig (2002) take this important point further and provide a shift of perspective by suggesting that the focal point of the brand community should be the consumer (instead of the brand). Consumers not only form relationships with the brand and other brand community members, but also attach importance to their relationships with their actual branded possessions (Belk, 1988; Holbrook & Hirschman, 1982) as well as with the marketing agents (Doney & Cannon, 1997; Dwyer, Schurr, & Oh, 1987) and institutions (Arnould & Price, 1993; Belk, 1988) which own and manage these brands. Hence, McAlexander et al. (2002) argue for a consumer-centric view on brand community where "the existence and meaningfulness of the community inhere [that is, is situated] in customer experience rather than in the brand around which that experience evolves" (McAlexander et al., 2002, p. 39). Brand communities can differ on a number of run brandfests which foster strong customer-centred relationships cultivating a well-integrated brand community. Members of such community are emotionally devoted to the welfare of the brand (and the organisation which owns and manages it); they become brand evangelists and missionaries who transfer brand messages to other communities, contributing to organisational and brand success (McAlexander et al., 2002).

Brand communities and convenience products

With many research studies exploring brand communities of 'quasi-deluxe' brands such as *Apple*, *Saab*, *Harley-Davidson*, and *Jeep*, one wonders whether or not it is possible for brand communities to develop around (more mundane) convenience products. Cova and Pace's (2006) study of *Nutella* (the hazelnut spread), sought to determine ways organisations, which own and manage such brands, can nurture brand communities, especially by utilising the Internet. *Ferrero* (the organisation-owner) achieved this through its *my Nutella The Community* website. However, as explained with the following, this community did not fully adhere to Muñiz Jr. & O'Guinn's (2001)

> predefined canons for a brand community: although members are marginally aware that they constitute a distinct group ('nutellari') and despite the materialisation of symbols and traditions, it is doubtful that any moral obligation of mutual assistance exists…[*Ferrero*] opted to facilitate individuals' exhibition of their para-social relationships instead of helping members to create real social relationships. In other words, the crux here is the fact that *Ferrero* has not offered online chatrooms or forums to facilitate interactions, encounters and dialogue amongst consumers (McWilliam, 2000), choosing instead to provide a sort of platform for 'personal pages' or blogs where action is more important than interaction and where consumers can produce the sub-cultural components that will make up their imaginary community.
>
> (Cova & Pace, 2006, p. 1100)

The above means that in brand communities of convenience products, the community is imagined instead of real, relationships are para-social instead of social, and web platforms with personal pages and blogs empower members to exhibit themselves and the brand's role in their life. On the basis of the principle of customer empowerment, "the company's role…is to facilitate this on-site self-exhibition by remaining as non-intrusive as possible" (Cova & Pace, 2006, p. 1101). Despite the fact that such communities are imagined, they are still capable of producing sub-cultural characteristics which contribute to maintaining a brand's following and adding to the daily lives of the brand enthusiasts (Cova & Pace, 2006). This consumer desire for self-display and publicity is also explored by Arvidsson and Caliandro's (2016) concept of brand publics, discussed later in this chapter.

Brand communities: Source and result of brand equity

The concept of the brand community, along with the other types of communities of consumption, recognises the social dimension of brands. Muñiz Jr. and O'Guinn suggest that "[b]rands are social objects and [are] socially constructed...Consumers are actively involved in that creation" (2001, p. 427). When discussing the concept of brand equity in Chapter 2, we explored how there are four categories of brand resonance (top layer of the CBBE pyramid model), one of which is a *sense of community* leading to a brand community (Keller, 2001). This means that brand loyalty can lead to the creation of a brand community. In our discussion in this section, we demonstrated that, a brand community can reciprocally lead to brand loyalty. A brand community can influence brand equity by creating brand awareness, developing unique, strong and favourable brand associations, improving the brand's perceived quality, and ultimately leading to brand loyalty (Aaker, 2010; Keller, 1993, 2001).

> Brand communities carry out important functions on behalf of the brand, such as sharing information, perpetuating the history and culture of the brand, and providing assistance. They provide social structure to the relationship between marketer and consumer. Communities exert pressure on members to remain loyal to the collective and to the brand...A brand with a powerful sense of community would generally have greater value to a marketer than a brand with a weak sense of community.
>
> (Muñiz Jr. & O'Guinn, 2001, p. 427)

Marketing risks and problems of brand communities

Despite the strong contributions of brand communities to the development of brand equity, organisations must consider some potential disadvantages and risks associated with them. There is a possibility that a brand community collectively rejects changes in the product or what brand marketers seek to achieve, and through communal channels of communications it disseminates this rejection (Muñiz Jr. & O'Guinn, 2001). In addition, competitors can spy on the brand community and its internal communication: "Brands could be sabotaged by competitors or brand terrorists misappropriating or subverting community values and interest" (Muñiz Jr. & O'Guinn, 2001, p. 427). It is important to bear in mind that the character of the brand community can influence people's perception of brand quality. In some cases, a strong brand community may indicate brand marginality (Muñiz Jr. & O'Guinn, 2001), which could deter people from using the product or service.

Cova and Pace (2006) list a number of problems brand communities can cause marketers. First, as we have already explored, consciousness of kind in a brand community can be maintained by oppositional brand loyalty. This means members of a brand community develop stronger connections toward each other by opposing another brand, and can encourage others to do so too. Second, with regards to legitimacy, devoted brand community members might view mere purchasers of the brand as illegitimate members, leading to animosity towards them. Third, brand community members might "actively try to keep the community small and marginal" (Cova & Pace, 2006, p. 1089). Fourth, a brand community might develop around a politicised brand (explored later in the chapter). Fifth, there is a potential for a brand community to develop around a product or brand, which has been abandoned by the organisation, such as the *Apple Newton* community (Muñiz Jr. & Schau, 2005). Finally, the social nature of brands implies that consumers see brands as shared cultural properties that do not privately belong to the organisation but to the community around them. This can lead to *brand hijack*, where organisations lose part of their control over the brand-to-brand community members who attempt to re-appropriate it (Cova & Pace, 2006). These risks, problems, and disadvantages associated with brand communities require a cautious approach from brand marketers.

CONSUMER TRIBES

Defining consumer tribes

The third type of consumption communities is *consumer tribes* which, unlike brand communities, "do not locate their socialisation around singular brands" (Canniford, 2011a, p. 594). More recent studies have explored the act of tribal consumption, which involves creating *linking value* during the shared use of a product or service in turn, generating social links with people (Cova, 1997; Cova & Cova, 2002). Consumers are both producers and users of this linking value; they generate the linking value attached to a brand which, as a consequence, is seen as more valuable. Hence, the linking value is the surplus enjoyed by organisations that have managed to develop a community of enthusiasts around their brands (Cova & White, 2010). The linking value is the "bonding or linking element that keeps people in the group" (Cova & Cova, 2002, p. 602). "If you are passionate about surfing, travelling, a TV show,…running,…a band or singer [etc.], the rise of social media…means that you can search for and find other like-minded devotees and *voilà* you will have the basis of a tribe" (Cova & Shankar, 2012, p. 178). Unlike a consumer segment, tribes are made of heterogenous individuals who act as advocates and are brought together by a shared passion (Cova & Cova, 2002). Indeed, collective identification, sharing experiences, passions, and emotions, and being able to engage in a collective action are the three main features of consumer tribes. When consumer tribes form around a specific organisation or brand, then they evolve to brand communities (Cova & Shankar, 2012). In consumer tribes, members form less structured and more ephemeral relations with each other and, similar to subcultures of consumption, consumer tribes focus on practices instead of brands (Arvidsson & Caliandro, 2016; Canniford, 2011b; Cova & Pace, 2006).

Characteristics of consumer tribes

According to Canniford (2011a) consumer tribes have four main characteristics (Figure 6.5). First, *multiplicity*, which means that if a person is a member of one consumer tribe it does not mean that he/she cannot be a member of another tribe or community (Elliott & Davies, 2006). Certainly, in post-modern society, one can belong to multiple consumer tribes, for example, a person can be a fan of a sport (e.g. football) (one tribe) and of an activity (e.g. cooking) (another tribe). Hence, each tribe can articulate a shared experience of a specific aspect of one's life (Cova & Cova, 2002). This means that "notions of [personal] identity are 'constructed' rather than 'given', and 'fluid' rather than 'fixed'" (Bennett, 1999, p. 599). Second, *playfulness*, in connection with this membership multiplicity and identity fluidity, is about the lack of long-term moral responsibility typically found in brand communities (Muñiz Jr. & O'Guinn, 2001) and a lack of "reverence afforded to social hierarchies and totemic activities felt in subcultures of consumption" (Canniford, 2011a, p. 595). Instead, consumer tribes generate 'active play', i.e. deconstruction and reassembling, of numerous resources found in the marketplace such as emotions, aesthetics, brands, places, media etc., without assigning reverence to specific brands (Canniford, 2011a; Cova, Kozinets, & Shankar, 2007). Any value generated relates to the potential of reviving passions and generating new forms of linking value (Canniford, 2011a).

Third, *transience* is concerned with the ability of consumer tribes to emerge, evolve, and vanish as different combinations of individuals and resources continuously develop. This adds to the unpredictability of consumer tribes where certain processes might be vital at some point, and then suddenly they lose their significance

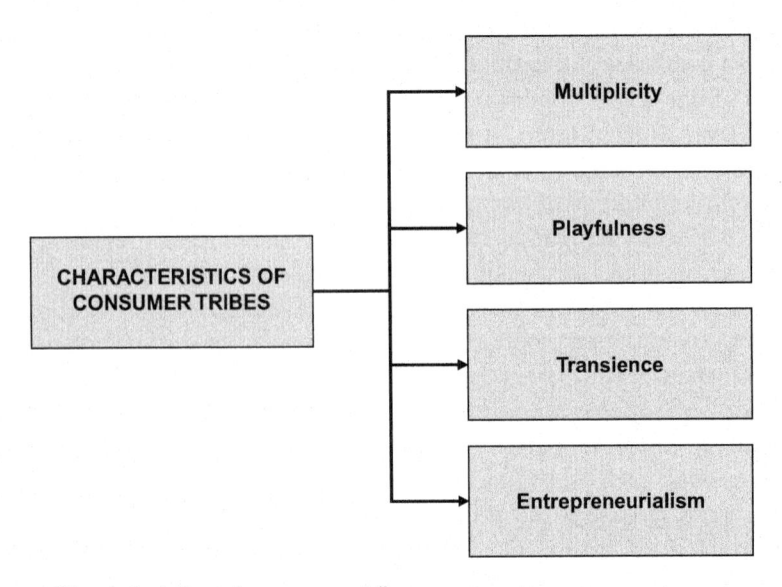

FIGURE 6.5 Characteristics of consumer tribes

and prominence: "Such a playful acceptance of rapidly changing, contradictory, and ambivalent meanings infers a power structure between consumers and the market that rapidly oscillates between manipulation and emancipation" (Canniford, 2011a, p. 595). Fourth, *entrepreneurialism* is about consumer tribes' ability to innovate based on their playfulness leading to new entrepreneurial ventures. For instance, Goulding, Shankar, Elliott, and Canniford (2009) explored the emergence of the 'club culture' "as a tribal reaction to changing aspects of the political environment in which raves were outlawed" (Canniford, 2011a, p. 595).

Seeding consumer tribes

The unpredictability and fluidity of consumer tribes is reinforced by the fact that nobody can control them and their processes. In fact, "the more marketers know about a tribe, the more likely the tribe will do something to break [the marketers'] rules" (Canniford, 2011a, p. 600). Yet many brand consultants recommend *brand tribes* as way to improve loyalty and brand equity. Thus, the vital question is whether or not consumer tribes can (or should) be managed. Any attempts to harness the power of consumer tribes must involve a recognition of their autonomy and integrity (Cova & Cova, 2001) and viewing marketing as "a boundless playing field from which consumers will select, interpret, and reject a profusion of cultural offerings" (Canniford, 2011a, p. 596). Failing to do so can lead to stifling the linking value of the consumer tribe and destroying a possible tribal marketing strategy.

Based on his research of 'board-sport tribes' (surfing and skate-boarding) and *Volcom*, a California-based board-sport brand, Canniford (2011a) recommends five interdependent ways brand marketers can 'seed' consumer tribes in a way that is respectful to their idiosyncrasies. First, there is a need to provide an offline and/or online *platform*, "a stage on which to improvise performances and assemble culture in a continual process of plundering, creativity, and innovation" (Canniford, 2011a, p. 598). Such platforms can include the Internet, social media, as well as physical places where consumers and organisations integrate different resources. Second, organisations need to foster a *hybrid culture* which recognises that "consumption communities are symbolically and emotionally constructed through shared product/ service on these platforms…[,and] consumers, products, services, spaces, places, and feelings are called into being through their interdependent associations" (Canniford, 2011b, p. 598). For example, over the years, the *BBC* has managed to replace a top-down information dissemination approach with a platform, which creates a "networked process of power sharing" between producers, viewers, and listeners (Canniford, 2011a, p. 599).

Third, brand marketers need to understand that consumer tribes assemble on the basis of *passion*. For instance, *Redbull* is not merely an energy drink brand, it has evolved to a brand which harnesses people's desire for peak performance and extreme sports, and provides the platforms for such passions to be dynamically articulated. Fourth, consumer tribes are *networks of heterogeneous individuals and things* brought together, thus brand marketers must attend to all elements of the constellation. Spaces, places, and material products provide the tools for consumer tribes' formation (Cova et al., 2007; Goulding et al., 2009). This means that instead of a brand marketer aiming to create a wholesale platform for the consumer tribe (based on his/her sole product or service), multiple organisations can simultaneously insert their different products and services in the consumer tribe, resulting in unique synergies and combinations (Canniford, 2011a). Hence a brand is not "the centralised locus of consumption (as is the case with brand community) [but]...a useful point of passage within a tribal network" (Canniford, 2011a, pp. 599–600). Finally, fifth, organisations must understand that consumer tribes are *dynamic*, they morph and evolve on a continuous basis, making their character an *identity-in-flux*. This requires from brand marketers to stay close to the consumer tribe to identify changes over time, and makes their job more difficult.

Bringing together these interdependent means of 'seeding' a consumer tribe, brand marketers can create a *seed network*, a hybrid constellation of people and resources, which enable consumers to create linking value (Canniford, 2011a). Over the years, *Volcom* has managed to harness the power of the board-sport consumer tribe by extending

> platforms of support, interest, and passion to consumers of art, music, and action sports culture...[Its] web presence is peppered with contributions from consumers who orbit around the skateboarding tribe. [It] recognises that tribal consumers exhibit multiple identities, and instead of seeking to place itself as the centre of any one identity, it seeks to permit hybrid networking opportunities...
> (Canniford, 2011a, pp. 601–602)

BRAND PUBLICS

The fourth type of consumption communities is *brand publics*. A brand public is defined as

> an organised media space kept together by a continuity of practices of mediation [such as *Twitter* hashtags]. Brand publics result from an aggregation of a large number of isolated expressions that have a common focus. Contrary to brand communities, they do not build on sustained forms of interaction or any consistent collective identity.
> (Arvidsson & Caliandro, 2016, p. 727)

This type of consumption communities is facilitated by widespread use of social media such as *Facebook*, *Twitter* and *Instagram*, which allow consumers to form less structured and more fleeting and ephemeral relationships with each other in comparison with the enduring social bonds found in brand communities (Arvidsson

& Caliandro, 2016). As discussed in Chapter 4, social media encourage a publicity-oriented consumer culture where individuals seek to create an attractive self-brand and achieve a micro-celebrity status (Khamis, Ang, & Welling, 2017; Marwick, 2015). Such culture is "oriented around appearance and visibility rather than identity and belonging,…[where] value co-creation is structured by private or collective affects, rather than deliberation and common values…Social media participation tends to give rise to publics rather than communities" (Arvidsson & Caliandro, 2016, pp. 727–728). This leads to what Belk (2014) called *pseudo-sharing* where although consumers share their opinions, perspectives, and experiences, they do so without expecting reciprocity or community formation (Arvidsson & Caliandro, 2016). The concept of brand publics bridges "the gap between the hard, physical, interpersonal, and social character of consumption communities however defined, and the fluid, digital, and communicative or conversational nature of consumers' collectives" (Cova & Dalli, 2018, p. 240).

Brand publics on social media can be viewed as digital crowds where online (instead of physical) aggregations of people are "energised by affectively driven 'waves' of imitation" (Arvidsson & Caliandro, 2016, p. 730) (similar to football fans celebrating when the home team scores), and "the possibility for public re-mediation without interaction creates a basic orientation toward publicity-oriented sharing of personal views or perspectives" (Arvidsson & Caliandro, 2016, p. 731). In their study of almost nine thousand tweets about the *Louis Vuitton* brand on Italian *Twitter*, Arvidsson and Caliandro (2016) identified three nuanced differences between brand communities and brand publics. First, in contrast with a brand community that is maintained by social interactions among its members, a brand public involves mediation, using devices such as a hashtag, which is continued with little or no interaction between participants. Second, unlike brand communities, which require communication, i.e. responding to and engaging with community members, in brand publics, participants do not engage with one another but merely imitate each other by sharing their views on specific issues. Third, unlike brand communities where members articulate a shared identity, brand publics are not a source of identification because they are simply spaces of public sharing perspectives and experiences that stem from a number of identities and practices that are not organised into clearly recognised shared values. In addition, a fourth distinction between brand communities and brand publics is that the units of analysis of the former are individuals and groups whereas that of the latter "is the medium and the flow of communication within it and therefore management is oriented towards this fluid dimension: social media, social networks, and the like" (Cova & Dalli, 2018, p. 239).

Based on these differences, Arvidsson, and Caliandro (2016) also determined four important characteristics of brand publics (see Figure 6.6).

[First,] a brand public is an organised media space kept together by a continuity of practices of mediation that are centred on a mediation device such as a hashtag…[Second, a brand public is] made up of structured aggregations of heterogeneous meanings without the formation of collective values…[Third,]… in brand publics participation is not structured by interaction but by private or collective affect…The function of the brand public is not to supply a focus for identification but a vehicle for visibility and publicity. [Fourth,] brand publics add publicity value to brands.

(Arvidsson and Caliandro, 2016, p. 742–744)

Brand publics can contribute to increased brand reputation because they facilitate the aggregation of a great number of disconnected individuals who sporadically contribute to online brand content. People tend to participate for their own gain because they can achieve social media fame for themselves. It is evident from the above that the publicity fostered by brand publics feeds into the attention economy, discussed in Chapter 4, and can be viewed as a new form of social capital (Bourdieu, 1986) which is more liquid and experience-oriented (Arvidsson & Caliandro, 2016). To summarise, drawing from Arvidsson and Caliandro (2016) and Canniford (2011a), we could argue that the *locus* of brand publics is mediation through social media. Similar to consumer tribes, their *power structure* can be characterised as a diffused, democratic, and hybrid network, with a fluid and fast moving structure. Like brand communities and consumer tribes, their *social position* is mobile and mainstreamed, however, their main *purpose* is visibility and publicity and they have a short-term and ephemeral *time span*. Table 6.1 provides a summary of the similarities and differences between the four types of communities of consumption.

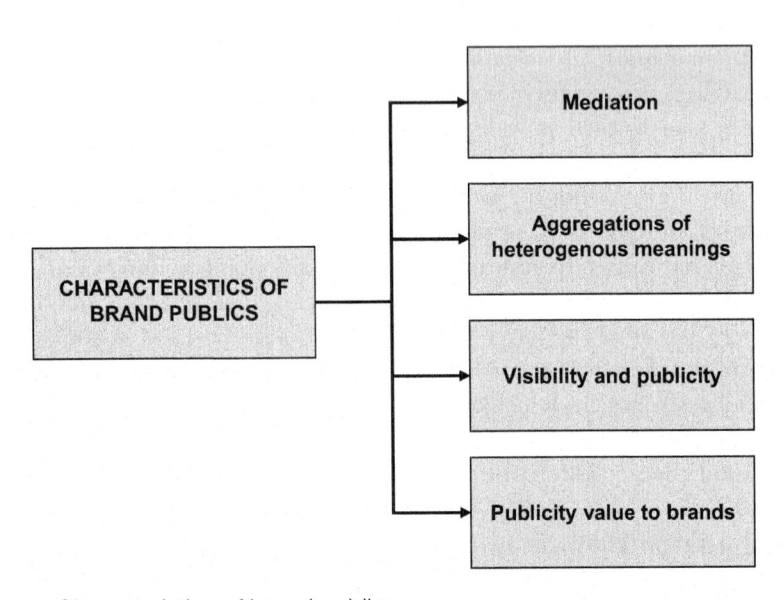

FIGURE 6.6 Characteristics of brand publics

BRAND AVOIDANCE AND ANTI-CONSUMPTION

Brand avoidance defined

As previously explored, one of the ways brand community members can develop a consciousness of kind is through oppositional brand loyalty, i.e. by opposing competing brands. This brings our discussion to the phenomenon of anti-consumption. The term encompasses a wide variety of attitudes and behaviours spanning "from harmless beliefs, such as negative perceptions of fast food, to violent and illegal behaviours, such as the act of vandalism and arson targeted at companies such as *McDonald's* and *Nike*" (Sandikci & Ekici, 2009, p. 208). Anti-consumption can be manifested by a mere preference to consume one brand over another or more profoundly by "a resistance to, distaste of, or even resentment or rejection of, consumption more generally" (Zavestoski, 2002, p. 121). An important question is of course what motivates people to engage in anti-consumption of certain brands and brand avoidance. *Brand avoidance* is consumers' active rejection of a brand and does not include situations where they reject the brand because they cannot afford it, or because it is not available or accessible.

Types of brand avoidance

Lee, Motion, and Conroy (2009) determined three types of brand avoidance that can explain the reasons consumers avoid certain brands (see Figure 6.7). First, with *experiential avoidance*, consumers avoid a brand because of negative first-hand experiences. It relates to *negative disconfirmation* "between what was expected by the consumer and what was delivered by the brand" (Lee et al., 2009, p. 172). Naturally, the most basic consumer expectation is about product functionality and performance; a product failing to function or perform as expected means that consumers may avoid the brand in the future. In addition, "the added hassle/inconvenience of a failed consumption experience and unpleasant store environment may also compound the brand avoidance incident" (Lee et al., 2009, p. 173).

Second, *identity avoidance* relates to cases when the brand cannot fulfil a person's symbolic identity requirements. This type of brand avoidance connects with the concepts of the *undesired self*, i.e. "an aspect of the negative self that a person is afraid of becoming" (Sandikci & Ekici, 2009, p. 210) and *disidentification*, whereby individuals cultivate their self-concept by disassociating themselves with organizations which are inconsistent with their own image and values (Lee et al., 2009). The undesired self is manifested by distastes and dislikes which can articulate as much about an individual as his/her preferences and likes (Banister & Hogg, 2001; Hogg & Banister, 2001). Karanika and Hogg (2010) discovered that the undesired self can be compatible or conflicting with one's desired self, leading to different identity-handling strategies. Their empirical study demonstrated that when there was *compatibility*, "consumers' pursuit of their desired self meant they succeeded

```
                                    ┌─────────────────────────┐
                                  ┌─│ Experiential avoidance  │
                                  │ └─────────────────────────┘
┌─────────────────────┐           │ ┌─────────────────────────┐
│  TYPES OF BRAND     │───────────┼─│  Identity avoidance     │
│  AVOIDANCE          │           │ └─────────────────────────┘
└─────────────────────┘           │ ┌─────────────────────────┐
                                  └─│  Moral avoidance        │
                                    └─────────────────────────┘
```

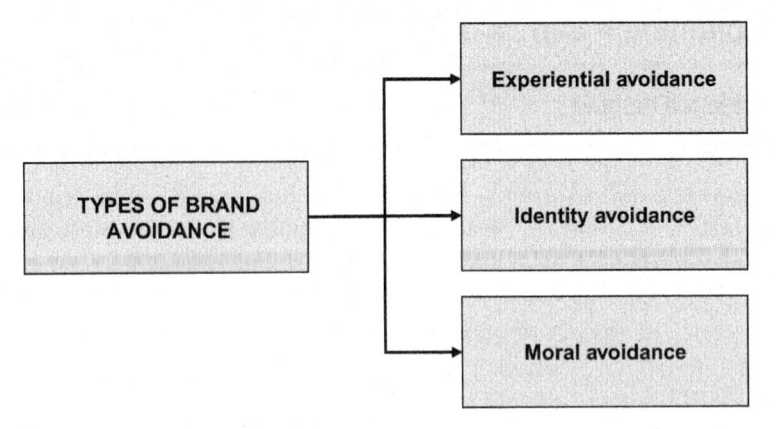

FIGURE 6.7 Types of brand avoidance

in avoiding an undesired self and vice versa" (Karanika & Hogg, 2010, p. 1102), whereas with *conflict* "consumers experience the dilemma of choosing between one pair of desired/undesired selves over another pair of desired/undesired selves" (Karanika & Hogg, 2010, p. 1097). The undesired self will cause the individual to avoid using a product or service that he/she associates with negative user stereotypes (Hogg & Banister, 2001).

> Negative symbolic meanings that the brand represents to the individual and how those meanings are incongruent with his or her self-concept motivate identity avoidance. For some participants, certain brands may represent a negative reference group, a lack of authenticity, or a loss of individuality, since all are aspects of an individual's undesired self, such brands are avoided accordingly.
> (Lee et al., 2009, p. 175)

Third, *moral avoidance* derives from ideological incompatibility, that is, when the brand and what it stands for is not compatible with a person's "political and socio-cultural sets of beliefs" (Lee et al., 2009, p. 175). Political ideology is "a belief system that explains and justifies a preferred political order for society, either existing or proposed, and offers a strategy for its attainment" (Christenson, 1971, p. 5). Consumers are often inclined to resist oppressive or dominating forces (anti-hegemony) by avoiding certain brands, for example, with anti-Americanism consumers avoid US brands because they want to defy their globally dominant power. Instead, consumers often feel a strong bond with local brands that are part of their community (financial patriotism) because this can lead to a stronger domestic economy and associated societal and individual benefits (consumer ethnocentrism) (Lee et al., 2009). Sandikci and Ekici (2009) tried to understand the reasons behind politically driven brand rejection in the context of *Coca-Cola* and *Cola Turka* (a Turkish cola brand). They discovered that some consumers rejected *Coca-Cola* because it was viewed as a manifestation of predatory globalisation, while other consumers rejected *Cola Turka* because it was associated with chauvinistic nationalism and religious fundamentalism. It is also possible that when consumers are frustrated with an organisation's behaviour, they form counter-brand communities that create spin-off products. For example when *Warhammer* (the table-top strategic battle game played with miniatures) community members felt exploited by *Games Workshop*, the organisation behind it, they started designing and selling their own counterfeit miniatures, and eventually developed their own game called *Confrontation*, forming a counter-brand community (Cova & White, 2010).

There are three ways organisations can manage brand avoidance. First, *avoidance barriers* make it difficult for consumers to avoid certain brands, including lack of alternatives, consumer inertia (cost of switching), influence of others (pressure to conform), and low product involvement (where a lack of perceived differences reduces the need to avoid specific brands). Second, *avoidance antidotes* include organisations genuinely changing their culture to become more responsible or "augmenting the value of the brand by either amplifying its perceived quality and/or attenuating its perceived costs" (Lee et al., 2009, p. 177). Third, antidotes can also include introducing a sub-brand, forming networks with other brands positively viewed by consumers, providing consumers with samples to re-experience the brand, and seeking to develop positive word-of-mouth (WOM) for the brand. However, it is important to admit that these activities can only go so far as "some feelings of hatred towards the brand may simply be too intense to remedy" (incurable avoidance) (Lee et al., 2009, p. 178).

POLITICAL CONSUMPTION

Moral avoidance, and ideological incompatibility as its source, exemplifies *political consumption* because it occurs when consumers view brand policies as having negative consequences on society (Lee et al., 2009). Political consumption has many forms: boycotts, buycotts, discursive, and lifestyle, political consumerism (Boström, 2019) (see Figure 6.8). First, *boycotting* a brand is different to brand avoidance because it

> builds from an implicit commitment, by the boycotter, to re-enter the relationship once certain conditions are met, such as a change of policy by the offending party...[whereas] in brand avoidance, there is no guarantee that the consumption relationship will resume in the future.
>
> (Lee et al., 2009, p. 170)

Boycotting can involve brands and organisations, as well as countries, regimes, and categories of products or services, which could indirectly impact brands (Boström, 2019).

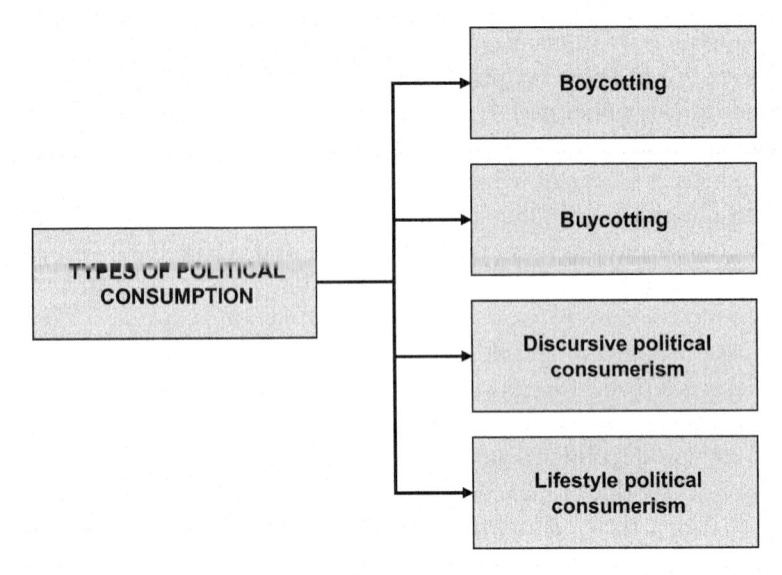

FIGURE 6.8 Types of political consumption

Second, *buycotting* connects with boycotting since a boycott of one brand comes with the promotion and choice of another brand. Buycotting relates to corporate social responsibility (CSR) and allows organisations to appeal to ethically and politically conscious consumers. One could argue that *Nike* sought to harness the power of buycotting by including in its advertising Colin Kaepernick, a former *National Football League* (NFL) player, who had made international headlines by kneeling during the American national anthem in order to promote social justice and had been subsequently accused of being unpatriotic by US President Donald Trump and dropped by *NFL* teams. The advert included a powerful message: "Believe in something. Even if it means sacrificing everything", and targeted consumers who disagreed with Trump's behaviour and *NFL* teams' decision to refrain from offering Colin Kaepernick a new contract. Of course, it is important to stress that organisations trying to target ethical consumers must do so in a way that is transparent to ensure legitimacy of their activities and avoid being accused of imitation, hypocrisy, and/or greenwashing (Boström, 2019). Perhaps critics of *Nike* would quickly point to the company's unimpressive record regarding sweatshops and its production practices in third world countries, and would reject such advertising messages as merely dishonest and disingenuous. "Critical literature suggests that ethical and green branding are often done more to seek legitimacy for one's business and increase profit than to actually open up space for politically conscious consumption" (Boström, 2019, p. 214).

The third type of political consumption is *discursive political consumerism*, which can be defined as

> the expression of opinions about corporate policy and practice in communicative efforts directed at business, the public at large, family and friends, and various

political institutions…It targets other vulnerable points within corporations, namely their image, brand names, reputation, and logos.

(Micheletti & Stolle, 2008, pp. 752–753)

In discursive political consumerism, activists, journalists, and social movements monitor and debate organisational practices to expose any dishonesty and misalignment between rhetoric and practice. According to Boström (2019), a major type of discursive political consumerism is *culture jamming*, which "targets and subverts the meanings of cultural logos and slogans" (Boström, 2019, p. 216) and picks on organisational vulnerabilities. Well-known culture jamming movements include *Adbusters* (an anti-consumerism, earth-friendly magazine and movement founded in the 1980s) and *Brandalism*, who act in urban spaces and install art works in bus stop advertising panels (Boström, 2019). Muñiz Jr. & O'Guinn (2001) have an optimistic view of brand communities as arenas "for (digital) discussion, consumer agency, and sharing of information, [however] in digital platforms, negative sentiments towards particular brands may escalate to levels that may be quite worrisome for brand marketers" (Boström, 2019, pp. 216–217).

In relation to current social movements, unlike the baby boomer generation who wanted to break the system, or generation X consumers who are often portrayed as apathic and individualistic, millennials are pragmatic because they believe that institutions in society can be improved, and seek to work within systems (Gafni, 2015). Millennials are empowered by technology that gives them the tools and platforms to drive this change, and "expect all aspects of their lives to be integrated" (Gafni, 2015, p.1). Hence, they engage in what Gafni (2015) calls *conscious movements*, which differ from other movements in three ways. First, they use both old and new forms of power. An example is the *Global Shapers Community*, which as part of

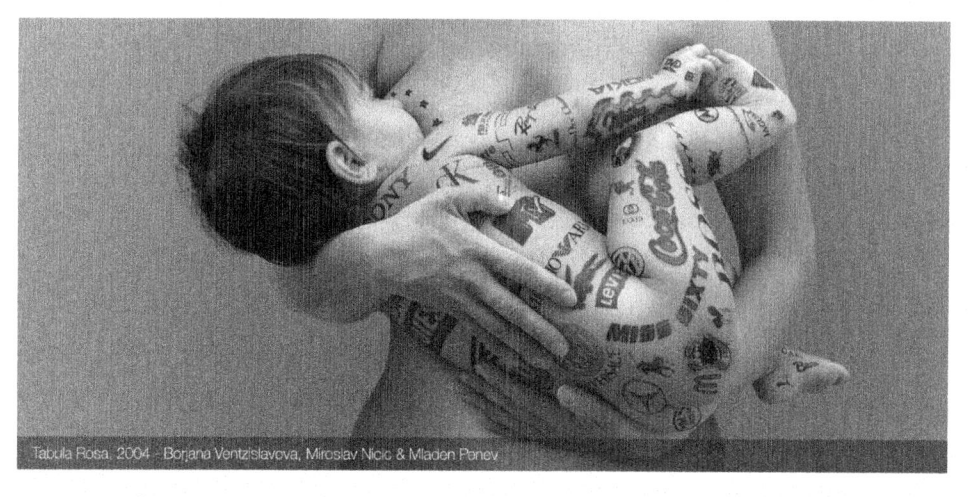

IMAGE 6.1 Culture-jamming (image courtesy of Adbusters Media Foundation)

Thinner than ever.

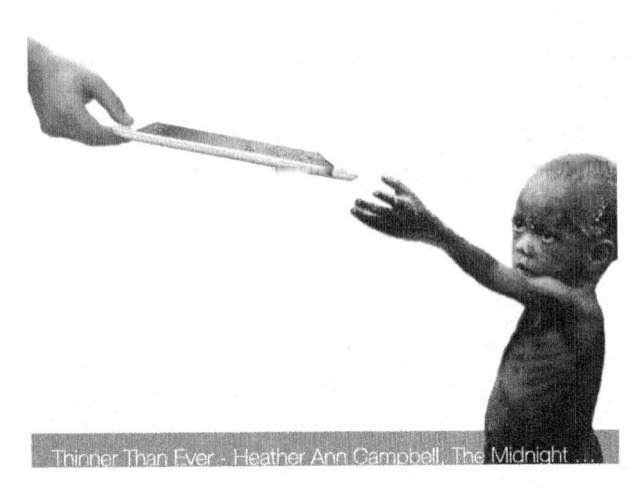

IMAGE 6.2 Culture-jamming (image courtesy of Adbusters Media Foundation)

the *World Economic Forum* in Davos, Switzerland, connects world leaders with shapers in cross-mentorship schemes. Second, such movements connect both online and in the physical world as they understand the importance of both in-person and online meetings. Third, they bring together global and local influence to solve world challenges. For example, the *+SocialGood* community, founded by organisations such as the *United Nations Foundation*, the *Bill & Melinda Gates Foundation*, and the *Rockefeller Foundation*, "unites changemakers around the power of innovation and technology to make the world a better place" (Gafni, 2015, p.2).

Finally, a fourth type of political consumption is *lifestyle political consumerism*, which involves a more holistic commitment on how a person leads his/her life. In this case, the focus might be a type of product or service, yet brands still play a very important role as they may act as both positive and negative references. Individuals make brand choices to include or exclude themselves from various lifestyles (Muñiz Jr. & O'Guinn, 2001). Through an extensive qualitative study, Thompson and Arsel (2004) explored the *anti-Starbucks* discourse and identified two types of local coffee shop consumption (as opposed to *Starbucks*): the *café flâneurs* and the *oppositional localists*, articulately explained with the following:

> *Café flâneurs* are acting upon a cosmopolitan desire to experience authentic local cultures, where authenticity is understood through a symbolic contrast to the commercialized experiences offered by conventional tourist sites and McDonaldized servicescapes…Rather than viewing Starbucks as a corporate colossus destroying local competition, they regard it as a boring, standardized, and mass-marketed meeting place, catering to the prosaic tastes of the corporate

world. They valorise local coffee shops as non-commercial environments where they can experience aesthetic and social stimulation, and enjoy, as a kind of gift from the establishments' proprietors, an authentic expression of local culture. [In contrast,] *oppositional localists* are acting upon an emancipatory desire to create communal spaces and exchange systems that offer an alternative to the profit-driven, commodity logic of corporate capitalism...They take the anti-Starbucks discourse as a socio-political gospel and regard the support of local coffee shops as a consequential rebuke to corporate power. Oppositional localists are fairly militant in their views about what constitutes a legitimate local coffee shop, questioning the social consciousness and motivations of any proprietor whose establishment does not display a strident anti-Starbucks's political sensibility.

(Thompson & Arsel, 2004, p. 639)

It is clear that these consumers developed their identity through their opposition to the *Starbucks* brand (Muñiz Jr. & O'Guinn, 2001; Thompson & Arsel, 2004).

Holt (2016) emphasises that branding in the digital age requires the pursuit of cultural branding, whereby organisations recognise the power of *crowdcultures*. These involve "subcultures which incubate new ideologies and practices, and art worlds which break new ground in entertainment" (Holt, 2016, p. 43). Crowdcultures were born out of youth subcultures of video gamers who shared and critiqued online content, and evolved to a number of different genres. Nowadays social media stars (e.g. *PewDiePie*, the Swedish YouTuber and online comedian) reach followings, which big brands such as *McDonald's*, *Coca-Cola*, and even *Red Bull*, the darling of branded content, have failed to achieve despite their efforts and investment. Evidently, consumers are disinterested in branded content which they view as clutter or spam. To be successful brands need to engage in cultural branding where they promote truly an innovative ideology that breaks product or service category conventions. Brands such as *Axe* (*Lynx* in the UK), *Dove*, and *Old Spice* have achieved this because

each engaged a cultural discourse about gender and sexuality in wide circulation in social media – a crowdculture – which espoused a distinctive ideology. Each acted as a proselytizer, promoting this ideology to a mass audience. Such opportunities come into view only if we use the prism of cultural branding – doing research to identify ideologies that are relevant to the category and gaining traction in crowdcultures...Companies need to shift their focus away from the [social media] platforms themselves and toward the real locus of digital power – crowdcultures...Companies can once again win the battle for cultural relevance with cultural branding, which will allow them to tap into the power of the crowd.

(Holt, 2016, p. 50)

CHAPTER REVIEW QUESTIONS

You can use the following questions to reflect on the material covered in Chapter 6:

1. Discuss the collectivist and constructivist aspects of consumption.
2. Critically explore the main characteristics of the four types of communities of consumption.
3. What are the differences and similarities of the four types of communities of consumption?
4. How can organisations harness the potential of communities of consumption?
5. What are the causes of brand avoidance and anti-consumption?
6. Define political consumption and explore the four types of political consumption.

RECOMMENDED READING

1. Schouten, J. W., & McAlexander, J. H. (1995). Subcultures of consumption: An ethnography of the new bikers. *Journal of Consumer Research*, 22(1), 43–61.
2. Muñiz Jr., A. M., & O'Guinn, T. C. (2001). Brand community. *Journal of Consumer Research*, 27(4), 412–432.
3. Canniford, R. (2011a). How to manage consumer tribes. *Journal of Strategic Marketing*, 19(7), 591–606.
4. Arvidsson, A., & Caliandro, A. (2016). Brand public. *Journal of Consumer Research*, 42(5), 727–748.
5. Boström, M. (2019). Rejecting and embracing brands in political consumerism. In M. Boström, M. Micheletti, & P. Oosterveer (eds), *The Oxford handbook of political consumerism* (pp. 205–225). Oxford: Oxford University Press.

CASE STUDY

Beyond the football borders: Going ahead to grow the relationship with fans and entertainment enthusiasts

Luca Adornato
Head of Marketing at *Juventus*

and Lidi Grimaldi,
Managing Director at Interbrand Milan

On the global market, sports brands now play a role that goes beyond just performing on the field, and have entered the broader sphere of entertainment. In this context, it suffices to say that sport is the second industry in terms of market share (€ 142 Bln, 21% of the share). As part of this movement, football is by far the lead player (€ 40 Bln, 28%). Indeed, entertainment and sporting performances co-exist within in an ecosystem of content and channels, moving seamlessly between physical and digital; the goal is to engage with local and international audiences by building a global community united by values that transcend individual sectors.

Apparently it's a symbol for a 'way of living' that represents the 'future of football'.

(*CNN.com*, 18 January 2017)

This was *CNN*'s take on the launch of *Juventus*' new branding and marketing strategy in 2017. Indeed, the Club masterfully anticipated changes in the market, as it undertook a growth process aimed at expanding its horizons beyond the football pitch, to become an entity with the potential to contribute to the everyday lives of us all. It is a brand that aims to offer unique experiences for its fans both in and outside the stadium but is also capable of creating relevant content about itself for people who are seemingly uninvolved in football. This long-term project was boosted by the creation of its marketing story LIVE AHEAD™, and puts *Juventus* at the forefront of a change of tack that is revolutionising the sector.

As part of this process, the new identity has a key role: to represent in an unmistakable and utterly distinctive way the DNA of *Juventus*, and its values of football tradition, excellence and ambition, through a new, transversal language. The logo — the universal expression of the Club's very essence through the initial J, the stripes of the jersey and the shield — is not just a symbol of allegiance to a soccer team: it is a lifestyle based on passion, on the courage to always look ahead and persevere,

IMAGE 6.3 New branding and marketing strategy launch event, Milan, 16 January, 2017 (image courtesy of Juventus)

IMAGE 6.4 *YourIcon* contest entry (image courtesy of Juventus)

something that the various communities of football fans around the world all have in common. Not by chance, recently the *YourIcon* contest was launched, challenging the football fan community to creatively reinterpret the Juventus logo.

The LIVE AHEAD™ marketing story is a platform that develops, strengthens and expands the positioning launched in 2017. It is a common thread that links together the brand's roots with the limitless opportunities for future projects and activities in which football will always be the origin, but not the limit. LIVE AHEAD™ completes and articulates the approach the brand has always had in all of its activities and communication, its wish to always be a leader with the ability to set new standards and point its peers in the right direction; but at the same time, it's a message that fans can identify with and trust. It is a statement that has relevance to a wider audience of entertainment enthusiasts, allowing them to recognise themselves among the many different facets that the brand is now able to express.

Over time, *Juventus* has won the hearts of more than 430 million football fans around the world, with a growing number of fans in Asia. For the first time in its history, Juventus has become the most-supported soccer team in an Asian country, namely Indonesia. Alongside this growth, its impressive feats on social networks have enabled it to engage with new target audiences in a quicker, deeper way, by offering storytelling about its core activities as well as initiatives that have been made possible by the club's repositioning and rebranding. The role of storytelling used on the Club's media channels is aimed at bringing together the global community of fans,

COLLECTIVES, AVOIDANCE, & CONSUMPTION **203**

IMAGE 6.5 *YourIcon* contest entry (image courtesy of Juventus)

IMAGE 6.6 *YourIcon* contest entry (image courtesy of Juventus)

204 COLLECTIVES, AVOIDANCE, & CONSUMPTION

IMAGE 6.7 *YourIcon* contest entry (image courtesy of Juventus)

IMAGE 6.8 *YourIcon* contest entry (image courtesy of Juventus)

COLLECTIVES, AVOIDANCE, & CONSUMPTION   205

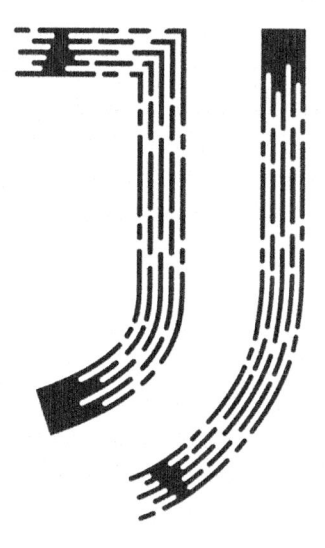

IMAGE 6.9 *YourIcon* contest entry (image courtesy of Juventus)

IMAGE 6.10 *Live Ahead* marketing story at the Allianz Stadium (image courtesy of Juventus)

206 COLLECTIVES, AVOIDANCE, & CONSUMPTION

enthusiasts, and brand lovers beneath a sole common denominator, represented by the brand's values.

The brand's new trajectory has allowed the Club to revise all of its points of contact in a substantial yet credible way. From the most traditional ones, such as its jersey, the Allianz Stadium, merchandising products, and fan engagement activities; to more apparently distant areas, by creating unique, distinctive experiences in strategic markets. The *JVillage* in Shanghai and the *Juventus Night* in Brooklyn (the first brand takeover of an NBA arena in history) are the most shining examples. This also enabled the Club to build outstanding collaborations such as the one it signed in November 2019 with *Adidas* and *Palace* for a capsule collection (which sold out on its first day of sales), redefining the benchmark for style in Italian and international football.

It might have seemed rather rash to imagine such an impactful result in just a few years, one that would break down the barriers of an entire sector. But time has proved *Juventus* and *Interbrand* right. Having anticipated shifts in the market and the desires of its own audience — and beyond — by courageously implementing what *Interbrand* defines as an 'Iconic Move', has brought rewards in terms of interaction with the public, collaborations and commercial results. Today, *Juventus* is one of the leading brands in the sports-entertainment industry; and it legitimately aspires to go

IMAGE 6.11 *Juventus* capsule collection in collaboration with *Adidas* and *Palace* (image courtesy of Juventus)

dimensions: geography, social context, temporality (enduring vs. periodic), and basis of identification (McAlexander et al., 2002).

McAlexander et al. studied the *Jeep* brand community and in particular *brandfests*, which are "geo-temporal distillations of a brand community [where] normally dispersed member entities [have] the opportunity for high-context interaction" (2002, p. 42), i.e. brand events that bring together the brand community. Brandfests provide benefits for both new brand owners and veterans; the former gain from the veteran's expertise and social approval, while the latter gain from the status conferred to them as assumed leaders of the community. In addition, during brandfests, brand marketers can actively foster Muñiz Jr. & O'Guinn's (2001) brand community characteristics of consciousness of kind, shared rituals and traditions, and sense of moral responsibility. Although brandfests take place over a specific period of time, they enable strong relationships due to their contextual richness, creating more stability and a greater sense of community longevity (McAlexander et al., 2002).

> Sharing meaningful consumption experiences strengthens interpersonal ties and enhances mutual appreciation for the product, the brand, and the facilitating marketers. Virtual ties become real ties. Weak ties become stronger. Strong ties develop additional points of attachment…Consumer-centric relationships with different entities in the brand community might be cumulative or even synergistic in forming a single construct akin to customer loyalty…More and stronger points of attachment should lead to greater integration in a brand community (IBC).
>
> (McAlexander et al., 2002, p. 44)

Through quantitative analysis, supported by additional ethnographic data, McAlexander et al. (2002) confirmed the multifaceted nature of brand communities which brandfests can help build. They determined that the integration in the brand community (IBC) is "the cumulative impact of four types of customer-centred relationships [focal customer with the brand, (another) customer, the branded product, and the marketer]" (McAlexander et al., 2002, p. 46). Despite the fact that these relationships are often portrayed as dyadic, they are inter-dependent and mutually reinforcing: "Each relationship connects to all the others through the central nexus of consumer experience, creating the holistic sense of a surrounding community…[,and] each relationship acts as a personal linkage to the brand community" (McAlexander et al., 2002, p. 46). The consumer becomes increasingly integrated into the brand community and more loyal to the brand when he/she internalises each relationship as part of his/her life experience (McAlexander et al., 2002). The marketing implication of this is that organisations should seek to differentiate their brands not only on the basis of the product or its positioning but also on the basis of the experience of ownership and consumption. Organisations can sponsor and

IMAGE 6.12 *Juventus* fans (image courtesy of Juventus)

beyond that sphere, to become a fully fledged global lovemark (in June 2020 *Juventus* became the Italian brand with the highest number of followers on *Instagram*).

Questions for discussion

1. Why should a sports brand transcend its own sector?
2. How must football fans' loyalty be won and revived?
3. How can we credibly champion and leverage a Club's identity to extend beyond the sports sector?
4. What can football learn from other sectors, and which sectors might learn from the football category?
5. Having undertaken this new direction, what are the next steps we can expect from *Juventus*, and which ones might we not expect (i.e. in line with what has been done so far, or 'out of the box')?

REFERENCES

Aaker, D. A. (2010). *Building strong brands*. London: Simon and Schuster.
Arnould, E. J., & Price, L. L. (1993). River magic: Extraordinary experience and the extended service encounter. *Journal of Consumer Research*, 20(1), 24–45.
Arvidsson, A., & Caliandro, A. (2016). Brand public. *Journal of Consumer Research*, 42(5), 727–748.

Avery, J. (2012). The relational roles of brands. In L. Peñaloza, N. Toulouse, & L. M. Visconti (eds), *Marketing management: A cultural perspective* (pp. 147–163). London: Routledge.

Banister, E. N., & Hogg, M. K. (2001). Mapping the negative self: From "so not me" ... to "just not me". *Advances in Consumer Research, 28,* 242–248.

Belk, R. W. (1988). Possessions and the extended self. *Journal of Consumer Research, 15*(2), 139–168.

Belk, R. W. (2014). You are what you can access: Sharing and collaborative consumption online. *Journal of Business Research, 67*(8), 1595–1600.

Bennett, A. (1999). Subcultures or neo-tribes? Rethinking the relationship between youth, style and musical taste. *Sociology, 33*(3), 599–617.

Boorstin, D. J. (1974). *The Americans: The democratic experience.* New York: Vintage.

Boström, M. (2019). Rejecting and embracing brands in political consumerism. In M. Boström, M. Micheletti, & P. Oosterveer (eds), *The Oxford handbook of political consumerism* (pp. 205–225). Oxford: Oxford University Press.

Bourdieu, P. (1984). *Distinction: A social critique of the judgement of taste* (Richard Nice, trans.). Cambridge: Harvard University Press.

Bourdieu, P. (1986). The forms of capital. In J. Richardson (ed.), *Handbook of theory and research for the sociology of education* (pp. 241–258). New York: Greenwood Press.

Canniford, R. (2011a). How to manage consumer tribes. *Journal of Strategic Marketing, 19*(7), 591–606.

Canniford, R. (2011b). A typology of consumption communities. In R. W. Belk, K. Grayson, A. M, Muñiz Jr., & H. Jensen Schau (eds), *Research in consumer behaviour* (Vol. 13) (pp. 57–75). London: Emerald.

Christenson, R. M. (1971). *Ideologies and modern politics.* New York: Dodd, Mead & Company.

Cova, B. (1997). Community and consumption: Towards a definition of the "linking value" of product or services. *European Journal of Marketing, 31*(3/4), 297–316.

Cova, B., & Cova, V. (2001). Tribal aspects of postmodern consumption research: The case of French in-line roller skaters. *Journal of Consumer Behaviour: An International Research Review, 1*(1), 67–76.

Cova, B., & Cova, V. (2002). Tribal marketing: The tribalisation of society and its impact on the conduct of marketing. *European Journal of Marketing, 36*(5/6), 595–620.

Cova, B., & Dalli, D. (2018). Prosumption tribes: How consumers collectively rework brands, products, services and markets. In O. Kravets, P. Maclaran, S. Miles, & A. Venkatesh (eds), *The Sage handbook of consumer culture* (pp. 235–255). London: Sage.

Cova, B., Kozinets, R., & Shankar, A. (eds) (2007). *Consumer tribes.* London: Routledge.

Cova, B., & Pace, S. (2006). Brand community of convenience products: New forms of customer empowerment – The case "my Nutella The Community". *European Journal of Marketing, 40*(9/10), 1087–1105.

Cova, B., & Shankar, A. (2012). Tribal marketing. In L. Peñaloza, N. Toulouse, & L. M. Visconti (eds), *Marketing management: A cultural perspective* (pp. 178–193). London: Routledge.

Cova, B., & White, T. (2010). Counter-brand and alter-brand communities: The impact of Web 2.0 on tribal marketing approaches. *Journal of Marketing Management, 26*(3–4), 256–270.

Doney, P. M., & Cannon, J. P. (1997). An examination of the nature of trust in buyer–seller relationships. *Journal of Marketing, 61*(2), 35–51.

Dwyer, F. R., Schurr, P. H., & Oh, S. (1987). Developing buyer-seller relationships. *Journal of Marketing, 51*(2), 11–27.

Elliott, R., & Davies, A. (2006). Symbolic brands and authenticity of identity performance. In J. E. Schroeder & M. Salzer-Mörling (eds), *Brand culture* (pp. 155–170). London: Routledge.

Fournier, S., & Lee, L. (2009). Getting brand communities right. *Harvard Business Review*, 87(4), 105–111.

Gafni, N. (2015). Why so many millennials aren't into protest movements. *Harvard Business Review: Generational Issues*. Available at: https://hbr.org/2015/10/why-so-many-millennials-arent-into-protest-movements [accessed 5 December 2019].

Goulding, C., Shankar, A., Elliott, R., & Canniford, R. (2009). The marketplace management of illicit pleasure. *Journal of Consumer Research*, 35(5), 759–771.

Hogg, M. K., & Banister, E. N. (2001). Dislikes, distastes and the undesired self: Conceptualising and exploring the role of the undesired end state in consumer experience. *Journal of Marketing Management*, 17(1–2), 73–104.

Holbrook, M. B., & Hirschman, E. C. (1982). The experiential aspects of consumption: Consumer fantasies, feelings, and fun. *Journal of Consumer Research*, 9(2), 132-140.

Holt, D. B. (1998). Does cultural capital structure American consumption? *Journal of Consumer Research*, 25(1), 1–25.

Holt, D. B. (2004). *How brands become icons: The principles of cultural branding*. Cambridge: Harvard Business Press.

Holt, D. B. (2016). Branding in the age of social media. *Harvard Business Review*, 94(3), 40–50.

Jannowitz, M. (1952). *The Community Press in an Urban Setting*. Glencoe: Free Press.

Karanika, K., & Hogg, M. K. (2010). The interrelationship between desired and undesired selves and consumption: The case of Greek female consumers' experiences. *Journal of Marketing Management*, 26(11–12), 1091–1111.

Keller, K. L. (1993). Conceptualizing, measuring, and managing customer-based brand equity. *Journal of Marketing*, 57(1), 1–22.

Keller, K. L. (2001). *Building customer-based brand equity: A blueprint for creating strong brands* (pp. 3–27). Cambridge: Marketing Science Institute.

Keller, K. L., & Swaminathan, V. (2020). *Strategic brand management: Building, measuring, and managing brand equity* (5th edn). London: Pearson Education.

Khamis, S., Ang, L., & Welling, R. (2017). Self-branding, "micro-celebrity" and the rise of social media influencers. *Celebrity Studies*, 8(2), 191–208.

Lee, M. S., Motion, J., & Conroy, D. (2009). Anti-consumption and brand avoidance. *Journal of Business Research*, 62(2), 169–180.

Marwick, A. E. (2015). Instafame: Luxury selfies in the attention economy. *Public Culture*, 27(1/75), 137–160.

Micheletti, M., & Stolle, D. (2008). Fashioning social justice through political consumerism, capitalism, and the internet. *Cultural Studies*, 22(5), 749–769.

McAlexander, J. H., Schouten, J. W., & Koenig, H. F. (2002). Building brand community. *Journal of Marketing*, 66(1), 38–54.

McWilliam, G. (2000). Building stronger brands through online communities. *MIT Sloan Management Review*, 41(3), 43–54.

Muñiz Jr., A. M., & O'Guinn, T. C. (2001). Brand community. *Journal of Consumer Research*, 27(4), 412–432.

Muñiz Jr., A. M., & Schau, H. J. (2005). Religiosity in the abandoned Apple Newton brand community. *Journal of Consumer Research*, 31(4), 737–747.

Sandıkcı, Ö., & Ekici, A. (2009). Politically motivated brand rejection. *Journal of Business Research*, 62(2), 208–217.

Schau, H. J., Muñiz Jr., A. M., & Arnould, E. J. (2009). How brand community practices create value. *Journal of Marketing*, 73(5), 30–51.

Schmitt, B. H. (1999). *Experiential marketing: How to get customers to sense, feel, think, act, relate*. New York: The Free Press.

Schouten, J. W., & McAlexander, J. H. (1995). Subcultures of consumption: An ethnography of the new bikers. *Journal of Consumer Research*, 22(1), 43–61.

Thompson, C. J., & Arsel, Z. (2004). The Starbucks brandscape and consumers'(anticorporate) experiences of glocalization. *Journal of Consumer Research*, 31(3), 631–642.

Townley, B. (2015). Exploring different forms of capitals: Researching capitals in the field of cultural and creative industries. In A. Tatli, M. Ozbilgin, & M. Karatas-Ozkan (eds), *Pierre Bourdieu, Organisation, and Management* (pp. 182–202). London: Routledge.

Vargo, S. L., & Lusch, R. F. (2004). Evolving to a new dominant logic for marketing. *Journal of Marketing*, 34(1), 1–17.

Zavestoski, S. (2002). Guest editorial: Anti-consumption attitudes. *Psychology & Marketing*, 19(2), 121–126.

CHAPTER 7

Brand ethics, social responsibility, and sustainable consumption

CHAPTER AIMS AND LEARNING OUTCOMES

This chapter corresponds to the second stage of Keller and Swaminathan's (2020) *strategic brand management process*, i.e. designing and implementing brand marketing programmes (see Figure 7.1), and explores branding and consumption from an ethical and societal perspective. In particular, it aims to achieve the following:

1. Define ethics and corporate social responsibility (CSR) and explore their implications for brands in postmodern society.
2. Discuss the two main traditions in moral philosophy and their implications for branding.
3. Explore the processes organisations can follow in order to incorporate ethics and CSR in their brand marketing.
4. Discuss the development of social marketing programmes based on theories from human behaviour sciences.
5. Provide an understanding of the concept of sustainability and its role in green marketing strategies.
6. Explore the development of cause-related marketing programmes (CPMs) and their implications for corporate and consumer philanthropy.

(POST)POSTMODERNISM AND SOCIAL RESPONSIBILITY

In the previous chapter, we explored the different types of communities of consumption, which are "a distinctively postmodern mode of sociality in which consumers claim to be doing their own thing while doing it with thousands of like-minded others" (Holt, 2002, p. 83). Challenging the modern view of brands as cultural blueprints, the postmodern context, which is characterized by scepticism and resistance (Butler,

ETHICS, SOCIAL RESPONSIBILITY, & SUSTAINABILITY

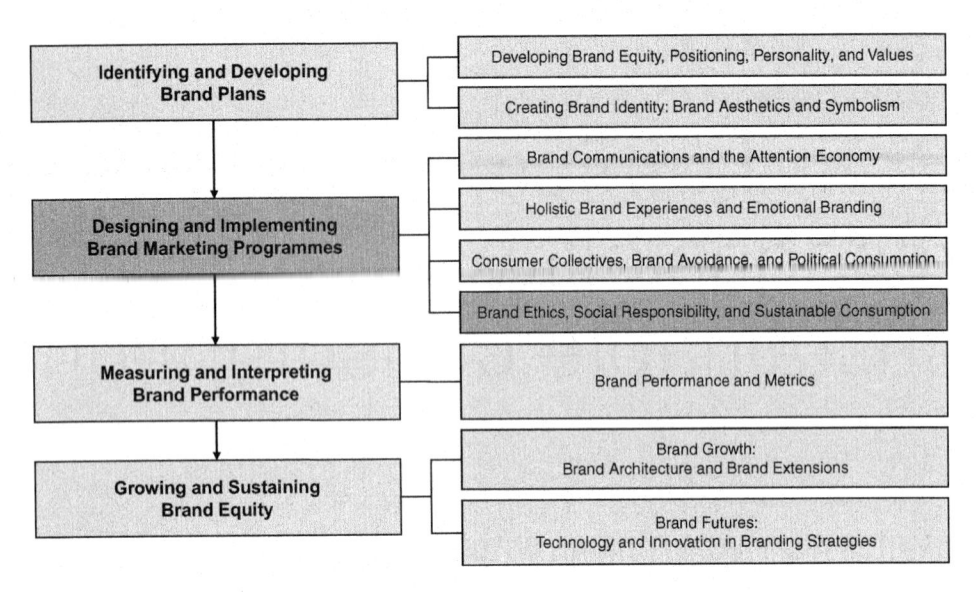

FIGURE 7.1 Strategic brand management process and book plan

2002), regards brands as cultural resources which consumers can use to construct their own identity and sense of self (Belk, 1988). However, brands can only act as valuable cultural resources if they are perceived to be *authentic*, which means that "brands must be disinterested; they must be perceived as invented and disseminated by parties without an instrumental economic agenda, by people who are intrinsically motivated by their inherent value" (Holt, 2002, p. 83). Subcultures of consumption, in particular, can act as an extra resource that allows brands to claim authenticity (Holt, 2002; Schouten & McAlexander, 1995).

As explored in Chapter 6, this postmodern paradigm is now challenged by political consumption. Nowadays, the *anti-branding movement* demands much more; it argues that for brands to be authentic, the organisations that own them must be *socially responsible*. Brands are only "trusted to serve as cultural source materials when their sponsors [organisations-owners] have demonstrated that they shoulder their civic responsibilities as would a community pillar" (Holt, 2002, p. 88). Otherwise, if this is not the case, consumers are willing to boycott brands until certain conditions are met (Lee, Motion, & Conroy, 2009). We have already explored how boycotting one brand means that consumers choose another one instead (buycotting). Indeed, organisations can harness this phenomenon by appealing to the increasingly ethically and politically conscious consumer with their own socially responsible brand offering. While culture jamming as a major type of discursive political consumerism (Boström, 2019) (e.g. *Adbusters*) initially "focused concerns with modern branding [i.e.] the manipulation of desires through advertising…[nowadays it is]…

more frequently used to attack disjunctures between brand promises and corporate actions" (Holt, 2002, p. 85). Savvy consumers now look for contradictions between the ideals adopted by brands and the real activities of the organisations who own them, and "a diverse coalition of self-appointed watchdogs monitors how companies act toward their employees, the environment, consumers, and governments" (Holt, 2002, p. 86). A prime example is the case of *Nike* in the 1990s when human rights groups accused the organisation of inhumane work conditions, insufficient wages, and child labour. The grassroots campaign attracted enormous media coverage forcing *Nike* to change its corporate policies. The company established routine independent inspections of its subcontracted operations becoming a very transparent organisation, which eventually enhanced its brand reputation.

> Of the brands that are able to make the transition to provide original cultural materials, consumers will carefully weed out those that they do not trust. Brands now cause trouble, not because they dictate tastes, but because they allow companies to dodge civic obligations. Postmodern branding is perceived as deceitful because the ideals woven into brands seem so disconnected from, and often contrary to, the material actions of the companies that own them… The antibranding movement is now forcing companies to build lines of obligation that link brand and company. As consumers peel away the brand veneer, they are looking for companies that act like a local merchant, as a stalwart citizen of the community.
>
> (Holt, 2002, p. 88)

Ethics and CSR are now paramount issues for organisations and brands. Drawing from moral philosophy, the following section seeks to define these concepts and provide an understanding of their implications for branding strategies.

MORAL PHILOSOPHY AND ETHICAL BRANDING

It is important to emphasise that the non-human nature of organisations does not imply firms are *amoral*; any suggestion that they do not need to adhere to moral principles and values is completely incorrect and unacceptable: "Business is human activity [therefore] it has…to be evaluated from a moral point of view" (Robin & Reidenbach, 1987, p. 49). Organisations as social systems embedded in the wider social structure, are established, owned, and run by individuals. They are legal entities, but as people are their legal agents and owners, they too have to adhere to moral standards. Organisations need to adopt a proactive approach toward their moral decision-making and should seek to balance profit and efficiency with adhering to ethical core values which should give a clear direction for the organisation's brand marketing strategy (Robin & Reidenbach, 1987).

Organisations as systems of stakeholder groups

An organisation can be defined as a *system of primary stakeholder groups* because it involves a multifaceted suite of relationships among various constituent groups with diverse rights, responsibilities, goals, and expectations (Clarkson, 1995).

> Stakeholders are persons or groups that have, or claim, ownership, rights, or interests in a corporation and its activities, past, present, or future. Such claimed rights or interests are the result of transactions with, or actions taken by, the corporation, and may be legal or moral, individual or collective.
> (Clarkson, 1995, p. 106)

Primary stakeholder groups include the organisation's internal audiences, that is, its employees, managers, shareholders, and investors, and the organisation's external audiences, i.e. its customers, distributors, and suppliers, as well as the "governments and communities that provide infrastructures and markets, whose laws and regulations must be obeyed, and to whom taxes and other obligations may be due" (Clarkson, 1995, p. 106). There is a vital interdependence between organisations and their primary stakeholder groups because they are the audiences whose continuing participation organisations need in order to stay in business (Clarkson, 1995). On the other hand, *secondary stakeholder groups* are defined "as those who influence or affect, or are influenced or affected by, the corporation, but they are not engaged in transactions with the corporation and are not essential for its survival" (Clarkson, 1995, p. 107). Media and other interest groups are secondary stakeholders as they are not crucial for the organisation's performance. However, they can enhance its strategy by being able to rally public opinion in favour of the firm, or cause important damage by encouraging opposition to the organisation among various audiences (Clarkson, 1995). This means that secondary stakeholders need to be considered in addition to primary stakeholder groups (Clarkson, 1995; Lindgreen, Maon, & Vallaster, 2016). The organisation needs to manage its relationships with all stakeholder groups. The development of a socially responsible brand is based explicitly on the brand promises to its primary and secondary stakeholders and implicitly on their trust (Kitchin, 2003).

Ethics and major traditions in moral philosophy

Ethics and CSR are different concepts despite the fact that they are often used interchangeably. *Ethics* are the moral principles and values that govern the actions and decisions of an individual or a group of individuals about what is right or wrong conduct (Robin & Reidenbach, 1987). These principles are expressed and supported through the process of *socialisation*, which occurs in a multiplicity of spaces such as schools, businesses, religious organisations, and clubs/social organisations (Peñaloza,

2012). *Business ethics* are concerned with the requirement and expectation from firms to operate in accordance with moral principles (Robin & Reidenbach, 1987). *Marketing ethics* relate to a number of issues: product safety and pricing, truthfulness in brand and marketing communications, honest relationships with primary and secondary stakeholders, and the impact of marketing decisions on environment and the wider society. Peñaloza recommends a cultural approach to market ethics, which emphasises "representations, discourses, and practices as the means through which a plurality of members of social and organisational groups *specify*, *enact*, and *police* ethical and unethical meanings and values in various fields that comprise a market system" (2012, pp. 511–512).

Drawing from moral philosophy, ethics can provide a solid direction about how organisations and brands ought to operate. There are two major traditions in moral philosophy: deontology and utilitarianism. *Deontology*, draws from the work of the German philosopher Immanuel Kant, and holds that there some *prima facie ideals* that can direct human thinking (Robin & Reidenbach, 1987). These ideals are universal in character yet not absolute, that is, they are applicable everywhere in the world but there might be circumstances where they do not apply. Robin and Reidenbach identify that "[t]he difference between absolute and universal is simply the recognition that situations sometimes arise in which one or more universal statements of 'right' and 'wrong' might be inappropriate" (1987, p. 46). According to Kant (1964), deontology is based on two important premises: 1) moral tradition can only be established on that basis of human reason or logic, and 2) only goodwill can be universalised (Robin & Reidenbach, 1987) as "one ought never to act unless one is willing to have the maxim on which one acts become a universal law" (Kant, 1964, cited in Robin & Reidenbach, 1987, p. 46): "Thus, a reasonable test for exceptions to universal rules is whether it is morally acceptable to market a product known to be potentially harmful to some individuals" (Robin & Reidenbach, 1987, p. 46).

This takes our discussion to the second major tradition in moral philosophy, *utilitarianism*, whose main premise is that if an act provides the greatest good for the greatest number of people then it can be considered ethical. This requires carrying out a social cost-and-benefit analysis where we contrast the cost of an act, its drawbacks, against the benefits it brings. If the net result of all benefits minus all costs is positive, then the act can be considered morally acceptable. This notion has been embraced by organisations due to its tradition in economic philosophy (Smith, 1776). Thus organisations seek to provide the greatest material good (utility) for the greatest number of people. However, there are two important problems with utilitarianism. First, there is the possibility of an *unjust distribution of utility* as utilitarianism might allow small social segments to be offset by "minor increases in utility to larger segments" (Robin & Reidenbach, 1987, p. 47). Second, utilitarianism can lead to lack of consistency because the result of the cost-and-benefit analysis cannot be generalised as it applies to a specific act; utilitarianism is *concerned with individual acts* and since each act is idiosyncratic, it is judged solely on its own cost-and-benefit analysis outcome. Hence, brand "marketers may argue that fraudulent advertising is all right if no one is worse off, and a rule against such practices becomes less tenable" (Robin & Reidenbach, 1987, p. 47). Despite these two main problems with utilitarianism, it is still a primary philosophical tradition regarding morality and is supported by many people and organisations. If we compare deontology and utilitarianism, we can see that they have a different focus and unit of analysis; deontology is concerned with the individual whereas utilitarianism is concerned with the welfare of society as a unit. This means that they can often be at odds with each other (Robin & Reidenbach, 1987).

Organisations as social systems capture aspects of both deontology and utilitarianism. However, what a given society perceives as the *appropriate blend* of these two moral philosophies is subject to evolutionary (not revolutionary) change (Robin & Reidenbach, 1987). This means that what a society believes to be ethical can change over time (i.e. gradually and not suddenly). There are two themes that can provide general direction with regards to the appropriate blend of the two moral philosophies.

> Marketing activities that have a foreseeable and potentially serious impact on individuals ought to be regulated by the values of deontological reasoning… [whereas]…for all marketing exchanges that do not have foreseeable serious consequences for individuals, the arguments of utilitarianism seem appropriate within capitalistic democracies.
> (Robin & Reidenbach, 1987, p. 50)

Of course an important question we must answer is how we can solve the 'level of performance' problem, that is, how do we determine what is and what is not 'serious impact' on the individual. To answer this fundamental question we must look at the work of ancient Greek philosopher Aristotle who argued that a moderation of prudence, in the way an individual behaves, is appropriate. Beauchamp articulated Aristotle's premise by explaining that "virtue is concerned with emotions and actions, where excess is wrong, as is deficiency, but the mean is praised and is right…Virtue…is a mean between two vices – one of excess, the other of deficiency" (1982, p. 161).

As the Norwegian author Jostein Gaarder explains in his best-selling novel 'Sophie's World', Aristotle believed that we must seek the *golden mean* in human relationships: "The ethics of both Plato and Aristotle contain echoes of Greek medicine: only by exercising balance and temperance will I achieve a happy or 'harmonious' life" (Gaarder, 2015, p. 97). Organisations need to apply the same moderation to the system of values adopted in their brand marketing. Neither excessiveness nor deficiency in organisational behaviour will be acceptable; organisations must also seek this golden mean (Robin & Reidenbach, 1987).

CORPORATE SOCIAL RESPONSIBILITY AND BRANDING

Social responsibility, responsiveness, and performance

Corporate social responsibility (CSR) is often viewed as an ambiguous term because it can mean different things to different people.

> To some it conveys the idea of legal responsibility or liability; to others it means socially responsible behaviour in an ethical sense; to still others, the meaning transmitted is that of 'responsible for', in a causal mode; many simply equate it with a charitable contribution.
>
> (Votaw, 1973, p. 11)

CSR is about the social contract between the organisation and community in which it operates (Robin & Reidenbach, 1987). The *social contract* is a set of "generally accepted relationships, obligations and duties between the major institutions and the people" (Steiner, 1972, p.18). Hence, there is a set of generally accepted relationships, obligations, and duties, which relate to the impact of the organisation on social welfare (Robin & Reidenbach, 1987).

Organisations can be evaluated on the basis of their social performance. *Corporate social performance* is about the impact of corporate behaviour on society, not only in terms of their policies and intentions but also the evaluation of their outcomes and results (Clarkson, 1995; Preston, 1988). This means that we judge organisations on the basis of how they deal with social issues. However, it is imperative we understand what we mean by the term *social issues*, as organisations cannot "be made responsible for dealing with all social issues" (Clarkson, 1995, p. 103). Indeed, we have to distinguish between social issues and stakeholder issues because some issues might be a concern for specific stakeholders but might not be of concern to the society as a whole. Clarkson (1995) explains that

> a particular society determines, usually over an extended period of time, what is a social issue, and when it is considered necessary, the relevant policy enacts legislation and regulation. When there is no such legislation or regulation, an issue may be a stakeholder issue, but it is not necessarily a social issue. A test of whether an issue has become a social issue is the presence or absence of legislation or regulation.
>
> (Clarkson, 1995, p. 103)

This means that not all stakeholder issues are automatically social issues; similarly, not all social issues are necessarily stakeholder issues (Clarkson, 1995). It is up to the organisation to acknowledge its obligations and responsibilities to its stakeholders and determine its response to its stakeholder issues. Wartick and

Cochran (1985) determined that an organisation's posture toward the management of stakeholder issues can be characterised as reactive, defensive, accommodative, and proactive. This was transformed to the *RDAP scale* (Clarkson, 1988, 1991, 1995) where 1) *reactive* is when the organisation denies responsibility, fights all the way (McAdam, 1973), and does less than it is required, 2) *defensive* is when the organisation admits responsibility, but fights it, and does the least that is required, 3) *accommodative* is when the organisation accepts responsibility, and does all that is required, and 4) *proactive* is when the organisation anticipates responsibility, leads the industry (McAdam, 1973), and does more than is required (Clarkson, 1988, 1991, 1995). Based on the above, it is clear that *corporate social performance* will be an interaction of 1) the categories of CSR (i.e. economic, legal, ethical, and discretionary), 2) the posture toward the management of stakeholder issues (corporate social responsiveness), and 3) the social issues involved in each case (Carroll, 1979; Clarkson, 1995; Wartick & Cochran, 1985).

Torres, Bijmolt, Tribó, and Verhoef (2012) explored the effects of CSR on global brand equity using a longitudinal database of fifty-seven global brands from a number of different sectors in ten countries. They determined that CSR positively affects global brand equity and both short-term and long-term brand equity values. In addition, the combination of *CSR toward customers* (which increases visibility) and *CSR toward community* (i.e. initiatives not directly related to the organisation's core business) has a larger impact on brand equity than CSR toward other stakeholders: investors, employees, and suppliers (Torres et al., 2012). On the other hand "the visibility of CSR initiatives may be less beneficial to the brand when CSR initiatives are related to the company's business (e.g. cigarette producer sponsoring a cancer fund)" (Torres et al., 2012, p. 15). Organisations should engage with CSR toward the community because it grants the firm with credibility and establishes it as one with an ethical stance to all of its primary and secondary stakeholders (Torres et al., 2012). Organisations which own global brands are usually complex entities characterised by information asymmetry, and consequently, a need for monitoring. Hence, "the implementation of credible CSR policies such as those targeted toward community will reduce opportunistic behaviours that emerge in information asymmetry contexts. The result is a creation of brand value" (Torres et al., 2012, p. 21).

Socially responsible brand framework

Lindgreen, Maon, Vallaster (2016) argue that organisations can harness CSR strategically to both benefit the society as well as achieve their own corporate objectives. They developed a *strategic CSR brand framework* where they distinguished four different types of socially responsible brands on the basis of: 1) strategic objectives, 2) level of integration of CSR in the organisation, and 3) the key initiators and drivers of the socially responsible brand development activities (Lindgreen et al., 2016) (see Figure 7.2). It is important to bear in mind that in all cases organisations harness desirable social causes to advance their interests, and they measure their

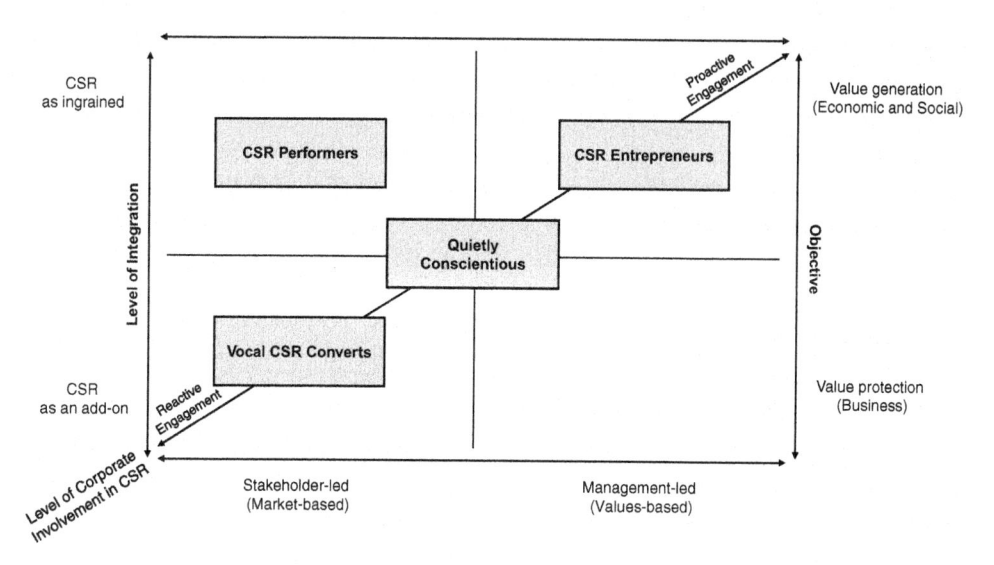

ETHICS, SOCIAL RESPONSIBILITY, & SUSTAINABILITY 219

FIGURE 7.2 Strategic CSR brand framework

success in shareholder value and profitability and not by the social improvements they deliver (Andreasen, 1994).

First, *CSR entrepreneurs* are organisations that have designed

> their corporate identity around CSR, because they have been founded with CSR in mind and embrace CSR as part of who they are and what they do…Their ethos often reflects the passion, vision and personality of their founders. Thus, their form of CSR goes beyond supportive systems and structures to include their overall identity and outlook.
>
> (Lindgreen et al., 2016, p. 239)

A great example is *Patagonia*, the outdoor clothing brand where environmental protection has been an important constituent part of its identity (Lindgreen et al., 2016). The organisation describes itself as an 'activist' company. It's website explains, "the protection and preservation of the environment isn't what we do after hours. It's the reason we're in business and every day's work" (Patagonia, 2020). CSR entrepreneur-brands have the ability to reconcile the need to benefit the society and the need to deliver results for organisational shareholders. Such organisations believe that being socially responsible does not contrast with the interests of shareholders, in fact it can enhance shareholder returns. CSR entrepreneur-brands tend to be smaller and younger as they can work from a clean slate and have not accumulated the difficulties of being large and global. However, larger organisations can also develop CSR entrepreneur-brands but in order to do so they need to embrace CSR wholeheartedly, holistically, and truthfully. They need to develop a code of ethics and have inspirational leaders who oversee the supply and value chains to ensure this code is always adhered to (Lindgreen et al., 2016).

Second, brands which are *CSR performers*

> are established, visible brands, with core environmental and social responsibility values, as well as the scale and ambition to transform their industries. Although CSR principles are ingrained in their organisational culture, they often engage in CSR not for values-based internal reasons but rather in response to stakeholder expectations. Despite an internal sense of CSR, these usually publicly owned companies adopt a shorter-term view, in pursuit of the goals of designing a CSR agenda and integrating CSR and branding activities to earn profits. Managers thus face pressures associated with accountability, limited resources and public governance; they also make more direct comparisons of the value of investing in CSR than to managers of privately owned companies.
>
> (Lindgreen et al., 2016, p. 240)

CSR performer-brands often seek to develop internal ownership by aligning their human resources policies with the desired brand positioning of socially responsible brand in order to integrate CSR in the corporate culture. *IKEA*, the Swedish furniture and furnishing brand, can be considered a CSR performer-brand which, based on a combination of reactive and proactive initiatives such as its collaboration with *UNICEF* or the *World Wildlife Fund* (*WWF*), has cemented its brand positioning as a socially responsible organisation (Lindgreen et al., 2016). However, there are some organisations which act half-heartedly; for instance, the reputation of *British Petroleum (BP)* was damaged (if not completely annihilated) after the 2010 Gulf of Mexico disaster which killed many workers and destroyed the regional ecosystem. The organisation's responsibility for, and handling of this disaster, completely weakened its positioning of 'going beyond petroleum' (Lindgreen et al., 2016). Critics could argue that *The Body Shop* founded by the late Dame Anita Roddick as CSR entrepreneur-brand became a CSR performer-brand when it was acquired in 2006 by *L'Oréal*, the French global personal care conglomerate (for £652m), because there was an increased focus on profits. Indeed, in 2017, the brand was sold to *Natura*, the Brazilian personal care organisation, in a €1bn deal.

Third, *vocal CSR converts* are brands which, reacting to the current growing importance of social responsibility, embrace CSR. These organisations

> have not convinced the public that their efforts are genuine or long-term [yet they continue] to integrate CSR into their business and brand strategy. [However] this reactive approach to doing what is good for business and a dominant emphasis on communication around peripheral CSR initiatives may not be sufficient to create brand value or overcome a legacy of irresponsibility in a context of generally increasing stakeholder expectations and scrutiny.
>
> (Lindgreen et al., 2016, p. 241)

In this case, organisations usually identify specific causes which can be strategically related to their products, e.g. as a prime water consumer, *Coca-Cola* has partnered with *Greenpeace* to conserve fresh water. Building a vocal CSR convert-brand can also be supported by a *cause-related marketing* strategy (explored later in this chapter), where an organisation offers to give part of its profits to specific charity or cause (Varadarajan & Menon, 1988). However, in order for organisations to thwart any stakeholder scepticism, they should not engage in CSR in a merely opportunistic manner but embrace social responsibility on a continuous basis in order to develop a vocal CSR convert-brand which delivers long-term business and societal value (Lindgreen et al., 2016).

Finally, *quietly conscientious* are organisations that do not promote their CSR activities

> perhaps out of fear that such publicity will invite criticism, or because they operate in markets or industries with lower visibility...[and] are subject to less stringent stakeholder demands...[Yet]...they work quietly in the background... to minimise their negative social and environmental impacts or contribute to the benefits of society.
>
> (Lindgreen et al., 2016, p. 241)

Quietly conscientious-brands use targeted communications activities to engage with specific stakeholder groups who have legitimate requirements that the organisation must address in its CSR strategy. *Hennes and Mauritz (H&M)* initially employed a quietly conscientious profile about its CSR activities based on the belief that CSR would not be a strong point-of-difference (POD). Subsequently, the Swedish fast-fashion brand has shifted to a CSR-performer profile, communicating more to its primary and secondary stakeholder groups about its CSR initiatives. This means that there is a need "for a dynamic perspective on firms' positions in [the] CSR framework for brand strategy [see Figure 7.2]. No strategic option is set in stone with regard to integrating CSR into the brand" (Lindgreen et al., 2016, p. 242).

INCORPORATING ETHICS AND CSR IN BRAND DEVELOPMENT AND MARKETING

Incorporating ethics in brand marketing

Robin and Reidenbach (1987) proposed a process that organisations can follow to integrate ethics in their brand marketing: "The basis of this integration process is the idea of ethical core values acting as guidelines for the development of marketing plans" (Robin & Reidenbach, 1987, p. 52). This will allow the organisation to balance the objectives of profitability and efficiency with being socially responsible. The process follows a "parallel planning approach by which ethical and socially responsible core values can be introduced into the organizational culture" (Robin & Reidenbach, 1987, p. 52).

As shown in Figure 7.3, in the first stage, the organisation's mission statement and ethical profile must guide the development of the organisation's marketing objectives. While developing these objectives "a feedback function also occurs, whereby the mission statement and the ethical profile are questioned, elaborated, and clarified" (Robin & Reidenbach, 1987, p. 52). The *ethical profile* is "a projection to external publics [stakeholders] with whom the organisation interacts, identifying how the organisation chooses to interact with those publics" (Robin & Reidenbach, 1987, p. 53). Brand marketers can look to numerous sources for inspiration when developing the ethical profile: 1) market opportunities and threats, 2) the organisation's history, mission, and current corporate image, 3) owners' and/or senior management's personal preferences, and 4) special marketing resources and competencies which can be harnessed to creatively communicate the ethical profile to the organisation's audiences (Robin & Reidenbach, 1987). For example, *The Body Shop* concentrated on the fight against animal testing, protection of the environment, and equal rights; all of these were issues championed by its founder, Dame Anita Roddick. This ethical profile can act as the standard to compare the marketing objectives against. It is important to determine whether the anticipated impact of the marketing objectives will be different with the dimensions of the profile. However, it is not always possible to predict all effects of a marketing programme. The ethical profile will essentially describe the organisation's customer and growth orientations, environmental concern, involvement in environmental protection, as well as its products' quality and reliability and its attitude toward innovation. Brand marketers

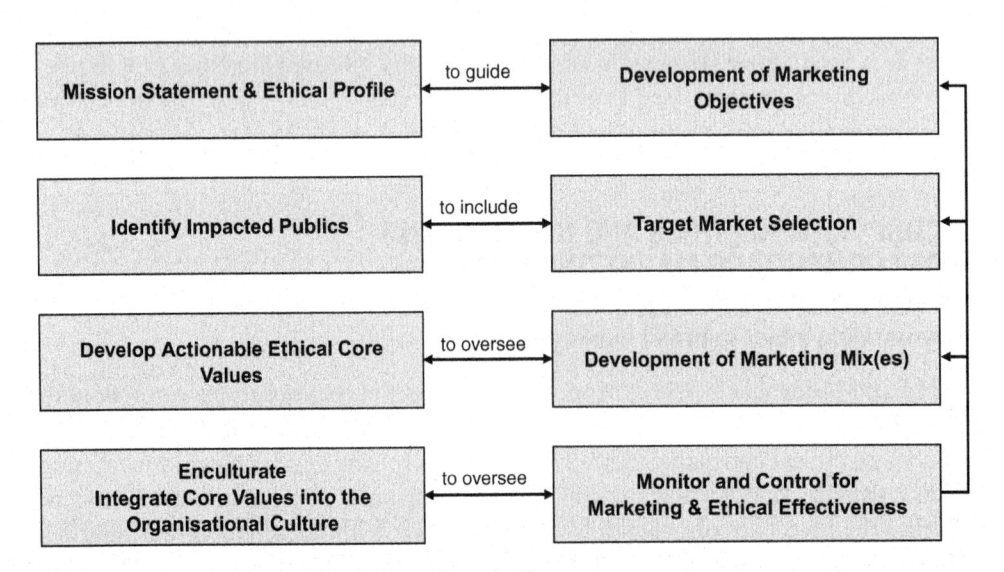

FIGURE 7.3 Integrating ethics in brand marketing

should focus their attention on the total dimension of the ethical profile, that is, how all parts fit together to produce a coherent profile (Robin & Reidenbach, 1987).

In the second stage an environmental analysis involving an understanding of the affected publics is pursued. These publics do not only include targeted consumers but also the other primary and secondary stakeholder groups we have previously explored. A dual emphasis is required because there is a reciprocal relationship between the stakeholder groups and the marketing strategy; we need to understand how the marketing strategy will impact these publics and how their actions will affect the marketing strategy (Robin & Reidenbach, 1987). The third stage of the integration process includes developing actionable ethical core values that should oversee the development of the brand's marketing mix. Again, there is a feedback process between the two because for "core values to be actionable and meaningful in daily marketing practices, their meaning must be explained in terms that apply to the marketing mix. Conversely, the marketing mix must satisfy the core values" (Robin & Reidenbach, 1987, p. 53). The ethical core values derive directly from the organisation's ethical profile and provide internal guidelines for developing marketing plans and balancing the goal of achieving profit and efficiency with maintaining the ethical profile. In order to construct these ethical core values, the organisation can combine deontological concern focusing on the individual with utilitarian concern seeking to achieve the greatest good for the greatest number of people. The ethical core values will provide guidance for the behaviour of organisational employees and the development of the brand's marketing mix. All values need to be tested to fit with each other and work well with the impacted stakeholder groups (Robin & Reidenbach, 1987).

In the final stage, the enculturation and integration of core values oversee the implementation of the organisation's marketing strategy. The "enculturation process instils the core values into each individual and integrates ethical and socially responsible concerns into the marketing planning process" (Robin & Reidenbach, 1987, p. 55). The organisation must run the necessary workshops and seminars to communicate these values to its workforce so that each staff member adopts these values when acting within his/her role. This requires that the core ethical values are concrete, that is, well established, and easy to understand. Brand marketers must monitor how effective the marketing strategy is in achieving marketing objectives as well as how effective the core values are in generating ethically and socially responsible behaviour (Robin & Reidenbach, 1987).

As with any strategic planning process, initial plans might not be entirely effective which requires the agility to go back to previous stages of the integration process and make changes at any required level (see Figure 7.3). It is important to recognise that the enculturation process must be an ongoing endeavour due to the fact that new staff continuously join the organisation and most importantly because of the dynamic nature of the market where societal values and public expectations about marketing practices change in an evolutionary manner. This means that old and new organisational members must be continuously briefed in the updated and ever-evolving ethical core values of the firm (Robin & Reidenbach, 1987).

One could argue that the above process assumes that the brand's ethical profile is influenced exclusively by the organisation's ethical marketing strategy; in fact this assumption does not consider the whole picture. Drawing from Kotler and Armstrong's (2004) product-attribute model who suggested that the product offering has three levels: the core, actual, and augmented products, Brunk (2016) explains that a brand's ethical strategy can add to the augmented product. This is crucial because the augmented product level is where most organisations compete for differentiation nowadays. This positive augmentation occurs when two conditions are met: 1) consumers are aware of this strategy, and 2) they believe that the ethical attributes involved in this strategy are important. Positive augmentation can be created directly or indirectly, and intentionally or unintentionally (i.e. internal or external locus of control respectively) (Brunk, 2016).

Developing a brand through CSR

Maon, Lindgreen, and Swaen (2009) developed a process organisations can follow to develop a socially responsible brand comprising of four stages and nine steps (see Figure 7.4).

First, in the *sensitising* stage the organisational awareness of CSR issues increases usually because of market-based factors such as consumer needs, market opportunities, and/or the need for differentiation (step 1) (Lindgreen et al., 2016; Lindgreen, Xu, Maon, & Wilcock, 2012; Maon et al., 2009). The core organisational task in this stage is to recognise that CSR can be harnessed in order to add brand value. Second, the *unfreeze* stage involves planning the development of a socially responsible brand. This stage includes four steps: assessing the organisation's societal context (step 2), establishing a corporate vision and definition for CSR (step 3), assessing

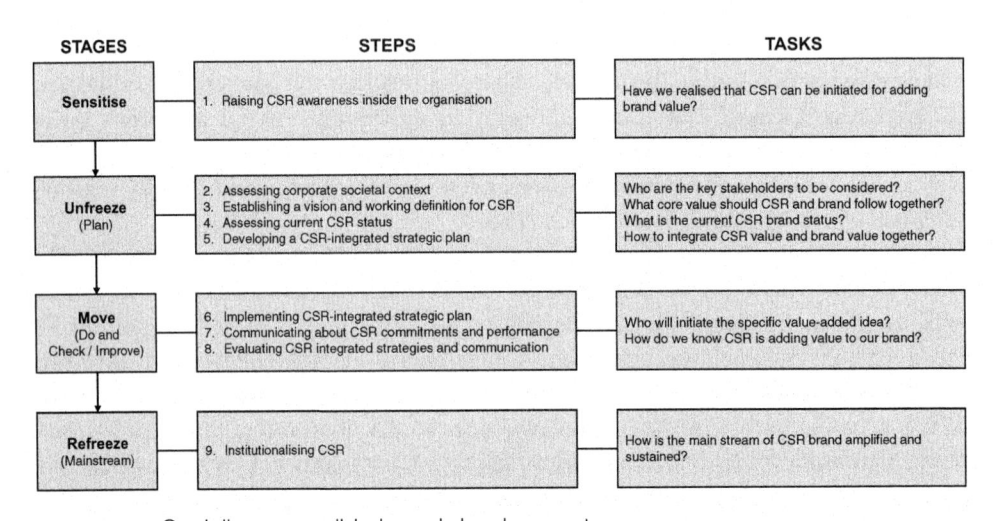

FIGURE 7.4 Socially responsible brand development process

the organisation's current CSR status (step 4), and developing a CSR-integrated organisational strategic plan (step 5). The tasks in this stage are to establish who the primary stakeholder groups are (step 2) as well as the core value the brand CSR strategy should follow (step 3). In addition, it is important to understand the current CSR brand status to benchmark it with competitors (step 4), and determine how to integrate the brand and CSR values (step 5) (Lindgreen et al., 2016; Lindgreen et al., 2012; Maon et al., 2009).

Third, the *move* stage involves three steps: The organisation implements the CSR-integrated plan (step 6), it communicates its CSR commitments and performance to its primary and secondary stakeholder groups (step 7), and then it evaluates the CSR strategy and communication (step 8). The organisation should determine who will be responsible for implementing the CSR strategy and then assess whether the CSR strategy adds value to the brand. We should note that communicating about the organisation's CSR commitments and performance (step 7) should be an ongoing activity that stretches onto the next and last stage too (Lindgreen et al., 2016; Lindgreen et al., 2012; Maon et al., 2009). Finally, in the *refreeze* stage, the CSR strategy and the multi-stakeholder approach should become institutionalised (step 9) (Werther Jr. & Chandler, 2005) and the organisation needs to determine how the mainstream ethos of CSR within its culture can be amplified and sustained (Lindgreen et al., 2016; Lindgreen et al., 2012; Maon et al., 2009).

SOCIAL MARKETING PROGRAMMES AND BRANDING

Besides socially responsible brand marketing, which seeks to harness social issues to achieve commercial interests, or *societal marketing* (ethically developed commercial marketing), which is concerned with the ethical and societal implications of commercial activity in order to deliver products and services that satisfy consumer needs (Andreasen, 1994), organisations and their brands can also engage in *social marketing*. The term was first coined by Kotler and Zaltman to describe "the design, implementation, and control of programmes calculated to influence the acceptability of social ideas" (1971, p. 5). However, social marketing's scope is greater than this. Andreasen defines social marketing as "the adaptation of commercial marketing technologies to programmes designed to influence the voluntary behaviour of target audiences to improve their personal welfare and that of society of which they are part" (Andreasen, 1994, p. 110). Such programmes include campaigns that seek to deal with social issues such as road safety, binge drinking, smoking, drug taking, obesity, sexual health, domestic abuse, homophobia, xenophobia, racism, bullying, and mental health stigmas.

Any organisation, be it commercial or a non-profit organisation (NPO) can pursue social marketing (SM); indeed, SM is *applied to programmes* (Andreasen, 1994). SM programmes often involve a collaboration of public sector with commercial organisations. For example, the UK's Department of Health and Social Care could collaborate with *Durex* to educate young people about safe sex in order to reduce the spread of HIV/Aids and other sexually transmitted diseases (STDs), or skin cancer charities could team up with *Nivea* to encourage the use of sun-protection. SM goes beyond communicating ideas and a change of attitudes as it focuses on *influencing behaviour*. It seeks to influence behaviour but not necessarily change it because there could be cases where the goal is to *discourage* a certain behaviour, e.g. using recreational drugs, or to *encourage* a certain behaviour, e.g. regular physical exercise. The *beneficiary of SM* is the individual, his/her family and friends, and the society, and not the institutions or organisations involved in these programmes; this means SM can never be a commercial activity (Andreasen, 1994).

Developing a social marketing programme

Human behaviour theories provide extremely useful insights for the development of successful SM programmes. The three theories organisations can draw from are: 1) the stages of change theory, 2) the social cognitive theory, and 3) the exchange theory. Let us explore these theories in more depth.

The stages of change theory

The *stages of change theory* draws from the Prochaska and DiClemente (1983) seminal transtheoretical model of behaviour change, which explains the stages that individuals go through to change their behaviour (Hastings & Domegan, 2018). Prochaska and DiClemente argue that people do not change our behaviour in a binary way: a smoker does not wake up one day a non-smoker (1983). Individuals go through five stages in order to change their behaviour (see Figure 7.5).

First, in the *pre-contemplation stage* people are aware of the new behaviour but are not interested in it. Therefore, participating organisations must demonstrate to them how the new behaviour is not antithetical to community values and will improve their health. Bringing in educators, public agencies and figures to increase awareness and understanding of the new behaviour, on popular communications media, can be a successful strategy (Hastings, 2007; Hastings & Domegan, 2018). This is the stage where smokers are aware of the non-smoking behaviour, and SM campaigns need to explain, in a subtle and well-thought manner, the benefits of this behaviour and how it does not run contrary to community values. Second, the *contemplation stage* requires from organisations to understand how individuals make complex behavioural decisions and how they can be motivated to undertake the desired behaviour. The primary goal at this stage is to change people's values so they change their behaviour. At this stage, smokers will start contemplating the benefits of the new behaviour (non-smoking) and how this can satisfy their desire to live a healthier life (changing values) (Hastings, 2007; Hastings & Domegan, 2018).

Third, the *preparation stage* is where individuals are motivated to change their behaviour and make the initial mental and practical preparations to do so. At this stage smokers will decide that they wish to try to give up smoking and will purchase

```
┌─────────────────────────┐     ┌──────────────────────────────────┐
│   PRE-CONTEMPLATION     │────▶│ Potential awareness of new behaviour │
└─────────────────────────┘     │    but no interest at this stage     │
            │                   └──────────────────────────────────┘
            ▼
┌─────────────────────────┐     ┌──────────────────────────────────┐
│     CONTEMPLATION       │────▶│   Evaluate personal relevance       │
└─────────────────────────┘     │       of the new behaviour          │
            │                   └──────────────────────────────────┘
            ▼
┌─────────────────────────┐     ┌──────────────────────────────────┐
│      PREPARATION        │────▶│    Decision to act and put in place │
└─────────────────────────┘     │ measures to carry out the new behaviour │
            │                   └──────────────────────────────────┘
            ▼
┌─────────────────────────┐     ┌──────────────────────────────────┐
│        ACTION           │────▶│           Take action                │
└─────────────────────────┘     └──────────────────────────────────┘
            │
            ▼
┌─────────────────────────┐     ┌──────────────────────────────────┐
│    CONFIRMATION OR      │────▶│   Commitment to behaviour and       │
│     MAINTENANCE         │     │  no desire or intention to regress  │
└─────────────────────────┘     └──────────────────────────────────┘
```

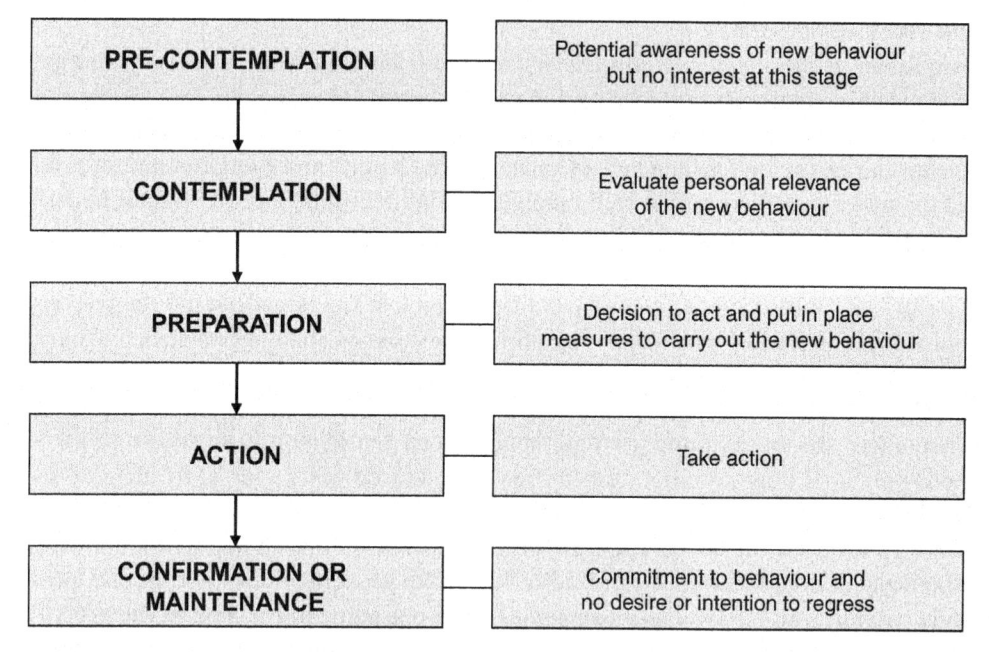

FIGURE 7.5 Stages of change theory

structural resources, e.g. *Nicorette* cigarette patches or chewing gums, to support them in doing so (Hastings, 2007; Hastings & Domegan, 2018). Fourth, the *action stage* is an important stage because individuals move from concluding that the new behaviour is a good idea (due to being personally rewarding or because social pressures make it imperative) to actually taking action. Individuals also need to believe that the desired new behaviour can actually be performed. This is determined by the individuals' *perceived behavioural control* which in turn is influenced by 1) *internal efficacy*, i.e. the individuals' perception that they have the knowledge and skills to carry out the behaviour, and 2) *external efficacy* which is the individuals' perception that the environment will permit this behaviour, manifested by other people's cooperation and having access to structural resources required. This is the stage where smokers stop smoking and expect the support of their surrounding environment (Hastings, 2007; Hastings & Domegan, 2018). Finally, in the confirmation or maintenance stage, individuals maintain the new behaviour. SM is primarily interested in sustained behaviour. At this stage, following a positive evaluation of actual consequences, individuals move from trialling the new behaviour to maintaining it. Hence, individuals move from trial to committed behaviour. For example, the (newly) smoke-free individuals experience the positive difference the new behaviour brings, and become committed to the non-smoking behaviour. There is, unfortunately, always the risk that individuals will drop out and return to their old behaviour but if SM initiatives remind them of the negative consequences of their old behaviour, then it is likely they will persist with their new behaviour (Hastings, 2007; Hastings & Domegan, 2018).

The social cognitive theory

According to the *social cognitive theory* human behaviour is influenced by internal and external environmental factors. Internal factors involve people's knowledge and self-efficacy, and external environmental factors include 1) their immediate environment, that is, the direct influence of their friends, family, and local community, and 2) the wider social context which involves the indirect influence of societal norms, cultural symbolism (e.g. media and advertising), structural issues (resources), and socio-economic conditions (Bandura, 1999; Hastings, 2007; Hastings & Domegan, 2018). The social cognitive theory can help social marketers understand the reasons individuals arrive at a particular stage (in the process of changing their behaviour). It recognises that there is a two-way relationship between the environment and people as both have an influence on each other. It is essential that the environment encourages the behavioural change, hence social marketers must adjust people's perceptions of how common and normal the desired behaviour is to increase its acceptability (through normative education) (Hastings, 2007; Hastings & Domegan, 2018). However, the social cognitive theory assumes that people merely knowing about the desired behaviour can lead to behaviour change; it does not, in fact, provide an indication of how to move people from one stage to the next in the process of adopting the new behaviour. This is provided by the exchange theory (Hastings, 2007; Hastings & Domegan, 2018).

The exchange theory

Exchange is at the heart of the marketing concept. According to Kotler and Zaltman, "marketing does not occur unless there are two or more parties, each with something to exchange and both able to carry out communications and distribution" (1971, p. 4). This exchange can be actual or symbolic, and what is transferred can be tangible or intangible respectively (Bagozzi, 1975). Commercial marketing involves both utilitarian exchange, i.e. product or service provision in exchange of money, and symbolic exchange through brands whose crucial role is to deliver symbolic and intangible benefits besides functionality. Similarly, according to Bagozzi (1975), SM involves a symbolic exchange, i.e. "the mutual transfer of psychological, social or other intangible entities" (Hastings, 2007, p. 30). Social marketers need to provide individuals with *appropriate incentives* in exchange of the behavioural change (and the success of the SM programmes) (Hastings, 2007; Hastings & Domegan, 2018). Failing to do so, i.e. providing inadequate rewards, or penalties, can be extremely counter-productive. Consequently, there is a need to consult the target group in order to identify incentives that will work with them (Hastings, 2007; Hastings & Domegan, 2018). The notion of exchange in SM is more challenging because the benefits to social marketers are more ambiguous than commercial marketers (profit). In addition, the social marketers' job is more demanding as they are asked to sell 'unseen' benefits, e.g. the benefits of not getting cancer (by refraining from smoking) or avoiding a car accident (by avoiding drink-driving) (Hastings, 2007; Hastings & Domegan, 2018).

Evidently, the aforementioned theories provide the three important steps of designing a SM programme. The stages of change theory helps social marketers to understand the *stage* that the target audience are at in relation to changing their behaviour, whilst social cognitive theory helps social marketers understand the *reasons* they are at that stage (i.e. what influences their behaviour), and the exchange theory helps social marketers to understand how to move the target audience from this stage to the next (until they reach confirmation or maintenance) (see Figure 7.5) (Hastings, 2007; Hastings & Domegan, 2018). SM's power and scope is enormous; organisations and brands can design and implement SM initiatives which seek to address many social issues such as encouraging sustainable consumption, which is a behaviour explored in the following section.

GREEN MARKETING AND SUSTAINABLE CONSUMPTION

Managing the paradox of green marketing with sustainability

Climate change and environmental protection have become mainstream issues in our post-modern society. Sustainability is a required societal endeavour embraced by regular people, not merely, the intellectual elite or people in the fringes of society. In response, organisations and brands can engage in *green marketing*, which is "the holistic management process responsible for identifying, anticipating and satisfying the needs of customers and society, in a profitable and sustainable way" (Peattie & Charter, 2003, p. 727). One could argue that green marketing is a paradoxical concept. A "paradox denotes contradictory yet inter-related elements – elements that seem logical in isolation but absurd and irrational when appearing simultaneously" (Lewis, 2000, p. 760). On the one hand, the green agenda calls for environmental concern and conservation, and on the other hand marketing, by definition, seeks to stimulate and facilitate consumption (Peattie & Charter, 2003). *Sustainability*, as the keystone of green marketing, assists organisations and societies in managing this paradox. Sustainability does not call for zero production and consumption but

> involves enjoying a material standard of living today, which is not at the expense of the standard of living of future generations. [This means] 1) using natural resources at a rate at which environmental systems or human activity can replenish them…[and] 2) producing pollution and waste at a rate which can be absorbed by environmental systems without impairing their viability.
> (Peattie & Charter, 2003, p. 728)

We must recognise that production and consumption are by definition detrimental to the environment, as organisations extract natural resources to produce their offerings, and during production, they generate pollution and by-products.

Hence, the concept of 'environmentally friendly products' is incorrect as production and consumption can never be environmentally friendly. What sustainability calls for is that production and consumption are *less environmentally harmful* by reducing the natural resources required to produce as well as reducing pollution and by-products in the process of doing so (Peattie & Charter, 2003). In addition, it is important to emphasise that organisations which continuously strive to be more environmentally responsible can claim green credentials even when they haven't yet achieved the highest levels of sustainability due to requirement for changes in their business model and industry which take time to plan and implement. As Rob Halkyard, *Friends of the Earth* Director of Marketing explains:

> sometimes we are talking to brands who, on the face of it, don't have the greatest environmental credentials. But, if we're reassured that there's an authentic leadership determined to make it happen, that's almost more valuable than marketing spend to put behind a single initiative.
> (cited in Cuddeford-Jones, 2019)

Fostering sustainable consumption

According to Fuchs and Lorek (2005) *sustainable consumption* requires two developments which are distinct yet interrelated: 1) increasing the efficiency of consumption through technological developments which facilitate production improvements or efficiency-friendly design, and 2) changing the levels and patterns of consumption which "requires changes in infrastructures and choices as well as questioning of the levels and drivers of consumption" (Fuchs & Lorek, 2005, p. 262). These two developments are therefore related to two concepts: efficiency and sufficiency respectively. *Efficiency* relies on technical innovations, whereas *sufficiency* depends on consumers changing their behaviour (which could be encouraged by SM programmes) and social innovation (Reisch & Scherhorn, 1999). However, Fuchs and Lorek (2005) argue that governments and international organisations have been concentrating on the former (efficiency) and have ignored the latter. In fact, many developed countries seek to increase instead of decrease the levels of consumption to stimulate growth (Marchand, 2013).

In response to the need for efficiency and sufficiency, organisations and brands can employ design thinking, which leads to innovation at the interception of business viability, technological feasibility, and human desirability (Brown, 2009). Design can help brands develop products and services which question the way consumer needs are satisfied and which are more resource-efficient and sustainable (Cooper, 2000; Fletcher, Dewberry, & Goggin, 2001). Sustainable product development involves designing product and service offerings that enable individuals to reduce the purchase, use, and disposal of these offerings without experiencing a loss of wellbeing (Cooper, 2000). This requires from consumers significant lifestyle changes to not only achieve efficiency but also sufficiency. They must avoid the *rebound effect* where greater efficiency of a given product or process may eventually increase consumer's desire to use more of that product, service or resource due its lower price [and] may also increase the amount of disposable income spent on other products and services.

(Marchand, 2013, p. 160)

Marchand (2013) distinguishes between *green consumers* who concentrate only on efficiency and opt for green products (weak sustainable consumption), and *truly sustainable consumers* who are interested in both efficiency and sufficiency and question the need for a product, and seek substitutes to traditional consumption, *before* they opt for green products (strong sustainable consumption). Etzioni (2003) suggests that consumers can become truly sustainable when they pursue *voluntary simplicity* whereby they willingly spend less on products and services and look for and find satisfaction and meaning in non-materialistic sources. This requires a number of elements: 1) a rejection of culture of consumption, 2) searching for autonomy on the basis of a social conscience, 3) revising one's consumption choices, 4) pursuing more environmentally responsible lifestyles, 5) being reflective rather than impulsive or unquestioning, 6) seeking spirituality, 7) maintaining interpersonal relationships based on empathy, and 8) living by values which display a global vision of health (Burch, 2012). By doing so they can avoid *mis-consumption* (Princen, 2005) which, like a vicious cycle, occurs when

> they purchase an item that provides only fleeting satisfaction, resulting in yet another purchase; when they overwork to meet this consumption pattern and, in turn, with more income but less time, attempt to compensate for overworking by using the additional income to consume more.
>
> (Marchand, 2013, p. 162)

Consumers who practice voluntary simplicity out of concern for the environment as well as their own self-interest, depend less on work and credit, like to give away objects, and spend less time and energy looking after material possessions. One could argue that this gives consumers a sense of freedom because they can feel less entangled with material possessions. The "dependence of things on humans draws humans deeper into the orbit of things. [Indeed] looking after things…traps humans into harder labour, greater social debts and duties, changed schedules and temporalities" (Hodder, 2012, p. 86). With voluntary simplicity people can reduce this dependence and the need for human investment.

However, some consumers might find disentangling themselves from their possessions quite hard. As already discussed, brands can be seen as cultural resources which consumers can utilise to construct their own identity and sense of self; indeed their possessions often become part of their extended self (Belk, 1988). In an extensive study on recycling and sustainability, Trudel, Argo, and Meng (2016) identified that when an everyday product is linked to a consumer's identity, he/she is more likely to recycle this item instead of disposing it. In addition, "the tendency to recycle an identity-linked product increases with the strength and positivity of the connection between the consumer and product (or brand)" (Trudel et al., 2016, p. 246). Their research study determined that such behaviour is due to the fact that disposing an identity-linked product is viewed by consumers as an identity threat. Trashing such products is symbolically similar to disposing a part of the self (Trudel et al., 2016). It seems that recycling provides consumers with an opportunity for painless disentanglement from their identity-linked possessions.

Pursuing voluntary simplicity can also be achieved by consumers buying second-hand products, as well as "opting for product-service systems that require investment of less energy, money, and time in a product's maintenance cycle as compared with owning a product" (Marchand, 2013, p. 163). The latter is the essence of the *sharing economy* in which consumers instead of purchasing material objects to own them, they purchase the right to use the product and service for a certain period of time avoiding the progressive over-accumulation of things. Indeed, in this post-materialistic sharing economy

> as we learn to share more and own less, we may realise that materialistic acquisitiveness imposes a great burden of ownership. To the extent that we can be happy with ready access to things rather than personally archiving, maintaining, and safeguarding them, sharing may truly offer a substantial step toward sustainability.
>
> (Belk, 2017, p. 168)

Sustainable consumption can also be fostered by communicating messages, which are suitable to consumers' political ideologies. Kidwell, Farmer, and Hardesty (2013) explored how tailoring messages about sustainability to suit consumers', either conservative or liberal, ideologies can lead to increased sustainable behaviours. Conservative consumers are driven toward the *binding* foundation for moral judgments because of their preference for authority, in-group loyalty, and purity. As a result, they feel a sense of duty and like to follow in-group social norms and maintain self-control. In contrast, liberal consumers focus more on caring and fairness and consequently are driven toward an *individualising* moral foundation with a greater concern for human rights and welfare (Graham, Haidt, & Nosek, 2009). In their study, Kidwell et al. (2013) designed different message appeals

> to tap unique moral foundations of each ideology, and when congruent [matching] with [consumers'] moral foundations, they elicited a 'feels right' fluent experience…that led to greater intentions. Fluency was characterised as 'ease of comprehension,' where consumers were persuaded effortlessly because the messages were compelling and easy to relate to based on their underlying beliefs and opinions.
>
> (Kidwell et al., 2013, p. 362)

The implications of this study is that designing communications messages which correspond to consumers' moral foundations and ideologies can be a powerful way to influence behaviour and can be used not only to achieve greater levels of sustainable consumption but also other desired behaviours (with SM initiatives). Of course, this route to persuasion can be applied in commercial marketing too, thus, the caveat is that consumers should develop persuasion knowledge connected with their own ideology, in order to identify (commercial) marketing attempts which appeal to their moral foundations, and avoid being inadvertently persuaded (Kidwell et al., 2013).

CAUSE-RELATED MARKETING AND CONSUMER PHILANTHROPY

As we mentioned earlier, building a vocal CSR convert-brand can be supported by *cause-related marketing programmes* (CRMPs). This is

> the process of formulating and implementing marketing activities that are characterized by an offer from the firm to contribute a specified amount to a designated cause when customers engage in revenue providing exchanges that satisfy organisational and individual objectives.
>
> (Varadarajan & Menon, 1988, p.60)

Kompella (2014) argues that CRMPs can add authenticity to the brand's positioning because the brand can demonstrate that it stands for a specific principle or belief and commits resources behind it.

Characteristics of cause-related marketing programmes

Understanding the characteristics of CRMPs can also help us explore their advantages to organisations, brands, and causes (e.g. charities). First, such CRMPs can achieve numerous *corporate objectives*: 1) increasing sales of the product or service, 2) enhancing the stature of the sponsoring organisation due to its association with a worthy cause, 3) countering negative publicity which can lead to the end of consumer boycotts (see Chapter 6), 4) consumer pacification leading to organisational reconciliation with offended groups, 5) facilitating market entry as partnerships can provide access to new markets and ease the introduction of new products and services, and 6) merchandising opportunities for the brand(s) involved in the programme (Varadarajan & Menon, 1988). In addition, CRMPs can deliver *cause-related objectives*: 1) collecting "funds for the cause by stimulating revenue-producing exchanges between the firm and its customers" (Varadarajan & Menon, 1988, p. 63) (which is the prime objective), 2) generating awareness of the cause among the brand's consumers regarding its mission and activities, 3) promoting direct contributions to the cause from individuals and organisations, and 4) encouraging people to become volunteers offering their services to the related cause (Varadarajan & Menon, 1988).

Other characteristics of CRMPs include the *proximity* between commercial organisations and causes, which can either be close or loose where there is strong or weak relationship between participating parties respectively, as well as the *timeframe* of the CRMPs; "[although partnerships] characterised by a short-term focus appear to be pervasive, the underlying characteristics of this evolving marketing tool suggest the desirability of a medium-term or long-term focus" (Varadarajan & Menon, 1988, p. 63). However, this is not to say that short-term CRMPs cannot be successful (e.g. during Christmas). Yet, long-term programmes are more desirable due to their higher PR and publicity potential, e.g. a programme delivering financial contributions to a cause on a continuous basis, and beyond this, even realising a more tangible end product, such as funding the construction of a new building.

The *number of participating parties* is crucial because the more partners involved, the more complex the CRMPs will be as they require organisational mechanisms (e.g. special units) to launch and effectively manage them. Brand-specific partnerships involve one brand working with one or more causes, whereas multi-brand partnerships involve multiple brands working with one or more causes. The latter can be an *intra-company partnership* where the multiple brands involved are owned by the same organisation, or an *inter-company partnership* where there is a "joint participation of two or more directly non-competing firms" (Varadarajan & Menon, 1988, p. 64). A good example of an inter-company partnership is *RED* (www.red.org), which has teamed up with brands such as *Apple*, *Moleskine*, *Vespa*, and *Montblanc* to name a few. In addition, the *level of association* can indicate whether the CRMPs are formed at the organisational, brand, or product levels.

Unsurprisingly in order for CRMPs to be *strategic* they need the support and involvement of senior management in keys decisions about these programmes, and considerable investment of time, financial and human resources toward their development and management (Varadarajan & Menon, 1988). CRMPs can of course be used as a tactical tool to be combined with the brand's sales promotions efforts (short-term in nature) which can increase the effectiveness of the latter, but the former might be deemed by consumers as opportunistic and merely a profit-generator (Varadarajan & Menon, 1988). Organisations must be very careful when *selecting which causes to support* as there ought to be a "match between the firm's customer profile…and the constituencies to which a cause appeals" (Varadarajan & Menon, 1988, p. 65). However, there have been partnerships which, on the surface, do not seem to be based on aligned values. For instance, Coca-Cola partnered with the UK's *National Obesity Forum* after it recognised the need for a low-sugar or no-sugar business model and chose to use sweetener Stevia (Cuddeford-Jones, 2019). Other factors that should influence the organisation's choice of cause are the characteristics of the product or service, the brand's image and positioning, as well as the sector to which the brand belongs. A cause appealing to numerous constituent groups provides greater media and publicity potential. Moreover, appealing to a portfolio of causes is suitable to cases where the organisation seeks to target multiple segments.

Kompella (2014) suggests that in order to choose a suitable cause to collaborate with, organisations should determine the social issues related to the positive and negative brand (and category) associations in consumers' minds, analyse brand-specific nuances, and explore how they could craft the cause in a brand-friendly way. They must also gauge support and commitment of internal stakeholders, and test the programme to ascertain "brand fit, relevance, memorability, distinctiveness, and stakeholder resonance" (Kompella, 2014, p. 192). Organisations must also develop criteria for evaluating the relative effectiveness of CRMPs on the basis of the social benefits delivered in comparison to alternative programmes which could achieve the same objectives (Varadarajan & Menon, 1988).

Implications of cause-related marketing programmes on philanthropy

With regards to the disadvantages of CRMPs, there have been major criticisms of such programmes, from a philanthropic perspective, because of their philosophy. Drawing from Gurin (1987), Varadarajan and Menon (1988) have identified possible negative effects on organisations, NPOs (charities), the general public, and consumers. First, CRMPs can lead to negative effects on *corporate philanthropy decisions* as organisations might make decisions about their philanthropic activities based merely on their marketing potential. Organisations might opt to target certain causes due to their popularity and ignore others that have equal (if not greater) need for support. In addition, CRMPs might simply replace corporate philanthropy instead of adding to it, and in the event where CRMPs are called into question, traditional philanthropy and fund-raising might be called into question too (Gurin, 1987; Varadarajan & Menon, 1988).

Second, CRMPs can lead to negative effects on the *mission and conduct of NPOs* as they might have to change their programme objectives to meet corporate demands and desires. Furthermore, with CRMPs "a charitable organisation must exploit its constituency and therefore compromise its integrity, because the [commercial organisation] must be convinced that the donors and members can be converted into consumers of its product or service" (Varadarajan & Menon, 1988, p. 70). Third, CRMPs might negatively affect the *general public's perception of, and the attitudes toward, causes*. This means that the public's understanding of what philanthropy is becomes unclear. The commercialising nature of CRMPs could compromise public approval of the charitable organisations involved, and damage their appeal among their most traditional supporters (Varadarajan & Menon, 1988). If the proximity between the commercial organisation and the charity is too close, the latter might be perceived as being owned by the former, which can predispose its appeal for support from other commercial organisations.

Finally, CRMPs could negatively influence *consumer's charitable giving behaviour* as they might feel that the pure form of philanthropy is the organisations' responsibility. They might also feel less inclined to look for other worthy causes, hence only donate to those charitable organisations participating in CRMPs (Varadarajan

& Menon, 1988). Most importantly such programmes could make consumers feel that they have fulfilled their philanthropic responsibilities by buying the product or service involved in the CRMPs. This reinforces the notion of *painless giving* where individuals seek to provide help with minimum effort. However, consumers participating in CRMPs, i.e. purchasing the product or service, does not mean they engage in a philanthropic act. By definition, this is not an altruistic behaviour as consumers gain economic value (extrinsic rewards) by purchasing the organisation's offering (Varadarajan & Menon, 1988). Being altruistic means that one is willing to help others without expecting any material reward in return. In fact, Chang and Chu (2020) determined that CRMPs can have an interesting impact on individuals' overall consumption. They found that

> mere exposure to cause-related marketing evokes in consumers a desire to be prosocial [benefiting others] and reduces the likelihood of self-indulgent choices. However, the act of purchasing cause-related marketing products may provide consumers with a 'warm glow' feeling from being prosocial. This feeling… licenses subsequent self-indulgent behaviours, especially when the product with a cause is hedonic (vs. utilitarian) in nature…When the warm glow feeling is misattributed to something else (e.g., weather), the licensing effect is reduced.
> (Chang & Chu, 2020, p. 1)

It becomes evident from the above that organisations must consider the implications of CRMPs carefully, and commit the necessary resources to effectively plan and manage them in a manner that benefits organisations and their consumers, charitable partners and their constituents, and most importantly, the society in general.

CHAPTER REVIEW QUESTIONS

You can use the following questions to reflect on the material covered in Chapter 7:

1. Explain the two major traditions in moral philosophy and discuss their implications for brand marketing.
2. Discuss the four types of socially responsible brands using the strategic CSR brand framework and provide appropriate examples.
3. Explain the processes for incorporating ethics in brand marketing. What are the stages organisations can follow to develop a brand through CSR?
4. How does social marketing differ from commercial marketing?
5. Discuss the three main theories in social marketing and explain how they can be used in the development of successful social marketing programmes.
6. How does sustainability help organisations manage the paradox of green marketing?

7. Discuss the concept of voluntary simplicity and explain how it can foster sustainable consumption.
8. Discuss the characteristics of CRMPs and explain their negative implications for philanthropy.

RECOMMENDED READING

1. Robin, D. P., & Reidenbach, R. E. (1987). Social responsibility, ethics, and marketing strategy: Closing the gap between concept and application. *Journal of Marketing*, 51(1), 44–58.
2. Lindgreen, A., Maon, F., & Vallaster, C. (2016) Building brands via corporate social responsibility. In F. Dall'Olmo Riley, J. Singh, & C. Blankson (eds), *The Routledge companion to contemporary brand management* (pp. 228–254). London: Routledge.
3. Brunk, K. H. (2016). Towards a better understanding of the ethical brand and its management. In F. Dall'Olmo Riley, J. Singh, & C. Blankson (eds), *The Routledge companion to contemporary brand management* (pp. 228–254). London: Routledge.
4. Varadarajan, P. R., & Menon, A. (1988). Cause-related marketing: A coalignment of marketing strategy and corporate philanthropy. *Journal of Marketing*, 52(3), 58–74.

CASE STUDY

Pukka Herbs: A budding brand creating change through commerce

Edward Latham
Pukka Life Lead

Pukka Herbs (*Pukka*) is an organic herbal well-being company founded in Bristol in 2001 by Tim Westwell, and herbalist, Sebastian Pole. The company produces and sells herbal teas, herbal lattes, and herbal food supplements made from certified organic plants sourced from over thirty countries. From its inception, the co-founders sought to create an ethical business, good for people, plants and planet, which advocates how plants can play a central role in everyday human health and well-being. The product range is rooted in the ancient Ayurvedic Indian medical system and the tradition of herbalism, including modern scientific herbalism. *Pukka* is currently available in over 40 markets, the largest of which is the UK.

In the UK, *Pukka* began by selling its premium organic products primarily through shops specialising in organic products and health foods. Over time *Pukka* has built a loyal niche following of shoppers who know and value *Pukka* as an organic, health- and well-being-focused sustainable brand with attractive packaging. In 2004, *Pukka* began to be distributed in mainstream grocery retailers, which unlocked new opportunities for the company to grow by making it available to a mainstream audience. *Pukka* is known and recognised for being a highly differentiated tea brand and for its beautiful packaging design[1] but has not achieved a high level of mass awareness

238 ETHICS, SOCIAL RESPONSIBILITY, & SUSTAINABILITY

IMAGE 7.1 *Pukka Herbs'* founders Tim Westwell and Sebastian Pole (image courtesy of Pukka Herbs)

IMAGE 7.2 *Pukka Herbs'* logo (image courtesy of Pukka Herbs)

(salience) or a clear brand image (meaning) with the general public yet[2]; this represents an opportunity for the company to grow further as more people begin to understand the value that *Pukka* offers and what the company stands for.

Pukka defines its purpose as: "nurture[ing] healthier, happier lives through powerful organic plants"[3]. The company states their mission, i.e. how they deliver their purpose, as follows: "Our [*Pukka*'s] herbal creations are crafted to connect as many people as possible to the beauty and power of nature. [*Pukka*] share[s] knowledge and campaign[s] for a healthier world, always trying to lead by example"[4]. The

IMAGE 7.3 *Pukka Herbs'* packaging (image courtesy of Pukka Herbs)

organisation has made an overt commitment to doing business in a way that helps people while not forgetting the impact of the company's operations on the planet. *Pukka* sets out an intention to share what the company knows and to campaign, positioning *Pukka* as an activist company. The purpose and mission are observable in the design of the products and packaging they make.

Pukka's products are designed to help people feel happier and healthier. Firstly, they are organic: research has shown organic foods to be more nutrient rich[5] and to have a smaller impact on the planet[6]. Furthermore, their products are crafted to support health and happiness, e.g. the night time herbal infusion is made using a blend of herbs known in traditional medicine for helping someone to sleep[7]. Closer inspection of the packaging shows the depth of the commitment: the boxes of tea and tags are printed using vegetable eco inks, all paper and card is sourced responsibly, certified by the Forest Stewardship Council, and is chlorine free, the tea bag is made from natural abaca fibres, the string for the teabag is organic cotton and the tea bag itself is folded and stitched rather than glued or stapled. *Pukka*'s purpose is also visible in their product design.

Pukka designed its company structure to support health and happiness by employing a team of herbal practitioners and researchers. The company employs a director of herbal, who is responsible for herbal education, supporting the multiple herbal practitioners that work for the business, the sustainability team and quality assurance team. *Pukka* invests heavily in herbal expertise and sponsors scientific research and clinical studies into the effects of herbs on people's health. Herbal expertise within the leadership team helps to ensure that herbal knowledge is involved in steering the company.

In 2017, *Pukka* became a B Corp[8], a business certified as a force for good, introducing an external certification programme alongside the company's existing governance structure to encourage ethical business decisions. *Pukka* meets every six months with an advisory board for the organisation specialising on health and sustainability, known as their 'mission council'. The mission council is tasked with ensuring *Pukka* maintains its commitment to strategically influencing sustainable healthcare, social impact, regenerative agriculture, and the climate crisis, as the company grows. In September 2017, *Pukka* was acquired by *Unilever*, the global FMCG business. The mission council, alongside their board of directors and B Corp status, continually challenges Pukka to be a positive force in the world.

To date *Pukka* has not participated in mass consumer campaigns to promote sustainability. In an age of extensive greenwashing by companies and heightened consumer interest in ethical businesses, *Pukka*, while deeply invested in responsible, ethical, sustainable business practices, has chosen not to drive mass awareness of their actions. Detailed accounts of the company's ethical business practices can be found in their annual sustainability report but is not actively communicated to a mass audience.

Pukka has multiple strategic partnerships around the world with like-minded organisations to reach people interested in supporting the natural world. *Pukka* partners with the *Eden Project*, Cornwall, where they have an educational sampling exhibit called the 'tea box'. The Eden project aims to "connect us with each other

IMAGE 7.4 *Pukka Herbs'* certifications (image courtesy of Pukka Herbs)

ETHICS, SOCIAL RESPONSIBILITY, & SUSTAINABILITY **241**

11% end of life
The carbon impact from recycling, composting and disposing of Pukka teas, supplements and their packaging.

25% our supply chain
Growing, drying and processing our herbs as well as the impact from other goods and services we purchase, including packaging.

pukka carbon footprint from crop to cup

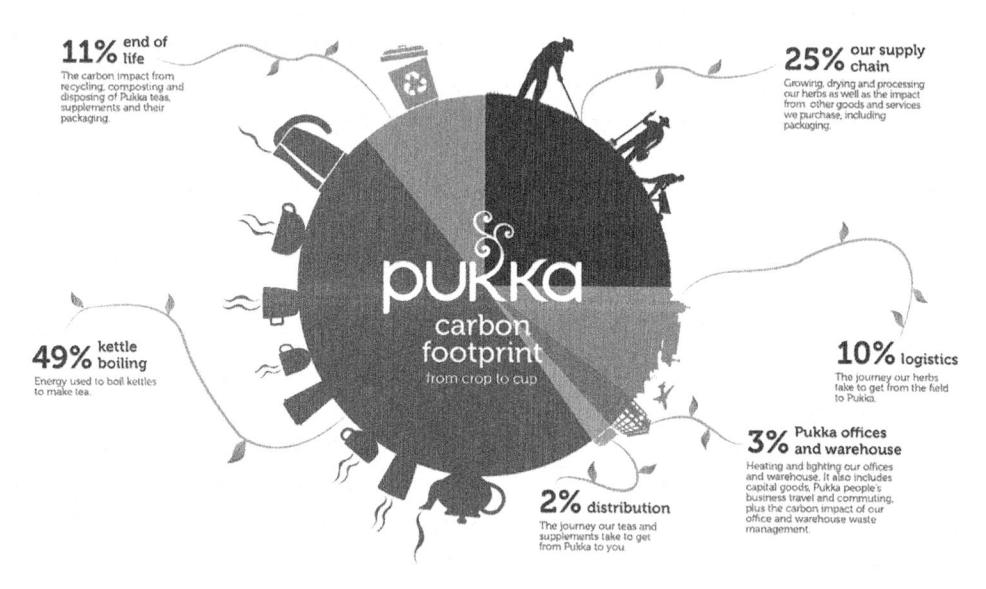

49% kettle boiling
Energy used to boil kettles to make tea.

10% logistics
The journey our herbs take to get from the field to Pukka.

3% Pukka offices and warehouse
Heating and lighting our offices and warehouse. It also includes capital goods, Pukka people's business travel and commuting, plus the carbon impact of our office and warehouse waste management.

2% distribution
The journey our teas and supplements take to get from Pukka to you.

IMAGE 7.5 *Pukka Herbs'* carbon footprint targets (image courtesy of Pukka Herbs)

IMAGE 7.6 *Pukka Herbs'* social activism (image courtesy of Pukka Herbs)

and the living world exploring how we can work towards a better future"[9] and they describe the Pukka tea box as "an educational and sampling station, as offering people a chance to discover the medicinal properties of herbs"[10]. Pukka invests a significant portion of its marketing budget on highly targeted access to audiences interested in plants, the planet, and the benefits of herbs.

In September 2019, *Pukka* declared a climate emergency to advocate for systemic change to minimise catastrophic effects of climate change[11]. To implement the commitment to be net carbon 0 by 2030, *Pukka* engaged an independent third party to audit and recommend how to achieve this, based on science-based targets for the reduction of carbon emissions. *Pukka* committed to reduce the emissions from crop to cup by 50% per million units of products by 2030 (i.e. including also emissions outside of their control from people, e.g. boiling kettles to make tea). This is an example of *Pukka* being an activist brand[12], turning the company's values into action to address one of society's most pressing needs.

Pukka is a deeply ethical company and can be considered as an activist brand but to date hasn't invested heavily in communicating at scale their sustainability credentials. *Pukka* challenges the status quo of a for-profit business by sourcing and producing products in the most ethical way possible, speaking out on issues it cares about, and by empowering its employees to make ethical decisions. The company acts on a shared concern for societal issues such as climate change and people's health and well-being, putting into action clear policies and practices to maximise the positive impact of the company.

Questions for discussion

1. How would you define *Pukka* – a CSR entrepreneur, CSR performer, vocal CSR converts, or quietly conscientious?
2. Based on what you've read about *Pukka*, what can a company do to incorporate ethics into its business decisions?
3. What cause-related marketing programme could *Pukka* credibly initiate?
4. Does *Pukka* miss an opportunity by not overtly communicating the company's work as sustainable? Why? Why not?
5. What is the role of business in saving our planet from the catastrophic impact of global warming over 1.5C net?
6. *Pukka* tries to act according its ethics. Should companies change their own behaviour or encourage others to act differently?
7. Do you believe companies should be held to the same moral standards that people are? Why? Why not?

Notes

1 Kantar Millward Brown (2019). *2019 UK Tea Review* (Kantar Millward Brown Report).
2 Kantar Millward Brown (2019). *2019 UK Tea Review* (Kantar Millward Brown Report).
3 Pukkaherbs.com (29 March 2020).
4 Pukkaherbs.com (29 March 2020).

5 Soil Association, www.soilassociation.org/organic-living/why-organic/its-nutritionally-different/.
6 Soil Association, www.soilassociation.org/organic-living/why-organic/better-for-the-planet/.
7 Pukka Herbs, www.pukkaherbs.com/products/organic-teas/night-time.html.
8 B Corp, https://bcorporation.net/.
9 Eden Project, www.edenproject.com/eden-story/our-ethos.
10 Eden Project, www.edenproject.com/visit/whats-here/pukka-tea-box.
11 Pukka Herbs, www.pukkaherbs.com/news/pukka-herbs-climate-emergency-declaration.html.
12 Kotler & Sarkar, www.activistbrands.com/what-is-brand-activism/.

REFERENCES

Andreasen, A. R. (1994). Social marketing: Its definition and domain. *Journal of Public Policy & Marketing*, 13(1), 108–114.

Bagozzi, R. P. (1975). Marketing as exchange. *Journal of Marketing*, 39(4), 32–39.

Bandura, A. (1999). Social cognitive theory of personality. In L. A. Pervin & O. P. John (eds), *Handbook of personality: Theory and research* (2nd edn) (pp. 154–196). London: The Guildford Press.

Beauchamp, T. L. (1982). *Philosophical Ethics*. New York: McGraw-Hill.

Belk, R. W. (1988). Possessions and the extended self. *Journal of Consumer Research*, 15(2), 139-168.

Belk, R. W. (2017). Sharing, materialism, and design for sustainability. In J. Chapman (ed.), *Routledge handbook of sustainable product design* (pp. 182–194). London: Routledge.

Boström, M. (2019). Rejecting and embracing brands in political consumerism. In M. Boström, M. Micheletti, & P. Oosterveer (eds), *The Oxford handbook of political consumerism* (pp. 205–225). Oxford: Oxford University Press.

Brown, T. (2009). *Change by design: How design thinking transforms organisations and inspires innovation*. New York: HarperCollins.

Brunk, K. H. (2016). Towards a better understanding of the ethical brand and its management. In F. Dall'Olmo Riley, J. Singh, & C. Blankson (eds), *The Routledge companion to contemporary brand management* (pp. 228–254). London: Routledge.

Burch, M. A. (2012). *Stepping lightly: Simplicity for people and the planet*. Gabriola Island: New Society Publishers.

Butler, C. (2002). *Postmodernism: A very short introduction*. Oxford: Oxford University Press.

Carroll, A. B. (1979). A three-dimensional conceptual model of corporate performance. *Academy of Management Review*, 4(4), 497–505.

Chang, C. T., & Chu, X. Y. M. (2020). The give and take of cause-related marketing: Purchasing cause-related products licenses consumer indulgence. *Journal of the Academy of Marketing Science*, 48(2), 203–221.

Clarkson, M. B. E. (1988). Corporate social performance in Canada, 1976–8. In L. E. Preston (ed.), *Research in corporate social performance and policy* (Vol. 10) (pp. 241–265). Greenwich: JAI Press.

Clarkson, M. B. E. (1991). Defining, evaluating, and managing corporate social performance: The stakeholder management model. In L. E. Preston (ed.), *Research in corporate social performance and policy* (Vol. 11) (pp. 331–358). Greenwich: JAI Press.

Clarkson, M. B. E. (1995). A stakeholder framework for analyzing and evaluating corporate social performance. *Academy of Management Review*, 20(1), 92–117.

Cooper, T. (2000). Product development implications of sustainable consumption. *The Design Journal*, 3(2), 46–57.

Cuddeford-Jones, M. (2019). Cause for effect: Purpose and profit need not be mutually exclusive. *Catalyst*. Issue 4. Chartered Institute of Marketing.

Etzioni, A. (2003). Voluntary simplicity: Psychological implications, societal consequences. In D. Doherty & A. Etzioni (eds), *Voluntary simplicity: Responding to consumer culture* (pp. 1–25). Lanham: Rowman and Littlefield Publishers.

Fletcher, K., Dewberry, E., & Goggin, P. (2001). Sustainable consumption by design. In M. Cohen, & J. Murphy (eds), *Exploring sustainable consumption: Environmental policy and the social sciences* (pp. 213–224). Oxford: Pergamon, Elsevier Science.

Fuchs, D. A., & Lorek, S. (2005). Sustainable consumption governance: A history of promises and failures. *Journal of Consumer Policy*, 28(3), 261–288.

Gaarder, J. (2015). *Sophie's world* (20th anniversary edition). London: Weidenfeld & Nicolson.

Graham, J., Haidt, J., & Nosek, B. A. (2009). Liberals and conservatives rely on different sets of moral foundations. *Journal of Personality and Social Psychology*, 96(5), 1029–1046.

Gurin, M. G. (1987). Cause-related marketing in question. *Advertising Age* (27 July), S-16.

Guy, B. S., & Patton, W. E. (1989). The marketing of altruistic causes: Understanding why people help. *Journal of Consumer Marketing*, 6(1), 19–30.

Hastings, G. (2007). *Social marketing: Why should the devil have all the best tunes?* Oxford: Butterworth-Heinemann.

Hastings, G., & Domegan, C. (2018). *Social marketing: Rebels with a cause*. London: Routledge.

Hodder, I. (2012). *Entangled: An archaeology of the relationships between humans and things*. Chichester: John Wiley & Sons.

Holt, D. B. (2002). Why do brands cause trouble? A dialectical theory of consumer culture and branding. *Journal of Consumer Research*, 29(1), 70–90.

Kant, I. (1964). *Groundwork for the metaphysics of morals* (H. J. Paton, trans.). New York: Harper and Row Publishers.

Keller, K. L., & Swaminathan, V. (2020). *Strategic brand management: Building, measuring, and managing brand equity* (5th edn). London: Pearson Education.

Kidwell, B., Farmer, A., & Hardesty, D. M. (2013). Getting liberals and conservatives to go green: Political ideology and congruent appeals. *Journal of Consumer Research*, 40(2), 350–367.

Kitchin, T. (2003). Corporate social responsibility: A brand explanation. *Journal of Brand Management*, 10(4), 312–326.

Kompella, K. (2014). Branding with a cause. In K. Kompella (ed.), *The definitive book of branding* (pp. 171–195). New Delhi: SAGE Publications India.

Kotler, P., & Armstrong, G. (2004). *Principles of marketing* (10th edn). Upper Saddle River: Pearson Education.

Kotler, P., & Zaltman, G. (1971). Social marketing: An approach to planned social change. *Journal of Marketing*, 35(3), 3–12.

Lee, M. S., Motion, J., & Conroy, D. (2009). Anti-consumption and brand avoidance. *Journal of Business Research*, 62(2), 169–180.

Lewis, M. W. (2000). Exploring paradox: Toward a more comprehensive guide. *Academy of Management Review*, 25(4), 760–776.

Lindgreen, A., Maon, F., & Vallaster, C. (2016) Building brands via corporate social responsibility. In F. Dall'Olmo Riley, J. Singh, & C. Blankson (eds), *The Routledge companion to contemporary brand management* (pp. 228–254). London: Routledge.

Lindgreen, A., Xu, Y., Maon, F., & Wilcock, J. (2012). Corporate social responsibility brand leadership: A multiple case study. *European Journal of Marketing*, 46(7/8), 965–993.

Marchand, A. (2013). Why sustainable consumers don't care much about green products. In S. Walker & J. Giard (eds), *The handbook of design for sustainability*. London: Bloomsbury.

Margolis, H. (1984). *Selfishness, altruism, and rationality*. Chicago: The University of Chicago Press.

Maon, F., Lindgreen, A., & Swaen, V. (2009). Designing and implementing corporate social responsibility: An integrative framework grounded in theory and practice. *Journal of Business Ethics*, 87(1), 71–89.

McAdam, T. W. (1973). How to put corporate responsibility into practice. *Business and Society Review/Innovation*, 6, 8–16.

Patagonia (2020). Environmental and social responsibility. Available at: https://eu.patagonia.com/gb/en/activism/ [accessed 17 April 2020].

Peattie, K., & Charter, M. (2003). Green marketing. In M. J. Baker (ed.), *The marketing book* (5th edn) (pp. 726–755). Oxford: Butterworth-Heinemann.

Peñaloza, L. (2012). Ethics. In L. Peñaloza, N. Toulouse, & L. M. Visconti (eds), *Marketing management: A cultural perspective* (pp. 505–526). London: Routledge.

Preston, L. E. (ed.) (1988). *Research in corporate social performance and policy* (Vol. 10). Greenwich: JAI Press.

Princen, T. (2005). *The logic of sufficiency* (Vol. 30). Cambridge: MIT Press.

Prochaska, J. O., & DiClemente, C. C. (1983). Stages and processes of self-change of smoking: Toward an integrative model of change. *Journal of Consulting and Clinical Psychology*, 51(3), 390.

Reisch, L. A., & Scherhorn, G. (1999). Sustainable consumption. In S. B. Dahiya (ed.), *The current state of economic science* (Vol. 2) (pp. 657–690). Knutsford: Spellbound Publications.

Robin, D. P., & Reidenbach, R. E. (1987). Social responsibility, ethics, and marketing strategy: Closing the gap between concept and application. *Journal of Marketing*, 51(1), 44–58.

Schouten, J. W., & McAlexander, J. H. (1995). Subcultures of consumption: An ethnography of the new bikers. *Journal of Consumer Research*, 22(1), 43–61.

Smith, A. (1776). *An inquiry into the nature and causes of the wealth of nations*. New York: The Modern Library.

Steiner, G. A. (1972). Social policies for business. *California Management Review*, 15(2), 17–24.

Torres, A., Bijmolt, T. H., Tribó, J. A., & Verhoef, P. (2012). Generating global brand equity through corporate social responsibility to key stakeholders. *International Journal of Research in Marketing*, 29(1), 13–24.

Trudel, R., Argo, J. J., & Meng, M. D. (2016). The recycled self: Consumers' disposal decisions of identity-linked products. *Journal of Consumer Research*, 43(2), 246–264.

Varadarajan, P. R., & Menon, A. (1988). Cause-related marketing: A coalignment of marketing strategy and corporate philanthropy. *Journal of Marketing*, 52(3), 58–74.

Votaw, D. (1973). Genius becomes rare. In D. Votaw & S. P. Sethi (eds), *The corporate dilemma: Traditional values versus contemporary problems* (pp. 11–45). Englewood Cliffs: Prentice Hall.

Wartick, S. L., & Cochran, P. L. (1985). The evolution of the corporate social performance model. *Academy of Management Review*, 10(4), 758–769.

Werther Jr., W. B., & Chandler, D. (2005). Strategic corporate social responsibility as global brand insurance. *Business Horizons*, 48(4), 317–324.

CHAPTER 8

Brand performance and metrics

CHAPTER AIMS AND LEARNING OUTCOMES

This chapter corresponds to the third stage of Keller and Swaminathan's (2020) *strategic brand management process*, i.e. measuring and interpreting brand performance (see Figure 8.1), and aims to achieve the following:

1. Explore a conceptual model for understanding the creation of brand value and identifying the sources and outcomes of brand equity (Brand Value Chain Model).
2. Discuss the two components of brand audit: Brand inventory and brand exploratory.
3. Explore the qualitative and quantitative techniques organisation can use when pursuing a brand exploratory.
4. Discuss ways organisations can understand the brand ecology by pursuing ethnographic studies.

ASSESSING BRAND VALUE

The Brand Value Chain Model (BVCM)

Nowadays brands are recognised as an important business asset, hence, there is a requirement for measuring brand performance in terms of the value it generates for the organisation (Lindemann, 2014). There is a growing need for accountability in branding which means that besides return-on-investment (ROI) measurements, organisations must find ways to identity brands' contribution to the generation of superior returns for organisations over time (Keller, Apéria, & Georgson, 2012; Knowles, 2005). In order for a brand to be considered a business asset in financial terms, it needs to be measured on the basis of whether or not it can generate a healthy cash flow. In addition, it is imperative to measure changes in actual consumer

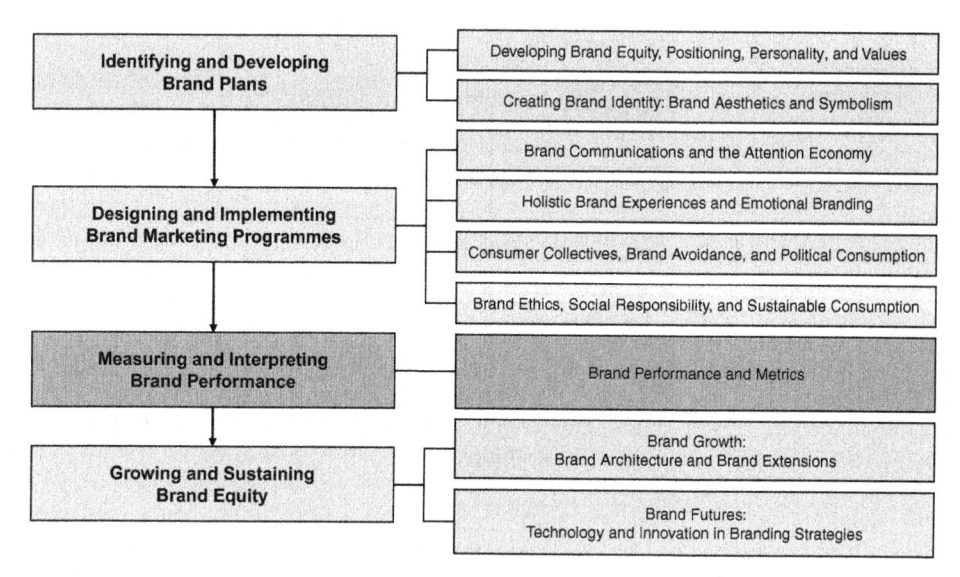

FIGURE 8.1 Strategic brand management process and book plan

behaviour instead of merely identifying changes in consumer attitudes because attitude improvements do not necessarily equate to more sales for the organisation. Finally, "brand equity needs to be measured in a way that captures the source and scale of the emotional augmentation that the brand provides to the underlying functionality of the product or service" (Keller et al., 2012, p. 380).

Keller and Lehmann developed a conceptual model that provides "a holistic, integrated approach to understanding the [financial] value created by brands" (2003, p. 26). According to the *Brand Value Chain Model* (BVCM), there are four stages in the creation of brand value. Value creation starts with the organisation's brand marketing campaign investment (stage 1), which influences the consumers' mindset (stage 2). The latter influences the brand's performance in the marketplace (stage 3), which, in turn, affects the way the brand is valued by investors and the financial community (stage 4) (Keller & Lehmann, 2003). The model also includes three *multipliers* which act as "linking factors [that] intervene between these stages…[and]…determine the extent to which value created at one stage transfers or 'multiplies' to the next stage" (Keller & Swaminathan, 2020, p. 128) (see Figure 8.2). Therefore, the BVCM is based on three assumptions: 1) the value of the brand resides with consumers (first and foremost), 2) the value creation process starts with the organisation making a marketing campaign investment targeted at current or potential customers, and 3) the multipliers intervene to moderate the value transfer from one stage to the next. It is essential to explore these stages and multipliers in more depth to understand the scope of this conceptual model.

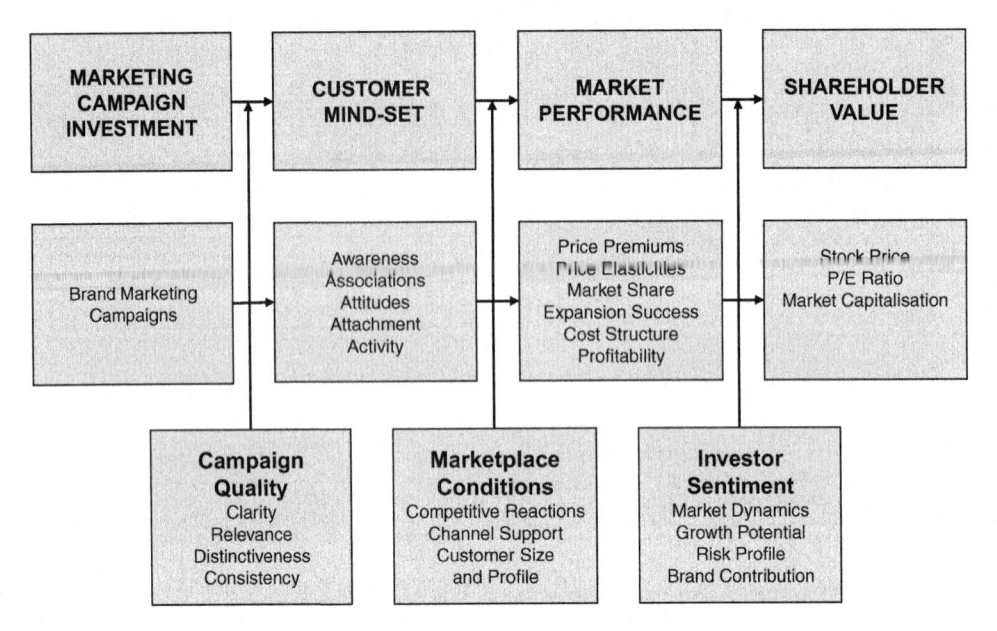

FIGURE 8.2 The brand value chain model

Marketing campaign investment

In the first stage we need to analyse any *marketing campaign investment* the organisation makes. This includes all investments that can be intentionally or unintentionally attributed to brand value development. Of course, this stage is not merely about the extent of the company's spending but about the quality of the campaign and the effectiveness of the brand marketing strategy pursued. Hence, the size of these investments cannot guarantee success; it is about quality, not quantity. The onus is on the firm to develop and implement successful brand marketing strategies; such strategies could involve concepts already explored in previous chapters of this book, e.g. brand IMC strategies, value co-creation activities, the development of holistic brand experiences, fostering consumer collectives (subcultures, brand communities, tribes, or brand publics), pursuing emotional branding, or developing socially responsible and ethical brands.

Campaign quality multiplier

As already mentioned, marketing campaign investments affect the consumers' mindset, however, such campaigns are moderated by the *campaign quality multiplier*. This multiplier includes four factors that determine the quality of the campaign. First, *clarity* is vital as the campaign must be clear and understandable to the intended target audience who need to be able to correctly interpret and evaluate the campaign's meaning. Second, the organisation must ensure *relevance*, that is, the campaign must be meaningful to the target audience in a way that makes them include the brand in their consideration set. Third, the campaign must be creative and differentiating enough to achieve a certain level of *distinctiveness*, i.e. it must be unique in comparison with its rivals. Fourth, *consistency* needs to be achieved, i.e. all aspects of the campaign must be well integrated to produce a cohesive message, which successfully influences consumer behaviour. The campaign must balance continuity and change by effectively relating to previous organisational campaigns while steering the brand in the right direction (Keller et al., 2012; Keller & Lehmann, 2003). In addition, the campaign must create short-term value (sales) and long-term value (brand equity), and must be designed to satisfy the highest industry standards expected for this specific type of marketing activity (Keller & Swaminathan, 2020).

Consumer mindset

A marketing campaign of sound quality will affect the *consumer mindset*. At this stage, the firm must understand the ways consumers have changed as a result of the campaign and how the changes manifest themselves in the consumers' mindset, including the audience's thoughts, feelings, experiences, images, perceptions, and beliefs. Keller and Lehmann (2003) have determined five ways to assess brand value at this stage. First, *brand awareness* involves the extent and ease of brand recall and recognition, as well as the extent and ease with which consumers can identify the products and/or services the brand is associated with. Second, *brand associations* is about how strong, favourable, and unique the perceived brand attributes and benefits are. Associations can be a source of brand value because they determine the ways consumers satisfy their needs. Third, *brand attitudes* includes the consumers' overall evaluations of the brand in relation to its quality and the satisfaction it provides. Fourth, *brand attachment* is concerned with how loyal consumers feel toward the brand. This is demonstrated by consumers' resistance to changing their brand preferences and the brand's ability to withstand bad news (adherence). Fifth, *brand activity* involves consumers actually using the brand, discussing it with others, and seeking out brand news, information, and events. Unquestionably, brand awareness is the prerequisite for all aforementioned factors. Consumers must be aware of the brand before they form any brand associations. This means that band value is created at this stage when consumers have deep and broad awareness, strong, favourable, and unique associations, positive brand attitudes, intense brand attachment and loyalty, and ultimately, high levels of brand activity (Keller & Lehmann, 2003; Keller & Swaminathan, 2020).

Marketplace conditions multiplier

As mentioned earlier, the consumer mindset will have an impact on the performance of the brand in the marketplace. However, the extent to which this happens, that is, the extent to which value transfers from stage 2 to stage 3 is determined by the *marketplace conditions multiplier*, which is based on three contextual factors external to the consumer: 1) competitive superiority, i.e. how effective the marketing investments of competing brands are, 2) channel and other intermediary support, i.e. the effectiveness of the selling efforts of marketing partners and the level of the resulting brand reinforcement, and 3) the size (how many) and profile (what type) of consumers (profitable or not) attracted to the brand (Keller & Lehmann, 2003; Keller & Swaminathan, 2020).

Market performance

The performance of the brand in the market, namely, how consumers react or respond, is influenced by the consumer mindset. Market performance can be measured by six specific outcomes. First, *price premiums*, which is about the fundamental question of how much extra consumers are willing to pay for a comparable product or service because of its brand. Second, *price elasticities*, which is concerned with how much consumers' demand increases or decreases when the product or service price changes. Third, changes in the *market share*, which demonstrates the campaign's ability to drive sales and improve market share. Fourth, *brand expansion*, which is about how successful the brand is "in supporting line and category extensions [explored in Chapter 9] and new product launches into related categories…[and]…its ability to add enhancements to the revenue stream" (Keller & Swaminathan, 2020, p. 130). Fifth, *cost structure*, which relates to the brand's ability to reduce expenditure on marketing campaigns due to a well-established positive consumer mindset. Sixth, *profitability* of the brand, which combines the previous five outcomes. The first three outcomes define the direct revenue stream which can be attributed to the brand; brand value is generated when the organisation enjoys higher market share, the brand can charge price premiums, consumers respond elastically to price decreases and inelastically to price increases (Keller & Lehmann, 2003; Keller & Swaminathan, 2020).

Investor sentiment multiplier

According to the BVCM, there are many external factors which influence the ability of the brand value created in the market performance stage (stage 3) to reach the final stage: shareholder value (stage 4). The *investor sentiment multiplier* includes factors considered by financial analysts and investors to determine brand valuations, these are: 1) financial markets dynamics including interest rates, investor sentiment, or supply of capital), 2) growth potential and prospects of the brand and its sector as well as how helpful or hindering the factors which constitute the organisation's economic, socio-cultural, physical (environmental), political, and legal environment, are, 3) risk profile of the brand in terms of its vulnerability to these factors, 4) brand contribution, that is, the level of importance of the brand in the organisation's portfolio and in relation to other brands the organisation might own. The financial value of the brand is reflected in shareholder value when 1) the organisation operates in a healthy sector with no environmental barriers, and 2) the brand contributes an important part of the organisation's revenues, and its prospects are positive (Keller & Lehmann, 2003; Keller & Swaminathan, 2020).

Shareholder value

In the final stage of the model, the shareholder value, the value of the brand is manifested in financial terms: the stock price the brand commands, the price/earnings multiples, and the market capitalisation for the organisation. Undoubtedly, the financial markets form opinions and generate assessments that can have direct financial implications for the organisation and the brand's value. Strong brands can generate greater returns on stockholder investments, and they can achieve this with lower risk (Keller & Lehmann, 2003; Keller & Swaminathan, 2020).

Assumption and implications
It is evident that the BVCM provides a structured way for organisations to identify where and how brand value is created, and determine where they have to focus to improve this value-creation process. Certainly, specific stages are of greater interest at different organisational management levels. Brand marketing managers are more concerned with the quality of the marketing campaign and how it affects the consumer mindset. Marketing directors focus on the impact of the consumer mindset on the performance of the brand in the marketplace. Managing directors are primarily interested in the influence of market performance on the shareholder value and consequently, the investment decisions.

An important implication of the BVCM is that although a well-funded, well-designed and well-implemented marketing campaign investment is the start of the process, it is merely a necessary but not a sufficient condition for the creation of value. Therefore, value creation involves more than the initial marketing campaign investment, as the aforementioned three multipliers can increase or decrease brand value as it moves from one stage to the next. The multipliers include factors that are mostly out with the control of the brand marketer. Recognising this means that we can put the relative success or failure of marketing campaigns to generate brand value in perspective. There is a set of measures that we can use to assess each stage and multiplier in the BVCM. Organisations can use their marketing plans and budgets to assess the marketing campaign investment (measure results against pre-determined marketing objectives), and quantitative and qualitative consumer research to determine the campaign quality multiplier and the consumer mindset. They can conduct market scans and calculate internal accounting measures to identify the marketplace conditions multiplier and the market performance (more on this in the next section), and draw from investors' analyses and interviews to determine the investor sentiment multiplier and shareholder value (Keller & Lehmann, 2003; Keller & Swaminathan, 2020).

In addition, certain modifications can be made to the BVCM, which can increase its relevance and applicability. First, feedback loops are possible, for instance, stock prices can influence morale and motivation among the organisation's staff, which can affect the quality of the work they produce (quality of marketing campaigns they plan and implement). Second, value creation does not necessarily have to occur sequentially as demonstrated in the BVCM. For example, advertising campaigns might directly influence investors who are exposed to these messages; the impressions these campaigns create in their minds can affect their brand valuations. A marketing campaign might not yield direct results; instead, results might be diffused in the long term, e.g. cause-related marketing programmes (explored in Chapter 7). Finally, "both the mean and variance of some brand value measures could matter" (Keller & Swaminathan, 2020, p. 132). For instance, in the case of consumer mindset, a niche brand might achieve great results but only across a narrow consumer range (niche) (Keller & Lehmann, 2003; Keller & Swaminathan, 2020).

The BVCM is well connected with Aaker's (1996) *Brand Equity Ten* model which is composed of ten measures organised into five categories: 1) loyalty measures (including price premium and satisfaction/loyalty), 2) perceived quality/leadership measures (including perceived quality and leadership), 3) associations/differentiation measures (including perceived value, brand personality, and organisational associations), 4) awareness measures (including brand awareness), and 5) market behaviour measures (including market share and price and distribution indices). Two terms from the Brand Equity Ten model need further explanation (as not explicitly discussed in the BVCM). *Brand leadership* relates to whether or not the brand is the market leader on the basis of its sales, its popularity (seen by trendy consumers as an up-to-date brand to own and use) and, technologically, its innovation record (Aaker, 1996). *Price and distribution indices* include, first, measuring "the *relative price* at which the brand is being sold…defined as the average price at which the brand was sold during the month divided by the average price at which all brands in that product class were sold" (Aaker, 1996, p. 116), and second, measuring *distribution coverage* calculated by "the percentage of stores carrying the brand, or the percentage of people who have access to it" (Aaker, 1996, p. 116).

Brand valuation methodologies

The BVCM explored in the previous section is a conceptual model which can be useful for brand marketers, marketing managers, and managing directors. However, the need for greater accountability and "as intangible assets displace tangible assets as sources of value creation, their growing relevance has generated a debate in terms of appropriate valuation methodologies" (Salinas, 2016, p. 48). The need for organisations to demonstrate the precise financial value of their brand as an intangible asset has called for more precise approaches to brand valuation. The latter can be a very challenging undertaking because the brand can be closely entwined with the rest of the organisation, hence trying to separate it from the rest of the business can be unfeasible and inappropriate. In addition, brand valuation requires combining financial and market research data as well as thorough comprehension of how consumer perceptions are formed. These perceptions can include "both factual (tangible) aspects and emotional (intangible) aspects. Depending on the brand, the emotional or factual aspects can be more pronounced" (Lindemann, 2014, p. 255). Brand valuation requires a multi-stakeholder approach because each constituent group views the brand from a different perspective. Moreover, brands are not only managed by the organisation's marketing function but also by human resources, research and development (R&D), sales, and investor relations, functions (Lindemann, 2014).

The importance of brand valuation has been recognised by the accounting profession, which has "overhauled the treatment of intangibles in order to align accounting values with business reality" (Lindemann, 2014, p. 256). Salinas and Ambler (2009) organise brand valuation methodologies in two categories: 1) technical valuations, and 2) managerial valuations. This corresponds to Lindemann's (2014) distinction between market-based valuation processes and brand-based valuation processes, respectively. Choosing the appropriate approach will depend on the objective of the valuation, in addition to the way the brand is defined by those who carry out the valuation exercise (Salinas, 2016).

Market-based valuation approaches (technical valuations)

Market-based valuation approaches concentrate on transaction values for comparable (similar) brands, which can provide a benchmark to value the brand in question (Lindemann, 2014). These approaches are followed by accounting firms for "balance sheet reporting and purchase price allocation, securitisation, mergers and acquisitions, or tax planning and intellectual property centralisation" (Salinas, 2016, p. 62). The main methodology in this category is

> the net present value (NPV) of discounted royalty incomes from brands for which licensing rates are available...The idea is that a market-based comparable royalty rate most appropriately represents the income stream from the brand to be valued. This is called the royalty relief method as it values the brand according to the NPV of the licensing fees that would have to be paid for the use of the brand. The value of the brand is calculated by forecasting the revenues the brand is expected to generate multiplied with the royalty rate of a comparable brand discounted to an NPV with the cost of capital of a business operating in the brand's sector or category.
>
> (Lindemann, 2014, p. 259)

Although this approach is simple the requirement is that an acceptably comparable royalty rate or transaction is identified. This constitutes the main flaw of this approach because in order to value the brand we need to find another comparable brand that has the potential to generate similar revenues in analogous markets. This might be impossible because even when brands operate in the same sector and involve similar production processes (e.g. *Coca-Cola* and *Pepsi*, *Nike*, and *Adidas*), the brands per se can never be similar; differentiation is among the main objectives of branding. Therefore this approach should only be used for transactional purposes where a financial value will suffice, as well as for crosschecking against brand-based valuation approaches (explained below). Nevertheless, in most cases, relying on a financial value is insufficient as it does not indicate the drivers of brand value and the strategies, which can be pursued to enhance this value further (Lindemann, 2014).

Brand-based valuation approaches (managerial valuations)

> Managerial brand valuations are conducted for brand portfolio optimisation, marketing budget allocation and measuring marketing effectiveness. The models that support this type of valuations are usually dynamic and focus on determining the role of the brand in terms of influencing the key variables of the model.
>
> (Salinas, 2016, p. 62)

The advantages of these approaches include their ability to determine a value (number) based on the earnings the brand in question is predicted to generate, as well as to indicate the drivers of brand value "as they are built from bottom up from the revenue generation of the specific brand" (Lindemann, 2014, pp. 262–263). The most used approach in this category is the methodology developed by *Interbrand*, the global brand consultancy, which produces its well-known annual global brand rankings. Described with the following, *Interbrand*'s methodology has three components, which are:

> the financial performance of the branded products or services,…the role the brand plays in purchase decisions, and…the brand's competitive strength. [First,] *financial analysis*…measures the overall financial return to an organization's investors, or its economic profit. Economic profit is the after-tax operating profit of the brand, minus a charge for the capital used to generate the brand's revenue and margins. [Second, the] *role of brand*…measures the portion of the purchase decision attributable to the brand as opposed to other factors (for example, purchase drivers such as price, convenience, or product features). The Role of Brand Index (RBI) quantifies this as a percentage. RBI determinations for Best Global Brands derive, depending on the brand, from one of three methods: commissioned market research, benchmarking against Role of Brand scores from client projects with brands in the same industry, or expert panel assessment. [Third,] *brand strength* measures the ability of the brand to create loyalty and, therefore, sustainable demand and profit into the future. Brand Strength analysis is based on an evaluation across ten factors that Interbrand believes constitute a strong brand. Performance in these areas is judged relative to other brands in the industry and relative to other world-class brands. The Brand Strength analysis delivers an insightful snapshot of the strengths and weaknesses of the brand and is used to generate a road map of activities to grow the brand's strength and value into the future.
>
> (*Interbrand*, 2020)

The ten factors in the Brand Strength analysis can be found in Table 8.1. Despite its popularity, Salinas (2016) provides a critique of this methodology. First, she argues that some of these factors are interconnected, for instance, responsiveness and relevance are two sides of the same coin. This means that these two factors need to be linked together because failing to do so, regardless of how much a brand tries to be responsive to shifting market needs, if consumers deem these efforts irrelevant, the brand will not be successful.

TABLE 8.1 Ten factors in brand strength analysis

Internal factors	
Clarity	Clarity internally about what the brand stands for in terms of its values, positioning, and proposition. Clarity too about target audiences, customer insights, and drivers.
Governance	The degree to which the organisation has the required skills and an operating model for the brand that enables effective and efficient deployment of the brand strategy.
Commitment	Internal commitment to the brand, and a belief internally in its importance. The extent to which the brand receives support in terms of time and influence.
Responsiveness	The organisation's ability to constantly evolve the brand and business in response to, or anticipation of, market changes, challenges and opportunities.

External factors	
Authenticity	The brand is soundly based on an internal truth and capability. It has a defined story and a well-grounded value set. It can deliver against the (high) expectations that customers have of it.
Consistency	The degree to which a brand is experienced without fail across all touchpoints or formats.
Relevance	The fit with customer/consumer needs, desires, and decision criteria across all relevant demographics and geographies.
Presence	The degree to which a brand feels omnipresent and is talked about positively by consumers, customers, and opinion formers in both traditional and social media.
Differentiation	The degree to which customers/consumers perceive the brand to have a differentiated proposition and brand experience.
Engagement	The degree to which customers/consumers show a deep understanding of, active participation in, and a strong sense of identification with, the brand.

Source: Interbrand (2020).

The only relevant indicator in terms of brand strength is thus public perception, and the impact that the internal activities have on this, consumer attitudes, and in turn, sales. The effort an analyst considers a brand to be making internally becomes irrelevant.

(Salinas, 2016, p. 57)

However, one could argue that it is still appropriate to explore responsiveness and relevance separately as organisations can take actions to improve these in different ways. Another criticism involves the fact that scores given to some of the factors in the brand strength analysis could be subjective (based on the analyst's judgment), in particular the scores for authenticity and clarity (Salinas, 2016). However, triangulating these scores with rigorous data can increase the objectivity of the results. Finally, Salinas (2016) argues that this model assumes the same factors and the same factor weights for every case, ignoring any nuances among brands or sectors. However, contrastingly, one could argue that using the same factors and weighting is actually preferable because it provides appropriate benchmark for comparisons among brands to consequently arrive at brand rankings. Of course, analysts could tailor the weighting of each factor for different brands based on the stage of these brands' development.

Implications of brand valuation methodologies

Salinas (2016) determined five important lessons that we can draw from an analysis of the available brand valuation methodologies. First, brand valuations are expert opinions, however they are not scientific results. The brand valuation the analyst arrives at is his/her opinion of the brand as an asset based on his/her analysis and hypothesis at a specific moment in time. Although this makes brand valuations subjective, "this doesn't matter, provided the methodologies employed are explicit, clear, and transparent" (Murphy cited in Salinas, 2016, p. 63). Second, brand valuations are based on predicted risk and returns of the brand in question. Third, connecting brand strength with the brand's forecasted risk and returns "assumes correctly that brand value is a function of brand strength or brand equity. [This means that]... we need to 'evaluate' a brand in order to 'value' it. The stronger the brand, all other variables constant, the higher its value" (Salinas, 2016, p. 63). Fourth, brand valuations need to include a legal analysis of the brand's properties in terms of the legal protection an organisation has secured for the brand's legal trademarks. Fifth, most importantly, as we have already emphasised, the main factor which should influence the choice of an appropriate methodology should be the purpose of the valuation, i.e. either technical for accounting and transactional purposes, or managerial for understanding the main drivers behind the brand's financial value (Salinas, 2016).

BRAND AUDIT

Brand marketers can carry out a comprehensive evaluation of the brand by conducting a *brand audit* defined by Keller and Swaminathan as a "consumer-focused exercise... to assess the health of the brand, uncover its sources of brand equity and suggest ways to improve and leverage its equity" (2020, p. 329). An effective brand audit will include assessing brand performance from both organisation and consumer perspectives. The former can be achieved through the brand inventory part of brand

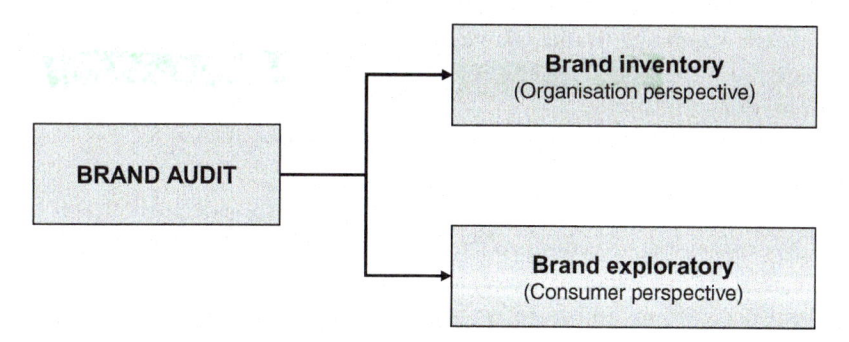

FIGURE 8.3 Components of brand audit

audit, and the latter with the brand exploratory part, which are discussed in detail in the following (Keller & Swaminathan, 2020) (see Figure 8.3).

Brand inventory

Brand inventory determines the performance of the brand from the organisation's perspective and involves brand marketers carrying out a detailed profiling of the organisation's products and/or services to determine how these are marketed and branded. This requires a thorough examination of brand elements and supporting marketing campaign materials. Hence, the brand inventory should catalogue the following: "the names, logos, symbols, characters, packaging, slogans or other trademarks used; the inherent product attributes or characteristics of the brand; the pricing, communications, distribution policies and any other relevant marketing activity related to the brand" (Keller & Swaminathan, 2020, p. 330). Brand marketers should present this information in both verbal and visual form (with relevant visual materials). It is important that the brand inventory is regularly updated to remain accurate and comprehensive. Brand marketers can also seek to profile all competing brands in the same sector or product/service category to determine their points-of-parity (POPs) and points-of-difference (PODs) associations (Keller & Swaminathan, 2020). Schmitt and Simonson's (1997) identity elements mix (see Chapter 3) and Schmitt's (1999a, 1999b) experience providers typology (see Chapter 5) are useful frameworks brand marketers can use when preparing the brand inventory.

Brand exploratory

Brand exploratory is "research directed to understanding what consumers think and feel about the brand and act toward it in order to better understand sources of brand equity, as well as any possible barriers" (Keller & Swaminathan, 2020, p. 332). This part of the brand audit explores the performance of the brand from the consumer perspective to reveal the true meaning of the brand to its target audience. Preliminary activities in the brand exploratory include collecting secondary data (existing data about the brand) as well as staff interviews to gauge their opinions and beliefs about the consumers' perceptions of the brand and its competitors (Keller & Swaminathan, 2020).

Qualitative techniques

The qualitative techniques used in brand exploratory are extremely useful because they allow respondents freedom of expression due to their relatively unstructured nature (Keller, 1993), which means that researchers can explore consumers' deeply held brand perceptions and feelings. Levy (1985) explains that the research goals can vary in terms of their direction, depth, and diversity (see Figure 8.4). *Direction* is about whether or not the questions asked focus on the consumer or the brand. This means that some questions could seek to understand consumers' psycho-social characteristics (without making reference to the brand in question) while other questions could aim to identify consumers' perceptions of the brand and their behaviour towards it (Levy, 1985). *Depth* is about whether consumer responses are specific, or deeper and more abstract which means that they would require extensive interpretation: "The more specific the question, the narrower the range of information given by the respondent. When the stimulus is more open and responses are freer, the information provided tends to be greater" (Levy, 1985, p. 68) but requires more interpretation. Quality research is interpretivist in nature, hence, it goes beyond what people explicitly say and seeks to understand what people mean. Finally, *diversity* is about how the data collected can relate to data gathered by other techniques (Keller et al., 2012).

There are three qualitative techniques that we need to explore in depth: free associations exercises, projective techniques such as completion and interpretation tasks (bubble exercises), and comparison tasks. As already discussed in Chapter 2, the free associations exercise is the simplest, yet most powerful way to identify consumer associations as respondents answer the following question: 'What comes to your mind when you think of the brand?' This helps brand marketers to generate a mental map of the brand (spider diagram), which displays the range of consumer's

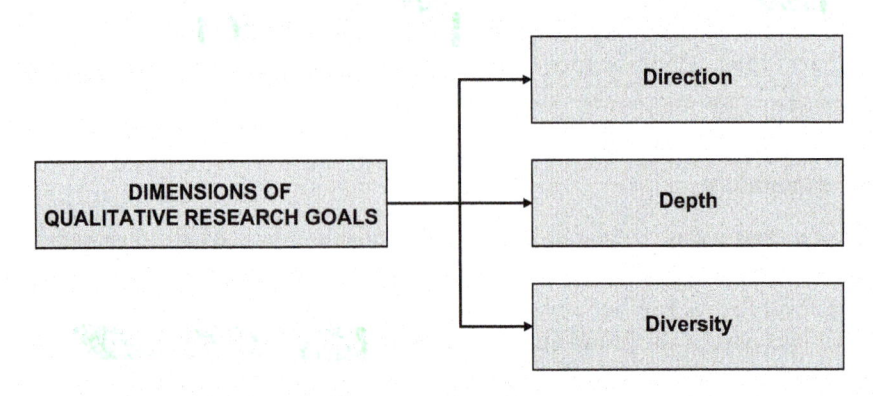

FIGURE 8.4 Dimensions of qualitative research goals

brand associations. This simple question can also provide some indication of *strength* of associations on the basis of "order of elicitation – whether they are early or late in the sequence" (Keller & Swaminathan, 2020, p. 364), for example, if the first association that come to consumer's mind when thinking of *Nike* is 'sport', then there is a strong connection between the brand and sport and fitness. Respondents' answers can also elicit an indication of *favourability* of associations by gauging how associations were stated and phrased by consumers, as well as their relative *uniqueness* when compared with other brands' associations (Keller & Swaminathan, 2020). Follow-up questions can include

> 'what do you like best about the brand?', 'what are its positive aspects?', 'what do you dislike?', 'what are its disadvantages?', 'what do you find unique about the brand?', 'how is it different from other brands?', 'in what ways is it the same?'
> (Keller et al., 2012, p. 447)

In addition, in a more unstructured format, respondents can be asked what the brand means to them by asking them about who, in their opinion, uses the brand (what type of person), when and where the brand is used (what kind of situations), the reasons people use the brand (the benefits they receive), and how is the brand used (what do people use the brand for) (Keller, 1993; Keller & Swaminathan, 2020).

Projective techniques include more advanced and comprehensive approaches in brand exploratory because they "are diagnostic tools to uncover the true opinions and feelings of consumers when they are unwilling or otherwise unable to express themselves on these matters" (Keller & Swaminathan, 2020, p. 366). There might be situations where consumers are embarrassed to reveal their behavioural choices or might be unaware of how they behave and why. With projective techniques, researchers present respondents with incomplete stimulus and are asked to complete it, or with ambiguous stimulus which are asked to make sense of, revealing individuals' genuine opinions and feelings. These techniques are extremely useful to brand marketers in cases where there are some deeply held personal motivations and/or topics which are personally or socially sensitive (Keller, 1993; Keller & Swaminathan, 2020). One of the projective techniques regularly used is the *completion and interpretation tasks*, also known as bubble exercises. They are based on images of people (or cartoons) in which characters are shown purchasing or using the product or service in question. Empty bubbles are placed on the images representing "the thoughts, words or actions of one or more of the participants in the scene" (Keller et al., 2012, p. 450). Respondents are then tasked to figuratively 'fill in the bubble' and explain what they think is taking place or is being said between participants in the scene. The respondents' explanations and interpretations of these images provide researchers with ways to understand consumers' user and usage imagery associations for the brand (Keller & Swaminathan, 2020).

Comparison tasks is another projective technique useful to researchers and brand marketers because

> in some instances, when discussing competitive brands, respondents have difficulty in directly articulating the different images they have of them. They can be helped to express their impressions by being asked to relate the brand to other kinds of objects. Often used are stimuli such as cars, animals, and human stereotypes to assist in bringing out the respondents' associative processes.
> (Levy, 1985, p. 69)

Thus, researchers could ask the following questions: 'If the brand were a car what would it be and why?', 'if the brand were an animal what would it be and why?', or "'looking at these people, which ones do you think would be most likely to use the following brands [and why]?'" (Levy, 1985, p. 69). The choices respondents make and the reasons they provide for them can provide a better understanding of consumers' mentality in relation to the brand as well as reveal the associations and inferences reflected by these choices, which can help brand marketers understand not only consumers' brand imagery associations, but also brand personality associations (Keller & Swaminathan, 2020).

According to Lannon and Cooper (1983), besides the free associations exercises, and projective techniques, other qualitative techniques which can be used by brand marketers to understand their target audiences' opinions, feelings, and actions toward their brand include: (1) *role playing*, where participants are asked to take on and act out a certain role, (2) *personal analogies*, where an "individual imagines him/herself to be object or material with which he/she is working and 'feels' like the object" (Lannon & Cooper, 1983, p. 210), (3) *direct analogies* used from other areas/topics, (4) *symbolic analogies* used to describe a problem or object, (5) *fantasy solutions/future scenarios*, where respondents define problems and imagine or dream up solutions, (6) *adjective ratings and checklists*, where respondents are asked to use adjectives to make associations with other areas or products, (7) *personifications*, where a brand is imagined as being alive and having its own personality and relationships, (8) *consumer drawings and photo-sorting*, and (9) *group conflict/competition*, where participants work in groups to compete in selling products and advocating their ideas (Lannon & Cooper, 1983).

Quantitative techniques

Tracking studies seek to collect consumer data over time and can be carried out using quantitative techniques. Such techniques can gather baseline information about the performance of the brand and its marketing strategies to enable brand marketers to make daily decisions. They also provide vital information about the effects of marketing campaigns on the consumer mindset, the performance of the brand in the market, and the shareholder value (i.e. the second, third, and fourth stages of BVCM as discussed earlier). This allows brand marketers to have a clear picture of the status of the brand's equity and understand the dynamics of the product/service category, consumer behaviour, how vulnerable the brand is to external factors, and the effectiveness and efficiency of marketing strategies (Keller & Swaminathan, 2020).

When the organisation has opted for a branded (brand-based) identity (see Chapter 3), i.e. when there is a corporate brand (e.g. *Procter and Gamble*) and product brands (e.g. *Pantene*, *Head & Shoulders* etc.), it is essential to pursue tracking studies for both the corporate brand and product brands, separately, concurrently (or both) (Keller & Swaminathan, 2020). Corporate brand tracking allows brand marketers to understand the dynamics between the corporate brand and the product brands and answer questions such as: 1) which product brands the corporate brand reminds the consumers of, 2) which product brands are the most influential in influencing consumer perceptions, and 3) which product brands consumers associate with the corporate brand (on an unaided basis). Of course, having a branded (brand-based) identity means that the organisation is known by its name and corporate brand elements to suppliers and distributors, and by its product brands to its consumers (Olins, 2008; Schmitt & Simonson, 1997), However, in recent years, corporate brands such as *Procter and Gamble*, *Unilever*, or *LVMH* have become more visible in consumers' eyes, in particular through community impact (CSR) programmes such as *Procter and Gamble*'s global *Children's Safe Drinking Water (CSDW)* programme (https://csdw.org) which seeks to provide clean water to children and their families around the world. This means that it is important that brand marketers determine consumer perceptions of corporate brands and their connections with product brands.

The quantitative techniques organisations can follow in order to track brand performance include methods measuring brand awareness, brand image, brand response (purchase intentions), brand relationship (behavioural loyalty and attitudinal attachment), and brand substitutability. Calculating *behavioural loyalty* involves determining how many consumers buy the brand in a period of time, how much they buy, and how often (Singh & Uncles, 2016). It also includes

> *the share of category requirements* which measures the share of an average buyer's total product category requirements that are accounted for by a specific brand, over an observation period (such as a year). [This is calculated as the] average purchase frequency per buyer for the brand during the period [divided by the] total amount of the product category bought in the period by buyers of the brand.
>
> (Singh & Uncles, 2016, p. 18)

According to Keller (1993) measuring brand awareness and brand associations (image) corresponds to the *indirect approach* to measuring brand equity whereby the brand marketer "attempts to assess potential sources of customer-based brand equity by measuring brand knowledge (i.e., brand awareness and brand image)" (Keller, 1993, p. 12). Consumer brand knowledge can be multidimensional and involves the cognitive representation of the brand in consumer's mind (Keller, 2003).

As explained in Chapter 2, *brand awareness* involves brand recall and brand recognition. With regards to brand recall, i.e. the ability of the consumer to retrieve the brand from his/her memory, we discussed two types: aided and unaided recall. *Unaided recall* is the most demanding from the consumer because it measures the extent to which consumers are able to retrieve the brand from their memory without the researcher providing specific cues. This means that 'all brands' are provided as a cue, which allows brand marketers to identify the strongest brands in consumers' minds (Keller & Swaminathan, 2020). Hence, the question researchers can ask is: 'Name five brands that come to your mind'. *Aided recall* is the exercise whereby the researcher provides a probe or cue such as a product category (e.g. washing detergents) or consumer need (transport and mobility): "Brand recall measures may use different sets of cues, such as progressively narrowly defined product category labels" (Keller, 1993, p. 12). Thus, the question asked could be: 'Name five washing detergent or automobile brands'. Besides being assessed in terms of consumers correctly recalling the brand, researchers can code brand recall results in terms of order, latency, and speed of recall (Keller & Swaminathan, 2020). "Order of recall [can] capture the extent to which the [brand] name is 'top of mind' and thus strongly associated with the product category in memory" (Keller, 1993, p. 12).

As far as brand recognition is concerned, this is about consumers' ability to recognise the brand name or other brand elements e.g. brand logo, colours, or symbols, as something they have seen or heard before (and connect it with the right brand). Brand recognition is not as demanding from consumers as brand recall because they are exposed to a visual stimuli and do not have to rely on their memory. The question is how confident they are in recognising the brand element as well as whether or not they can match the brand element with the correct brand. Therefore, similar to brand recall, apart from correctly recognising the brand, researcher can measure response latencies "to provide a fuller picture of memory performance with respect to the brand" (Keller, 1993, p. 12). As mentioned before, brand recognition data can be very useful for decisions on product packaging, which needs to be recognisable from a certain distance.

Brand image quantitative techniques can build on qualitative results (e.g. free association exercise results) in order to quantitatively measure the strength, favourability, and uniqueness of consumers' brand associations by using appropriate scales. Consumers can be asked to rate their associations by asking questions such as:

'what are the strongest associations you have with the brand? (strength),…'what do you like about it?',…'what do you dislike about it?' (favourability), 'what is unique about the brand?', and 'what characteristics or features does it share with other brands?' (uniqueness).

(Keller et al., 2012, p. 493)

Alternatively, researchers can also provide statements about the brand (possible associations) and ask consumers to rate them on *Likert* scales (1–5) (from 'strongly disagree' to 'strongly agree').

As regards to *brand response*, this is about the *direct* approach to measuring customer-based brand equity, which "attempts to measure…brand equity more directly by assessing the impact of brand knowledge [as explained above] on consumer response to different elements of the firm's marketing programme" (Keller, 1993, p. 12). Brand response is primarily concerned with consumers' purchase intentions, hence, "the likelihood of buying the brand or the likelihood of switching from the brand to another" (Keller et al., 2012, p. 498). "Purchase intentions can provide better forecasts than a simple extrapolation of past sales trends" (Armstrong, Morwitz, & Kumar, 2000, p. 383). In order for purchase intentions to provide accurate predictions of actual purchase there must be

> correspondence between…two in the following dimensions: action (e.g. buying for own use or to give as a gift), target (e.g. specific type of product and brand), context (e.g. in what type of store based on what prices and other conditions), [and] time (e.g. within a week, month, or year).
>
> (Keller & Swaminathan, 2020, p. 383)

This means that researchers should provide exact specification of the circumstances involved (purpose, location, time, etc.) when asking respondents to predict their likely purchase of the brand.

In addition, Keller (1993) proposes an experimental research technique to directly measure the impact of brand knowledge on consumer responses to brand marketing campaign whereby

> one group of consumers responds to an element of the marketing programme when it is attributed to the brand and another group of consumers responds to that same element when it is attributed to a factiously named or unnamed version of the product or service…Comparing the responses of the two groups thus provides an estimate of the effects due to the specific knowledge about the brand that goes beyond basic product or service knowledge.
>
> (Keller, 1993, p. 13)

As far as *brand relationship* is concerned, researchers should try to measure behavioural loyalty and attitudinal attachment. Researchers can ask consumers questions such as "what percentage of their last purchases in the [product] category went to the brand (past purchase history) and what percentage of their planned next purchases will go to the brand (intended future purchases)" (Keller et al., 2012, p. 499). Table 8.2 provides an extensive list of the questions brand marketers can ask to measure brand usage (behavioural loyalty) and brand attitudes (attitudinal attachment), determine gaps with competing brands, and identify which brands are

TABLE 8.2 Questions for assessing consumers' brand usage and brand attitudes

Behavioural loyalty

Which brand of <product category or class> do you usually buy?
Which brand of <product category or class> did you buy last time?
Do you have any <product category or class> at home? Which brand?
Which brands of <product category or class> did you consider buying?
Which brand of <product category or class> will you buy next time?
Do you expect to buy <product category or class> in the next two weeks?
Have you consumed any <product category or class> in the last two weeks?

Source: Based on Keller, Apéria, & Georgson (2012).

included in consumers' consideration sets. Researchers can use open-ended questions, but to make data more quantitative, they could ask dichotomous questions where consumers are made to choose between two brands, provide multiple choices, or ask consumers to rate their responses. Following purchase intention exercises, the organisation should compare the data gathered with actual purchase data to evaluate whether or not consumers (and these techniques) have been accurate in predicting behaviour (Keller et al., 2012).

Finally, *brand substitutability* is an important measure because it can be a successful indicator of brand equity as it determines the extent to which consumers are willing to accept a substitute brand. Researchers can ask two important questions: "1) 'which brand did you buy last time?', and 2) 'if the brand had not been available, what would you have done?'" (Keller et al., 2012, p. 500): a) would you have waited (until it becomes available), b) 'would you have gone to another store to find it?', or c) 'would you have purchased another brand, and if so, which brand?'. The less people are willing to substitute the brand with another, the greater the likelihood they will purchase it again, and the stronger their relationship with the brand (Keller et al., 2012). Table 8.3 summarises the qualitative and quantitative techniques organisations can use to conduct the brand exploratory.

UNDERSTANDING THE BRAND ECOLOGY: CONSUMER ETHNOGRAPHY

As mentioned earlier, consumers are often unaware of their behaviour, unable to explain the reasons behind their choices, or simply unwilling to share this information with researchers. Consumers might be unable to predict what they will want or consume in the future, to identify any problems with products or services, or to imagine future product or service use (Cooper & Evans, 2006). This means that consumers do not always behave in the way they say they do (Fellman, 1999) resulting in the *say/do gap bias* (Liedtka, 2015). In addition, traditional marketing research techniques can often be limiting as they rely on consumer responses, and often focus on predicting consumers' behaviour instead of trying to understand and explain

TABLE 8.3 Brand exploratory: Qualitative and quantitative techniques

Qualitative techniques	Quantitative techniques
Free associations exercises	Brand awareness measures
Projective techniques	Brand image measures
Role playing	Brand response measures (purchase
Personal analogies	intentions)
Direct analogies	Brand relationship measures (behavioural
Symbolic analogies	loyalty and attitudinal attachment)
Fantasy solutions / future scenarios	Brand substitutability
Adjective ratings and checklists	
Personifications	
Consumer drawings and photo-sorting	
Group conflict / competition	

their behaviour. Based on an extensive study where he compared purchase intentions data (as explained above) with actual subsequent sales, Ovans (1998) discovered that "people are generally not reliable predictors of their own long-term purchasing behaviour for any type of good" (1998, p.12).

To compensate for the aforementioned shortcomings, over the last few decades, organisations have pursued ethnographic studies to better understand consumers' behaviour toward their brands (Liedtka, 2015; Malefyt, 2009). In contrast with quantitative marketing research, which seeks to generate generalisations that hold truth across time and in different contexts, ethnography aims to explore "social phenomena in situ or in particular contexts" (Moisander & Valtonen, 2012, p. 252). *Ethnography*, originally used in anthropology, is "the research approach that produces a detailed, in depth observation of people's behaviour, beliefs, and preferences by observing and interacting with them in a natural environment" (Ireland, 2003, p. 26). Ethnography has been widely used in academic research in the fields of consumer culture theory (e.g. Kates, 2002, 2004; Thompson, 1997) and design studies (e.g. Squires & Byrne, 2002; Wasson, 2000, 2002) (see Chapter 2 in Lalaounis, 2017, for a comprehensive overview of design ethnography). It has also been pursued in commercial consumer research by organisations that seek to delve deeper in human behaviour and lifestyles (Zukin, 2004). Ethnography is adaptable to different circumstances due to the richness of its findings and the open-endedness of its approach (Kozinets, 2002). It produces particularised understanding and 'grounded knowledge' (Glaser & Strauss, 1967), which is inductively generated from the collected data. Ethnography allows brand marketers to understand the *brand ecology* (Percy, Rossiter, & Elliott, 2001), which involves

> studying the lived experience of the consumer as a social being, and which considers not just the attitudinal, emotional, and behavioural aspects of brand consumption, but explores how this brand-related behaviour integrates with wider social and cultural experience in the life-world of the active consumer.
>
> (Elliott & Jankel-Elliott, 2003, p. 215)

Traditionally, when anthropologists conduct an ethnography study, they spend a very long time with the social group under study to immerse themselves in the lives of these individuals. This allows researchers to 'go native' and become accepted as part of the social group in order to minimise their influence on what is being observed, and to identify behaviours which even those under study are not able to explain or articulate themselves (Malinowski, 1922; Plowman, 2003). However, we must recognise that spending such lengthy periods of time with consumers can be extremely expensive or even impossible for organisations that usually operate in tight time schedules and budgets. Consequently, organisations must follow a more applied version of ethnography when pursuing consumer or design research (Elliott & Jankel-Elliott, 2003; Lalaounis, 2017; Wasson, 2000, 2002).

Notwithstanding the applied nature of consumer ethnography for branding, researchers must still adhere to the requirement of 'going native' in order to become part of the social group and to identify consumers' symbolic and cultural meanings, values, and patterns of consumption. The ethnographic study must take place in natural settings, e.g. in consumers' homes, or in stores, to achieve a significant level of *empathy*, i.e. being able to "[see] the world through their eyes, and using their meanings" (Elliott & Jankel-Elliott, 2003, p. 216). Consumer researchers should seek to spend extensive periods of time in the field to achieve the necessary "immersion in context [which] increases the likelihood of spontaneously encountering important moments in the ordinary events of consumers' daily lives and of experiencing revelatory incidents" (Arnould & Wallendorf, 1994, p. 485). Ethnographic studies seek to achieve depth instead of breadth, and understanding instead of prediction unlike other traditional marketing research methods (Elliott & Jankel-Elliott, 2003). Hence, ethnography applied to gain consumer market insight is

> the research process in which the researcher participates in the daily life of consumers in a particular social setting and collects data using a set of ethnographic fieldwork methods (particularly participant observation, and personal, in-context interviews) and then writes accounts of this process.
>
> (Moisander & Valtonen, 2012, p. 251)

Observations are ideal for identifying inconsistencies between what people say they do and what they actually do (Leblanc, 2012) and eliminating the say/do gap bias (Liedtka, 2015). Ethnography can be employed in brand development to study consumer collectives such as subcultures of consumption, brand communities, and consumer tribes (as discussed in Chapter 6), in order to identify ways organisations can harness their power.

Ethnography can help organisations gather what technology ethnographer and business consultant Tricia Wang described in her 2016 *TEDxCambridge* talk (in Boston, USA) as 'thick data' (as compared to big data). *Thick data* provides organisations with "precious, unquantifiable insights from actual people to make the right business decisions and thrive in the unknown" (Wang, 2016). While at *Nokia* in 2009, around the time when *iPhones* had just come out, Tricia Wang sought to understand the technology consumption behaviour of low-income Chinese social groups through an extensive ethnographic study. She discovered that these consumers were willing to spend half of their income to buy a smartphone. When she presented the results of her study to *Nokia* business executives, they were not convinced because her research findings were not based on big data and because her sample (100 participants) was, in their eyes, insignificant. Needless to say that *Nokia* missed a great opportunity and its business completely collapsed in four years.

Besides *field ethnography*, which involves an individual or social group being observed by a researcher in their natural setting while they go about their daily lives, there are other techniques or types at the researcher's disposal. *Digital ethnography* involves generating digital recordings of people's behaviour which are then analysed by the researcher, and *photo ethnography* involves participants being asked to capture (using digital cameras or smartphones) aspects of their daily lives with photos or videos which then they have to explain with personal notes. As far as the design of new products or services is concerned, researchers can also pursue *'real world' ethnographic enactments* (inspired by *MTV's Real World Series*) where participants are placed in a purpose-built environment and are monitored with regards to their use of digital appliances and distributed computing. They can also pursue *personas* which involve developing "scenarios or profiles...to inspire and guide design... [including] visual and textual descriptions" (Ireland, 2003, p.?), and *ethno-futurism* which combines a futures perspective, i.e. identifying future global trends (e.g. health and medical issues, communications etc.) (Cooper & Evans, 2006), with digital ethnography to identify daily activities with wider trends that can influence and morph culture and society (see Belk, Fischer, & Kozinets (2012), Coughlan & Prokopoff (2004), and Ireland (2003) for a comprehensive discussion of human-centred ethnographic techniques).

Given the proliferation of social media as platforms where consumers can communicate with each other, share their thoughts and experiences, and build online communities, it is important for organisations to find ways to study consumers' online behaviour. Online communities contribute to *consumer advocacy* because they act as online social gatherings where consumers can discuss brands and influence each other's brand perceptions. Hence online communities can have a significant impact on the equity of one brand over another (Kozinets, 2002). In his seminal paper, Kozinets presented *netnography*,

> a new qualitative research methodology that adapts ethnographic research techniques to study the cultures and communities that are emerging through computer-mediated communications. [Netnography] uses the information that is publicly available in online forums to identify and understand the needs and decision influences of relevant online consumer groups.
>
> (Kozinets, 2002, p. 62)

Compared with other types of consumer ethnography, netnography can be unobtrusive if the researcher chooses to not participate in the interaction taking place in the online context. Hence, in a non-participant observation manner, the researcher observes the setting by 'lurking', that is, monitoring without interfering, which is important for understanding the online community rules and norms (Maclaran & Catterall, 2002). This allows observing consumers' behaviour in an online context which is not influenced by the researcher. In addition, in comparison with traditional ethnography, netnography is less time-consuming and elaborate but it allows "continuing access to informants in a particular online situation" (Kozinets, 2002, p. 62). However, researchers should not ignore the

> limitations of netnography [which] draw from its more narrow focus on online communities, the need for researcher interpretive skill, and the lack of informant identifiers present in the online context that leads to difficulty generalizing results to groups outside the online community sample. Marketing researchers wishing to generalize the findings of a netnography of a particular online group to other groups must therefore apply careful evaluations of similarity and employ multiple methods for triangulation.
>
> (Kozinets, 2002, p. 62)

Needless to say that, regardless of which type of ethnography brand marketers and researchers choose to pursue to understand consumer behaviour, raw data is useless unless it is rigorously analysed and interpreted to produce knowledge. As Moisander and Valtonen (2012) explain

> the use of interpretive data *per se* does not ensure valuable insights into the cultural complexity of consumer experience and marketplace activity. Only practitioners and researchers who are able to make insightful *interpretations* of those data may gain knowledge that is valuable for designing [and developing successful brands].
>
> (Moisander & Valtonen, 2012, p. 257)

In addition, brand marketers must recognise empirical phenomena can be interpreted in different ways depending on the interpretive frameworks and approaches followed to make sense of these phenomena (Moisander & Valtonen, 2012). Finally, when practitioners assess the data reports provided to them by ethnographers, they must refrain from being preoccupied with quantifying and predicting behaviour, but, instead, embrace ethnography's "insightfulness of interpretive frame,…variety and quality of empirical materials [depth and 'thickness' of data],…[and] creativity in drawing up conclusions" (Moisander & Valtonen, 2012, p. 258). Despite these managerial challenges in deploying an interpretive approach, it is evident from our aforesaid discussion that "ethnographic methods [can be] appropriate for apprehending a wide variety of consumption and use situations with implications for market segmentation and targeting; product and service positioning; and product, service, and brand management" (Arnould & Wallendorf, 1994, p. 484).

CHAPTER REVIEW QUESTIONS

You can use the following questions to reflect on the material covered in Chapter 8:

1. Explain the components of the Brand Value Chain Model and discuss its scope and implications.
2. Discuss the two parts of the brand audit: Brand inventory and brand exploratory.
3. What are the quantitative and qualitative techniques used in brand exploratory?
4. Choose a brand and conduct the following survey by asking 50 respondents the following questions:
    i. Name five brands that come to your mind.
    ii. Name five brands in the <product category / usage situation>.
    iii. Do you recognise this brand element (e.g. show logo without brand name, or product design)? If yes, name the brand.
    iv. What comes to your mind when you think of <the brand> (produce a mental map).
    v. What do you like best about the brand? What are its positive aspects?
    vi. What do you dislike? What are its disadvantages?
    vii. What do you find unique about the brand? In what ways is it the same?
    viii. What does the brand mean to you?
    ix. What percentage of your last purchases in the category went to the brand?
    x. What percentage of your planned next purchases will go to the brand?
    xi. If you cannot find the brand – will you wait, go somewhere else to find it, or buy another brand?

RECOMMENDED READING

1. Keller, K. L., & Lehmann, D. R. (2003). How do brands create value? *Marketing Management*, 12(3), 26–32.
2. Belk, R., Fischer, E., & Kozinets, R. V. (2012). *Qualitative consumer and marketing research*. London: Sage (Chapter 4).
3. Kozinets, R. V. (2002). The field behind the screen: Using netnography for marketing research in online communities. *Journal of Marketing Research*, 39(1), 61–72.
4. Wasson, C. (2000). Ethnography in the field of design. *Human Organization*, 59(4), 377–388.

CASE STUDY

From measuring to impacting performance

Mathilde Leblond
Senior Design Researcher

When working at an insights and innovation agency, a food delivery company approached us with the aim of driving more frequent use of their app. The company was doing relatively well, but was facing increased competition from newer players and saw stagnating sales through its app. It was no stranger to quantitative research – they had a brand tracker which highlighted the occasions people chose to order through them over competitors, had conducted a segmentation study which had helped them define their user base demographically and attitudinally, and had recently sent a survey to lapsed customers.

This had armed them with data to describe the current situation – but they lacked generative insights to inspire their brand marketing teams. One issue was that the research had focused so much on the brand and its direct competition because quantitative surveys force respondents to consider a pre-populated list to select from. However, real-life is much more fluid than that – for the same occasion, customers may be weighing up different take-away providers, but also whether to cook, snack, go to a restaurant, have a beer, go to the cinema, etc (see Christensen, Hall, Dillon, & Duncan's (2016) 'Jobs-To-Be-Done' framework for more on this). Another issue was that the quantitative data lacked the deeper, more granular understanding of *how* customers use their app, but also, what it means to them, what emotional state they find themselves in when ordering, and what influences their choices.

Rather than designing a research plan asking people about their takeaway habits, what the brand meant to people, or even giving them money in order to encourage ordering from a new restaurant, we decided to go broad and explore the food habits of fourty British consumers – both current users and non-users of the app.

We invited them to an online diary study, which we told them focused on food habits in general. For several weeks, we asked them to record their moods and cravings, send us photos of what they were eating, what they were planning to eat, etc. When someone serendipitously ordered a takeaway, we were also able to contact them straight away to talk more at length about it – we wanted to get as close to real behaviour as possible (as opposed to claimed behaviour). Using this technique, we got a wealth of information about the drivers and triggers that led people to use our client's app or get takeaway some other way, but we also found out what might lead them to cook, eat out, or simply snack instead.

We got a rich tapestry of their lives, for example, how some methodically planned their weekly meals, only for it to go out the window on a particularly stressful evening. They sent us photos of their monthly family curry nights, and were privy to the organisation of a baby shower. They told us about the stress, the guilt, the happiness, and the celebrations associated with food. And they also told us of days when they would consider treating themselves to a takeaway, only to give up when confronted with too much choice.

We also discussed with them other products that helped them discover new things. Analogous industries can provide a wealth of inspiration when it comes to people's motivations and preferences. They told us of their *Spotify* Discover Weekly playlist, which would keep them coming back, and how their understanding of how the algorithm works made them trust the recommendations. They described the peer pressure that led them to watch certain *Netflix* documentaries or shows simply to be able to get in on the conversation.

By the end of the project, we were able to map out four main customer journeys, including barriers to ordering food at all, and barriers to ordering food on the platform. By cross-examining the results with the quantitative data from previous studies, we spotted several opportunities for the brand to become closer to their customers. Furthermore, the understanding we had gained by deep diving into people's lives helped inspire radical recommendations. The product team was able to take away a set of features for A/B testing and for further development, while the marketing team launched a campaign targeting one of the customer journeys we had uncovered.

Questions for discussion

1. In your opinion, how might researching brand performance differ from researching product performance?
2. What are the limitations of quantitative research? What are the limitations of qualitative research?
3. Can research ever avoid observation bias? Name some methods you think might lead to more bias, and some that would lead to less bias in the results.
4. How might researching an app differ from researching a fast-moving consumer good (FMCG) (e.g. shampoo)? Do you think branding would be more, less, or equally important? Why?

Glossary

Digital product teams use A/B testing to learn which version of a specific feature / message drives most engagement from their users. They push different versions of the element to randomly selected users, and closely track usage metrics to determine effectiveness.

Further reading

Christensen, C. M., Hall, T., Dillon, K., & Duncan, D. S. (2016). Know your customers' jobs to be done. *Harvard Business Review*, 94(9), 54–62.

REFERENCES

Aaker, D. A. (1996). Measuring brand equity across products and markets. *California Management Review*, 38(3), 102–120.

Armstrong, J. S., Morwitz, V. G., & Kumar, V. (2000). Sales forecasts for existing consumer products and services: Do purchase intentions contribute to accuracy? *International Journal of Forecasting*, 16(3), 383–397.

Arnould, E. J., & Wallendorf, M. (1994). Market-oriented ethnography: Interpretation building and marketing strategy formulation. *Journal of Marketing Research*, 31(4), 484–504.

Belk, R., Fischer, E., & Kozinets, R. V. (2012). Ethnography and observational methods. In *Qualitative consumer and marketing research*. London: Sage.

Chaudhuri, A., & Holbrook, M. B. (2001). The chain of effects from brand trust and brand affect to brand performance: The role of brand loyalty. *Journal of Marketing*, 65(2), 81–93.

Cooper, R., & Evans, M. (2006). Breaking from tradition: Market research, consumer needs, and design futures. *Design Management Review*, 17(1), 68–74.

Coughlan P., & Prokopoff I. (2004). Managing change by design. In R. J. Boland, & F. Collopy (eds), *Managing as designing*. Palo Alto: Stanford University Press.

Elliott, R., & Jankel-Elliott, N. (2003). Using ethnography in strategic consumer research. *Qualitative Market Research: An International Journal*, 6(4), 215–223.

Fellman, M. (1999). Breaking tradition. *Marketing Research*, 11(3), 20–25.

Glaser, B. G., & Strauss, A. L. (1967). *The discovery of grounded theory*. Chicago: Aldine.

Hirschman, E. C., & Holbrook, M. B. (1982). Hedonic consumption: Emerging concepts, methods and propositions. *Journal of Marketing*, 46(3), 92–101.

Interbrand (2020). Brand valuation methodology. Available at: www.interbrand.com/best-brands/best-global-brands/methodology/ [accessed 11 February 2020].

Ireland, C. (2003). Qualitative methods: From boring to brilliant. In B. Laurel (ed.), *Design research: Methods and perspectives*. Cambridge: MIT Press.

Kates, S. M. (2002). The protean quality of subcultural consumption: An ethnographic account of gay consumers. *Journal of Consumer Research*, 29(3), 383–399.

Kates, S. M. (2004). The dynamics of brand legitimacy: An interpretive study in the gay men's community. *Journal of Consumer Research*, 31(2), 455–464.

Keller, K. L. (1993). Conceptualizing, measuring, and managing customer-based brand equity. *Journal of Marketing*, 57(1), 1–22.

Keller, K. L. (2001). *Building customer-based brand equity: A blueprint for creating strong brands* (pp. 3–27). Cambridge: Marketing Science Institute.

Keller, K. L. (2003). Brand synthesis: The multidimensionality of brand knowledge. *Journal of Consumer Research*, 29(4), 595–600.

Keller, K. L., Apéria, T., & Georgson, M. (2012). *Strategic brand management: A European perspective*. London: Pearson Education.

Keller, K. L., & Lehmann, D. R. (2003). How do brands create value? *Marketing Management*, 12(3), 26–32.

Keller, K. L., & Swaminathan, V. (2020). *Strategic brand management: Building, measuring, and managing brand equity* (5th edn). London: Pearson Education.

Knowles, J. (2005). In search of a reliable measure of brand equity. *Marketing NPV*, 2(3).

Kozinets, R. V. (2002). The field behind the screen: Using netnography for marketing research in online communities. *Journal of Marketing Research*, 39(1), 61–72.

Lalaounis, S. T. (2017). *Design management: Organisation and marketing perspectives*. London: Routledge.

Lannon, J., & Cooper, P. (1983). Humanistic advertising: A holistic cultural perspective. *International Journal of Advertising*, 2(3), 195–213.

Leblanc, T. (2012). Problem finding and problem solving. In S. Garner & C. Evans (eds), *Design and designing: A critical introduction* (pp. 32–49). London: Bloomsbury.

Levy, S. J. (1985). Dreams, fairy tales, animals, and cars. *Psychology & Marketing*, 2(2), 67–81.

Liedtka, J. (2015). Perspective: Linking design thinking with innovation outcomes through cognitive bias reduction. *Journal of Product Innovation Management*, 32(6), 925–938.

Lindemann, J. (2014). Brand valuation: Identifying and measuring the economic value creation of brands. In K. Kompella (ed.), *The definitive book of branding* (pp. 253–271). New Delhi: Sage.

Maclaran, P., & Catterall, M. (2002). Researching the social web: Marketing information from virtual communities. *Marketing Intelligence & Planning*, 20(6), 319–326.

Malefyt, T. D. W. (2009). Understanding the rise of consumer ethnography: Branding technomethodologies in the new economy. *American Anthropologist*, 111(2), 201–210.

Malinowski, B. (1922). *Argonauts of the Western Pacific*. New York: E.P. Dutton.

Moisander, J., & Valtonen, A. (2012). Interpretive marketing research: Using ethnography in strategic market development. In L. Peñaloza, N. Toulouse, L. M. Visconti (eds), *Marketing management: A cultural perspective* (pp. 246–260). London: Routledge.

Olins, W. (2008). *Wally Olins: The brand handbook*. London: Thames & Hudson.

Ovans, A. (1998). The customer doesn't always know best. *Harvard Business Review*, 76(3), 12–14.

Percy, L., Rossiter, J., & Elliott, R. (2001). *Strategic advertising management*. Oxford: Oxford University Press.

Plowman T. (2003). Ethnography and critical design practice. In B. Laurel (ed.), *Design research: Methods and perspectives*. Cambridge: MIT Press.

Salinas, G. (2016). Brand valuation: Principles, applications, and latest developments. In F. Dall'Olmo Riley, J. Singh, & C. Blankson (eds), *The Routledge companion to contemporary brand management* (pp. 228–254). London: Routledge.

Salinas, G., & Ambler, T. (2009). A taxonomy of brand valuation practice: Methodologies and purposes. *Journal of Brand Management*, 17(1), 39–61.

Schmitt, B. H. (1999a). Experiential marketing. *Journal of Marketing Management*, 15(1–3), 53–67.

Schmitt, B. H. (1999b). *Experiential marketing: How to get customers to sense, feel, think, act, relate*. New York: The Free Press.

Schmitt, B. H., & Simonson, A. (1997). *Marketing aesthetics: The strategic management of brands, identity, and image*. New York: Simon and Schuster.

Singh, J., & Uncles, M. (2016) Measuring the market performance of brands: Applications in brand management. In F. Dall'Olmo Riley, J. Singh, & C. Blankson (eds), *The Routledge companion to contemporary brand management* (pp. 13–31). London: Routledge.

Squires, S., & Byrne, B. (2002). An introduction to the growing partnership between research and design. In S. Squires, & B. Byrne (eds), *Creating breakthrough ideas: The collaboration of anthropologists and designers in the product development industry*. Westport: Bergin & Garvey.

Thompson, C. J. (1997). Interpreting consumers: A hermeneutical framework for deriving marketing insights from the texts of consumers' consumption stories. *Journal of Marketing Research*, 34(4), 438–455.

Wang, T. (2016). The human insights missing from big data. TEDxCambridge talk. Available at: www.ted.com/talks/tricia_wang_the_human_insights_missing_from_big_data [accessed 15 February 2020].

Wasson, C. (2000). Ethnography in the field of design. *Human Organization*, 59(4), 377–388.

Wasson, C. (2002). Collaborative work: Integrating the role of ethnographers and designers. In S. Squires, & B. Byrne (eds), *Creating breakthrough ideas: The collaboration of anthropologists and designers in the product development industry.* Westport: Bergin & Garvey.

Zukin, S. (2004). *Point of purchase: How shopping changed American culture.* New York: Routledge.

CHAPTER 9

Brand growth: Brand architecture and brand extensions

CHAPTER AIMS AND LEARNING OUTCOMES

This chapter corresponds to the fourth stage of Keller and Swaminathan's (2020) *strategic brand management process*, i.e. growing and sustaining brand equity (see Figure 9.1), and aims to achieve the following:

1. Understand the concepts of brand architecture and brand hierarchy.
2. Explore the characteristics of the two types of brand extensions: line and category extensions.
3. Discuss the advantages and disadvantages of brand extensions and their impact (spillovers) on the parent brand.
4. Understand the psychological processes consumers follow in evaluating brand extensions.
5. Provide a thorough discussion of the consumer-, brand-, culture-, and competitor-related factors which moderate brand extension evaluations.

BRAND ARCHITECTURE AND BRAND HIERARCHY

Brand architecture

One of the strategies organisations can follow to achieve further growth is developing and introducing new products, and potentially new brands, within their portfolio. Maintaining a portfolio of products and brands can be demanding and organisations must identify ways to organise and manage this portfolio in the most effective way to ensure maximum returns and profitability. This calls for a *brand architecture*

```
┌─────────────────────────┐   ┌──────────────────────────────────────────────────────────┐
│                         │──▶│ Developing Brand Equity, Positioning, Personality, and Values │
│ Identifying and Developing│   ├──────────────────────────────────────────────────────────┤
│      Brand Plans        │──▶│ Creating Brand Identity: Brand Aesthetics and Symbolism  │
└─────────────────────────┘   └──────────────────────────────────────────────────────────┘
            │
            ▼
┌─────────────────────────┐   ┌──────────────────────────────────────────────────────────┐
│                         │──▶│ Brand Communications and the Attention Economy           │
│                         │   ├──────────────────────────────────────────────────────────┤
│ Designing and Implementing│──▶│ Holistic Brand Experiences and Emotional Branding       │
│ Brand Marketing Programmes│   ├──────────────────────────────────────────────────────────┤
│                         │──▶│ Consumer Collectives, Brand Avoidance, and Political Consumption │
│                         │   ├──────────────────────────────────────────────────────────┤
│                         │──▶│ Brand Ethics, Social Responsibility, and Sustainable Consumption │
└─────────────────────────┘   └──────────────────────────────────────────────────────────┘
            │
            ▼
┌─────────────────────────┐   ┌──────────────────────────────────────────────────────────┐
│ Measuring and Interpreting │──▶│ Brand Performance and Metrics                            │
│   Brand Performance     │   └──────────────────────────────────────────────────────────┘
└─────────────────────────┘
            │
            ▼
┌─────────────────────────┐   ┌──────────────────────────────────────────────────────────┐
│                         │──▶│ Brand Growth:                                            │
│ Growing and Sustaining  │   │ Brand Architecture and Brand Extensions                  │
│     Brand Equity        │   ├──────────────────────────────────────────────────────────┤
│                         │──▶│ Brand Futures:                                           │
│                         │   │ Technology and Innovation in Branding Strategies         │
└─────────────────────────┘   └──────────────────────────────────────────────────────────┘
```

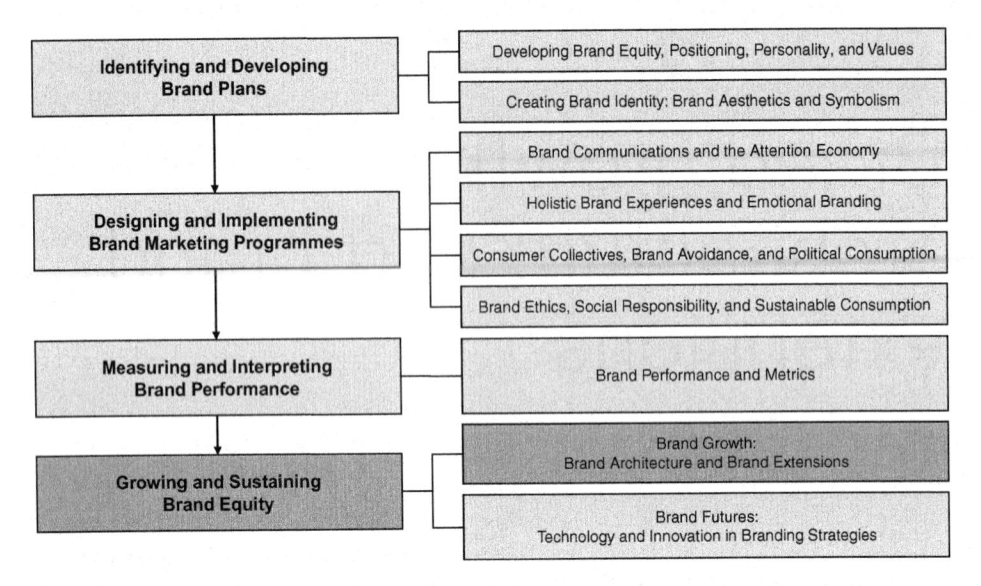

FIGURE 9.1 Strategic brand management process and book plan

design defined as the "organising structure of the brand portfolio that specifies the brand roles and the relationships between brands" (Aaker & Joachimsthaler, 2000, p. 8). Brand architecture design is essential as it can influence the external face of the organisation's strategy and should ideally align with the corporate objectives. When organisations strongly integrate their brands in their portfolio and clearly define their roles in delivering the corporate goals, they are able to articulate their overall business strategy more effectively. This also enables organisations to proactively manage their portfolio, make appropriate growth decisions, successfully shape the way they are perceived by their respective target audiences, and provide employees and investment communities an understanding of their positioning and strategic vision (Park, MacInnis, & Eisingerich, 2016).

Branded house vs. house of brands
When developing their brand architecture design, organisations must determine: 1) which brand names, logos, and symbols should be used for which products within the portfolio, 2) which products should have the same brand name and whether or not there should be variations of this brand name, and 3) the nature of new and existing brand elements which will be assigned to any new products (Keller, Apéria, & Georgson, 2012). A fundamental decision firms must make is whether they will pursue a *branded house* approach, which involves the organisation applying an umbrella corporate (or family) brand to all of its products, or a *house of brands* approach where the organisation develops a collection of individual brands (with different brand names). Consider, for instance, *Samsung*, which follows a branded

IMAGE 9.1 *Samsung* shipyard (image courtesy of Samsung)

house approach because it applies the same corporate name on all of its products and services including consumer electronics products (e.g. mobile phones, mp3 players, and TVs), white goods (e.g. refrigerators and washing machines), and industrial services (e.g. shipyards), in contrast with *Unilever* and *Procter and Gamble (P&G)* which own and manage a plethora of different brands such as *Dove*, *VO5*, *Hellman's*, and *Cif (Unilever)*, or *Pampers*, *Pantene*, *Always*, and *Ariel (P&G)*. Following the branded house approach, organisations capitalise on their corporate name's connotations of "quality, dependability, and value, [so that] each new product gains immediate positive brand associations. However, an unfavourable product issue, accident or recall might taint the entire line" (Pitta & Katsanis, 1995, p. 57). When organisations follow the house of brands approach, "each brand has its own brand identity [branded (or brand-based) identity – see Chapter 3] and can develop its own brand equity. In the unlikely event of a…product catastrophe, each brand would be rather insulated from adverse publicity" (Pitta & Katsanis, 1995, p. 56).

The brand–product matrix

The *brand–product matrix* graphically represents the brands and products sold by the organisation where the rows represent its brands and the columns represent the

IMAGE 9.2 Procter and Gamble's (P&G) portfolio of brands

corresponding products (Keller & Swaminathan, 2020) (see Figure 9.2). Keller and Swaminathan (2020) explain this matrix with the following:

> The rows of the matrix represent *brand–product relationships*. They capture the firm's brand extension strategy in terms of the number and nature of products sold under its different brands. A *brand line* consists of all products – original as well as line and category extensions [explored later in this chapter] – sold under a particular brand. Thus, a brand line is one row of the matrix...The columns of the matrix represent *product–brand relationships*. They capture the brand portfolio strategy in terms of the number and nature of brands to be marketed in each category. The *brand portfolio* is the set of all brands and brand lines that a particular firm offers for sale to buyers in a particular category. Thus, a brand portfolio is one column of the matrix...A *product line* is a group of products within a product category that are closely related...[and] may include different brands, a single family brand, or individual brand that has been line extended. A *product mix*...is the set of all product lines and items [sold]. Thus, product lines represent different sets of columns...that, in total, make up the product mix...A *brand mix* is the set of all brand lines sold [which represent different sets of rows].
>
> (Keller & Swaminathan, 2020, p. 427)

Based on the above, the organisation might have a deep or broad brand architecture (or both). *Depth of brand architecture* involves the number and nature of brands marketed by the organisation within a product category or class, while the *breadth*

		PRODUCTS			
BRANDS		1	2	3	...N
	A				
	B				
	C				
	...M				

FIGURE 9.2 Brand–product matrix

```
                    BRAND
                 ARCHITECTURE
                   /        \
              DEPTH          BREADTH
   Product–Brand Relationships    Brand–Product Relationships
   & Brand Portfolio Strategy     & Brand Extension Strategy
```

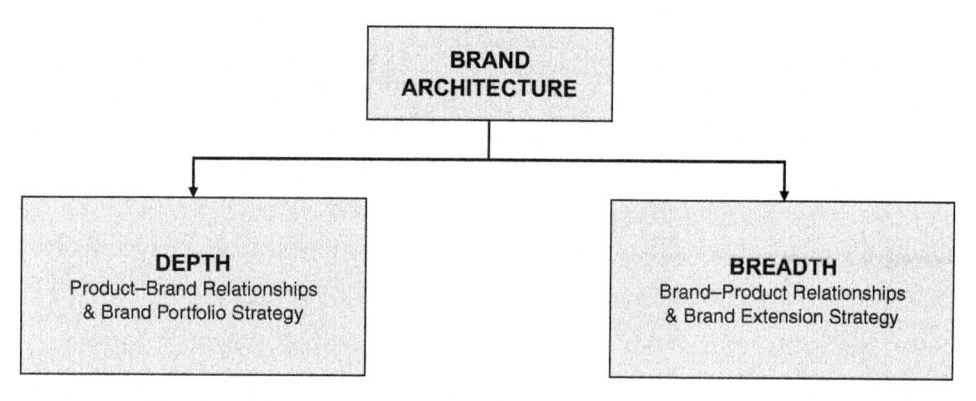

FIGURE 9.3 Brand architecture

of brand architecture is all about the number and nature of product categories linked to a brand sold by the organisation (Keller & Swaminathan, 2020) (Figure 9.3). For example, *The Coca-Cola Company* and the *Heineken Group* are organisations with a deep brand architecture as they own and manage a number of brands in one product category each, i.e. within the soft drinks and beer categories, respectively. In contrast, *Philips*, *Samsung*, or *Apple*, each have a broad brand architecture because each brand involves products across many different product categories. A company will have a deep *and* broad brand architecture when it owns and manages many brands across many different product categories (e.g. *Unilever* and *P&G*).

Brand hierarchy

It is imperative that the organisation determines a clear *brand hierarchy* in order to summarise its brand architecture. It should seek to connect its products and brands to demonstrate to consumers how these are related with each other. Brand hierarchy displays "the number and nature of common and distinctive brand elements across the firm's products, revealing their explicit ordering" (Keller & Swaminathan, 2020, p. 436). Similar to any other hierarchy, as you move from top to bottom there are more entries, i.e. more brands. A brand hierarchy might include the following levels from top to bottom. First, the *corporate or company*

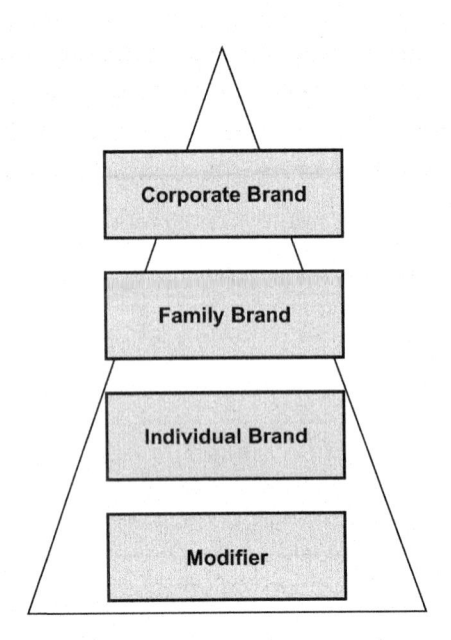

FIGURE 9.4 Brand hierarchy

brand which, in some cases, might be the only brand an organisation uses. In other cases, the organisation might give no attention to the corporate brand in its marketing campaigns, although it is still technically part of its brand hierarchy. For legal reasons, the corporate brand must almost always feature somewhere on the product packaging (either prominently or at the back of the packaging). Second, the *family brand* is used in more than one product class or category but it is not the corporate name itself. Most organisations will only support few family brands because having too many can get confusing for the organisation's stakeholders (i.e. consumers, suppliers, distributors, etc.): "If the corporate brand is applied to a range of products, then it functions as a family brand too, and the two levels collapse to one for those products" (Keller & Swaminathan, 2020, p. 437). Third, the *individual brand* is limited to effectively one product category, however, it can be used for numerous products within this category. Individual brands enable the organisation to achieve a dominant position within a particular product category. Finally, the *modifier*, at the lowest level of the brand hierarchy, describes a specific item, i.e. a product model, type, version, or configuration (Keller & Swaminathan, 2020) (see Figure 9.4).

BRAND EXTENSIONS

Types and characteristics

When organisations seek to launch a new product, they have three options: 1) develop a new brand, 2) launch the new product under an existing brand, or 3) combine a

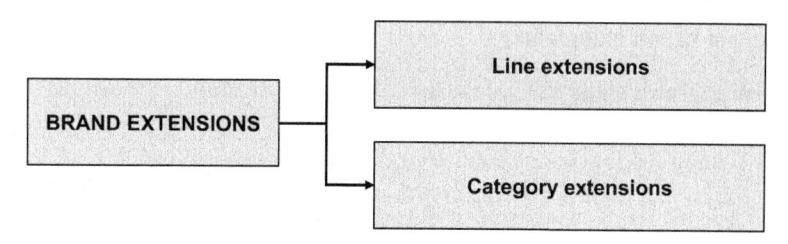

FIGURE 9.5 Types of brand extensions

new brand name with an existing one. Using an existing brand name to introduce a new product can be a successful strategy for expanding the organisation's product portfolio and for achieving growth (Hayran & Gürhan-Canli, 2016). In this case, the new product is called a *brand extension* and the brand that lends its name to this new product is the *parent brand*. Keller explains that "[b]rand extensions capitalise on the [parent] brand image…to efficiently inform consumers and retailers about the new product or service" (1993, p. 15). When the organisation combines a new brand name with an existing one, the result is called a *sub-brand*.

There are two types of brand extensions: line extensions and category extensions (see Figure 9.5). The following discusses their characteristics and provides relevant examples.

Line extensions

Organisations develop a *line extension* when they use an existing brand name to launch a new product in the parent brand's product category (Farquhar, 1989; Hayran & Gürhan-Canli, 2016; Pitta & Katsanis, 1995). In this case, firms can target a new market segment by launching a different flavour, ingredient variety, form, or size of the product. For example, when *The Coca-Cola Company* launched *Fanta Strawberry* using the Fanta (orange) brand name, or when *Molson Coors Beverage Company* used the *Coors* brand name to launch *Coors Light*.

Category extensions

With category extensions, organisations use an existing brand name to launch a new product in a category different to that of the parent brand (Farquhar, 1989; Hayran & Gürhan-Canli, 2016; Pitta & Katsanis, 1995). For example, consider the case of the *Armani* brand extended to the hotel and hospitality category with *Armani Hotels and Resorts* (in Milan and Dubai), and *Ferrari* or *Mercedes-Benz* clothing. There are three requirements for successful category extensions: 1) *perceptual fit*, that is, consumers should perceive the new product to be consistent with the parent brand, 2) *competitive leverage*, i.e. the new product "must be comparable or superior to other products in the [new] category" (Farquhar, 1989, p. 31), and 3) *benefit transfer*, which means that the benefit "offered by the parent brand must be desired by consumers of products in the new category" (Farquhar, 1989, p. 31).

Advantages of brand extensions

It is important at this stage to explore the advantages of brand extensions, which can be organised in two overarching categories: (1) facilitating new product acceptance, and (2) providing feedback to parent brand and organisation (see Figure 9.6).

As far as the new product is concerned, using an existing brand name can improve the image of the new product because consumers use their established knowledge of the parent brand to make conclusions about the performance of the new product, which leads to an improvement of the strength, favourability, and uniqueness of consumers' associations of the new product (Keller & Swaminathan, 2020). Keller (1993) explains that new product acceptance achieved by brand extensions can provide two benefits: 1) *higher awareness* because consumers connect the new product with an existing brand node in their memory, and 2) *inferences*, that is, expectations about the new product based on their existing knowledge about the parent brand.

As mentioned in Chapter 1, brands are important to consumers because they can reduce the risks associated with purchase and consumption (i.e. the functional, physical, financial, psychological, social, and time risks) (Roselius, 1971). By purchasing brands that they already know and trust, consumers can feel more confident about the quality of the acquired product or service. Brand extensions, as new products using an existing brand name, reduce these risks as they link with the reputation and credibility of the parent brand. Consequently, this risk reduction enhances the potential of a new product's adoption by the consumers (Keller & Aaker, 1992; Milewicz & Herbig, 1994). In addition, consumers are not the only external stakeholders needing persuasion; retailers need to be convinced to stock and promote a new product. Due to their higher potential for increased consumer demand because of the reputation

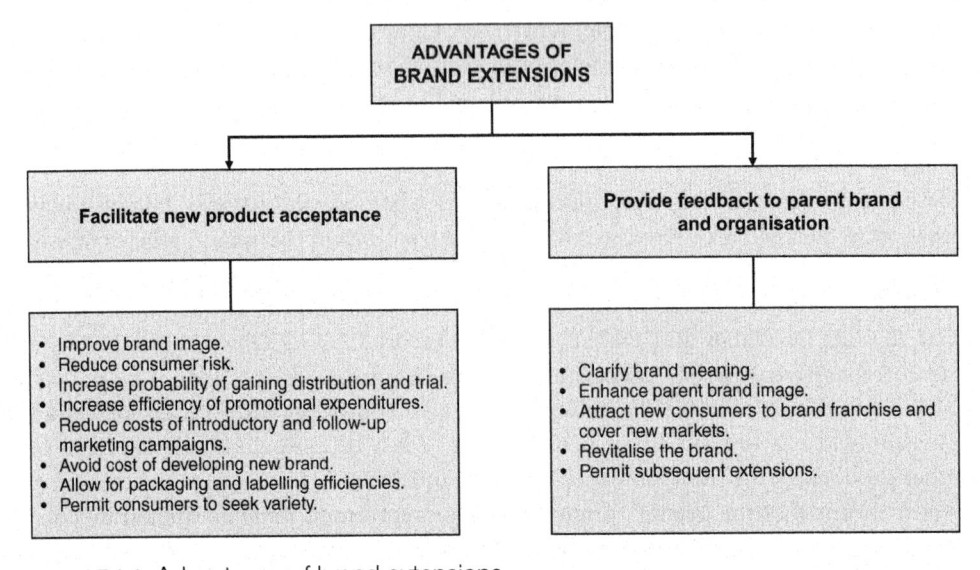

FIGURE 9.6 Advantages of brand extensions

of the parent brand, retailers are more likely to give brand extensions the required retail space.

Advertising campaigns introducing brand extensions do not need to create awareness about the brand but can concentrate on introducing the new product. This means that organisations can leverage consumers' existing brand knowledge (without having to start building brand equity from scratch). Of course, it is important that these advertising campaigns make the necessary connections between the new product and the thoughts, feelings, and attitudes consumers have toward the parent brand (Aaker & Carmon, 1992). Furthermore, "when a brand becomes associated with multiple products, advertising can become more cost-effective for the family brand as a whole" (Keller & Swaminathan, 2020, p. 474). Using similar packaging and labelling for a brand extension can lead to lower costs of production. In addition, when retailers display all products of the parent brand together, they can create the *poster or billboard effect* increasing the parent brand's prominence in store (Keller & Swaminathan, 2020).

Consumers might want to try a new flavour, ingredient, or variant within the product category because they are bored or feel satiated with the original product. Brand extensions allow consumers to satisfy their desire for variety without having to leave the brand family, which is extremely important for organisations. Providing variants within a product category (through line extensions) can also motivate consumers to use the brand more and in different ways. Finally, brand extensions enable organisations to launch a new product without having to incur the costs of developing a completely new brand. Despite the availability of digital technology, which allows organisations to develop and manage brand identities in a cost-efficient way (from an aesthetics perspective) (see Chapter 3) (Schmitt & Simonson, 1997), building brand equity from scratch requires substantial financial resources and time (Keller & Swaminathan, 2020).

In relation to the advantages of brand extensions to the organisation and the parent brand, new products under existing brand names can provide the organisation with vital information about market opportunities and threats. They can also enhance the image of the parent brand because they can strengthen, and improve the favourability of, existing brand associations, as well as add new associations. Brand extensions can clarify the parent brand's meaning, core values, and associations, as well as increase the organisation's credibility. In particular with regards to the parent brand's meaning to consumers, brand extensions can define with more clarity the types of markets the parent brand can compete in. Brand extensions can broaden the meaning of the parent brand, can ensure that organisations do not become vulnerable to competitors' strategies, and can help them avoid *marketing myopia* whereby they miss out on market opportunities (Levitt, 1960) because they narrowly define boundaries around their brand and category (Keller & Swaminathan, 2020). In addition, "line extensions can benefit the parent brand by expanding market coverage, such as by offering a product benefit whose absence may have prevented consumers from trying the brand" (Keller & Swaminathan, 2020, p. 476). Finally, brand extensions can revitalise the parent brand by renewing interest in, and liking for, it, as well as can become the basis for subsequent brand extensions in the future (Keller & Swaminathan, 2020).

Disadvantages of brand extensions

Brand extensions can also have a number of disadvantages that organisations should consider carefully (see Figure 9.7). First, providing consumers more product options under the same brand does not necessarily equate to greater sales or success. Line extensions can potentially confuse or even frustrate consumers (Schwartz, 2004) making them buy less. In addition, the growth on the number of products available can outpace the expansion of retail space. This means that retailers might not have the required space to stock the brand extension leading to disappointed consumers who are unable to purchase the new product (Keller & Swaminathan, 2020).

Of course, if an organisation introduces a brand extension which consumers consider inappropriate, they may doubt the parent brand's integrity and competence. Indeed, the most devastating situation involves the brand extension failing and hurting the image of the parent brand. This would be a catastrophe that must be, by all means, avoided.

Even if an extension initially succeeds, by linking the brand to multiple products, the firm increases the risk that an unexpected problem or even tragedy with one

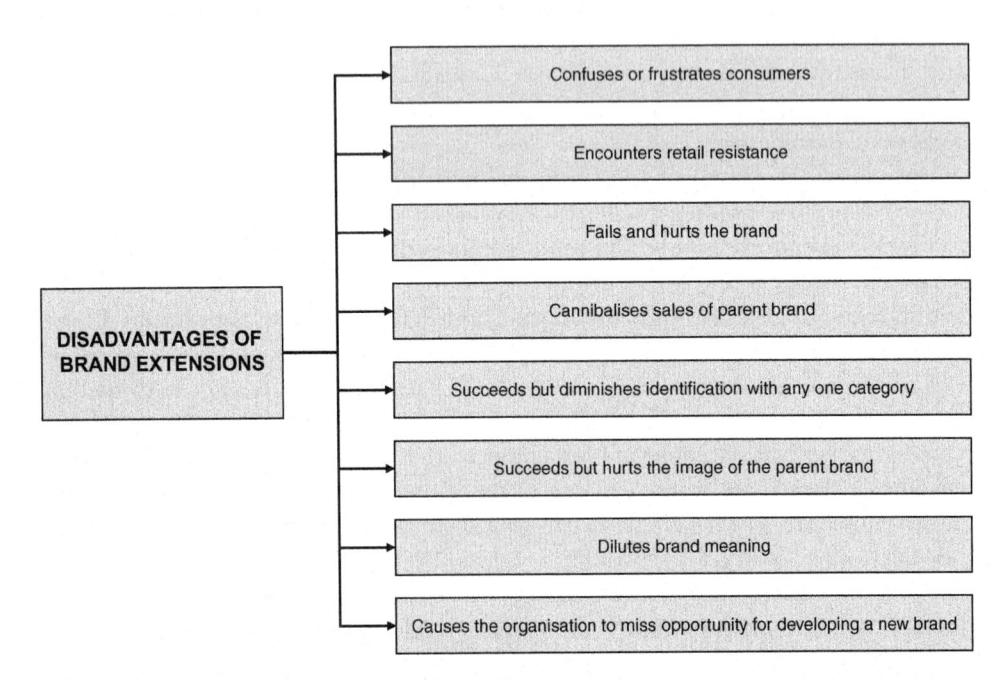

FIGURE 9.7 Disadvantages of brand extensions

product in the brand family can tarnish the image of some or all of the remaining products.

(Keller & Swaminathan, 2020, p. 478)

In addition, the brand extension could cannibalise the sales of the original product because consumers might choose to buy the former instead of the latter, resulting in decreased sales for the original product. For example, consumers might purchase *Sprite No Sugar* instead of the original *Sprite* product. After all, line extensions are designed to establish points-of-parity associations (POPs) (see Chapter 2) with the parent brand. Nevertheless, this is not entirely a problem because it means that consumers have (at least) stayed with the brand family instead of purchasing, for example, *7Up Free*.

Furthermore, brand extensions might weaken the parent's brand association with a specific category, as explained by Keller (1993) with the following:

Successful brand extensions may potentially harm the core brand image if they weaken existing associations in some way. If the brand becomes associated with a disparate set of products or services, product category identification and the corresponding product associations may become less strong.

(Keller, 1993, p. 16)

This dilution effects with regards to category correspondence can reduce the levels consumer awareness of the parent brand. Moreover, there can be cases where the brand extension is successful but consumers change their perceptions of the parent brand if the brand extension is associated with attributes or benefits which are considered inconsistent or conflicting with those of the parent brand (Keller & Swaminathan, 2020). The absence of clear category identification and a weakened image can lead to dilution of the parent brand's overall meaning to consumers. An unsuccessful brand extension can damage the image of the parent brand by generating undesirable associations; this is most likely when there is not much of a difference between the parent brand and the brand extension (Keller, 1993). Finally, brand extensions can lead to the organisation missing out on the opportunity of developing a new brand which might have been successful with the target audience (Keller & Swaminathan, 2020), e.g. *Lexus* (introduced by *Toyota*), *Infiniti* cars (developed by *Nissan*), and *Cos* (an *H&M* brand).

Keller (1993) urges brand marketers to assess possible extension options for their viability and impact on the image of the parent brand by following three important steps. First, determine possible extension alternatives based on overall similarity to the parent brand, as well as on core brand associations, and in particular, in relation to brand positioning and core benefits. Second, assess the potential of these alternatives by "measuring the salience, relevance, and favourability of core brand associations in the proposed extension context and the favourability of any inferred associations" (Keller, 1993, p. 16). Third, evaluate the possible impact of each extension alternative on the image of the parent brand and the strength, favourability, and uniqueness of core brand associations (Keller, 1993).

Impact on the parent brand: Spillover effects

Many empirical research studies have delved deeper into the impact of brand extensions on the parent brand. Hayran and Gürhan-Canli (2016) explain that although some scholars have identified an immunity of parent brands to spillover effects (e.g. Keller & Aaker, 1992; Romeo, 1991), others argue that spillover effects can considerably enhance or weaken attributes of the parent brand. Some studies (e.g. Ahluwalia & Gürhan-Canli, 2000; Lane & Jacobson, 1997; Milberg, Park, & McCarthy, 1997; Swaminathan, Fox, & Reddy, 2001) have discovered that "when the parent brand and the extension are perceived dissimilar in terms of categorical fit or brand image attributes, parent brand image may get diluted" (Hayran & Gürhan-Canli, 2016, p. 148). However, these spillover effects are minimised when beliefs about the parent brand become more global and indistinctive; brand extensions cannot easily change global attribute beliefs that are more resistant to change (Loken & John, 1993). In addition, an organisation's flagship product, that is, the product "most closely associated with the parent brand" (John, Loken, & Joiner, 1998, p. 20), e.g. *iPhone* (*Apple*), shows higher level of resistance to negative spillovers than the parent brand itself because of the fact that consumers are abundantly exposed to this flagship product leading to greater familiarity with it (John et al., 1998).

Three factors moderate the spillover effects on the parent brand: (1) whether or not the brand extension is considered typical or atypical of the parent brand (Loken & John, 1993), i.e. whether or not it has common characteristics with the parent brand, (2) the accessibility of the extension information to the consumer's mind (Ahluwalia & Gürhan-Canli, 2000), and (3) the level of processing motivation (Gürhan-Canli & Maheswaran, 1998). Analytically, when consumers consider a brand extension atypical of the parent brand, these dilution effects are less likely (Loken & John, 1993). In contrast,

> dilution effects are more likely to occur when the extension information is highly accessible (i.e. salient) to the consumer's mind, facilitating the use of that information in evaluating the parent brand. When the extension information is less accessible, however, individuals tend to rely on the diagnosticity of that information. Unless the extension information is perceived as diagnostic, consumers may not incorporate that information in judging the parent brand.
> (Hayran & Gürhan-Canli, 2016, p. 148)

Diagnosticity relates to Feldman and Lynch's (1988) *accessibility-diagnosticity model* and

> in the context of [the impact to the parent brand], the extension information would be diagnostic to the extent that it indicates the quality of the family brand…A brand extension's diagnosticity for [parent] brand evaluation is likely to be jointly determined by its valence [power] and category similarity with the [parent] brand name.
> (Ahluwalia & Gürhan-Canli, 2000, pp. 371)

With regards to the level of processing motivation, when consumers are highly motivated, they will consider all information available to them and will be very attentive to product attributes, whereas when they are not, they will not pursue such effortful processing (Gürhan-Canli & Maheswaran, 1998). Under low levels of motivation, typical extensions have higher spillover effects in comparison with atypical extensions. However, it is important to note that cultural differences influence the interaction between processing motivation and extension typicality. Ng (2010) determined that in relation to typical extensions, Eastern consumers experience more dilution effects when highly motivated because they focus on the negative information in contrast with Western consumers who experience more dilution effects under low motivation levels.

As mentioned earlier, *sub-branding* involves the strategy by which the organisation combines an existing brand name with a new one when launching a new product or service. Sood and Keller (2012) argue that consumers evaluate a sub-brand on the basis of both names, which can generate a perception of distance between the extension and its parent brand. This means that sub-brands have an advantage over regular (family) brand extensions in distant categories (category extensions) because consumers tend to form their evaluations of category extensions only on the basis of the parent brand, which means there is more emphasis on the perceived fit between the parent brand with the extension category (Hayran & Gürhan-Canli, 2016; Sood & Keller, 2012). Consequently, sub-brands can reduce potential negative spillovers to the parent brand because of this perception of distance between the parent brand and its extension. Consumers might think that the sub-brand is produced by another organisation than the parent brand (Milberg et al., 1997).

Consumer processes for evaluating brand extensions

Consumer processes for evaluating brand extensions can be organised under three overarching themes: (1) categorisation processes, (2) motivational processes, and (3) thinking styles (Hayran & Gürhan-Canli, 2016) (see Figure 9.8). We structure the discussion of these processes accordingly.

Categorisation processes

Categorisation processes are centred on the concept of the *perceived fit* (perceptual fit) whereby

> the new product is judged according to the suitability of its membership in a category…[and the] beliefs and affect associated with this brand category may transfer to an extension when consumers perceive the extension as fitting with the brand category.
>
> (Park, Milberg, & Lawson, 1991, p. 185)

Perceived fit implies a match between the parent brand and the extended category and it enables transfer of affect from the parent brand to the product extension (Boush, Shipp, Loken, Gencturk, Crockett, Kennedy, Minshall, Misurell, Rochford, & Strobel, 1987). This means that

```
                    ┌─────────────────────────────┐
                  ┌→│  Categorisation processes   │
┌──────────────┐  │  └─────────────────────────────┘
│  EVALUATING  │  │  ┌─────────────────────────────┐
│    BRAND     │──┼→│   Motivational processes    │
│  EXTENSIONS  │  │  └─────────────────────────────┘
└──────────────┘  │  ┌─────────────────────────────┐
                  └→│       Thinking styles       │
                    └─────────────────────────────┘
```

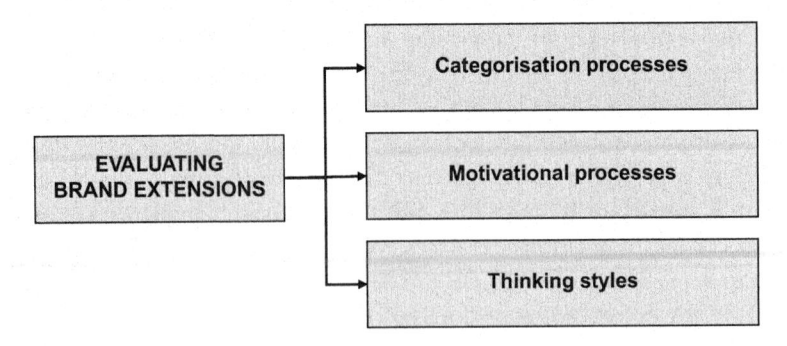

FIGURE 9.8 Consumer processes for evaluating brand extensions

consumers' positive or negative evaluations about a parent brand are more likely to transfer to the new extension when two categories are perceived consistent. When perceived fit is low, consumers' affect toward the parent brand is less likely to influence extension evaluations.

(Hayran & Gürhan-Canli, 2016, p. 137)

Aaker and Keller (1990) discovered that the perceived fit is higher when three dimensions are in place: 1) *the complement dimension*, when two products are perceived by consumers as complementary to each other, 2) *the substitute dimension*, when two products can replace each other and satisfy similar needs, and 3) *the transfer dimension*, when the parent brand is considered as capable of producing the extension product. Although most scholars recognise the importance of perceived fit, there have been successful brand extensions that lacked the required perceived fit (e.g. *Arm & Hammer* toothpaste) and unsuccessful cases where the perceived fit was high (e.g. *Campbell's* tomato sauce) (Hayran & Gürhan-Canli, 2016). Indeed, some scholars have identified exceptions to this general rule of perceived fit. Dimitriu, Warlop, and Samuelsen discovered that

> high level of similarity between parent brand and extension category can be detrimental if consumers have the goal of choosing a product that performs well on a specific attribute, rather than a product with an overall good performance on all its attributes.

(Dimitriu et al., 2017, p. 851)

They explain this by drawing from two theoretical perspectives that can be applied on the case of brand extensions.

First, according to Chernev (2007), when consumers have to choose between an 'all-in-one' option and a 'specialised' option, the latter is perceived as superior on that specific attribute in comparison with the former, even when both alternatives' performance on this specific attribute is objectively the same. This is a form of *compensatory reasoning* (Chernev, 2007) "where consumers equate the overall attractiveness of the alternatives in the choice set under the form of a zero-sum heuristic" (Dimitriu et al., 2017, p. 853). Second, the *dilution effect* stipulates that any perception that a product possesses an attribute is weakened by any information irrelevant to this attribute; consumers look for information which provides evidence that the product delivers a benefit, any information irrelevant to this benefit is deemed as disconfirming that the product possesses the benefit (Dimitriu et al., 2017; Meyvis & Janiszewski, 2004). The above have "implications for how consumers assess the attribute performance of 'all-in-one' compared to 'specialised' products" (Dimitriu et al., 2017, p. 853). Dimitriu et al. (2017) conducted an empirical study which compared two brand extension options: laptop–to–mobile-phone extension (higher similarity and 'all-in-one' positioning) versus TV–to–mobile-phone extension (lower similarity and 'specialised' positioning). Their argument is that the degree of similarity of a brand extension influences the product's positioning in that high similarity means that the parent brand and the extension category share many common attributes (hence 'all-in-one') whereas low similarity indicates a limited set of similar attributes (hence 'specialised'). Their experiments confirmed that

> compared to a low similarity brand extension that specialises on a specific attribute, a high similarity brand extension is perceived to perform worse on the attribute on which the low similarity extension specialises. [In addition] compared to a low similarity brand extension that specialises on a specific attribute, a high similarity brand extension is perceived to perform better on overall performance (i.e. across all attributes).
>
> (Dimitriu et al., 2017, p. 854)

The above was also the case when the two alternatives were not presented together as well as when the specific attribute was of an abstract/imagery-related nature. This means that in cases where consumers look for something specific, high similarity can have detrimental effects. Their study indicates an exception to the widely accepted canon of perceived fit. It explains why *Arm & Hammer* toothpaste has been successful despite being a low similarity brand extension. This brand extension has leveraged a specific attribute the parent brand has been widely connected to (in the US), i.e. the baking soda ingredient, with advanced tooth-whitening properties. It also provides an explanation for other category extensions' success such as *Armani* and *Bulgary* extending to the hotel sector by capitalising on their personality of luxury and sophistication (Dimitriu et al., 2017).

Another exception to the traditional categorisation process of perceived fit has been identified by Sood and Drèze (2006) who explored brand extensions of experiential goods, and in particular, film sequel evaluations. They explain that consumers have a propensity to satiate on experiential attributes, which means that, in the case of a film sequel, they prefer that experiential characteristics such as the film plot to be different from the original film (different genres) as they do not want to see the original again in the sequel film. Sood and Drèze (2006) discovered

> that dissimilar extensions are rated higher than similar extensions. This reversal is moderated by the name of the sequel; numbered sequels (Daredevil 2) are influenced by similarity more than named sequels (Daredevil: Taking It to the Streets). [This] reversal arises because numbered sequels invoke a greater degree of assimilation with the parent movie, thereby increasing consumers' level of satiation of experiential attributes.
>
> (Sood & Drèze, 2006, p. 352)

The feelings consumers have towards the parent brand can also influence their evaluation of brand extensions. Even when the perceived fit is low, when consumers have positive feelings towards the parent brand, they may consider the brand extension favourably (Bhat & Reddy, 2001) because these feelings influence their assessment before they get involved in a cognitive evaluation of perceived fit (Yeung & Wyer, 2005). In addition, affect transfers more easily from the parent brand to typical extensions, i.e. extensions that have more common characteristics with the parent brand (Boush & Loken, 1991). Moods, which are more ambient affective states than emotions, can have an impact on extension evaluations too. A positive mood allows people to identify relations between a moderately dissimilar extension and the parent brand (Barone, Miniard, & Romeo, 2000). However, if the parent brand is undesirable, Barone and Miniard (2002) argue that its "extensions are likely to be evaluated unfavourably regardless of any mood effects" (Hayran & Gürhan-Canli, 2016, p. 138). Finally, repeated exposure to the brand extension in store and on advertising media enables consumers to find more common characteristics between the parent brand and the extension, which, in consequence, can increase consumers' perception of fit between the two (Klink & Smith, 2001). The implication is that brand marketers should seek to achieve repeated consumer exposure to advertising messages that highlight the fit between the parent brand and the extension. In fact, "repeated ad exposure is shown to enhance fit perceptions even for incongruent extensions" (Hayran & Gürhan-Canli, 2016, p. 138).

Motivational processes
Motivational processes are the second set of processes that can influence consumers' evaluation of brand extensions. First, different cognitive concentration in assessing brand extensions is generated by different types of *self-regulatory focus* (Yeo & Park, 2006). Consumers with a *promotion focus* tend to "concentrate more on the positive consequences of events and on the hedonic attainment of objects, [hence] they are likely to seek hedonic value in evaluating an extension...[and] tend to underestimate the negative effects of low fit in extension evaluations" (Hayran & Gürhan-Canli, 2016, p. 138). The exact opposite occurs when consumers have a *prevention focus*; these consumers concentrate on the negative outcomes and all the risks involved in

assessing brand extensions (Hayran & Gürhan-Canli, 2016). In addition, individuals' *feelings of control* can influence brand extension evaluations. People who feel they have low levels of control prefer order and structure in their lives and in their consumption choices, hence, they evaluate less favourably low-fitting extensions. However, high-fitting extensions tend to be assessed similarly regardless of individuals' feelings of control (Cutright, Bettman, & Fitzsimons, 2013).

Brand extension evaluations are also influenced by consumers' level of *brand attachment*; consumers who feel attached to the parent brand evaluate its extensions more positively. This does not, nevertheless, apply in cases where there is low fit between parent brand and extension; the affect toward the parent brand does not transfer to the extension (Fedorikhin, Park, & Thomson, 2008). Like brand attachment, the *ownership effect* needs to be considered too. When consumers own the parent brand, they evaluate line extensions of the brand more favourably (Kirmani, Sood, & Bridges, 1999). This does not apply on the case of downscale extensions of prestigious brands (lower quality versions) because consumers want these brands to maintain their exclusivity. Pitta and Katsanis explain that "functional products seem to allow downscale but not upscale extension. Conversely, prestige products allow upscale but not downscale extensions" (1995, p. 62).

Another difference in extension evaluations can be found between *fixed-mindset individuals* who believe in the fixed nature of human traits and *growth-mindset individuals* who, in contrast, believe in the fluid nature of human traits. Growth-mindset consumers tend to be more accepting toward brand extensions in new and dissimilar categories than fixed-mindset consumers (Yorkston, Nunes, & Matta, 2010). Hence, organisations should try to motivate a specific mindset that increases consumers' perception of brand extension's compatibility with the parent brand in order to increase their acceptance of this extension. Finally, Monga and Gürhan-Canli (2012) discovered that a "*mating mindset*...[enables] male individuals to express more creativity and to involve more easily in relational processing, which facilitates finding novel ways to link a parent brand with its extension" (Hayran & Gürhan-Canli, 2016, p. 139). This means that advertising campaigns that stimulate mating mindsets through sex appeal can make male consumers evaluate extensions more favourably. Of course, in light of ethical implications, one would argue against such subliminal messaging and objectifying sexual images.

Thinking styles

Extant literature has determined that different thinking styles can lead to different brand extension evaluations. Research studies have explored the differences between holistic and analytic thinking styles, low and high involvement information processing, and the amount of information provided. First, a person with a *holistic thinking style* focuses on the relationships between objects and their contexts and emphasises the whole, in contrast with those with an *analytic thinking style* who seek to detach an object from its context and emphasise the object's specific attributes (Nisbett, Peng, Choi, & Norenzayan, 2001). Consumers with holistic thinking style (usually a characteristic of Eastern consumers) evaluate brand extensions more favourably because they are able to identify more associations between the parent brand and the extension (higher perception of extension fit) (Monga & John, 2007). Mong and John (2010) furthered our understanding by exploring different brand types (prestigious brands in comparison with functional brands) and their interaction with consumers' thinking styles. They determined that consumers with holistic and analytic styles evaluate extensions of prestigious brands similarly whereas

> in evaluating extensions of functional brands, holistic thinkers are able to find more brand-related associations between the parent brand and the extension, than analytic thinkers, who tend to focus on the more restrictive product level linkages. As a result, holistic (vs. analytic) thinkers' fit perceptions are shown to be higher for functional brand extensions.
> (Hayran & Gürhan-Canli, 2016, p. 140)

When brand extensions are extremely typical, or extremely atypical, consumers find it easier to find commonalities, or differences, respectively, hence the information processing style is faster and less thoughtful. In comparison, moderately typical brand extensions tend to be processed more thoughtfully, including situations where the consumer gradually considers the brand extension through piecemeal processing (i.e. gradual processing) (Boush & Loken, 1991).

Second, the *level of consumer involvement* can also influence brand extension evaluations. Interestingly, individuals who are highly involved with the evaluation task, hence, those who engage in deeper information processing, experience mental satisfaction when they are able to resolve some amount of incongruency (Mandler, 1981). This enhances highly involved consumers' judgements of moderately incongruent extensions (vs. highly congruent or highly incongruent). In contrast, in the case of low-involved consumers the favourability of extension evaluations increases in a parallel way to fit perceptions (Maoz & Tybout, 2002). In addition, Barone (2005) determined that low-involvement individuals' extension evaluations can be directly influenced by their mood. Finally, as far as *the amount of information* is concerned, the relative impact of the perceived fit in the evaluation process is reduced when brand marketers provide more information about the extension product (Klink & Smith, 2001).

Moderating factors
Following the discussion of consumers' processes of brand extension evaluations, we now turn to the factors moderating these processes. The moderating factors can be organised in four categories: (1) consumer-related, (2) brand-related, (3) culture-related, and (4) competitor-related moderating factors, which are explored in the following section (Hayran & Gürhan-Canli, 2016) (see Figure 9.9).

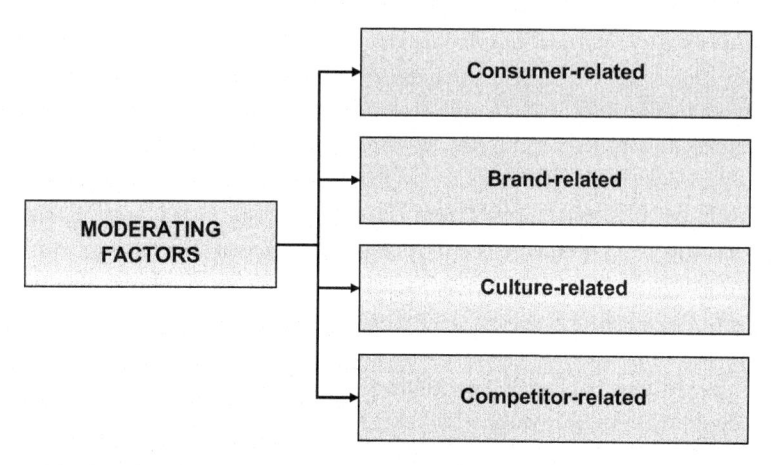

FIGURE 9.9 Moderating factors of brand extension evaluations

Consumer-related moderating factors

The first set of moderating factors involves consumer characteristics. First, Broniarczyk and Alba (1994) explored how the *consumers' level of parent brand knowledge* can influence their evaluations of brand extensions. Some consumers might be considered *experts* because they have a high level of parent brand knowledge, while others are *novices*, having a low level of parent brand knowledge. Experts pay more attention to the relevance of brand-specific associations in the extension category, in contrast with novices whose "extension judgements appeared to be driven by brand affect or brand awareness" (Broniarczyk & Alba, 1994, p. 226). This is because experts can more easily make sense of the extension as they can identify the relevance of brand-specific associations in the extension category.

Another consumer-related moderating factor is individuals' *tendency to adopt* new products. Consider the distinction between early and late adopters; the former are more innovative and less risk-averse consumers than the latter (see Rogers, 1962). Extensions with lower perceived fit can be considered riskier, hence, early adopters will be more tolerant toward them than late adopters (Hayran & Gürhan-Canli, 2016; Klink & Smith, 2001). In addition, an individual's *age* can also influence brand extension evaluations as shown by Zhang and Sood's (2002) experimental study with children. They determined that

> children, relative to adults, evaluate brand extensions by relying more on surface cues (e.g. brand name characteristics used to launch the extension) and less on deep cues (e.g. category similarity between the parent and the extension category). [In particular, in relation to brand name characteristics], children rated extensions with a rhyming name (e.g. 'Coca-Cola Gola' iced tea; 'Wrigley's Higley' toffee) more positively than extensions with a non-rhyming name (e.g. 'Coca-Cola Higley' iced tea; 'Wrigley's Gola' toffee), whereas adults rated them similarly.
>
> (Zhang & Sood, 2002, p. 129)

An *individual's construal level* is also an interesting moderating factor for brand extension evaluations. Trope and Liberman's (2003) *construal level theory* stipulates that "people can perceive events, objects, and other individuals in the environment as either close or distant" (Hayran & Gürhan-Canli, 2016, p. 147). Consumers with high-level construals view their environment as more distant, create abstract concepts about it, and pay more attention to perceived fit when assessing a brand extension because they perceive the associations between the abstract parent brand and the extension as more diagnostic (i.e. relevant for judgement). Therefore, they tend to view high-fitting extensions more favourably (Hayran & Gürhan-Canli, 2016; Kim & John, 2008). Furthermore, whether or not consumers view themselves as independent, or interdependent, to others can have an impact on brand extension evaluations (Ahluwalia, 2008). Those with an *interdependent view*, have a higher relational processing ability, thus, "perceive higher fit judgments between a parent brand and its extension resulting in more favourable evaluations" (Hayran & Gürhan-Canli, 2016, p. 147). Brand marketers can stimulate interdependent consumers' relational processing through appropriate advertising messages, which, in turn, will enhance those consumers' brand extension evaluations (Ahluwalia, 2008; Hayran & Gürhan-Canli, 2016).

Brand-related moderating factors

With regards to brand-related moderating factors, besides, the three dimensions of fit, Aaker and Keller (1990) discovered that consumers' *perception of parent brand quality* can influence their evaluation of brand extensions. Based on an experimental study, they determined that the

> attitude toward the extension was higher when (1) there was both a perception of 'fit' between the two product classes along one of three dimensions and a perception of high quality for the [parent] brand or (2) the extension was not regarded as too easy to make.
>
> (Aaker & Keller, 1990, p. 27)

In addition, they also found that expanding on the attributes of the brand extension can neutralise any negative associations more successfully than "reminding consumers of the positive associations with the [parent] brand" (Aaker & Keller, 1990, p. 27).

High-quality parent brands can be stretched further than average-quality brands because consumers evaluate high-quality parent brand extensions more favourably even when these are in dissimilar categories (Hayran & Gürhan-Canli, 2016; Keller & Aaker, 1992). This is also the case of parent brands with a higher reputation because they are viewed as more capable by consumers (Chun, Park, Eisingerich, & MacInnis, 2015). The parent brand's perceived quality can also transfer to the brand extension (Kim & Sullivan, 1998). Reciprocally, with regards to the impact to the parent brand, Heath, DelVecchio, and McCarthy (2011) have, more recently, found that high-quality extensions can improve the evaluations of the parent brand more than how low-quality brand extensions can harm parent brand evaluations.

There are two bases that can be used by consumers to evaluate an extension's perceived fit with the parent brand. First, *product feature similarity*, i.e. the similarity of the parent brand product category and the brand extension, as already mentioned, can mediate the evaluation of brand extensions and/or purchase intentions (Chakravarti, MacInnis, & Nakamoto, 1990; Farquhar, Herr, & Fazio, 1989; Park et al., 1991). Second, *brand concept consistency* goes beyond product characteristics to understand how the concept of the brand or the brand image in consumers' minds can influence consumers' perceptions of the fit between the parent brand and the extension (Park et al., 1991).

> Brand concepts are brand-unique abstract meanings (e.g., high status) that typically originate from a particular configuration of product features (e.g. high price, expensive-looking design, etc.) and a firm's efforts to create meanings from these arrangements (e.g., 'the...pursuit of perfection' by *Lexus*).
>
> (Park et al., 1991, p. 186)

Hence *brand concept consistency* is about the ability of the brand extension to accommodate the parent brand concept. Park et al. (1991) argue that when the brand extension shares the same concept as the parent brand, consumers perceive greater fit between the parent brand and the extension (Park et al., 1991). They considered the difference between functional brand concepts, which emphasise product performance (e.g. *Dyson*) and prestige (symbolic) brand concepts, which are defined in relation to their ability to express consumers' self-concepts or self-images (e.g. *Chanel*) and confirmed that

> [c]onsumers react more favourably to the extensions of a functional brand name when the extension products reflect a functional concept than when they reflect a prestige concept. [Similarly,] consumers react more favourably to extensions of a prestige brand name when they reflect a prestige concept than when they reflect a functional concept.
>
> (Park et al., 1991, p. 187)

A more nuanced finding of their study, and one with an interesting implication for brand marketers, is that concept consistency can have a greater influence on the prestige brand than on the functional brand due to the unique characteristics of prestige brands in consumers' memories. This means that prestige brands might have greater extendibility to dissimilar product categories as long as these categories share the prestige concepts (Park et al., 1991). In addition, "since these readily accessible, prestige brand concepts (e.g. luxury, status) are more abstract than functional concepts (e.g. reliability, durability), they may be able to accommodate a more diverse set of objects that share fewer features" (Park et al., 1991, p. 192).

Similarly, in a later study, Hagtvedt and Patrick (2009) determined that luxury brands are more extendable than value brands because of their hedonic perceptions in consumers' minds.

However, as previously mentioned, brand associations can relate to any brand attribute and characteristic. Broniarczyk and Alba explained that "consumers assess the ability of the extension to satisfy their needs and such assessments are driven primarily by the specific associations of the brand" (1994, p. 215). These scholars view brand-specific associations as the key determinant of the extendibility of the parent brand.

> [The] relevancy (or diagnosticity) of brand-specific associations in an extension strategy facilitates consumers to make meaning of an extension. Extensions in dissimilar product categories are shown to be evaluated more favourably than extensions in similar product categories when the brand's specific associations are relevant in those categories.... Even extensions of less liked brand [can be] evaluated more favourably when their specific brand attributes [are] perceived relevant in the extended category.
> (Hayran & Gürhan-Canli, 2016, p. 142)

Scholars have also explored the relationship between brand extension typicality, that is, the perceived similarity of the extension with the parent brand's products and *brand breadth*. Narrow brands have products in similar categories (e.g. *Nike* or *Adidas*), in contrast with broad brands that have products in varied categories (e.g. *Zara* or *Ralph Lauren*). Studies have concluded that the relationship between brand extension typicality and brand breadth is opposite, which means that "typical extensions make up a narrow brand and atypical extensions make up a broad brand. [This means that] due to similarity among existing products, a typical extension is more likely to succeed in a narrow category" (Hayran & Gürhan-Canli, 2016, p. 144). Being strongly associated with a specific category can increase or decrease the parent brand's extendibility subject to the extension structure.

Apart from the *diagnosticity* (relevancy for judgement) of benefit associations (explored earlier), Meyvis and Janiszewski (2004) state that the success of the brand extension is also subject to the *accessibility* of benefit associations, i.e. the ability to retrieve them from memory. They add that accessibility is dependent on the extent of interference by competing brand associations, such as category associations. This means that the benefit associations of broad brands tend to be more accessible than those of narrow brands. Hence, broad brands can pursue more successful brand extensions than narrow brands, even when the latter have greater similarity with the extension category (Meyvis & Janiszewski, 2004). However, as Meyvis & Janiszewski argue "when benefit associations are equally accessible and diagnostic, the evaluation of brand extensions will instead be dictated by the similarity between brand and extension category associations" (2004, p. 346).

Many organisations, such as the *Virgin Group* or the *easyGroup*, have grown by pursuing a *multiple extension* strategy. Such strategy, when carefully planned and implemented, can enhance the parent brand's image because consumers may view the "higher number of products in a brand's portfolio as a higher backing, and in turn increase their confidence in the brand's extensions" (Hayran & Gürhan-Canli, 2016, p. 145). However, a multiple extension strategy may weaken the parent brand's image when the organisation has many products with different levels of perceived quality. In this case, the parent brand cannot create a consistent image in consumers' minds (see our earlier discussion of the disadvantages of brand extensions), leading to decreased consumer confidence in the overall quality of the parent brand (Dacin & Smith, 1994). Therefore, it is imperative that organisations consider carefully the perceived quality image of their products when introducing extensions to achieve the required consistency.

Keller and Aaker (1992) determined that the extension's evaluation is also subject to whether the parent brand has other *intervening extensions*. The results of their experimental study show that intervening extensions had an effect on the proposed extension evaluation only when there was substantial difference

> between the perceived quality of the intervening extension (as judged by its success or failure) and the perceived quality of the [parent] brand. A successful intervening extension increased evaluations of a proposed extension only for an average quality [parent] brand; an unsuccessful intervening extension decreased evaluations of a proposed extension only for a high-quality [parent] brand. [In addition] an unsuccessful intervening extension did not decrease [parent] brand evaluations regardless of the quality level of the [parent] brand.
> (Keller & Aaker, 1992, p. 35)

Organisations should also be systematic about the *sequence* they follow in introducing multiple extensions. The order of introduction can also influence the evaluation of brand extensions. Research has shown that firms should gradually increase the similarity gap with the parent brand, hence, they should start with more similar extensions, and progress to moderately similar extensions later as this will increase the likelihood that the extension will be accepted (Dawar & Anderson, 1994). If organisations plan to introduce extensions simultaneously as opposed to sequentially, they must launch complementary extensions (e.g. bicycle and cycling helmet) instead of similar (e.g. two bicycles) or unrelated extensions (e.g. a bicycle and a skateboard) as they are evaluated more favourably (Shine, Park, & Wyer Jr., 2007).

Culture-related moderating factors

As far as culture-related moderating factors are concerned, first, by comparing Western with Eastern consumers, Han and Schmitt (1997) determined that *cultural differences* can moderate brand extension evaluations. They discovered that perceived fit is important for Western consumers, while Eastern consumers seem to concentrate more on the size of the organisation behind the brand extension. Hence,

Eastern consumers tend to evaluate brand extensions of larger organisations more favourably even when the perceived fit is low. In addition, *cultural symbolism* is an important moderating factor in brand extension evaluations. According to Torelli and Ahluwalia (2012), a culturally symbolic brand can automatically trigger in consumers' minds the cultural schemata it is associated with; consider, for example, how *Emporio Armani* will remind consumers of Italy, or *IKEA*, of Sweden.

> When the extension product category is also associated with this activated cultural schema (i.e., the brand and extension product category are culturally congruent), the extension is likely to be processed fluently, generating a feeling of ease, resulting in a pleasing processing experience. This ease of processing experience is likely to result in a more favourable evaluation of the extension.
> (Torelli & Ahluwalia, 2012, p. 934)

Therefore, this activation of cultural schemata can be stronger than the perceived fit, leading to more favourable brand extension evaluations. The implication for brand marketers is that culturally symbolic brands can extend into culturally congruent product categories even when the perceived fit between parent brand and extension category is low (Hayran & Gürhan-Canli, 2016). Perhaps this explains the success of *Emporio Armani Caffè & Ristorante*, and *IKEA* meatballs as culturally congruent brand extensions in categories of lower perceived fit. Finally, *brand extension authenticity* is a cultural construct, which can also act as a moderating factor. A brand extension is deemed as authentic when it incorporates the parent brand's unique meaning, heritage, and values, hence it is deemed as a genuine and culturally congruent extension of the parent brand (Spiggle, Nguyen, & Caravella, 2012). Brand extension authenticity increases the favourability of extension evaluations, and leads to higher purchase intentions, and more consumer recommendations, whereas inauthentic extensions have the opposite effects (Hayran & Gürhan-Canli, 2016; Spiggle et al., 2012).

Competitor-related moderating factors
The evaluation of the brand extension will also be influenced by the parent brand's competitive environment. Product/service categories with no, or more unknown, competitors offer more advantages than those dominated by familiar competitors (Hayran & Gürhan-Canli, 2016). This argument is based on the following reasons: (1) extensions have a higher effect on the parent brand's market share when there are fewer competing offerings (Smith & Park, 1992), (2) the perceived fit of the extension with the parent brand is influenced by the familiarity of competing brands in the extension category (Milberg, Sinn, & Goodstein, 2010), and (3) consumers evaluate brand extensions more favourably when these have unfamiliar competitors in the extension category (Hayran & Gürhan-Canli, 2016).

In addition, a brand which is the *market leader* in a certain product or service category, e.g. *Nike* (sports trainers and apparel), *American Express* (financial services), and *Qatar Airways* or *Singapore Airlines* (air travel) have an advantage over their competitors as far as brand extensions are concerned. This is because the number of consumers who purchase the brand compared with competitor brands is related to the pre- and post-extension image of the parent brand, and the extension perceived fit and evaluation (Dall'Olmo Riley, Hand, & Guido, 2014). Furthermore, *entry order* can also influence the evaluation of brand extensions, namely the extension, which is introduced first (pioneering) appears to be evaluated by different processes than subsequent extensions (follower) (Oakley, Duhachek, Balachander, & Sriram, 2008). Hayran and Gürhan-Canli (2016) explain the reasons with the following:

> Pioneering extensions induce a singular evaluation process in which the extension is evaluated by itself; whereas follower extensions induce a comparative evaluation process with the existing (pioneering) offers in the market. Therefore, follower high-fitting extensions can benefit from the existence of pioneering poor-fitting extensions and induce relatively favourable evaluations. By similar means, when the pioneering extensions are better-fitting, follower lower-fitting extensions are likely to be evaluated less favourably due to a comparative judgement. These findings support an early entrance strategy for low-fitting extensions and a follower entrance strategy for high-fitting extensions.
> (Hayran & Gürhan-Canli, 2016, p. 146)

However, this seems to contradict Dawar and Anderson's (1994) argument that a firm should gradually increase the similarity gap between successive extensions and the parent brand. Finally, competitors in the extension category might counter-attack the parent brand by extending in the parent brand's own category. This strategy is called *counter-extension* and the way the parent brand can avoid this is by following a co-branded extension strategy, i.e. by partnering with another brand when creating an extension into a new category. This is because if the parent brand extends into a new category by itself, although this increases the perceived fit of the parent brand with the extension category, it also means that, at the same time, any potential counter-extension is more likely to be accepted and favoured by consumers (Hayran & Gürhan-Canli, 2016, Kumar, 2005).

CHAPTER REVIEW QUESTIONS

You can use the following questions to reflect on the material covered in Chapter 9:

1. What are the organisational benefits of a clear brand architecture?
2. Explain the difference between the 'branded house' and the 'house of brands' approaches to brand architecture design and provide appropriate examples.
3. Discuss the advantages and disadvantages of brand extensions.

4. What are the potential positive and negative spillover effects of brand extensions to the parent brand?
5. Define the concept of the perceived fit and explain its three dimensions.
6. What are the processes consumers follow when evaluating brand extensions?
7. Discuss the consumer-, brand-, culture-, and competitor-related factors moderating brand extension evaluations.

RECOMMENDED READING

1. Aaker, D. A., & Joachimsthaler, E. (2000). The brand relationship spectrum: The key to the brand architecture challenge. *California Management Review*, 42(4), 8–23.
2. Aaker, D. A., & Keller, K. L. (1990). Consumer evaluations of brand extensions. *Journal of Marketing*, 54(1), 27–41.
3. Hayran, C., & Gürhan-Canli, Z. (2016). Brand extensions. In F. Dall'Olmo Riley, J. Singh, & C. Blankson (eds), *The Routledge companion to contemporary brand management* (pp. 136–152). London: Routledge.
4. Park, C. W., MacInnis, D. J., & Eisingerich, A. B. (2016). Brand architecture design and brand naming decisions. In F. Dall'Olmo Riley, J. Singh, & C. Blankson (eds), *The Routledge companion to contemporary brand management* (pp. 109–119). London: Routledge.

CASE STUDY

A case for divergent brand extensions?

Radu Dimitriu
Associate Professor in Marketing
Trinity College Dublin, Dublin, Ireland

Brands are among the most valuable assets on a company's balance sheet. Consequently, companies have been seeking to create value by leveraging such assets as extensions to new markets or categories. Managerial wisdom and a significant body of research (see the current chapter) suggest that a brand extension strategy is likely to be successful when the extension logically fits (or is similar) to the parent brand. For instance, *Whirlpool*'s range spans white goods and kitchen appliances, including washing machines, driers, fridges, hobs, microwaves, or extractors. *Colgate*'s expertise lies in oral care, including a large range of toothbrushes, toothpastes, mouthwashes, or flossing products.

Ventures outside the logical brand realm are seldom encouraged: for instance, *Colgate* failed miserably when extending the brand into kitchen entrees (Huffington Post, 2014). However, there are several examples of brands that seem to have found market success with low fitting and dissimilar extensions. *Catterpillar (CAT)*, the brand of earth moving machinery, launched Caterpillar boots. These days, consumers can buy *Coca-Cola* and *Sprite* lip smackers. Eager parents can carry their kids around in *Jeep* strollers. Launching poor fitting brand extensions seems, more often than not, to result in failure. However, examples of successes as the ones above cast doubt on the principle that brands should just remain close to their natural base.

What is apparent is that such dissimilar extensions are often launched through licence agreements. The *Caterpillar* brand does not have a natural expertise to manufacture boots; instead, the *CAT* boots are manufactured and marketed through an exclusive licencing agreement by *Wolverine Worldwide*. However, the presence of licencing agreements does not explain market reactions to such products. Consumers are seldom aware about the licensing agreements behind the new offerings; they normally just witness a product and the brand that it bears.

A careful examination reveals such dissimilar brand extensions meet an important criterion: they leverage brand benefits into new, albeit distant, categories (see Farquhar, 1989, as well as the current chapter). The *Caterpillar* boots benefit from the brand's association with ruggedness, endurance and ability to handle rough terrain. If you are into lip smackers, you would most probably not mind one that has the flavour of *Coca-Cola* or *Sprite*. Not least, as a parent you might want to take your kid around in a stroller with an edgy, cool, and all-terrain-suitable image; just like *Jeep*. Surprisingly, by leveraging relevant associations to distant categories, the said brand extensions have built strong positions as delivering such particular attractive benefits in the respective categories (see Dimitriu et al., 2017, as well as the current chapter).

Brand scholars and managers have also been at pains to explain the brand extension success of brands such as *Virgin*. The British brand spans categories as diverse as airlines, financial products, cruises, radio, gyms, balloon flights, mobile, or broadband (in many cases, via licence agreements). In another example, the '*Easy*' brand is not just behind *easyJet*; its portfolio includes car and van rentals, hotels, bus services, or pizza deliveries. The portfolio of the *Co-operative (Co-op)* brand spans supermarkets, funeral care, legal services, and insurance. The question that arises is therefore: What kind of benefits have brands like *Virgin*, *Easy* or *Co-op* leveraged to such different categories? Do these brands hold any special properties? *Virgin*'s aggressive brand extension strategy has actually also resulted in numerous failures, e.g., *Virgin Cola*, *Virgin Vodka*, *Virgin Makeup*, or *Virgin Bridalwear* (Business Insider, 2012). A careful examination nevertheless reveals that the Virgin brand has been successful when applied to a variety of new services, but not new products.

Specifically, Dimitriu and Warlop (2014) demonstrate that brands that essentially stand for services have heightened latitude to extend to dissimilar categories as long as they remain within a service domain. The authors explain that service brands are likely to carry service associations, including employee friendliness and expertise, the ambiance, design, and functionality of the physical or online environment of service delivery, the promptness or the quality of service experience; such associations can be applied as relevant associations to a diversity of service domains. The rationale builds on service quality research, according to which "regardless the type of service, consumers use basically the same general criteria in arriving at an evaluation of service quality" (Parasuraman, Zeithaml, & Berry, 1988, p.6).

Extensions to dissimilar markets appear to hold yet other distinct advantages. Poor fitting extensions can offer a brand the opportunity to update and enhance its personality, especially in the eyes of consumers who think that brand (like human) personality is malleable (Mathur, Jain, & Maheswaran, 2012). Other evidence points out that high reputation brands increase liking for their brand extensions and benefit most from spillover effects by launching low (rather than high) fit extensions while introducing and proactively communicating benefits that are innovative in the respective extension markets (Chun et al., 2015). Real-life examples of such a principle include *Google* home security solutions, or *Amazon* unmanned supermarkets. Unlike high reputation brands, low reputation brands stand most to gain by launching high (rather than low) fit extensions which introduce innovative benefits; consumers would simply not trust low reputation brands' ability to launch innovative innovations in dissimilar categories.

A brand that successfully extends into dissimilar categories essentially increases its breadth (see the chapter discussion on brand breadth); in turn, a broad (compared to a narrow) brand has an enhanced capacity to further stretch into non-typical categories (Boush & Loken, 1991), not least as broad brands have significantly more accessible benefit associations which can be applicable across both similar and dissimilar extension markets (cf., Meyvis & Janiszewski, 2004). Brands such as *Ralph Laurent*, *Apple*, or *Virgin* are cases in point.

While the success of 'divergent' brand extensions is by no means a given, carefully planning and executing extensions into dissimilar categories can significantly enhance the competitive stature of a brand in the markets where it operates, by helping the brand consolidate or construct associations that are appealing, meaningful and innovative; the brand can thus avoid complacency and make sure it stays 'relevant' in the markets that it spans (cf., Aaker, 2012).

Questions for discussion

1. Why do certain brands succeed with extensions into dissimilar / low fit categories?
2. What explains the extension success of brands such as *Virgin* or *'Easy'*?
3. Why would a brand want to extend into a 'divergent' category? Enumerate several of the advantages that a brand could incur from such an extension strategy.

References

Aaker, D. A. (2012). Win the brand relevance battle and then build competitor barriers. *California Management Review*, 54(2), 43–57.

Business Insider (2012). Richard Branson's fails: 14 Virgin companies that went bust. Available at: www.businessinsider.com/richard-branson-fails-virgin-companies-that-went-bust-2016-5?r=US&IR=T [accessed 25 April 2020].

Boush, D. M., & Loken, B. (1991). A process-tracing study of brand extension evaluation. *Journal of Marketing Research*, 28(1), 16–28.

Chun, H. H., Park, C. W., Eisingerich, A. B., & MacInnis, D. J. (2015). Strategic benefits of low fit brand extensions: When and why? *Journal of Consumer Psychology*, 25(4), 577–595.

Cutright, K. M., Bettman, J. R., & Fitzsimons, G. J. (2013). Putting brands in their place: How a lack of control keeps brands contained. *Journal of Marketing Research*, 50(3), 365–377.

Dimitriu, R., & Warlop, L. (2014). The broader boundaries: The importance of service-specific associations in service brand extensions. European Marketing Academy Conference (EMAC), Valencia, Spain, 4–6 June.

Dimitriu, R., Warlop, L., & Samuelsen, B. M. (2017). Brand extension similarity can backfire when you look for something specific. *European Journal of Marketing*, 51(5/6), 850–868.

Farquhar, P. H. (1989). Managing brand equity. *Marketing Research*, 1(3), 24–33.

Huffington Post (2014). 6 hilarious food and drink product fails. Available at: www.huffpost.com/entry/6-hilarious-food-and-drin_b_5055465 [accessed 25 April 2020].

Kirmani, A., Sood, S., & Bridges, S. (1999). The ownership effect in consumer responses to brand line stretches. *Journal of Marketing*, 63(1), 88–101.

Mathur, P., Jain, S. P., & Maheswaran, D. (2012). Consumers' implicit theories about personality influence their brand personality judgments. *Journal of Consumer Psychology*, 22(4), 545–557.

Meyvis, T., & Janiszewski, C. (2004). When are broader brands stronger brands? An accessibility perspective on the success of brand extensions. *Journal of Consumer Research*, 31(2), 346–357.

Parasuraman, A., Zeithaml, V. A., & Berry, L. L. (1988). SERVQUAL: A multiple-item scale for measuring consumer perceptions of service quality. *Journal of Retailing*, 64(1), 12–40.

REFERENCES

Aaker, D. A. (1996). Measuring brand equity across products and markets. *California Management Review*, 38(3), 102–120.

Aaker, D. A., & Carmon, Z. (1992). The effectiveness of brand name strategies at creating brand recall. University of California at Berkeley.

Aaker, D. A., & Joachimsthaler, E. (2000). The brand relationship spectrum: The key to the brand architecture challenge. *California Management Review*, 42(4), 8–23.

Aaker, D. A., & Keller, K. L. (1990). Consumer evaluations of brand extensions. *Journal of Marketing*, 54(1), 27–41.

Ahluwalia, R. (2008). How far can a brand stretch? Understanding the role of self-construal. *Journal of Marketing Research*, 45(3), 337–350.

Ahluwalia, R., & Gürhan-Canli, Z. (2000). The effects of extensions on the family brand name: An accessibility-diagnosticity perspective. *Journal of Consumer Research*, 27(3), 371–381.

Barone, M. J. (2005). The interactive effects of mood and involvement on brand extension evaluations. *Journal of Consumer Psychology*, 15(3), 263–270.

Barone, M. J., & Miniard, P. W. (2002). Mood and brand extension judgments: Asymmetric effects for desirable versus undesirable brands. *Journal of Consumer Psychology*, 12(4), 283–290.

Barone, M. J., Miniard, P. W., & Romeo, J. B. (2000). The influence of positive mood on brand extension evaluations. *Journal of Consumer Research*, 26(4), 386–400.

Bhat, S., & Reddy, S. K. (2001). The impact of parent brand attribute associations and affect on brand extension evaluation. *Journal of Business Research*, 53(3), 111–122.

Boush, D. M., & Loken, B. (1991). A process-tracing study of brand extension evaluation. *Journal of Marketing Research*, 28(1), 16–28.

Boush, D. M., Shipp, S., Loken, B., Gencturk, E., Crockett, S., Kennedy, E., Minshall, B., Misurell, D., Rochford, L., & Strobel, J. (1987). Affect generalization to similar and dissimilar line extensions. *Psychology & Marketing*, 4(3), 225–241.

Broniarczyk, S. M., & Alba, J. W. (1994). The importance of the brand in brand extension. *Journal of Marketing Research*, 31(2), 214–228.

Chakravarti, D., MacInnis, D. J., & Nakamoto, K. (1990). Product category perceptions, elaborative processing and brand name extension strategies. *Advances in Consumer Research*, 17, 910–916.

Chernev, A. (2007). Jack of all trades or master of one? Product differentiation and compensatory reasoning in consumer choice. *Journal of Consumer Research*, 33(4), 430–444.

Chun, H. H., Park, C. W., Eisingerich, A. B., & MacInnis, D. J. (2015). Strategic benefits of low fit brand extensions: When and why? *Journal of Consumer Psychology*, 25(4), 577–595.

Cutright, K. M., Bettman, J. R., & Fitzsimons, G. J. (2013). Putting brands in their place: How a lack of control keeps brands contained. *Journal of Marketing Research*, 50(3), 365–377.

Dacin, P. A., & Smith, D. C. (1994). The effect of brand portfolio characteristics on consumer evaluations of brand extensions. *Journal of Marketing Research*, 31(2), 229–242.

Dall'Olmo Riley, F., Hand, C., & Guido, F. (2014). Evaluating brand extensions, fit perceptions and post-extension brand image: does size matter? *Journal of Marketing Management*, 30(9–10), 904–924.

Dawar, N., & Anderson, P. F. (1994). The effects of order and direction on multiple brand extensions. *Journal of Business Research*, 30(2), 119–129.

Dimitriu, R., Warlop, L., & Samuelsen, B. M. (2017). Brand extension similarity can backfire when you look for something specific. *European Journal of Marketing*, 51(5/6), 850–868.

Farquhar, P. H. (1989). Managing brand equity. *Marketing Research*, 1(3), 24–33.

Farquhar, P. H., Herr, P. M., & Fazio, R. H. (1989). Extending brand equity to new categories, working paper. Center for Product Research, Carnegie Mellon University.

Fedorikhin, A., Park, C. W., & Thomson, M. (2008). Beyond fit and attitude: The effect of emotional attachment on consumer responses to brand extensions. *Journal of Consumer Psychology*, 18(4), 281–291.

Feldman, J. M., & Lynch, J. G. (1988). Self-generated validity and other effects of measurement on belief, attitude, intention, and behavior. *Journal of Applied Psychology*, 73(3), 421–435.

Gürhan-Canli, Z., & Maheswaran, D. (1998). The effects of extensions on brand name dilution and enhancement. *Journal of Marketing Research*, 35(4), 464–473.

Hagtvedt, H., & Patrick, V. M. (2009). The broad embrace of luxury: Hedonic potential as a driver of brand extendibility. *Journal of Consumer Psychology*, 19(4), 608–618.

Han, J. K., & Schmitt, B. H. (1997). Product-category dynamics and corporate identity in brand extensions: A comparison of Hong Kong and US consumers. *Journal of International Marketing*, 5(1), 77–92.

Hayran, C., & Gürhan-Canli, Z. (2016). Brand extensions. In F. Dall'Olmo Riley, J. Singh, & C. Blankson (eds), *The Routledge companion to contemporary brand management* (pp. 136–152). London: Routledge.

Heath, T. B., DelVecchio, D., & McCarthy, M. S. (2011). The asymmetric effects of extending brands to lower and higher quality. *Journal of Marketing*, 75(4), 3–20.

John, D. R., Loken, B., & Joiner, C. (1998). The negative impact of extensions: Can flagship products be diluted? *Journal of Marketing*, 62(1), 19–32.

Keller, K. L. (1993). Conceptualizing, measuring, and managing customer-based brand equity. *Journal of Marketing*, 57(1), 1–22.

Keller, K. L., & Aaker, D. A. (1992). The effects of sequential introduction of brand extensions. *Journal of Marketing Research*, 29(1), 35–50.

Keller, K. L., Apéria, T., & Georgson, M. (2012). *Strategic brand management: A European perspective*. London: Pearson Education.

Keller, K. L., & Swaminathan, V. (2020). *Strategic brand management: Building, measuring, and managing brand equity* (5th edn). London: Pearson Education.

Kim, H., & John, D. R. (2008). Consumer response to brand extensions: Construal level as a moderator of the importance of perceived fit. *Journal of Consumer Psychology*, 18(2), 116–126.

Kim, B. D., & Sullivan, M. W. (1998). The effect of parent brand experience on line extension trial and repeat purchase. *Marketing Letters*, 9(2), 181–193.

Kirmani, A., Sood, S., & Bridges, S. (1999). The ownership effect in consumer responses to brand line stretches. *Journal of Marketing*, 63(1), 88–101.

Klink, R. R., & Smith, D. C. (2001). Threats to the external validity of brand extension research. *Journal of Marketing Research*, 38(3), 326–335.

Kumar, P. (2005). The impact of cobranding on customer evaluation of brand counterextensions. *Journal of Marketing*, 69(3), 1–18.

Lane, V., & Jacobson, R. (1997). The reciprocal impact of brand leveraging: Feedback effects from brand extension evaluation to brand evaluation. *Marketing Letters*, 8(3), 261–271.

Levitt, T. (1960). Marketing myopia. *Harvard Business Review*, July–August, 45–46.

Loken, B., & John, D. R. (1993). Diluting brand beliefs: When do brand extensions have a negative impact? *Journal of Marketing*, 57(3), 71–84.

Mandler, G. (1981). The structure of value: Accounting for taste. In M. S. Clark & S. T. Fiske (eds), *Affect and cognition: The 17th Annual Carnegie Symposium* (pp. 3–36). Hillsdale: Erlbaum.

Maoz, E., & Tybout, A. M. (2002). The moderating role of involvement and differentiation in the evaluation of brand extensions. *Journal of Consumer Psychology*, 12(2), 119–131

Meyvis, T., & Janiszewski, C. (2004). When are broader brands stronger brands? An accessibility perspective on the success of brand extensions. *Journal of Consumer Research*, 31(2), 346–357.

Milberg, S. J., Park, C. W., & McCarthy, M. S. (1997). Managing negative feedback effects associated with brand extensions: The impact of alternative branding strategies. *Journal of Consumer Psychology*, 6(2), 119–140.

Milberg, S. J., Sinn, F., & Goodstein, R. C. (2010). Consumer reactions to brand extensions in a competitive context: does fit still matter? *Journal of Consumer Research*, 37(3), 543–553.

Milewicz, J., & Herbig, P. (1994). Evaluating the brand extension decision using a model of reputation building. *Journal of Product & Brand Management*, 3(1), 39–47.

Monga, A. B., & Gürhan-Canli, Z. (2012). The influence of mating mind-sets on brand extension evaluation. *Journal of Marketing Research*, 49(4), 581–593.

Monga, A. B., & John, D. R. (2007). Cultural differences in brand extension evaluation: The influence of analytic versus holistic thinking. *Journal of Consumer Research*, 33(4), 529–536.

Monga, A. B., & John, D. R. (2010). What makes brands elastic? The influence of brand concept and styles of thinking on brand extension evaluation. *Journal of Marketing*, 74(3), 80–92.

Nisbett, R. E., Peng, K., Choi, I., & Norenzayan, A. (2001). Culture and systems of thought: Holistic versus analytic cognition. *Psychological Review*, 108(2), 291–310.

Ng, S. (2010). Cultural orientation and brand dilution: Impact of motivation level and extension typicality. *Journal of Marketing Research*, 47(1), 186-198.

Oakley, J. L., Duhachek, A., Balachander, S., & Sriram, S. (2008). Order of entry and the moderating role of comparison brands in brand extension evaluation. *Journal of Consumer Research*, 34(5), 706–712.

Park, C. W., MacInnis, D. J., & Eisingerich, A. B. (2016). Brand architecture design and brand naming decisions. In F. Dall'Olmo Riley, J. Singh, & C. Blankson (eds), *The Routledge companion to contemporary brand management* (pp. 109–119). London: Routledge.

Park, C. W., Milberg, S., & Lawson, R. (1991). Evaluation of brand extensions: The role of product feature similarity and brand concept consistency. *Journal of Consumer Research*, 18(2), 185–193.

Pitta, D. A., & Katsanis, L. P. (1995). Understanding brand equity for successful brand extension. *Journal of Consumer Marketing*, 12(4), 51–64.

Rogers, E. (1962). *Diffusion of innovations*. New York: Free Press.

Romeo, J. B. (1991). The effect of negative information on the evaluations of brand extensions and the family brand. *Advances in Consumer Research*, 18(1), 399–406.

Roselius, T. (1971). Consumer rankings of risk reduction methods. *Journal of Marketing*, 35(1), 56–61.

Schmitt, B. H, & Simonson, A. (1997). *Marketing aesthetics: The strategic management of brands, identity, and image*. New York: Simon and Schuster.

Schwartz, B. (2004). The paradox of choice: Why more is less. New York: Ecco.

Shine, B. C., Park, J., & Wyer Jr., R. S. (2007). Brand synergy effects in multiple brand extensions. *Journal of Marketing Research*, 44(4), 663–670.

Smith, D. C., & Park, C. W. (1992). The effects of brand extensions on market share and advertising efficiency. *Journal of Marketing Research*, 29(3), 296–313.

Sood, S., & Drèze, X. (2006). Brand extensions of experiential goods: Movie sequel evaluations. *Journal of Consumer Research*, 33(3), 352–360.

Sood, S., & Keller, K. L. (2012). The effects of brand name structure on brand extension evaluations and parent brand dilution. *Journal of Marketing Research*, 49(3), 373–382.

Spiggle, S., Nguyen, H. T., & Caravella, M. (2012). More than fit: Brand extension authenticity. *Journal of Marketing Research*, 49(6), 967–983.

Swaminathan, V., Fox, R. J., & Reddy, S. K. (2001). The impact of brand extension introduction on choice. *Journal of Marketing*, 65(4), 1–15.

Torelli, C. J., & Ahluwalia, R. (2012). Extending culturally symbolic brands: A blessing or a curse? *Journal of Consumer Research*, 38(5), 933–947.

Trope, Y., & Liberman, N. (2003). Temporal construal. *Psychological Review*, 110(3), 403–421.

Yeo, J., & Park, J. (2006). Effects of parent-extension similarity and self regulatory focus on evaluations of brand extensions. *Journal of Consumer Psychology, 16*(3), 272–282.

Yeung, C. W., & Wyer Jr., R. S. (2005). Does loving a brand mean loving its products? The role of brand-elicited affect in brand extension evaluations. *Journal of Marketing Research, 42*(4), 495–506.

Yorkston, E. A., Nunes, J. C., & Matta, S. (2010). The malleable brand: The role of implicit theories in evaluating brand extensions. *Journal of Marketing, 74*(1), 80-93.

Zhang, S., & Sood, S. (2002). "Deep" and "surface" cues: Brand extension evaluations by children and adults. *Journal of Consumer Research, 29*(1), 129–141.

CHAPTER 10

Brand futures: Technology and innovation in branding strategies

CHAPTER AIMS AND LEARNING OUTCOMES

The final chapter of this book corresponds to the fourth stage of Keller and Swaminathan's (2020) *strategic brand management process*, i.e. growing and sustaining brand equity (see Figure 10.1) and seeks to explore brand futures by considering innovation and technology applications in branding strategies. In particular, this chapter aims to achieve the following:

1. Explore the three dimensions of consumer engagement: cognitive, emotional, and behavioural.
2. Discuss the characteristics of big data, as well as its contribution to value creation and competitive advantage.
3. Explain various metrics which can be employed to measure consumer engagement and suggest ways brand marketers can facilitate consumer engagement.
4. Critically discuss the anti(social) consequences of consumer analytics and data mining.
5. Explore the Internet of Things (IoT) and its implications for branding strategies.
6. Define the concept of neuromarketing, explore its application in branding, and consider the associated ethical implications.

CONSUMER ENGAGEMENT AND ITS DIMENSIONS

Defining consumer engagement

As explored in Chapter 4, in what is known as the attention economy, firms compete for consumers' attention in a market that assigns "value according to something's

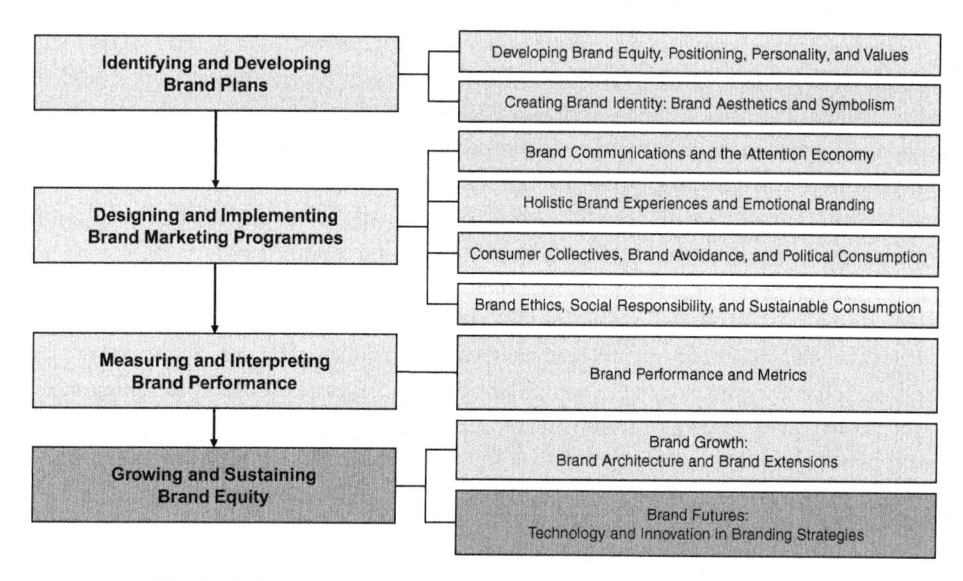

FIGURE 10.1 Strategic brand management process and book plan

capacity to attract 'eyeballs' in a media-saturated, information-rich world" (Marwick, 2015, p. 138). Consumer engagement has, nowadays, become the brand marketer's holy grail; it is of outmost importance if the brand is to succeed in a fiercely competitive digital landscape. Practitioners have defined *consumer engagement* as "establishing a strong and enduring bond between brand and consumers based on ongoing effort of the brand to activate consumers through interactions, shared values, experiential content and rewards" (Schultz, 2007, p. 7). However, this definition, although easy to comprehend, does not represent the multifaceted nature of the construct. Consumer engagement, besides its behavioural part, involves psychological elements such as consumer involvement and loyalty (Borel & Christodoulides, 2016). A scholarly definition of consumer engagement has been provided by Brodie, Hollebeek, Juric, and Ilic (2011), who explain that:

> Consumer engagement is a psychological state that occurs by virtue of interactive, co-creative, customer experiences with a focal agent / object (e.g. brand) in focal service relationships. It occurs under a specific set of context dependent conditions generating differing consumer engagement levels; and exists as a dynamic, iterative process within service relationships that co-create value. Consumer engagement plays a central role in a nomological network governing service relationships in which other relational concepts (e.g. involvement, loyalty) are antecedents and / or consequences in iterative consumer engagement processes. It is a multi-dimensional concept subject to a context and/or stakeholder-specific expression of relevant cognitive, emotional and / or behavioural dimensions.
>
> (Brodie et al., 2011, p. 11)

The level of consumer engagement achieved in digital spaces depends on the social, cultural, and political context of the co-creation activity between a consumer and the brand (Brodie et al., 2011; Vibert & Shields, 2003). The collaborative nature of the digital landscape requires a transformation of branding strategies employed by organisations. As we explored in Chapter 5, Vargo and Lusch's (2004, 2008) seminal work on the *service-dominant logic* highlighted the prominent role of consumers in co-creating value by taking part in value-creation networks (Baron & Harris, 2008; Tynan & McKechnie, 2009). Nowadays, brand marketers recognise that they need to relinquish some control to consumers because brands, although legally a property of their organisations, are, in essence, owned by consumers; it is primarily what consumers think of, and feel toward, a brand which contributes to the development of brand and its meaning. Branding in our digital society involves organisations facilitating positive brand conversations. To do so, brand marketers must create attractive content which consumers read, watch, or listen to, and are willing to share with others (see Chapter 4). *Content marketing* is "a strategic marketing approach focused on creating and distributing valuable, relevant, and consistent content to attract and retain a clearly defined audience — and, ultimately, to drive profitable customer action" (Content Marketing Institute, 2020).

Dimensions of consumer engagement

Scholars have determined three levels or dimensions of consumer engagement: cognitive, emotional, and behavioural (Brodie et al., 2011; Fredricks, Blumenfeld, & Paris, 2004) (see Figure 10.2). Patterson, Yu, and de Ruyter (2006) describe the intensity of consumer interaction as a continuum of cognitive, emotional, and/or behavioural engagement, which can vary from non-engaged to highly-engaged consumers. Indeed, Borel and Christodoulides (2016) argue that the engagement process starts with the consumers looking for information about the brand, that is, the engagement process originates from cognition as the first stage. *Cognitive engagement* relates to the notion of cognitive investment, whereby an individual makes the effort to understand complex ideas and learn difficult skills (Fredricks et al., 2004): "Online engagement is characterised as a cognitive and affective commitment to an active relationship with the brand as personified by…computer-mediated entities [website, social media pages, blogs etc.] designed to communicate brand value" (Borel & Christodoulides, 2016, p. 258). With cognitive engagement, consumers cognitively identify a co-creating opportunity and provide their resources to others (i.e. organisations) (Frow, Nenonen, Payne, & Storbacka, 2015).

Second, *emotional engagement* requires higher levels of involvement, the development of brand trust, leading to emotional commitment (Borel & Christodoulides, 2016). This means that consumers feel passion for the brand, want to spend time and effort with it (Hollebeek, 2011), developing high levels of brand loyalty (brand resonance) (Brodie, Ilic, Juric, & Hollebeek, 2013; Van Doorn, Lemon, Mittal, Nass, Pick, Pirner, & Verhoef, 2010). Consumers might form relationships with other brand enthusiasts, developing a community around the brand (see Chapter 6). Emotional engagement means that consumers *feel* committed toward co-creating

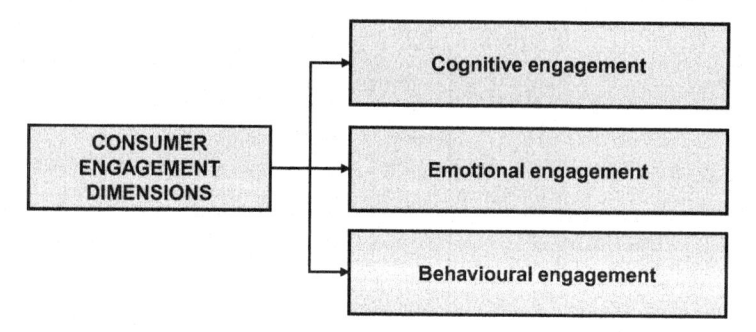

FIGURE 10.2 Dimensions of consumer engagement

brand meaning and put more effort in engaging with others (fellow consumers and organisations) (Frow et al., 2015).

Third, *behavioural engagement* is all about actions and interactions between consumers and the brand (Prahalad & Ramaswamy, 2004). It is about active engagement, i.e. the highest form of brand resonance (see Chapter 2), where consumers are willing to spend time, effort, and financial resources beyond purchasing and consuming the brand, to interact with the brand and other brand enthusiasts, participate in brand-related events, and become brand evangelists seeking to persuade others to purchase and consume the brand (Keller, 2001). At this stage, consumers, given a specific frame of reference, might change their behaviour as a result of the co-creation activity (Frow et al., 2015).

> Active engagement in the form of membership continuance, participation, giving and receiving recommendations from other community members and creating brand-related user-generated content often lead to positive brand outcomes such as higher levels of brand equity, brand loyalty and customer advocacy.
> (Borel & Christodoulides, 2016, p. 258)

BIG DATA AND CONSUMER ANALYTICS

Defining big data and its dimensions

Nowadays, organisations have recognised the importance of *big data* for making brand marketing decisions, as well as for measuring and facilitating the aforementioned consumer engagement.

> *Big data* is a term that primarily describes data sets that are so large (terabytes to exabytes), unstructured, and complex (from genome-analysis, political science, sensor, social media, or smartphone apps, to Internet-based gadgets data) that require advanced and unique technologies to store, manage, analyse, and visualise.
> (Xu, Frankwick, & Ramirez, 2016, p. 1562)

```
                    ┌─────────────┐
                 ┌─▶│   Volume    │
                 │  └─────────────┘
                 │  ┌─────────────┐
                 ├─▶│  Velocity   │
 ┌─────────────┐ │  └─────────────┘
 │DIMENSIONS OF│ │  ┌─────────────┐
 │  BIG DATA   │─┼─▶│   Variety   │
 └─────────────┘ │  └─────────────┘
                 │  ┌─────────────┐
                 ├─▶│  Veracity   │
                 │  └─────────────┘
                 │  ┌─────────────┐
                 └─▶│    Value    │
                    └─────────────┘
```

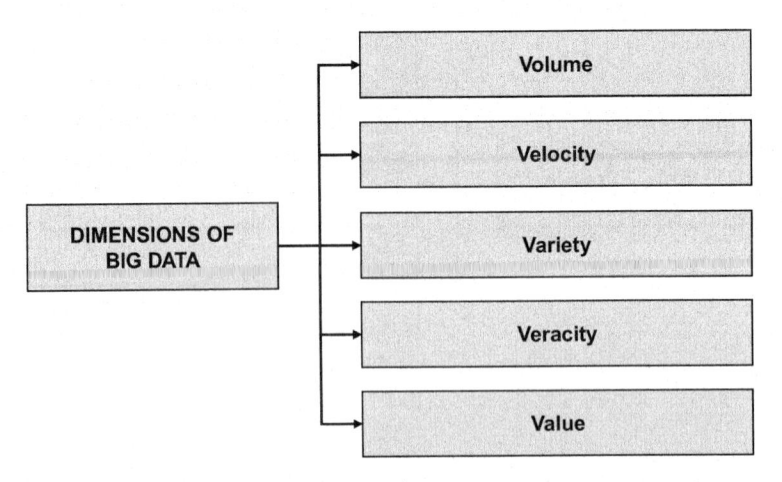

FIGURE 10.3 Dimensions of big data

Big data provides organisations with tremendous volume of personal consumer data that brand marketers can interpret, using consumer analytics, to generate behavioural patterns leading to a competitive advantage for the brand and the organisation. Consumer analytics provide organisations the tools of extracting latent consumer behavioural insights and exploiting them to their advantage (Erevelles, Fukawa, & Swayne, 2016).

Scholars have indicated five dimensions that define big data: volume, velocity, variety, veracity, and value (Erevelles et al., 2016; Lycett, 2013; Zikopoulos & Eaton, 2011) (see Figure 10.3). First, *volume* relates to the magnitude of big data, and is "currently measured in petabytes, exabytes or zettabytes. One petabyte is equivalent to 20 million traditional filing cabinets of text" (Erevelles et al., 2016, p. 898). Organisations face the challenge of storing and analysing ever-increasing volume of big data, and as a result the size of the global market for digital software and hardware doubles every two years (Erevelles et al., 2016). Second, *velocity* is about the persistent speed of data creation. Brand marketers can make better decisions on the basis of evidence generated by real time consumer data (Erevelles et al., 2016). Third, *variety* refers to the diverse richness of big data. For example, social media can capture personal and behavioural information which consumers share with their followers. With big data there is a

> shift from structured transactional data to unstructured behavioural data. [This] unstructured data include textual data (e.g., from blogs and text messages) and non-textual data (e.g., from videos, images, and audio recordings)…Semi-structured data incorporate various types of software that can bring order to the unstructured data. For instance, Standard Generalized Mark-up Language (SGML) software enables the viewing of videos to determine common elements that an organization wants to capture (e.g., of the videos posted on *YouTube* showing people using its product, how many of them seem to be happy?).
>
> (Erevelles et al., 2016, p. 898)

Fourth, *veracity* emphasises the need for data quality; it highlights the fact that some big data about consumers might not be as accurate as brand marketers might think. As the volume, velocity, and variety of big data increases, its veracity becomes a major challenge. Finally, *value* relates to the usefulness and relevance of big data. The onus is on the organisation to distinguish relevant from irrelevant data and interpret valuable data in a timely manner (Erevelles et al., 2016; Lycett, 2013).

Big data, value creation, and competitive advantage

Erevelles et al. (2016) developed a conceptual framework that explains the contribution of big data to (brand) value creation and organisational competitive advantage. According to their framework, the firm uses its resources to interpret big data captured by consumers' online activities in order to generate consumer insights. In turn, the latter leads to the organisation's dynamic capability and adaptive capability, and both generate value and sustainable competitive advantage for the brand and the organisation. The process of generating consumer insights and developing dynamic capability and adaptive capability is moderated by organisational resource characteristics (see Figure 10.4) (Erevelles et al., 2016). Let us explore the components of this framework in more depth.

The organisation's resources involve physical capital (software), human capital (data scientists and strategists), and organisational capital (structure), resources. Big data includes structured, semi-structured, and unstructured data (as explained above). The characteristics of the organisation's resources include two constructs, ignorance and creative intensity, which play an important moderating role. First, *ignorance* refers to an individual understanding what he/she does not know instead of merely focusing on what he/she already knows (Proctor & Schiebinger, 2008; Sammut & Sartawi, 2012). Ignorance is essential for the discovery of new knowledge (Smithson, 1985) because it

> facilitates latitude and freedom that are critical for stimulating creativity within an organisation…Thus, as the source of competitive advantage moves from the knowledge itself to the speed of generating creative ideas, ignorance is likely to become a crucial cultural orientation for facilitating creativity within an organisation.
>
> (Erevelles et al., 2016, p. 899)

Ignorance requires *inductive reasoning* which, as a methodological approach, stipulates that a scientific inquiry should start by observing a phenomenon before trying to form hypotheses on the basis of what we already know, i.e. existing theory. Such inductive reasoning enables consumer analysts to observe online phenomena and, using algorithms, find behavioural patterns in big data without depending on existing knowledge. Xu et al. (2016) suggest that organisations should pursue a *knowledge fusion perspective* that combines bid data analysis (BDA) with traditional

314 BRAND FUTURES

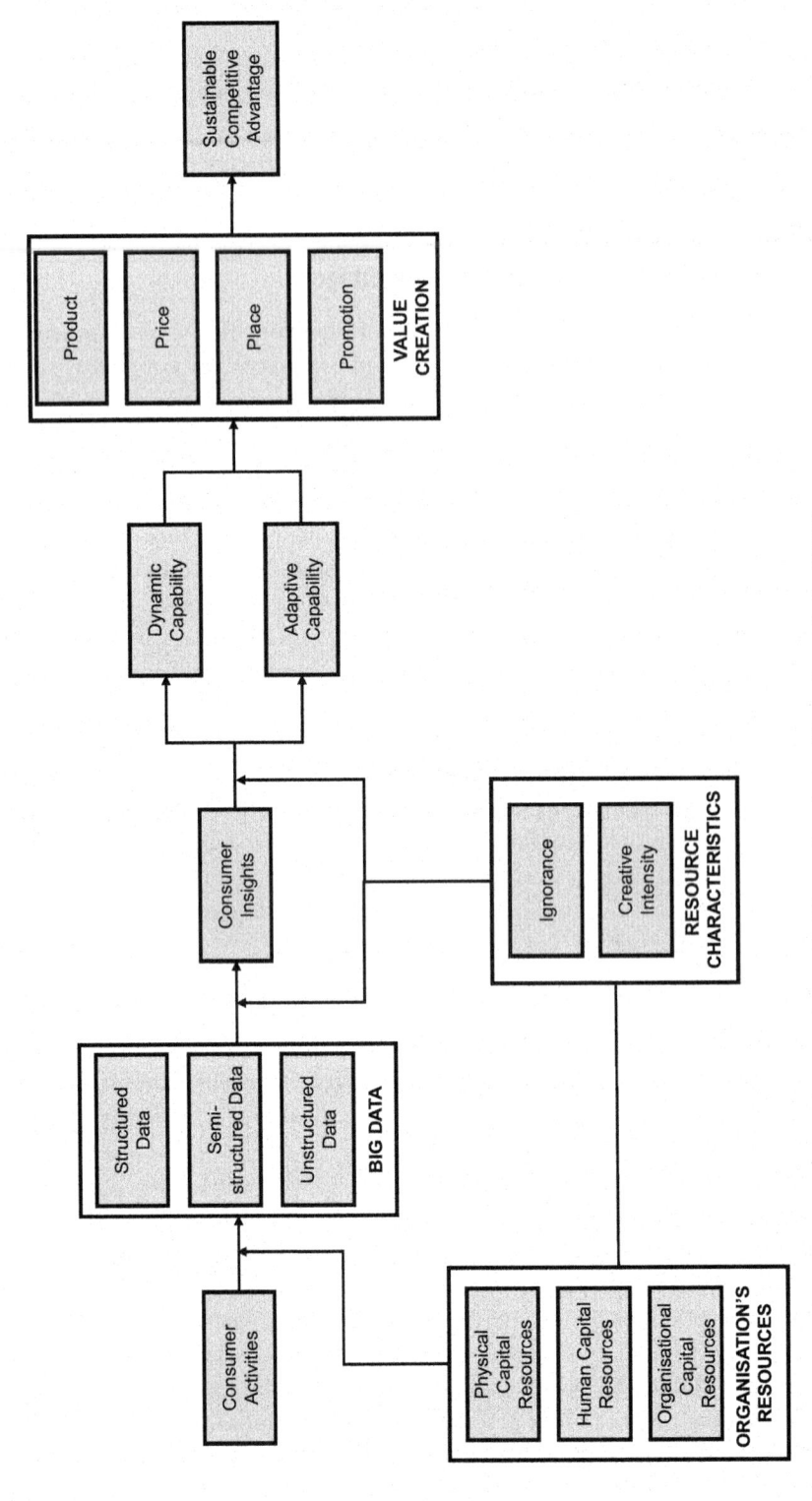

FIGURE 10.4 Big data, value creation, and competitive advantage (Erevelles et al., 2016)

marketing analysis (TMA) (which concentrates primarily on improving key performance indicators to generate better insights), in order to improve new product success. The organisations that blend the highest levels of BDA and TMA are *pioneers*, as they manage to achieve a synergy between IT capabilities, and generate new knowledge (Xu et al., 2016).

Second, *creative intensity* is about the organisation's ability to formulate new ways of analysing big data to generate new consumer insights and implement new brand marketing activities. Such creative intensity can lead to radical innovation and "lies in the skills of an organisation's members who generate innovative ideas (human capital resources), plus in organisational culture that enables the firm to utilize innovative ideas (organisational capital resources)" (Erevelles et al., 2016, p. 901).

As mentioned earlier, ignorance and creative intensity moderate the process of generating consumer insights and developing the organisation's dynamic capability and adaptive capability. *Dynamic capability* is about the organisation's ability to respond to dynamic changes in the market by transforming its resources to create new value. Consumer insights generated by big data enable the organisation to understand the unmet needs of the brand's target audience which enhances the organisation's dynamic capability. In addition, "*adaptive capability* derives not from a specific change in organisational structure but from the overall ability to capture consumer activities and extract hidden insights. When successfully exploited, big data provides firms with opportunities to enhance adaptive capability" (Erevelles et al., 2016, p. 899).

Dynamic and adaptive capabilities enable the organisation to generate value through the four elements of the marketing mix. First, organisations can gather fast consumer feedback about *product* concepts (e.g. potential brand extensions – see Chapter 9) due to the velocity of big data (without having to wait for insights from traditional focus groups and surveys) enabling rapid prototyping and radical innovation. For example, *Netflix* harnessed big data captured from its millions of users to analyse and predict viewing preferences and develop new content, e.g. the hit drama *House of Cards* (Erevelles et al., 2016). In addition, organisations can use data mining methods to automatically gather online textual comments about current products for the purposes of product reputation management (Fan, Lau, & Zhao, 2015). Second, drawing from big data, the organisation can adopt a flexible *pricing* strategy on the basis of dynamic consumer demands. This enables the organisation to change its pricing according to consumers' willingness to pay more for the brand (brand equity – see Chapter 2) (Erevelles et al., 2016). Fan et al. argue that data mining methods can be used for "automated competitor analysis…[which] does not simply identify the potential competitors of a company, [but also] effectively discovers the potentially competitive products and the product contexts" (2015, p. 30).

Third, organisations can improve their product distribution strategies (*place*) by drawing from big data. As an example, Erevelles et al. (2016) cite *Amazon*'s anticipatory shipping process whereby the firm can predict when a consumer will put an order by using big data such as his/her product search, order, and shopping cart history, and it starts product shipping before the consumer has even placed his/her online order. Location-based data captured by smartphone technology enable location-based advertising, which provides consumers with "timely advertisements or product recommendations based on their current position or predicted future position" (Fan et al., 2015, p. 30). Indeed, geospatial information can accurately predict where a consumer will be and when (Sadilek & Krumm, 2012) so that the organisation can customise its communications messages (*promotion*) accordingly. With methods that are based on user ratings and content-based associations, organisations can develop recommendation systems that improve brand awareness. However, it can be difficult to scale up such systems to cope with the ever-increasing volume of big data to "generate appropriate recommendations to potential customers in real time as expected in e-commerce settings. This is the reason why velocity is one of the most challenging issues for the 'promotion' perspective in the context of marketing intelligence" (Fan et al., 2015, p. 30).

(Anti)social consequences of consumer analytics and data mining

The omnipresent use of smartphones in daily life means that every single consumer is now a valuable data source; using a variety of mobile social media and other apps, consumers allow organisations access to their location and mobile activity, generating a constant flow of personal data. Even though social media are thought to be democratising marketing by giving consumers greater power and control over the flow of marketing information (see Chapter 4) (Kaplan & Haenlein, 2010; Smith & Zook, 2012), Kaplan (2011) argues that mobile social media allow organisations to claim some of that power back. In addition, Pridmore and Zwick (2013) believe that the digitalisation of information and the advent of data mining have enabled organisations to pursue *consumer surveillance*.

> While the digital code deconstructs complex, idiosyncratic, and often erratic behaviour into individualised and individualising data points, the algorithm reconstructs this data into standardised, rationalised, and comparable structure, making it possible for marketers to identify 'right' and 'wrong' targets for professional marketing intervention.
> (Pridmore & Zwick, 2013, p. 105)

Organisations need to be extremely careful when using algorithmic models for decision-making. As discussed earlier, Erevelles et al. (2016) argue that when an organisation follows an ignorance-based approach, "researchers [can] observe phenomena using inductive reasoning without being biased by existing knowledge to facilitate the discovery of hidden insights in big data" (2016, p. 900). However, according to mathematician and data scientist, Cathy O'Neil, in fact, algorithms can often involve human bias and misunderstandings leading to destructive results. She coins the term *weapons of math destruction* (WMDs) to describe such harmful algorithmic models (O'Neil, 2016) (their characteristics include opacity, scale, damage), and articulately explains this term with the following:

> [WMDs]...define their own reality and use it to justify their results. This type of model is self-perpetuating, highly destructive – and very common...In WMDs, many poisonous assumptions are camouflaged by math and go largely untested and unquestioned...Ill-conceived mathematical models now micromanage the economy, from advertising to prisons. WMDs [are] opaque, unquestioned, and unaccountable, and they operate at a scale to sort, target, or 'optimise' millions of people.
>
> (O'Neil, 2016, pp. 7–12)

Indeed, some organisations ignore the social consequences of their data mining practices (Danna & Gandy, 2002). Such practices can often discriminate against, and exclude, certain consumer groups (Zwick & Dholakia, 2004). Hence, it is imperative that firms "consider more than the bottom line when engaging in marketing based on data mining practices" (Pridmore & Zwick, 2013, p. 106). A brand perceived by consumers as over-relying on flawed algorithmic analyses to discriminate and exclude poor and vulnerable individuals will see its equity diminish as negative associations in consumers' minds will lead to negative feelings and reduced brand resonance.

MEASURING AND FACILITATING CONSUMER ENGAGEMENT

Organisations should harness the power of big data analytics in order to make societally informed brand marketing strategy decisions, and sustain and grow brand equity further. It is essential that brand marketers monitor and measure consumer engagement across all three dimensions: cognitive, emotional, and behavioural. By doing so, they can "evaluate the effectiveness of social [media] programmes, and optimise brand campaigns for their target audience by understanding what type of content is successful or not for their brands" (Borel & Christodoulides, 2016, p. 259). Different online marketing communications channels involve different metrics. For example, the organisation can measure performance of: (1) unique and return visitors' numbers of brand websites, including webpage views, dwell time, and conversions, (2) emails sent to registered consumers based on open and click-through rates, and (3) social media posts based on 'likes' and 'shares' (Borel & Christodoulides, 2016).

In particular, measuring cognitive engagement involves mapping changes in brand awareness, in consumers' interest in the brand (related to the first level of the Customer-Based Brand Equity (CBBE) pyramid model (Keller, 2001)), and in purchase intentions, by using metrics such as link clicks and photo/video viewings (Borel & Christodoulides, 2016). Measuring emotional engagement would concentrate on determining how brand-related content, including advertising messages and online posts, make users feel towards the brand, i.e. determining brand associations and brand feelings (related to the second and third level of the CBBE pyramid model (Keller, 2001)). This can be done by mining data for positive consumer comments, blog posts, and brand recommendations (Borel & Christodoulides, 2016). Finally, measuring behavioural engagement requires brand marketers to monitor user-initiated interactions by using metrics such as consumers 'following' a brand, liking and sharing online brand posts on social media, and using brand-related hashtags (Borel & Christodoulides, 2016) (related to the fourth level of the CBBE pyramid model – brand community membership and active engagement (Keller, 2001)).

A simple scale of consumer–brand engagement across all three dimensions has been provided by Hollebeek, Glynn, and Brodie (2014). The scale includes a number of statements consumers can rate their answers on (for example by using *Likert* scales, 1 for 'strongly disagree' and 5 for 'strongly agree') (see Table 10.1). It is important to note that this scale relies on consumers' *perceptions* of their cognitive, emotional, and behavioural engagement, instead of *actual* engagement (Borel & Christodoulides, 2016). Nevertheless, the results of such surveys can be combined with the other measures discussed earlier. By triangulating data, brand marketers can more accurately predict consumers' purchase intentions of specific brands within an organisation's portfolio (Hollebeek et al., 2014).

It is essential that organisations monitor very closely consumers' brand-related conversations, i.e. online word-of-mouth (WOM), because this can help brand marketers understand consumers' brand perceptions (Christodoulides, Jevons, & Bonhomme, 2012), proactively tailor brand communications messages, respond to any possible negative comments, and avoid online brand crises. Tools such as *Synomos*, *Brandwatch*, or *Radian 6* can "scrape the web for brand mentions using Boolean queries, in other words, complex keyword searches, that can include or exclude

TABLE 10.1 Measuring consumer–brand engagement

Engagement dimension	Scale items
Cognitive processing	Using [brand] gets me to think about [brand]. I think about [brand] a lot when I am using it. Using [brand] stimulates my interest to learn more about [brand].
Affective (emotional)	I feel very positive when I use [brand]. Using [brand] makes me happy. I feel good when I use [brand]. I am proud to use [brand].
Activation (behavioural)	I spend a lot of time using [brand], compared to other [category] brands. Whenever I am using [category], I usually use [brand]. [Brand] is one of the brands I usually use when I use [category].

Sources: Based on Borel & Christodoulides (2016) and Hollebeek, Glynn, & Brodie (2014).

certain keywords to return the most accurate results" (Borel & Christodoulides, 2016, p. 262). There are four types of analysis that brand marketers can pursue when monitoring consumers' brand-related conversations. First, *sentiment analysis* involves manually analysing the sentiment of each post to determine how consumers feel about the brand. For example, from a dataset of more than two million tweets which included the keyword *Starbucks*, Shirdastian, Laroche, and Richard (2019) used big data analytics to examine

> sentiments toward [the] brand, via brand authenticity, to identify the reasons for positive or negative sentiments on social media…[By verifying] the robustness of previous findings with an in-lab experiment, [they demonstrated] high accuracy for both the brand authenticity dimensions' predictions and their sentiment polarity.
>
> (Shirdastian et al., 2019, p. 291)

Second, *topic analysis* is about brand marketers analysing brand online mentions to determine how consumers talk about the brand. Third, *media type analysis* involves identifying on which social media platform consumers are discussing the brand the most. Finally, with *share of voice analysis* brand marketers can benchmark the number of brand mentions against those of the competitors' brands (Borel & Christodoulides, 2016).

In the past, critics of online brand metrics often pointed to the fact that one of the challenges with such measurements had been that they cannot attribute social media marketing on the bottom line, i.e. "although engagement metrics can help measure a brand's success in social media, these metrics do not provide marketers with accurate sale figures, making it difficult to report on a social media campaign's ROI" (Borel & Christodoulides, 2016, pp. 262–263). To tackle this, social media platforms sought to improve the accuracy of measuring the ROI of their services so that advertisers are more confident that their social media campaigns do contribute to sales beyond merely increasing engagement. For instance, few years ago, *Facebook* introduced the 'purchase' button in its posts, enabling brand marketers to directly measure social media ROI in an accurate way, and *Twitter* added conversion tracking in their advertising which enables organisations to track likes, re-tweets, and favourites.

Improving social media ROI measurements means that brand marketers can now use big data analytics to tailor their sales promotion campaigns to achieve higher financial returns for the organisation. However, according to brand consultants, Peter Horst and Robert Duboff, this does not necessarily imply that the brand marketers' job has become easier. In fact, the opposite is true; their job is now harder. They explain that because of big data analytics, organisations might find it harder to

> Achieve…the right balance between short-term revenue pursuit and long-term brand building…If it was difficult before to defend branding investments with indefinite and distant payoffs, it is doubly so now that near-term sales can be

so precisely engineered. Analytics allows a seeming omniscience about what promotional offers customers will find appealing. Big data allows impressive amounts of information to be obtained about the buying patterns and transaction histories of identifiable customers. Given marketing dollars and the discretion to invest them in either direction, the temptation to keep cash registers ringing is nearly irresistible.

(Horst & Duboff, 2015, p. 81)

They caution organisations against over-relying on sales promotions, and cite *Time*, the US weekly news magazine, as a classic example of a brand that 'sales-promoted' itself to obscurity. There can be a tension between building brand equity, which requires a long-term strategy, and achieving short-term sales so they make the following four recommendations. First, brand marketers should "make every message do double duty" (Horst & Duboff, 2015, p. 82), which means that the brand's online messages should trigger more instant sales *and*, at the same time, contribute to building brand equity. For example, *Subway*, the sandwich brand, has used big data analytics to identify sales relationships among its different products to grow the consumers' repertoire (the sandwiches they choose more than once) instead of merely pushing to the customer (with sales promotions) whatever he/she has ordered most often, since this would have been destructive in the long run because the greater the repertoire the greater the consumer's loyalty to the brand (Horst & Duboff, 2015). Second, brand marketers should harness digital analytics to make a case for long-term brand development investments. Using big data analytics to understand consumers' brand perceptions can help organisations identify specific problems they need to solve in the short term to improve sales, while improving brand positioning in consumers' minds in the long term. Third, organisations should refrain from pursuing sales offers which are off-brand, i.e. offers which the organisation cannot defend: "Taking a follow-the-data approach could lead to marketing initiatives that generate strong ROI but unwittingly expose the company to allegations of inappropriate targeting, or unfair exclusion, or using data-driven correlations that in hindsight appear discriminatory" (Horst & Duboff, 2015, p. 85). This echoes O'Neil's (2016) concerns about marketing algorithms and data analytics turning into WMDs. Brand marketers should use their deontological reasoning (see Chapter 7) when making decisions about what offers to pursue. As Tariq Shaukat, Chief Marketing Officer of *Caesar Entertainment* explains, "if the data tells us to do something that doesn't make intuitive sense, we won't do it" (cited in Horst & Duboff, 2015, p. 85). Finally, organisations should facilitate effective collaboration between brand marketers and data scientists to jointly work towards growing and sustaining brand equity.

Generally speaking, Borel and Christodoulides (2016) argue that measuring engagement can help brand marketers to: 1) determine successful and unsuccessful content to optimise the brand online content strategy, 2) identify the success of their social media campaigns in relation to social media ROI, 3) benchmark brand's social media efforts against its competitors' efforts by using engagement metrics or WOM referrals metrics (as explained earlier), 4) drive online traffic to the brand website in order to increase consumers' purchase consideration and brand sales, 5) report on ROI figures to senior executives for future budget allocation and planning purposes (Borel & Christodoulides, 2016).

In order to facilitate cognitive engagement, brand marketers should develop content that is cognitively engaging and informative, as well as make sure this content is easily searchable on social media. This can include photo albums, custom-built forums, FAQ tabs on *Facebook*, pinned posts, *YouTube* playlists, as well as harnessing the use of hashtags (Borel & Christodoulides, 2016). To facilitate emotional engagement brand marketers should develop online platforms where brand enthusiasts can submit their stories and photos. For example, as discussed in Chapter 6, *Nutella* achieved this through its *my Nutella The Community* online platform (Cova & Pace, 2006). Emotionally engaged consumers should also be able to submit their ideas on how to develop better products, how to improve consumer experience, as well as how to encourage even more community involvement. As discussed in Chapter 4, earned media involve fan pages developed and run by brand enthusiasts for their favourite brands (Edelman, 2010). Brand marketers should collaborate with brand enthusiasts to maintain these unofficial pages to facilitate positive online brand discussions (Borel & Christodoulides, 2016).

Finally, brand marketers can facilitate behavioural engagement by harnessing the power of gamification (developing online brand-related games), encouraging WOM referrals and the development of user generated content, and using branded hashtags. Consumers tend to engage with branded hashtags because of their entertainment value, their emotional value, and because they allow consumers to be creative. However, branded hashtags should involve a clear call-to-action to achieve brand objectives. Table 10.2 highlights consumer–brand engagement metrics for *Facebook*, *Twitter*, *YouTube*, and WOM referrals, and provides a summary of how the engagement dimensions can be measured.

THE INTERNET OF THINGS (IoT)

A factor that has significantly contributed to the massive growth in the volume of big data is the *Internet of Things* (IoT) which enables organisations to incorporate computerisation in their products, be they home appliances, automobiles, engines, toys, and consumer electronics (Erevelles et al., 2016). With the rise of the IoT we witness the development of interconnected networks of people, organisations, and objects leading to greater consumer connectivity (Verhoef et al., 2017). Technology, and in particular smartphones, provide the platform upon which multiple connections and interactions can occur. Thanks to this network facilitated by the IoT, consumers can now make bank transactions, share social information, and seamlessly interface with their wearable devices. Verhoef et al. (2017) developed a conceptual framework to understand the interactions enabled by the IoT and the useful data that these

TABLE 10.2 Consumer–brand engagement metrics for the main social networking sites

Social networking site	Engagement dimension	Measurement metric	Additional information
Facebook – post engagement	Cognitive	Website clicks (Traffic) Photo / Video views Tab views Post comments	*Post engagement* • Post reach is the number of people who have seen a post. • Post reach can be segmented by fans/non-fans and organic reach vs paid reach. *Page engagement* • Page engagement is the total amount of engagement-related actions on a *Facebook* page. • Page engagement actions include: post likes, post comments, post shares, offer claims, question follows, website clicks, photo views, video views, page likes, check-ins, page mentions, tab views, question answers, question follows. • Figures are for the first 28 days after a post was created and include people viewing a post on desktop and mobile.
	Emotional	UGC upload Page mentions Page likes	
	Behavioural	Post likes Post shares Check-ins UGC upload	
Twitter	Cognitive	Reach Impressions Website clicks	• Typically measured via listening tools / statistic tools such as *Sysomos*, *Tweetreach*, *Hootsuite*. • For advertisers, data provided by *Twitter* within the analytics dashboard for both organic and paid tweets: https://analytics.twitter.com/
	Emotional	Brand mentions (@ replies) Following a brand	
	Behavioural	Re-tweeting 'Favouriting' a tweet	
YouTube	Cognitive	Video views Audience attention Traffic sources Audience demographics Geographic impact	• Statistics available from the *YouTube* analytics panel.
	Emotional	Commenting Sharing Remixing a video through UGC	
	Behavioural	'Favouriting' a video Sharing a video	

TABLE 10.2 Cont.

Social networking site	Engagement dimension	Measurement metric	Additional information
WOM Referrals	Emotional	Sentiment analysis Topic analysis Share of voice analysis Media type analysis (e.g. *Twitter*, *Facebook*, blogs, mainstream media)	• Third party tools e.g. *Sysomos*, *Brandwatch*, *Radian 6*. • Searches conducted through Boolean queries, complex keyword searches set up within the third party tool.

Source: Based on Borel & Christodoulides 2016).

interactions can generate for organisations. Their framework helps us to understand consumer connectivity and its relation to marketing value and examines

> connectivity both from the conventional perspective where a consumer is *actively* engaged in a network through devices (particularly mobile or wearable), interacting with other consumers, firms, or objects; and also from an emerging perspective where a consumer is *passively* engaged in a network through objects such as IoT sensors and appliances that form networks and communicate with each other to 'sense' consumers' locations, characteristics, needs, behaviours, and even moods and, then trigger actions or information transmissions that can create some form of value for consumers.
>
> (Verhoef et al., 2017, p. 2)

The framework of consumer connectivity has three components: people, objects, and their physical environments (see Figure 10.5). First, consumers can communicate with other *people* vocally, visually (through *FaceTime*, *Skype*, or *Zoom*), and virtually (through social media platforms). People can also monitor others: senior managers can monitor their employees' behaviour and performance, and parents can look after their children using camera technology. Using wearable technology, e.g. *Fitbit*, consumers can also monitor themselves, with instant access to health metrics, which can help them change their lifestyle and improve their health.

As consumers connect with each other across multiple dimensions—text, image, audio and video—the created content can be analysed to uncover content-based network structures. For example, there could be strong networks of brands within the content shared by people. A mapping between social networks of people and networks of brands identified in the content could be very helpful for identifying competitive brand maps and associated segments of consumers. Such

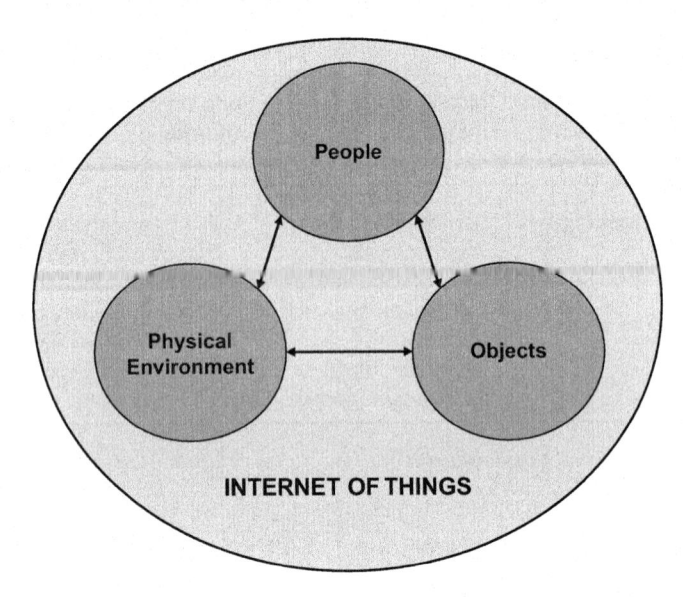

FIGURE 10.5 Framework of consumer connectivity

content networks can extend beyond brands to interests, experiences and needs, representing a treasure trove of information relevant for marketers.

(Verhoef et al., 2017, p. 3)

Identifying strong networks of brands can help organisations pursue an experiential marketing strategy. As discussed in Chapter 5, experiential marketers do not narrowly define product category and competition but view their brands as part of consumption experiences that involve other products (even when these are competitors' products). Experiential marketers seek to make synergies between their brands and other products situated in these consumption experiences (Schmitt, 1999a, 1999b). In addition, identifying social networks of people with similar interests, experiences, and needs, can help brand marketers harness the marketing potential of consumer collectives, and in particular, of subcultures (Schouten & McAlexander, 1995), and consumer tribes (Canniford, 2011), which do not centre around one brand in particular, but are related to lifestyles, and passions, respectively (see Chapter 6).

Second, consumers can connect with the *objects* they own as well as other products and sensors in public and private spaces. For instance, consumers can control their cars as well as their home heating appliances, track parcels, and sync information from one device to another. The IoT enables many-to-many interactions "between smart products – passively, without active human interventions – and interactions between smart products and consumers that are more active" (Verhoef et al., 2017, p. 2). This demonstrates how the IoT can contribute to higher levels of entanglement, i.e. stronger relationships of dependence (or dependency) between humans and things, among humans, and among things (see Hodder, 2012). Drawing from Belk (2013), Verhoef et al. emphasise that the meaning of objects consumers use in their daily lives can change on the basis of "who is connecting them, what they are being connected to, and where they are being connected" (2017, p. 4).

According to Hoffman and Novak (2018) smart products entail three unique elements which affect consumers' interactions with them: 1) *agency*, which relates to the fact that by definition smart objects have the ability to act and interact, to influence and to be influenced, 2) *autonomy*, which is about the role of smart products as active partners in these interactions and their ability to autonomously express their agency to consumers through their actions, both when consumers closely or remotely command these objects or when these objects act autonomously, and 3) *authority*, which is about the fact that smart products have the power "to interact with each other, without direct interaction from consumers" (Verhoef et al., 2017, p. 4). These three elements of smart products can influence the types of potential interactions in the IoT.

Third, consumers can connect with *physical environments* including locations, local weather, traffic conditions, current events, and public transport. Using mobile apps, they can navigate themselves in 'smart cities' (e.g. *Google Maps* or *Waze*), they can instantly check on the weather conditions (e.g. *BBC weather* app), and track train journeys (e.g. *Trainline* app) and flights (e.g. *Flight tracker* app). With wearable technologies they can monitor themselves in the physical environments to calculate the distance they have run or walked and the speed at which they have done so (Verhoef et al., 2017). Connecting to their surroundings enables consumers to be more informed and feel more empowered as they can learn about product prices and have access to brand reviews on a real time basis. Connecting the physical store with digital platforms provides tremendous opportunities for retailers. Some consumers engage in *webrooming* where they make their brand choices on the basis of online reviews and their actual purchases in the physical store, while others treat physical stores as showrooms and make their purchases online. However,

> the importance of theory in guiding any systematic search for answers to retailing questions, as well as for streamlining analysis remains undiminished, even as the role of big data and predictive analytics in retailing is set to rise in importance aided by newer sources of data and large-scale correlational technique.
> (Bradlow, Gangwar, Kopalle, & Voleti, 2017, p. 79)

Mobile advertising can also become more effective by personalising messages to individual consumers based on GPS data captured by smartphone apps used on personal devices. Not only organisations but also governments can "respond to consumer actions and shape their demands to increase the profitability or system efficiency from a public policy perspective" (Verhoef et al., 2017, p. 3).

The above demonstrate how the IoT can increase the volume, velocity, variety, veracity, and value of big data captured, providing excellent opportunities for organisations to grow and sustain brand equity. However, we must note that there can be a 'dark side' of smart products. For instance, consumers might use drones to invade other people's privacy, or use monitoring devices to snoop on their neighbours. In addition, although organisations can use big data captured by IoT to improve consumer brand experience, powerful firms, such as *Apple, Amazon*, or *Google*, might also exploit this data. This, of course, raises important questions regarding privacy, security, and data ownership. There is an ongoing debate about who owns and controls this big data. This has made the European Union disallow third party cookies without explicit consumer consent. This issue will "get even thornier [as] devices inside people's homes start collecting and sharing data on a larger scale" (Verhoef et al., 2017, p. 7).

NEUROMARKETING AND BRANDING

Definition and process

As discussed in Chapter 8, a drawback of conventional marketing research methods has been the fact that they over-depend on what people *say* they do or like. Consumers can often be unaware of their own *actual* behaviour, can find it difficult to explain the reasons behind their actual choices, or simply they might not want to share personal information with researchers. Ethnography can mitigate these problems, as it enables consumer researchers to embed themselves in natural settings, and observe and understand individuals' actual behaviour and brand consumption. Recently, organisations have also turned to another discipline, neuroscience, to deal with the weaknesses of traditional marketing research techniques. With neuromarketing, organisations can directly probe consumers' "minds without requiring demanding cognitive or conscious participation" (Morin, 2011, p. 131). Using advancing neuro-imaging technology to track consumers' thoughts and feelings toward brand communication messages, can help remove the greatest problem with conventional advertising research which has been to trust that research participants have the inclination and ability to articulate how they are influenced by a specific advertising message.

Neuromarketing combines neuroscience with marketing to study consumer behaviour from the perspective of the human brain: "Ignoring neuro-imaging as a way to understand consumer behaviour would be as absurd as astronomers refusing to use electronic telescopes" (Morin, 2011, p. 132). The emerging field provides great opportunities for organisations seeking to understand their target audiences better and grow and sustain the equity of their brands. However, the scope and application of neuromarketing is not limited to consumer behaviour. A broader definition is as follows:

> neuromarketing as a field of study [is] the application of neuroscientific methods to analyse and understand human behaviour in relation to markets and marketing exchanges. Such a definition has two main upshots: firstly, it moves consideration

of neuromarketing away from being solely the use of neuroimaging by commercial interests for their benefit; secondly, the scope of neuromarketing research is widened from solely consumer behaviour, to include many more avenues of interest, such as inter and intra-organisational research, which are common in the marketing research literature.

(Lee, Broderick, & Chamberlain, 2007, p. 200)

The basic *process* used in a typical neuromarketing research study involves the participants

[performing] an experimental task (E) and a control task (C) while 'wired up' to a variety of high tech devices that produce colourful, real-time electronic images of a working brain. By comparing differences between the images taken during the performance of the (E) task and the (C) task, the researcher can see what part of the brain is differentially activated by the (E) task.

(Fugate, 2007, p. 386)

Therefore the design of such event- or stimulus-based studies implies that the brain is a reactive system. This system receives sensory inputs that trigger neural activity, which then cause a cognitive, affective, or behavioural response (Lee, Brandes, Chamberlain, & Senior, 2017). Despite the popularity of the aforementioned process, it has one significant limitation. Scholars have determined that responses to the same stimulus can vary across multiple trials (Braeutigam, Lee, & Senior, 2019). This may be due to *intrinsic brain activity* (also called *endogenous* or *spontaneous activity*), which is required for an individual to maintain basic *homeostasis* in order to stay alive (Braeutigam et al., 2019; Lee et al., 2017). Hence, it is essential that neuromarketing research also include pre-stimulus research designs to measure brain activity before a participant is exposed to the experimental stimuli (Lee et al., 2017).

Cognitive methodologies in neuromarketing

Over the years, neuromarketing research studies have pursued three neuroscience methodologies to generate neurological images: electroencephalography (EEG), magnetoencephalography (MEG), and, the most popular technique, functional magnetic resonance imaging (fMRI) (Lee et al., 2017; Morin, 2011) (see Figure 10.6). It is important to note that all techniques are non-invasive, thus can be safely pursued in consumer research studies.

Electroencephalography (EEG)

First, *electroencephalography* (EEG) uses electrodes placed on the participant's scalp to measure his/her brainwaves in response to a particular stimulus (e.g. an advertising message). The EEG technique is explained with the following:

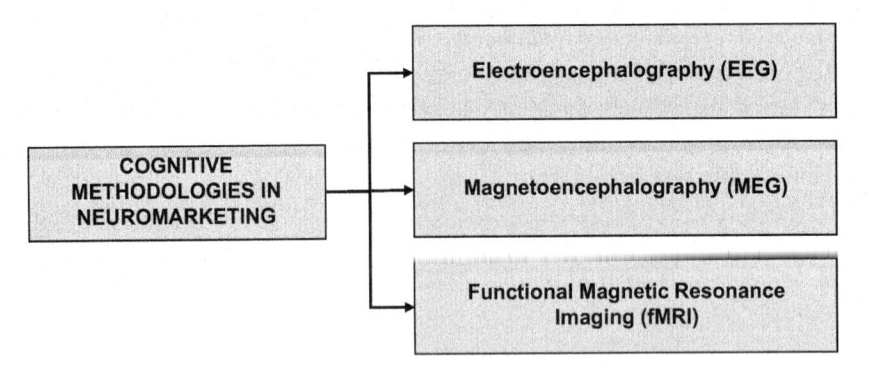

FIGURE 10.6 Cognitive methodologies in neuromarketing

> The cells responsible for the biological basis of our cognitive responses are called neurons...In the presence of a particular stimulus like a piece of advertising, neurons fire and produce a tiny electrical current that can be amplified. These electrical currents have multiple patterns of frequencies called brainwaves which are associated with different states of arousal.
>
> (Morin, 2011, p. 133)

The main limitation of this technique is its lack of effective *spatial resolution* because it cannot identify the exact location of the neurons firing in the brain. In addition, as eighty per cent of our brain activity is devoted to intrinsic brain activity, it would not be appropriate to argue that the generated brainwaves are entirely produced by the stimulus (e.g. the advertising message) (Morin, 2011). Generally speaking, electrical activity in the left frontal lobe is correlated with positive emotions and is believed to be a good predictor of motivation to act, whereas electrical activity in the right frontal lobe is associated with negative emotions, which prepare an individual to withdraw from a situation. Thus, based on which area 'lights up', researchers can make assumptions about the participant's unconscious thought patterns.

Magnetoencephalography (MEG)

Second, *magnetoencephalography* (MEG) has made significant improvements in neuro-imaging because it not only has good temporal resolution (like EEG) but also better spatial resolution than EEG. However this technique, like EEG, is only able to record activity at the brain's surface and can be very expensive. However,

> a few valuable studies have demonstrated that specific frequency bands correlate to controllable cognitive tasks such as recognizing objects, accessing verbal working memory, and recalling specific events. This in fact suggests that the best way to use MEG is to measure activity in areas known or expected to produce activity given specific tasks rather than to conduct exploratory experiments.
>
> (Morin, 2011, p. 134)

Functional Magnetic Resonance Imaging (fMRI)

The aforementioned technique (MEG) has been mostly used in combination with *functional magnetic resonance imaging* (fMRI), the most widely used technique in neuromarketing, "in order to optimise both temporal and spatial resolution issues and/or provide the added value of time stamping critical cognitive sequences at the incredible speed of just a few milliseconds" (Morin, 2011, p. 134). It is important to emphasise that the way fMRI is used in neuromarketing does not measure brain activity *per se* but *blood oxygenation level dependent* (BOLD) response. Lee et al. explain that "[t]his relies on the idea that increased brain activity in a given [brain] region results in increased blood flow to the active area. However,…this response is not actually the brain activity itself, but in essence a proxy" (2017, p. 882). Despite fMRI's strength in terms of spatial resolution, it lacks good temporal resolution. This means that using fMRI on its own is not suitable for studying very quick or transient processes but more appropriate for exploring processes lasting a few seconds or longer, such as watching a TV advert which requires from the participant considerable attention to the advert's design (i.e. its message and creative strategies – see Chapter 4). This is the reason fMRI is usually combined with MEG, as previously mentioned. Other important issues with fMRI studies have been the great number of statistical comparisons required, issues with the software used to analyse data, and the sample sizes involved in such studies (Lee et al., 2017).

Neuromarketing: Applications in branding

As mentioned earlier, based on which area of the brain 'lights up', researchers can make assumptions about the participant's unconscious thought patterns. This can be particularly useful for advertising research. For instance, if the organisation aims to create a specific emotion (e.g. excitement) for its brand through an advert's creative strategy, then "it can be matched to the approximate area of brain where these concepts are processed. If that brain area is unaffected after exposure to the advertising stimulus, it is obvious that the advertisement has failed this crucial test" (Fugate, 2007, p. 387). Of course, if there is a measurable change in the identified brain area, then the advertising message has generated the intended emotion, although this does not mean that the consumer will actually purchase the brand (Fugate, 2007). Neural scanning might also provide a prediction of advertising messages' recall, but it cannot necessarily provide an indication of postponed purchase influence (Schäfer, 2005).

In addition, neuro-imaging can be used for studying neurological responses to sensory stimuli such as smell, touch, sound, or layout of a store. As explored in Chapter 3, a person's cognitive activity is partly generated by the mental processing of sensory perceptions, which lead to the neural activation of associated brain areas (Barsalou, 2008; Krishna, 2012). Fugate highlights that "[s]tudying neural responses to the sense of smell is particularly intriguing since odor-generated impulses travel to the limbic (emotive) region of the brain and have profound effects on memories and feelings" (2007, p. 387). As previously discussed, the anatomical reason for the strong influence of smell on memory and emotion is the fact that olfaction is very close to the memory system in our bodies (i.e. the amygdala and the hippocampus) (Cahill, Babinsky, Markowitsch, & McGaugh, 1995; Eichenbaum, 1996). However, similar to the case of advertising stimuli, there is not a direct link between arousal and behaviour; after all, only toddlers cannot stop themselves from acting on arousal (James, 2004).

Organisations can pursue neuromarketing research studies during the design of a new product (e.g. a brand extension – see Chapter 9). Using brain-imaging devices, product designers can gather unbiased consumer responses to product concept prototypes (Friedman, 2006). For example, brain scans of male consumers indicated that showing participants pictures of sports cars activated the self-reward area in the brain; this area was aroused by the release of mental substances related to lust and pleasure (Britt, 2004). Perhaps this activation is not enough to guarantee purchase but "all things being equal, product designs that are thought to produce pleasure are probably more likely to be purchased than those that do not" (Fugate, 2007, p. 388); indeed, humans are pleasure-seeking creatures. However, developing a very strong brand image in consumers' minds is as important as product development. This was shown by a seminal neuromarketing research study, which compared the taste of *Coke* and *Pepsi* (McClure, Li, Tomlin, Cypert, Montague, & Montague, 2004). These scholars identified that when participants were told they were drinking *Coke*, they preferred *Coke* to *Pepsi* and affect-related brain regions were recruited. However, this was not the case when there was blind testing, i.e. participants were not told they were drinking *Coke*. This study "[reinforced] the complexity of choice-making, as well as the value of emotional, situational, and informational resources" (Lee et al., 2007, p. 201).

Neuromarketing research studies have also explained the reason celebrity endorsements can contribute positively to the development of brand equity. When a consumer is exposed to a familiar face (e.g. a celebrity), hormones such as dopamine and phenylethylamine are released in his/her brain, leading to positive emotional states, which encourage trust in the promotional message communicated to him/her by this familiar face (Mucha, 2005). This might also explain the effectiveness of favourable WOM recommendations from family and friends (Fugate, 2007). In addition, neuro-imaging has explained the reason consumer satisfaction cannot guarantee brand loyalty. The human brain can easily get used to new stimuli (satisfaction) and has a propensity for reacting only to the unexpected (Coy, 2005). Hence, organisations should not only seek to satisfy consumers, but also to delight them in order to increase loyalty. This echoes Schmitt's (1999b) suggestion that sensory marketing should not merely stimulate consumer senses but delight target audiences with stimuli they love: "To elevate customers to that point where they deliver value back to the firm, marketers must find the crucial emotional connections…that create customer engagement and passion – emotions that can be discovered and tracked as neural activity" (Fugate, 2007, p. 390) (see Figure 10.7).

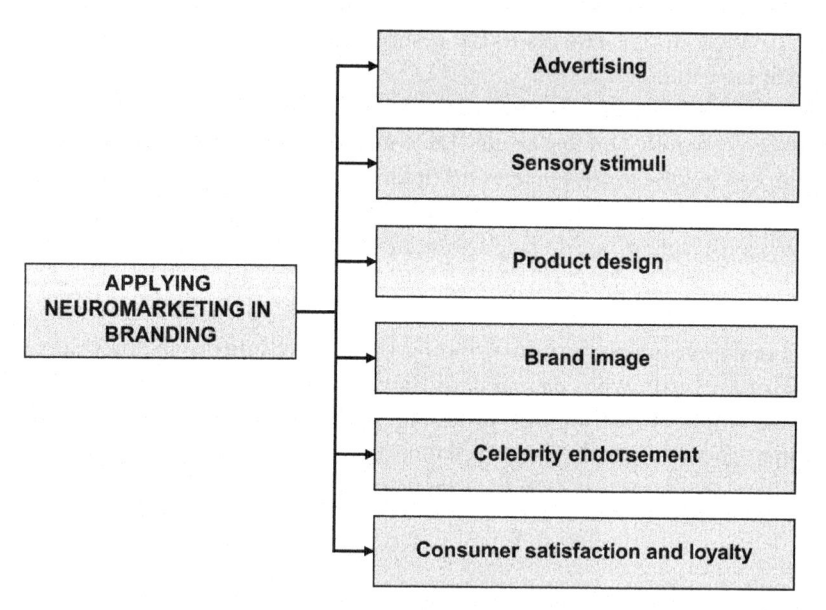

FIGURE 10.7 Applications of neuromarketing in branding

Neuromarketing implications for consumer research

The aforementioned neuromarketing research techniques help brand marketers monitor brain reactions to marketing stimuli. However, scholars still do not know what all these reactions actually mean. Lee et al. (2017) highlight many questions that remain unanswered:

> is there anything more to mental experience than brain activity? What exactly are these psychological processes that our theories refer to? Do they have some independent reality over and above their physical manifestations (i.e. brain activity etc.), or are terms like 'emotion', 'attitude', 'thought' or any subjective experience at all, simply metaphors or folk-terms that have been developed to describe what was heretofore mysterious? If so, should we now devote all our attention to further study of their physical manifestations and phase out theories which refer to these metaphorical entities or properties, since we now have little justification to consider them real?
>
> (Lee et al., 2017, p. 886)

There is a possibility that subjective mental states might actually be different to brain states (Kripke, 1980). Bagozzi and Lee (2019) suggest that these questions need to be explored in the future as they will have an impact on how consumer researchers ought to approach neuromarketing and social sciences in general. Some neuroscientists are displeased by the commercialisation of their scientific field. They argue that technology is still imprecise and that extant neuroscientific literature has not yet provided all the answers to the complex question of the connection between mental response and behaviour.

Furthermore, many have questioned the morality of using neuromarketing studies in consumer research and branding. Of course, ethical standards are increasingly being adopted by research agencies and organisations, to ensure that such studies are conducted with respect to human life and with high levels of transparency. Lee et al. (2007) argue that neuromarketing can actually contribute to improving marketing ethics. First, with regards to advertising effectiveness, it

> can contribute more than just finding the… 'buy button' in the brain. In fact, exploring exactly what elements of an advertisement are critical to awareness, attitudes and evaluations of products, and whether these differ for different groups, should reduce firms' reliance on the 'blunt instruments' of blanket coverage, shock tactics, or sexual imagery.
>
> (Lee et al., 2007, p. 203)

Second, with regards to sales practices, neuromarketing could assist in distinguishing between the mental activity of highly ethical salespeople and those who follow a less ethical approach. A study by Rilling, Gutman, Zeh, Pagnoni, Berns, and Kilts (2002) explored altruism and discovered that cooperation is associated with the activation of reward brain regions. Perhaps neuromarketing can determine whether these brain regions are activated when an unethical salesperson performs an unethical activity (Lee et al., 2007). Finally, neuromarketing could also lead to better understanding why certain aspects of brand marketing campaigns lead to negative effects, such as compulsive purchasing, over-consumption, or even addictive behaviours (Lee et al., 2007; Morin, 2011). This means that besides neuromarketing's commercial application to grow and sustain brand equity, it can also be adopted in designing social marketing campaigns (e.g. public health campaigns) which (as explored in Chapter 7) seek to influence the behaviour of target audiences to improve their, and society's welfare (Andreasen, 1994).

CHAPTER REVIEW QUESTIONS

You can use the following questions to reflect on the material covered in Chapter 10:

1. Define consumer engagement and explain its three important dimensions.
2. What are the five dimensions of big data?
3. How can big data lead to value creation and competitive advantage? Explain the process.
4. Discuss the negative aspects of consumer analytics and data mining.
5. What are the metrics organisations can use to measure cognitive, emotional, and behavioural engagement?

6. Discuss the three components of the framework of consumer connectivity (IoT) and their characteristics.
7. Explain the techniques used in neuromarketing research and consider their strengths and weaknesses.
8. How can neuromarketing research studies be applied in branding strategies?
9. Discuss the ethical implications of neuromarketing.

RECOMMENDED READING

1. Borel, L., & Christodoulides, G. (2016). Branding and digital analytics. In F. Dall'Olmo Riley, J. Singh, & C. Blankson (eds), *The Routledge companion to contemporary brand management* (pp. 255–268). London: Routledge.
2. Fugate, D. L. (2007). Neuromarketing: A layman's look at neuroscience and its potential application to marketing practice. *Journal of Consumer Marketing, 24*(7), 385–394.
3. Lee, N., Broderick, A. J., & Chamberlain, L. (2007). What is "neuromarketing"? A discussion and agenda for future research. *International Journal of Psychophysiology, 63*(2), 199–204.

CASE STUDY

Village Hotels and the Internet of Things (IoT)

Martin Jordan
Innovation Director
Equator, Glasgow, UK

The UK hotel market is a highly competitive and cluttered market. It is broadly broken down into three markets; luxury, mid-market, and value. At the luxury end, you have experiential, destination-driven locations such as *Gleneagles,* the *Ritz, Rocco Forte Hotels* and so on – places people go to *as* the experience. At the value end of the market you have the dominant brands (*Premier Inn* and *Travelodge*), offering a straightforward and consistent experience for a modest price point (as well as a long tail of B&Bs and small guest houses). Invariably, you are in this market because you need/want to be in a location. The hotel *is not* the destination. And in the middle, being increasingly squeezed, is the (typically) three- and four-star hotels across dozens of brands. From the global *Marriott, Hilton,* and *Radisson* properties to UK-specific players such as *Malmaison, Village Hotels, Macdonald, Hallmark,* and so on. It is here where the market is especially challenged.

Without the luxury trappings of a 'destination experience' of the five-star locations and often without the sheer size of *Premier Inn* and *Hilton,* many mid-market brands struggle to get brand cut-through and recognition. In a modern market fuelled massively by the Online Travel Agents (OTA) (*Booking.com, Expedia, Hotels.com* and so on), it is increasingly the case that brand recognition for these middle market players is being further eroded by the OTA's dominance. For it is with their sites that many hotel companies have become just a "bed in a place on a date" and price and service reputation becomes the only lever. But it is here in this viciously competitive marketplace that IoT and other contemporary technology stacks are making their mark in delivering brand differentiation and cut-through for mid-market players looking to standout.

Digital service without additional cost

In the hotel mid-market, you are looking to attract those from the value sector with a better quality of service, room, and facilities without the perceived unnecessary extravagance of the 5-star market. At the same time, encourage those who may reside in luxury brands to your hotel in the hope they bring their wallets with them without outrageous expectations of upscale service. All in a space that is highly competitive and commoditised by the OTAs. This means you typically have very narrow margins to work with but still with a need to deliver an elevated service to ensure loyalty and positive reviews.

High service in the middle market means ensuring you have customer service staff available at all times, quick service in the bars and restaurants, and a slicker experience all round. Traditionally, the only way to achieve this level of service would be with adding headcount – more people to work the front desk, more people behind the bars, and more people working the floor in the restaurants. But of course, this adds a LOT of cost – costs that either cause room rates to go up, rendering the hotel less competitive, or the margins to go down – which is untenable as the OTAs have already likely taken 15–25% of the room sale cost away from you as well as squeezing your rate further down to allow you to remain visible and moderately competitive.

Enter technology. In every situation, IoT technology, mobile and artificial intelligence technology can step up and take the place of costly staff whilst still augmenting and improving service.

A different arrival and departure experience

Technology and the IoT are changing the hotel arrivals and departure experience. With modern self-check-in technologies, the typical hotel reception has been transformed. As Images 10.1, 10.2, and 10.3 show, the guest can check-in using a simple, tablet-driven platform, setup their room key, and head straight to their room. This self-service approach continues to be further enhanced for many brands with digital room keys in-app, allowing guests to arrive at a hotel, check-in on their phone, and bypass reception areas altogether. This again is achieved with a mix of technologies. Mobile apps mixed with *ibeacon* technology allow brands to more tightly *geolocate* guests to their reception areas. These Bluetooth-powered micro transmitters allow compatible apps and mobile phones to know a much more accurate location for guests without high cost or disruption.

However, for mid-market brands such as *Village Hotels*, removing staff from this equation completely was not a consideration. With most guests self-checking in, the

BRAND FUTURES 335

IMAGE 10.1 *Village Hotels* arrival and departure experience (image courtesy of Village Hotels)

IMAGE 10.2 *Village Hotels* arrival and departure experience (image courtesy of Village Hotels)

front-of-house staff were 'cut loose' from a fixed desk location, made mobile with a smartphone and tablet, and able to service a wider group of guests, not just those checking in or out, as was the previous limitation. This has improved the overall guest experience without an uptick in staff and, in a post-COVID-19 environment,

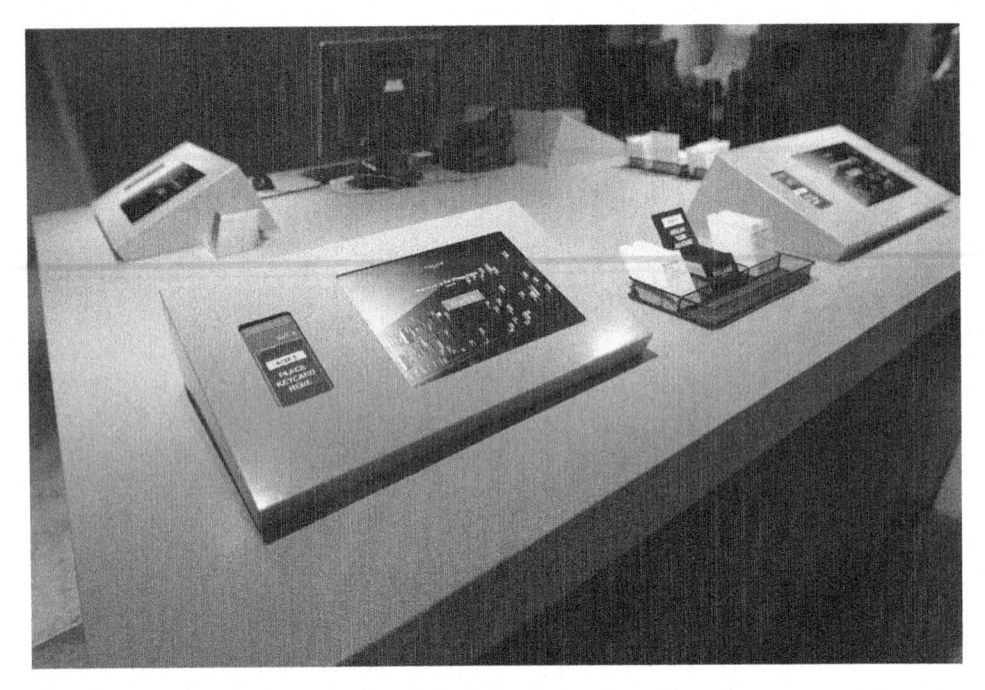

IMAGE 10.3 *Village Hotels* arrival and departure experience (image courtesy of Village Hotels)

further improves guest perceptions. Of course, it is likely many brands will move past these shared-screen environments soon to further enhance hotel hygiene.

A better food and beverage experience

As mentioned previously, a raised level of service without higher overheads is the goal in any food and beverage (F&B) environment in mid-market hotels. Again, multiple technologies can be used here. Similarly with the touchless check-in experience described above, the bar and restaurant experience is augmented with mobile and beacon technology. Again, beacons connected through a mobile app can better locate guests in a bar or restaurant and allow an app to accurately place a guest for ordering. Then, in a lightweight interface, all requests for food and drink can be taken, as well as payment when connected to *ApplePay* or *GooglePay* services. And if a guest wants to summon a waiter, they can do so in-app and the waiting staff can easily locate the guest within their partner app.

Critically here, there are other technology stacks at play. With the guest ordering their food and drinks directly, there is no need for order taking; requests go straight to the kitchen or bar and payments are taken directly without the need for till receipts, card machines, or human intervention. Again, a guest can receive a high level of service with 80% less human engagement, meaning the hotel brand can either deliver a higher quotient of service with the same people or deliver a consistent service with less people. Again, post COVID-19, this will move from the exception to the norm as more people look to maintain social distancing and look to brands with self-serve capabilities in place.

In-room service

For mid-market brands, the in-room service experience can again be raised without large human or infrastructure costs. Another example from *Village Hotels* is their world-first fully integrated deployment of the *Amazon Echo* (mini) into their hotel rooms. A massively popular device, the *Echo* (commonly referred to by its platform name – *Alexa*) in an inexpensive and lightweight device that can be purchased for as low as £20/unit. These devices are, in themselves, dumb. They are little more than a microphone and a wi-fi connection. The smarts occur in the cloud.

And it is in the cloud where *Village Hotels* exploited multiple connections to make the in-room capabilities of the *Echo* come alive. With a connection to the F&B system, this enables guests to order room service directly from the kitchen or bar (just as in the restaurant). With integration into the hotel's booking system, they are able to request late checkouts with just a few simple interactions (a key revenue boost for the brand). And with another few simple commands, they can order a taxi to come as and when they need. This is on top of the *Echo* knowing most hotel facts including check-out times, bar opening times, football matches on the TV, and so on. Whilst some may consider this a novelty, this smart and simple device massively reduces calls to reception (every interaction it can handle would have previously been dealt with by reception) and improves guest satisfaction as they no longer have to wait for their call to be answered. Of course, the capabilities can expand silently in the background without any disruption to the rooms or the hotels systems.

Summary

The IoT and mobile technologies are changing what service means in mid-market hotels. In a future with more social distancing and a higher emphasis on hygiene set to become the norm, the adoption of these technologies has moved from the early adopter to the mainstream, and it is likely that every brand will look to grow out these capabilities as the demand moves from the balance sheet to the customer.

Questions for discussion

1. As the technologies discussed become more mainstream, how can a mid-market hotel brand such as those mentioned remain differentiated? Are there other emerging technologies that could be applied here for lower cost / better service?
2. At what point does service cease to define a brand and, instead technology does? When does technology move from pervasive to invasive in a customer service environment?
3. What will be the demands of the hotel guest five years from now? What will it require of the companies of today to meet those needs, both technologically and through service and product?

REFERENCES

Andreasen, A. R. (1994). Social marketing: Its definition and domain. *Journal of Public Policy & Marketing*, 13(1), 108–114.

Bagozzi, R. P., & Lee, N. (2019). Philosophical foundations of neuroscience in organizational research: Functional and nonfunctional approaches. *Organizational Research Methods*, 22(1), 299–331.

Baron, S., & Harris, K. (2008). Consumers as resource integrators. *Journal of Marketing Management*, 24(1–2), 113–130.

Barsalou, L. W. (2008). Grounded cognition. *Annual Review of Psychology*, 59(1), 617–645.

Belk, R. W. (2013). Extended self in a digital world. *Journal of Consumer Research*, 40(3), 477–500.

Borel, L., & Christodoulides, G. (2016). Branding and digital analytics. In F. Dall'Olmo Riley, J. Singh, & C. Blankson (eds), *The Routledge companion to contemporary brand management* (pp. 255–268). London: Routledge.

Bradlow, E. T., Gangwar, M., Kopalle, P., & Voleti, S. (2017). The role of big data and predictive analytics in retailing. *Journal of Retailing*, 93(1), 79–95.

Braeutigam, S., Lee, N., & Senior, C. (2019). A role for endogenous brain states in organizational research: Moving toward a dynamic view of cognitive processes. *Organizational Research Methods*, 22(1), 332–35.

Britt, B. (2004). Automakers tap consumer brains. *Automotive News Europe*, 9(1), 1–22.

Brodie, R. J., Hollebeek, L. D., Juric, B., & Ilic, A. (2011). Customer engagement: Conceptual domain, fundamental propositions, and implications for research. *Journal of Service Research*, 14, 252–271.

Brodie, R. J., Ilic, A., Juric, B., & Hollebeek, L. (2013). Consumer engagement in a virtual brand community: An exploratory analysis. *Journal of Business Research*, 66(1), 105–114.

Cahill, L., Babinsky, R., Markowitsch, H. J., & McGaugh, J. L. (1995). The amygdala and emotional memory. *Nature*, 377(6547), 295–296.

Canniford, R. (2011). How to manage consumer tribes. *Journal of Strategic Marketing*, 19(7), 591–606.

Christodoulides, G., Jevons, C., & Bonhomme, J. (2012). Memo to marketers: Quantitative evidence for change: How user-generated content really affects brands. *Journal of Advertising Research*, 52(1), 53–64.

Content Marketing Institute (2020). What is content marketing. Available at: https://contentmarketinginstitute.com/what-is-content-marketing/ [accessed 6 April 2020].

Cova, B., & Pace, S. (2006). Brand community of convenience products: New forms of customer empowerment – The case "my Nutella The Community". *European Journal of Marketing*, 40(9/10), 1087–1105.

Coy, P. (2005). Why logic often takes a backseat, *Business Week*, 28 March, 94–95.

Danna, A., & Gandy, O. H. (2002). All that glitters is not gold: Digging beneath the surface of data mining. *Journal of Business Ethics*, 40(4), 373–386.

Edelman, D. C. (2010). Branding in the digital age. *Harvard Business Review*, 88(12), 62–69.

Eichenbaum, H. (1996). Olfactory perception and memory. In R. Llinás & P. S. Churchland (eds), *The mind-brain continuum: Sensory processes* (pp. 173–202). Cambridge: MIT Press.

Erevelles, S., Fukawa, N., & Swayne, L. (2016). Big Data consumer analytics and the transformation of marketing. *Journal of Business Research*, 69(2), 897–904.

Fan, S., Lau, R. Y., & Zhao, J. L. (2015). Demystifying big data analytics for business intelligence through the lens of marketing mix. *Big Data Research*, 2(1), 28–32.

Fredricks, J. A., Blumenfeld, P. C., & Paris, A. H. (2004). School engagement: Potential of the concept, state of the evidence. *Review of Educational Research*, 74(1), 59–109.

Friedman, R.A. (2006). What's the ultimate? Scan a male brain, *New York Times*, Vol. 156, No. 53743, G10.

Frow, P., Nenonen, S., Payne, A., & Storbacka, K. (2015). Managing co-creation design: A strategic approach to innovation. *British Journal of Management*, 26(3), 463–483.

Fugate, D. L. (2007). Neuromarketing: A layman's look at neuroscience and its potential application to marketing practice. *Journal of Consumer Marketing*, 24(7), 385–394.

Hodder, I. (2012). *Entangled: An archaeology of the relationships between humans and things*. Chichester: John Wiley & Sons.

Hollebeek, L. (2011). Exploring customer brand engagement: Definition and themes. *Journal of Strategic Marketing*, 19(7), 555–573.

Hollebeek, L. D., Glynn, M. S., & Brodie, R. J. (2014). Consumer brand engagement in social media: Conceptualization, scale development and validation. *Journal of Interactive Marketing*, 28(2), 149–165.

Hoffman, D. L., & Novak, T. P. (2018). Consumer and object experience in the Internet of Things: An assemblage theory approach. *Journal of Consumer Research*, 44(6), 1178-1204.

Horst, P., & Duboff, R. (2015). Don't let big data bury your brand. *Harvard Business Review*, 93(11), 78–86.

James, S. (2004). Neuromarketing is no brainwave if you just think about it. *Precision Marketing*, 24(9), 12–13.

Kaplan, A. M. (2011). If you love something, let it go mobile: Mobile marketing and mobile social media 4x4. *Business Horizons*, 55(2), 129–139.

Kaplan, A. M., & Haenlein, M. (2010). Users of the world, unite! The challenges and opportunities of social media. *Business Horizons*, 53(1), 59–68.

Keller, K. L. (2001). *Building customer-based brand equity: A blueprint for creating strong brands* (pp. 3–27). Cambridge: Marketing Science Institute.

Keller, K. L., & Swaminathan, V. (2020). *Strategic brand management: Building, measuring, and managing brand equity* (5th edn). London: Pearson Education.

Kripke, S. (1980). *Naming and necessity*. Oxford: Blackwell.

Krishna, A. (2012). An integrative review of sensory marketing: Engaging the senses to affect perception, judgment and behavior. *Journal of Consumer Psychology*, 22(3), 332–351.

Lee, N., Brandes, L., Chamberlain, L., & Senior, C. (2017). This is your brain on neuromarketing: Reflections on a decade of research. *Journal of Marketing Management*, 33(11–12), 878–892.

Lee, N., Broderick, A. J., & Chamberlain, L. (2007). What is "neuromarketing"? A discussion and agenda for future research. *International Journal of Psychophysiology*, 63(2), 199–204.

Lycett, M. (2013). "Datafication": Making sense of (big) data in a complex world. *European Journal of Information Systems*, 22(4), 381–386.

Marwick, A. E. (2015). Instafame: Luxury selfies in the attention economy. *Public Culture*, 27(1/75), 137–160.

McClure, S. M., Li, J., Tomlin, D., Cypert, K. S., Montague, L. M., Montague, P. R. (2004). Neural correlates of behavioral preference for culturally familiar drinks. *Neuron*, 44(2), 379–387.

Morin, C. (2011). Neuromarketing: The new science of consumer behavior. *Society*, 48(2), 131–135.

Mucha, T. (2005). Why the caveman loves the pitchman. *Business, 2*, 37–9.
O'Neil, C. (2016). *Weapons of math destruction: How big data increases inequality and threatens democracy*. London: Penguin Random House UK.
Patterson, P. G., Yu, T., & de Ruyter, K. (2006). Understanding customer engagement in services. Advancing theory, maintaining relevance. *Proceedings of ANZMAC 2006 Conference*, Brisbane, Australia, December.
Prahalad, C. K., & Ramaswamy, V. (2004). Co-creating unique value with customers. *Strategy & Leadership, 32*(3), 4–9.
Pridmore, J., & Zwick, D. (2013). The rise of customer database: From commercial surveillance to customer production. In R. W. Belk & R. Llamas (eds), *The Routledge companion to digital consumption* (pp. 102–112). London: Routledge.
Proctor, R. N., & Schiebinger, L. (2008). *Agnotology: The making and unmaking of ignorance*. Stanford: Stanford University Press.
Rilling, J. K., Gutman, D. A., Zeh, T. R., Pagnoni, G., Berns, G. S., & Kilts, C. D. (2002). A neural basis for social cooperation. *Neuron, 35*(2), 395–405.
Sadilek, A., & Krumm, J. (2012). Far out: Predicting long-term human mobility. Twenty-Sixth AAAI Conference on Artificial Intelligence, Toronto, Canada, July.
Sammut, G., & Sartawi, M. (2012). Perspective-taking and the attribution of ignorance. *Journal for the Theory of Social Behaviour, 42*(2), 181–200.
Schäfer, A. (2005). Buy this. *Scientific American Mind, 16*(2), 72–75.
Schmitt, B. H. (1999a). Experiential marketing. *Journal of Marketing Management, 15*(1–3), 53–67.
Schmitt, B. H. (1999b). *Experiential marketing: How to get customers to sense, feel, think, act, relate*. New York: The Free Press.
Schouten, J. W., & McAlexander, J. H. (1995). Subcultures of consumption: An ethnography of the new bikers. *Journal of Consumer Research, 22*(1), 43–61.
Schultz, D. E. (2007). Focus on brand changes rules of engagement. *Marketing News, 15*(8), 7-8.
Shirdastian, H., Laroche, M., & Richard, M. O. (2019). Using big data analytics to study brand authenticity sentiments: The case of Starbucks on Twitter. *International Journal of Information Management, 48*, 291–307.
Smith, P. R., & Zook, Z. (2012). *Marketing communications: Integrating offline and online with social media*. Philadelphia: Kogan Page.
Smithson, M. (1985). Toward a social theory of ignorance. *Journal for the Theory of Social Behaviour, 15*(2), 151–172.
Tynan, C., & McKechnie, S. (2009). Experience marketing: A review and reassessment. *Journal of Marketing Management, 25*(5–6), 501–517.
Vargo, S. L., & Lusch, R. F. (2004). Evolving to a new dominant logic for marketing. *Journal of Marketing, 68*(1), 1–17.
Vargo, S. L., & Lusch, R. F. (2008). Service-dominant logic: Continuing the evolution. *Journal of the Academy of Marketing Science, 36*(1), 1–10.
Van Doorn, J., Lemon, K. N., Mittal, V., Nass, S., Pick, D., Pirner, P., & Verhoef, P. C. (2010). Customer engagement behavior: Theoretical foundations and research directions. *Journal of Service Research, 13*(3), 253–266.
Vibert, A. B., & Shields, C. (2003). Approaches to student engagement: Does ideology matter? *McGill Journal of Education, 38*(2), 221–240.
Verhoef, P. C., Stephen, A. T., Kannan, P. K., Luo, X., Abhishek, V., Andrews, M., Bart, Y., Datta, H., Fong, N., Hoffman, D. L., Hu, M. M., Novak, T., Rand, W., Zhang, Y. (2017). Consumer connectivity in a complex, technology-enabled, and mobile-oriented world with smart products. *Journal of Interactive Marketing, 40*, 1–8.

Xu, Z., Frankwick, G. L., & Ramirez, E. (2016). Effects of big data analytics and traditional marketing analytics on new product success: A knowledge fusion perspective. *Journal of Business Research*, 69(5), 1562–1566.

Zikopoulos, P., & Eaton, C. (2011). *Understanding big data: Analytics for enterprise class hadoop and streaming data.* New York: McGraw-Hill/Osborne Media.

Zwick, D., & Dholakia, N. (2004). Consumer subjectivity in the Age of Internet: the radical concept of marketing control through customer relationship management. *Information and Organization*, 14(3), 211–236.

Index

Aaker D. A. 25, 28–9, 44, 50, 55–6, 60, 95, 186, 207, 252, 272, 276, 282–3, 286, 288, 294, 297, 300, 302–3, 305
Aaker J. L. 4, 6, 14, 19, 37, 49–50, 52, 151, 158, 167
advertising 3, 9, *10*, 13, 27, 33, 36, 45, 47, *48*, 54–5, 57, 61, 70, 74, 78–9, 81, **82**, 83, 85, **86**, 95–6, 102–5, 107–13, 116–17, 130–1, 133–4, 146–7, 157–8, 161, 170, 196–7, 212, 216, 228, 251, 272–3, 283, 290–1, 294, 306, 316–17, 319, 325–30, *331*, 332
aesthetics 17, 18, *24*, 34–5, 59, *60*, 61, 65, 71–2, 79, **86**, 89, 95, 97–9, *101*, *136*, 145, 158, 160, 168, 170, *172*, 188, *212*, 247, 273, 276, 283, 306, *309*
attention economy 17, 18, *24*, *60*, 100, *101*, 126–8, 131–3, *136*, *172*, 192, 209, *212*, 247, 276, 308, *309*, 339

Belk R. W. 2, 13, 14, 20, 87, 95, 120–1, 128, 131, 133, 148–9, 155, 168, 183, 191, 208, 212, 231, 232, 243, 267, 269, 272, 325, 338, 340
big data 19, 266–7, 273, 308, 311–13, *314*, 315–17, 319–21, 325–6, 332, 338–41
boycott(s) 195–6, 212, 233
brand architecture 17, 19, *24*, *60*, *101*, *136*, *172*, *212*, 247, 275, 276, 278–9, 299–300, 303, 306, *309*
brand audit 18, 246, 256–7, 269
brand avoidance 17, 18, *24*, *60*, *101*, *136*, 171, *172*, 193, *194*, 195, 200, 209, *212*, 244, 247, 276, *309*
brand awareness 25, 27–9, 57, 65, 105, 109, 147, 186, 249, 252, 261–2, 265, 293, 316–17
brand communications 17, 18, *24*, 53, 54, *60*, 70, 88, 100–2, 105, 109, 115, 116, 128, *136*, *172*, *212*, 247, 276, *309*, 318, 326

brand community 3, 18, 20–2, 40, 58, 150, 160–1, 169, 172, *173*, 177–80, **181**, 182–8, 190–3, 195, 197, 200, 208–10, 248, 266, 318, 338
brand equity *13*, 15, *17*, 18–21, 23–8, 33–6, 51, 55–9, *60*, 97, 100–1, 104, 109–10, 125, 128, 133, *136*, 153, 169, *172*, 180, 182, 186, 189, 209, *212*, 218, 244–7, 249, 252, 256–7, 261, 263–4, 272, 275, 276, 277, 283, 303–6, 308, *309*, 311, 315, 317, 320, 325, 330, 332, 339
brand essence 55, 91–2, 160–1, *162*, 169; *see also* brand mantra
brand experiences 17, *24*, *60*, *101*, 135, *136*, 137, 150–1, *172*, 179, *212*, 247, 248, 276, *309*
brand exploratory 246, 257–9, 264, **265**, 269
brand extensions 17, 19, *24*, 25, *60*, *101*, *136*, *172*, *212*, 247, 275, 276, 280–307, *309*, 315
brand feelings 38, 318
brand hierarchy 19, 275, 279–80
brand identity 4, 11, *17*, 18, 21, *24*, 25–6, 34, 37–9, 56, 59–64, 66, 69, 72, 74, 79, 83, 88, 90, 95–6, 98–9, *101*, 109, 110, 123, 132–3, *136*, 160, *172*, *212*, 247, 276, 277, *309*
brand imagery associations 26, 27, 29, 34, 36, 38, 42, 260
brand inventory 246, 256, 257, 269
brand judgments 38; *see also* consumer judgments
brand mantra 45, 48, 55, 66, 100; *see also* brand essence
brand metrics 319
brand performance 17, 18, *24*, 32, 56, 58, *60*, *101*, *136*, *172*, *212*, 246, 247, 256, 261, 271, 272, 276, *309*; associations 26, 27, 29, 34, 36, 42

INDEX

brand personality 6, 8, 9, 11, 18–19, 23, 37, 49–50, 52, 55–6, 72, 110–11, 113, 132, 151, 167, 252, 260, 303
brand publics 18, 172, *173*, 185, 190–2, 248
brand resonance 26, *27*, 39–40, 55, 153, 186, 310–11, 317
brand salience 26, *27*, 28, 59
brand values 18, 23, 49, 50, 51, 55, 160
buycotts 195; buycotting 196, 212

consumer judgements 38, 99
consumer tribes 18, 20, 172, *173*, 187–90, 192, 200, 208, 266, 324, 338

direct marketing 27, 103–4

emotional 4, 11, 13, 15, 25–7, 30, 38–9, 45, **46**, 47, 51, 59, 65, 86, 87, 96, 102, 116, 138, 140, 144–5, 148, 152, 169, **181**, 182, 247, 252, 265, 270, 304, 308–10, *311*, 317–18, 321, **332**, *323*, 330, 332, 338; branding *17*, 18, *24*, 37, 39, *60*, 96, *101*, 135, *136*, 146, 152, 168, 172, 212, 247, 248, *276*, *309*
emotions 18, 39, 58, 81–2, 87, 88, 91, 102, 138, 139, 145–6, 149, 152–4, 169–70, 187, 188, 216, 290, 328, 330
ethics *17*, 18, *24*, *60*, *101*, *136*, 172, 211, *212*, 213–16, 219, 221, 222, 236–7, 242–3, 245, 247, *276*, *309*, 332
ethnography 200, 210, 245, 264–9, 272, 273, 326, 340
experience economy 18, 98, 135, 139, 140, 142–4, 163, 166, 170
experiences 3, 13, 15, *17*, 18, *24*, 35–7, *60*, 71–2, 74, *101*, 106, 119–23, 135, *136*, 137, 139–46, 148–53, 155–6, 161–3, 168, 170, 172, 174, 177, 179, 184, 187, 191, 193, 198, 201, 206, 209–10, *212*, 247, 248–9, 267, *276*, *309*, 324
experiential marketing 18, 58, 98, 135, 143–4, 150, 153, 162–3, 170, 177, 210, 273, 324, 340

innovation 8, *17*, 19, *24*, *31*, 44, **46**, 55, *60*, *101*, 128, *136*, 172, 189, 198, *212*, 222, 230, 243, 247, 252, 270, 273, *276*, 308, *309*, 315, 333, 339; *see also* technology
Internet 3, 9, 27, 43, 81, 105, 108, 112, 120–1, 123–4, 132–3, 161, 172, 185, 189, 209, 311, 341; Internet of Things (IoT) 19, 308, 321, *324*, 333, 339

Keller K. L. 4, 12, 17–18, 21, 23–6, 28–30, 33–49, 51, *57*, 59, 68, 95, 97, 100–3, 107, 109–13, 115–17, 128, 133, 135, 153, 160, 169, 171, 186, 209, 211, 244, 246–7, 249–52, 256–64, 269, 272, 275–6, 278–88, 294, 297, 300, 303, 305–6, 308, 311, 317–18, 339

moral philosophy 211, 213–15, 236

neuromarketing 19, 308, 326, 327, *328*, 329, 330–3, 339

pay-per-click (PPC) 108, *109*, 132
personal selling 27, 103–4
points-of-difference (PODs) associations 37, 54, 55, 100, 109, 111, 257
points-of-parity (POPs) associations 37, 55, 100, 109, 111, 257, 285
political consumption *17*, 18, *24*, *60*, *101*, *136*, 171, 172, 195–6, 198, 200, 212, 247, *276*, *309*
positioning 18, 23, *24*, 37, 41–2, 44–5, 52, 54–8, *60*, 62, 66, 67, 72, 90, 95, *101*, 109, 111, 119, *136*, 172, 184, 202, *212*, 220, 233–4, 239, 247, *255*, 269, *276*, 285, 289, *309*, 320
primary elements 61, 64–6, 70–1, 74, 83, 89, 95
publicity *see* public relations
public relations 27, 104, 131, 132, 134

radio 81, 112, 114, 301

sales promotions 27, 103, *104*, 234, 320
Schmitt, B. H. 39, 58, 60–7, 70–7, 79, **80**, 81, 83, **84**, 87–9, 98, 136, 137, 142–5, 147–53, 163, 168, 170, 177, 210, 257, 261, 273, 283, 297, 305, 306, 324, 340
search engine optimisation (SEO) 108, *109*
social media 3, 9, 11, 18, 21, 27, 40, 57, 74, 100, 105–8, *109*, 113–14, 118–34, 161, 163, 167, 172, **173**, 183, 187, 189–92, 199, 209, **255**, 267, 310–12, 316–21, 323, 339–40
social responsibility 18, 196, 211–13, 217–21
subcultures of consumption 172, *173*, 174–8, 187–8, 200, 210, 212, 245, 266, 340
sustainability 18, 77, 130, 211, 229–32, 236, 240, 242–3, 245
symbolism *17*, 18, 22, *24*, 59, *60*, 61, 62, 68, 70, 77, 80, 97, *101*, *136*, 172, 212, 228, 247, *276*, 298, *309*

technology 5, 16, *17*, 19, *24*, 44, *60*, 67, 71, 81, 95, *101*, 106, 114, *136*, 146, 148, 158, 160,

163, 169, *172*, 197–8, *212*, 247, 266, 267, 276, 283, 308, *309*, 316, 321, 323, 326, 331, 334, 336, 337, 340; *see also* innovation
TV 29, 35, 81, 84, 111, 114, 124, 158, 187, 289, 329, 337

value 2–6, 8–10, 15–16, 19, 22–4, 32, 34–5, 38, 50, 52, 57, 71–2, 98, 101, 126–7, 129–30, 138–40, 142–3, 145, 154, 172, **173**, 174, 177, 180, 182, 186, 188, 191–2, 195, 209, 212, 219–21, 224, 225, 236–8, 246–54, **255**, 256, 260, 269, 272–3, 277, 290, 296, 300, 305, 308–10, 312–13, *314*, 315, 321, 323, 325, 329–30, 332–34, 340; brand value 18, 54, 218, 220, 224, 246–54, 256, 310; brand value chain model (BVCM) 18, 246, 247, 248, 269; linking value 187–90, 208